SUNDAYS AT SINAI

HISTORICAL STUDIES OF URBAN AMERICA

Edited by Timothy J. Gilfoyle, James R. Grossman, and Becky M. Nicolaides

ALSO IN THE SERIES:

Sundays at Sinai

A JEWISH CONGREGATION IN CHICAGO

Tobias Brinkmann

The University of Chicago Press

CHICAGO AND LONDON

Tobias Brinkmann is the Malvin E. and Lea P. Bank Associate Professor of Jewish Studies and History at the Pennsylvania State University.

The University of Chicago Press, Chicago 60637
The University of Chicago Press, Ltd., London
© 2012 by The University of Chicago
All rights reserved. Published 2012.
Printed in the United States of America

21 20 19 18 17 16 15 14 13 12   1 2 3 4 5

ISBN-13: 978-0-226-07454-2 (cloth)
ISBN-10: 0-226-07454-4 (cloth)

Library of Congress Cataloging-in-Publication Data

Brinkmann, Tobias.
Sundays at Sinai : a Jewish congregation in Chicago / Tobias Brinkmann.
p. cm.
Includes bibliographical references and index.
ISBN-13: 978-0-226-07454-2 (hardcover : alkaline paper)
ISBN-10: 0-226-07454-4 (hardcover : alkaline paper)   1. Chicago Sinai Congregation—
History.   2. Reform Judaism—Illinois—Chicago—History.   I. Title.
BM225.C52C493 2012
296.09773'11—dc23
2011038189

♾ This paper meets the requirements of ANSI/NISO Z39.48-1992
(Permanence of Paper).

CONTENTS

ACKNOWLEDGMENTS

I am grateful to many people and institutions that supported me during the research and writing of this book. Howard Sulkin, a former president of the Chicago Sinai congregation, first suggested the topic to me. The current president of Sinai, Peter B. Bensinger Jr.; his predecessors, Alec Harris and Jack D. Tovin; and the board graciously opened the congregation's archive, even though they knew that I would write a critical history. I am grateful to the executive director of the Chicago Sinai congregation, Susan Solomon, and her staff for assisting me during the research I conducted at the temple archive. I am also appreciative of the many conversations I had with members and officers of the congregation, notably Donna Barrows, Jim Deutelbaum, Norm Hirsch, Scott Kumer (the congregations's director of music) Robert A. Sideman, and especially William Marks. I spent three weeks in June 2009 with Miriam and Malvin Letchinger in Hyde Park to get a better understanding of Sinai's postwar development. One of the most moving moments during the research was when we visited the former temple of Sinai in Grand Boulevard where Pastor Joseph Jackson of Mt. Pisgah Missionary Baptist Church gave us a tour through the former social center and the enormous sanctuary.

I am particularly grateful to Michael A. Meyer, who read several draft chapters and made very constructive suggestions for improvements. The two reviewers, who both identified themselves, also made very important suggestions. I profited enormously from Jonathan Sarna's unrivaled knowledge of American Jewish history. Martin Marty's input was particularly valuable, because he has shaped the emerging field of the history of American congregations. I received useful advice from Yaakov Ariel, Dean Bell, Kathleen Conzen, Karla Goldman, Bernice Heilbrun, Miriam Joyce, Richard S. Levy, Evan Moffic, Eric Novotny, Walter Roth, Rima Lunin Schultz, and Norma Spungen. Liz Bentley helped me with the editing during the early stages of the writing. I want to thank Virginia N. Dick, Lisa Silverman, and, last but not least, Norma and Kenneth Spungen for their friendship and hospitality during my repeated stays in Chicago.

Jim Grossman showed an interest in this project early on. I had a number of intriguing discussions with him and several members of the Newberry community, notably with Daniel Greene, who alerted me to Jacob I. Weinstein. I am grateful to the editors of the Historical Studies of Urban America series for their inclusion of this book. At the University of Chicago Press, Robert P. Devens, Mary Gehl, Anne Goldberg, and Russ Damian provided much support.

The Rabbi Harold D. Hahn Memorial Fellowship at the American Jewish Archives in Cincinnati in 2007 and a short-term research fellowship at the Newberry Library in Chicago in 2009 enabled me to conduct a crucial part of the research for this project. The British Academy provided a travel grant for a conference that enabled me to spend a few days doing research in Chicago in early 2006. A research leave at the University of Southampton, where I taught until 2009, provided me with the necessary time for writing. Penn State University funded the final stage of the research.

I am very grateful to the staff at the American Jewish Archives, particularly Kevin Proffit and Camille Servizzi, as well as Kathy Block, Joy Kingsolver, and Ilana Segal at the Chicago Jewish Archives and Asher Library at the Spertus College of Jewish Studies in Chicago. I also relied on the help of the staff at the Klau Library at Hebrew Union College in Cincinnati, the American Jewish Historical Society and the Center of Jewish History in New York, the Newberry Library in Chicago, and Widener Library at Harvard. At the Sinai congregation, my research would not have been possible without Joy Kingsolver. She carefully organized the collection remaining at the temple and prepared an inventory. Without her help I would have never been able to navigate the collection.

Acknowledgments

INTRODUCTION

Any visitor to a residential neighborhood in a midwestern or northeastern city will notice churches and (former) synagogues built during the nineteenth and early twentieth centuries. As urban neighborhoods have transformed, sometimes beyond recognition, new residents representing different faiths and religions have reinvented houses of worship. Catholic churches, erected by eastern and southern European immigrants before 1914, frequently serve parishioners from Latin America; former synagogues have become African American Baptist churches; other buildings have been transformed into Muslim mosques or Buddhist temples. Sometimes several congregations are cohabiting. The Calvary United Methodist Church in West Philadelphia, for instance, remains in the church built in 1906 but provides space to the Jewish Reconstructionist Kol Tzedek congregation, as well as three Christian congregations: West Philadelphia Mennonite Fellowship, Grace Chapel Church of God in Christ, and Thompson's Temple of Faith.[1] The continuous and creative use of houses of worship is testament as much to the forces of segregation and economic inequality as to the promise of America for immigrants from around the world and to the vibrancy and diversity of religious life in the American city.

The recently published *Encyclopedia of Chicago* features several maps on the religious geography of the city, illustrating the enormous diversity and mobility of religious congregations over the last 150 years. The map on the distribution of Presbyterian churches in 1920 and 2000, for instance, highlights the impact of suburbanization after 1945. A heavy concentration of Buddhist, Hindu, and Muslim congregations on Chicago's North Side betrays the area's role as gateway for immigrants from east and south Asia. The movement of Jewish congregations within metropolitan Chicago is particularly striking. On a first glance, the map "Jewish Congregations on the Move" resembles a partly disentangled ball of wool depicting former locations in the central business district on the West and South Sides, and current locations on the Near North and Far North Sides. Admittedly, even the most experienced mapmaker would struggle to track the high mobility of Jewish congregations.[2]

Retracing the path of Jewish (and other) congregations from their current location to former houses of worship takes researchers on a tour through the respective city in time and space. Chicago's oldest Jewish houses of worship, mostly former churches, were largely destroyed in the 1871 fire. In the 1960s, the University of Illinois campus on the Near West Side replaced the remnants of the former "ghetto," the large Jewish immigrant neighborhood that experienced its heyday in the first two decades of the twentieth century. Former synagogues can still be found in North Lawndale on the West Side, and across the South Side. One of Chicago's most beautiful houses of worship, KAM Isaiah Israel on Hyde Park Boulevard, closely resembles a mosque but has served as synagogue since its dedication in 1924. Nearby on Drexel Boulevard stands one of two surviving former synagogues of Chicago's oldest Jewish congregation, KAM (Kehilath Anshe Ma'ariv). When KAM merged with Isaiah Israel in 1971, it sold its synagogue to Operation PUSH (People United to Serve Humanity), which still uses the edifice as its headquarters.[3]

Chicago's largest former synagogue, a grand neoclassical structure, is located in the heart of the South Side. Adjacent to the name "Mount Pisgah Missionary Baptist Church," a prominent inscription from Isaiah 56:7 greets the visitor: "MINE HOUSE SHALL BE A HOUSE OF PRAYER FOR ALL NATIONS." Inconspicuous Stars of David and depictions of the menorah still adorn the interior walls of the enormous sanctuary, next to Christian symbols. In the hundred years of its existence, this house of worship has hosted several of America's most influential religious leaders and other illustrious figures. It was here, on a Sunday morning in late August 1967, that Martin Luther King Jr. preached one of his last major sermons to the Mt. Pisgah congregation. In its earlier life, as the temple of Chicago Sinai congregation, theologian Reinhold Niebuhr; rabbis Stephen S.

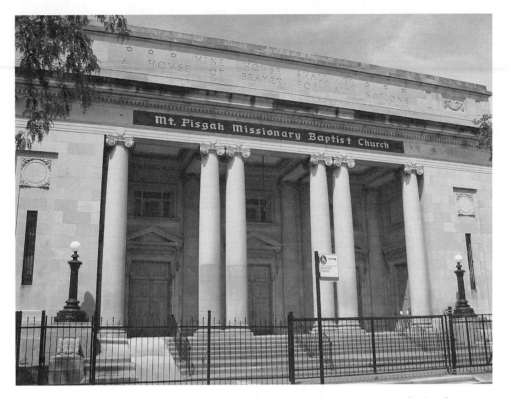

FIGURE I. Mt. Pisgah Missionary Baptist Church, on S. Martin Luther King Jr. Drive in the Grand Boulevard neighborhood, Chicago, 2009. Photo by the author.

Wise, Abba Hillel Silver, and Kaufmann Kohler; social reformer Jane Addams; writers Israel Zangwill, Thomas Mann, and Theodore Dreiser; composer Leonard Bernstein; First Lady Eleanor Roosevelt; lawyer Clarence Darrow; and many others addressed large crowds from the imposing podium.[4]

When Mt. Pisgah bought the building in 1962 from the Catholic Archdiocese of Chicago, the Grand Boulevard neighborhood had been in decline for almost two decades. In the early 1920s, the corner of 47th Street and Grand Boulevard (later South Park, and today Martin Luther King Jr. Drive) emerged as the crossroads of the thriving African American entertainment district of Bronzeville. The Depression, the loss of industrial jobs after World War II, segregation, and the effects of Chicago's public housing policy hit the neighborhood hard. In the late 1960s, at the time of King's visit, dozens of homes were boarded up. America's largest public housing project at its completion in 1962, the soon-notorious Robert Taylor Homes, dominated the western skyline. By the 1980s, many homes in the vicinity of Mt. Pisgah had been razed. Yet even today, as the scarred area is reviving and small residential units fill conspicuous gaps in many locations, a few older buildings betray traces of former splendor.[5]

In 1912, when Chicago Sinai congregation moved into the new building, Grand Boulevard was one of Chicago's most prestigious neighborhoods. Sinai, then one of the largest Jewish congregations in the country, counted almost one thousand members. The new temple was a status symbol of a congregation strongly committed to Chicago. Architect Alfred S. Alschuler designed a large sanctuary with more than two thousand seats. An adjacent building, the Sinai Social Center, accommodated a meeting hall, basketball courts, and a swimming pool. In a typical week during the 1920s up to ten thousand people passed through the state-of-the-art complex. The new temple and the social center represented the highpoint in the career of Sinai's rabbi, Emil Gustav Hirsch, a widely respected progressive reformer, Jewish theologian, and renowned speaker. The sentence from Isaiah 56:7 over the entrance was no empty promise: the sermons Hirsch preached regularly attracted up to two thousand Christians and unaffiliated Jews. Only weeks after its dedication in 1912, Sinai's temple served as opening venue of the fourth annual conference of the National Association for the Advancement of Colored People (NAACP).[6]

In theological terms, Chicago Sinai congregation never belonged to (or regarded itself as part of) the Jewish mainstream. From its founding in 1861, the congregation provoked acerbic criticism for its radical reinterpretation and seeming disregard for the Jewish tradition. Sinai was the first Jewish congregation in America to permanently adopt Sunday services in 1874. The congregation reached out to many Chicagoans, supporting in particular civic institutions devoted to education. From its earliest days, Sinai initiated a dialogue with Christians, and the leaders of a congregation comprising some of the city's wealthiest businessmen spoke up on behalf of the working class. Even though Sinai appeared to be more committed to assimilation—and indeed, Americanization—than almost any other Jewish congregation in and beyond the United States, it has endured. Today the congregation is based on Chicago's Near North Side. Sunday services are still celebrated, and the congregation, again counting almost one thousand members, is flourishing. Against the backdrop of Chicago's rapid transformation since the 1860s and the quickly changing American religious landscape, the 150th anniversary of a Jewish congregation that persists and has remained within the city requires explanation. Closely related are the questions of how the relationship between Sinai and Chicago evolved and how the congregation defined (and redefined) its place in the urban society.

To examine these questions, this book will analyze the impact of rabbinic leadership and the idiosyncratic theology of the congregation. Much attention will be devoted to the wider social context, especially to the many relationships the congregation forged in and beyond Chicago: to Jewish immigrants who arrived after 1880, to working-class Chicagoans, to African Americans, to other Jewish and Christian congregations, and to civic institutions.

The religious congregation has long played a significant role in the lives of Americans. Academic historians, however, have neglected the congregation and focused instead on theology, denominations, illustrious ministers, and rabbis. There is certainly no lack of congregation histories. Some are surprisingly detailed and well researched. Most, however, have a narrow focus and reflect the viewpoint of the respective congregation, since the intended audience is often the membership. The institution, ministers, prominent supporters, and committed members take center stage, while the social and cultural context fades into the background. More important, controversies, critical moments, and potentially embarrassing "scandals" are glossed over.

The recent academic interest is driven by the recognition that the congregation has long been a crucial part in the diverse fabric of American society. Following the definition of James P. Wind and James W. Lewis, "congregation" is defined here as a group of "people who regularly gather to worship at a particular place." From the earliest days, congregations have brought people together and played a mediating role—admittedly, not always successfully or constructively—between tradition and modernity, between past and future, between young and old, between private and public, between *Gemeinschaft* and *Gesellschaft*, between immigrants and America, and between people of different backgrounds, to name but a few. The history of congregations reflects the impact of social and economic transformation and the influence of divisive forces but also attempts to overcome social isolation.[7]

Sinai's relationship to African Americans illustrates this point forcefully. Rabbi Hirsch was one of the founders of the NAACP and repeatedly spoke up against racial discrimination. His congregant, Julius Rosenwald, devoted much of his philanthropy to African Americans, and Sinai built ties to a large African American congregation, Bethel Church. But after 1920, this relationship deteriorated, not coincidentally when Sinai moved from being an important player in Chicago and within the Jewish Reform movement to the margins. Lately, however, the congregation has tried to reconnect with its older tradition of social action.[8]

Conforming to the general trend, the social history of Judaism in the United

States remains sorely understudied. Naomi W. Cohen's recently published *What the Rabbis Said*, a well-informed discussion of important sermons by famous nineteenth century rabbis, is a typical example of the traditional emphasis on "big men" rather than actual congregations (let alone women). In contrast, the almost simultaneously published historical survey of Orthodox Judaism in America by Jeffrey S. Gurock hints at a new trend. He devotes much attention to the grassroots, gender, and everyday life.[9] Apart from two detailed histories of Jewish congregations, however, both commissioned by the respective congregations, a few authors have examined the social history of Jewish congregations, such as the rise of the synagogue-center and the role of women in the nineteenth-century synagogue. Particularly noteworthy is the chapter on Cincinnati's Rockdale Temple by Karla Goldman and Jonathan D. Sarna in the essay collection *American Congregations*, a rare example of a critical history of a Jewish congregation.[10]

The theological and intellectual history of the Reform movement in the United States is well researched; Michael A. Meyer's authoritative survey of the Reform movement especially stands out. Unlike other historians of American Reform Judaism, Meyer analyzes the central European origins of the movement highlighting the close ties between two usually separately treated fields, German and American Jewish history. Until recently, scholars in American Jewish history paid only scant attention to the European background and transnational ties of Jewish immigrants. Surprisingly few authors rely on sources in Yiddish, German, Polish, and other languages widely spoken by immigrant Jews.[11] Chicago Sinai congregation was founded as a "German" congregation. "German," however, only superficially referred to a geographically defined space—a unified German state was only formed in 1871. Sinai's founders understood Germanness not in ethnic or national but primarily in spiritual and transnational terms and as a synonym for modernity. Indeed, Sinai was one of the first Jewish congregations in America, and one of the first congregations of any denomination in Chicago that explicitly described itself as modern. To understand the trajectory of the congregation, especially in its formative phase, it is indispensable to look beyond America's shores.

Sundays at Sinai is as much a history of Chicago and Jewish immigrants in urban America as it is a history of a social institution and its members. The period from 1870 to 1920 stands at the center of this book, largely because Sinai's influence as a congregation culminated in this dramatic phase of Chicago's short history. This was no coincidence: Sinai's development was closely intertwined with Chicago's spectacular growth to one of America's principal cities—and the city's decline during the middle decades of twentieth century. In fact, the high mobility rates of Jewish and Protestant congregations are one indicator of Chicago's socioeconomic development in the last 150 years. In American urban history, however, religion is often passed over. *Challenging Chicago*, an extensive and well-researched study of everyday life in Chicago between 1837 and 1920, to give only one example, does not even touch on religion. Notable exceptions are studies dealing with ethnic groups, such as Polish immigrants, for whom religion constituted an important part of their social milieu. But the ethnic lens imposes constraints and an artificially narrow perspective. A model study that transcends the ethnic paradigm without dismissing ethnicity is John T. McGreevy's *Parish Boundaries*, an in-depth examination of the nexus between religion, urban space, and race. Indeed, as Kathleen N. Conzen has argued for German-speaking Catholics, religion may have been a more important point of reference for immigrants and their American-born descendants than ethnicity.[12]

From its earliest days, Sinai's board members carefully archived documents and other materials they considered as valuable. The deep appreciation of the congregation's specific history and mission largely explains why Sinai's rabbis and lay leaders treated the archive with great care.[13] During the 1970s, the congregation deposited most of the remaining pre-1940 files at the American Jewish Archives in Cincinnati, Ohio. Twentieth-century documents, images, and other materials are kept at the current temple. This collection has recently been cataloged. Apart from a few gaps, notably for the 1940s and the decade before the Great Chicago Fire in 1871, the board minutes are almost complete. Internal documents—letters, sermons, and reports—were frequently written in German well into the 1880s. In addition to archival collections in Chicago, Cincinnati, and New York, *Sundays at Sinai* relies extensively on daily and weekly newspapers. These range from German- and English-language dailies in Chicago and New York to Jewish weeklies in the United States and Germany.

The congregation graciously opened its archive and provided me with space in the library for conducting research. Between 2007 and 2009, I spent much time talking to several members; current and former officers; the current rabbi, Michael P. Sternfield; former associate rabbi Evan Moffic; his successor, David Levinsky; and the former senior rabbis Howard Berman and Samuel E. Karff. Early on I decided to concentrate on the older history of the congregation. The influence of Sinai in Chicago and on Reform Jews throughout the United States culminated in the period between 1880 and 1920. Surprisingly little has been written on this part of Sinai's history, although, as I hope this study shows, it mattered for Chicago but also for the Reform movement, and for the history of the Jewish-Christian dialogue. Moreover, in American Jewish history the so-called German Jews have not been sufficiently studied. Of course, another very different book could—and hopefully will be—written on the post-1920 phase of Sinai's history. Such a monograph would concentrate more on race, on the history of the South Side, on other Jewish and Christian congregations, and the controversial urban renewal program in Hyde Park during the 1950s and 1960s. This phase is summarized in the final chapter of this book. Even when I began this study a few years ago, very few members were still alive who could remember the period before 1940. Therefore, I decided not to conduct formal interviews, with one exception. In the summer of 2009, I spent three weeks with Miriam and Malvin Letchinger to get a better understanding of postwar developments. Both are longtime members; Miriam was Sinai's first female president.

The study traces the history of Sinai congregation from its beginnings as a migration network from the Palatinate in central Europe to the early 1960s. The first part of the book examines the background of migration and emancipation in the German states, and the long founding process of the congregation. During the 1860s and 1870s, the first two decades after Sinai's founding, the members displayed a high social mobility and enjoyed much respect by their Christian peers. But until 1880, they could not find a religious leader who matched their expectations. The second and central part of the study concentrates on the tenure of Emil G. Hirsch. During the forty-two years of his leadership, Sinai emerged as one of the largest Jewish congregations in the country with several hundred members. Hirsch, a brilliant intellectual and charismatic speaker (but also a difficult and eccentric figure), pulled large audiences to his famous sermons, successfully translating radical Reform Judaism into the social context of a rapidly growing city. Hirsch fostered many relationships, to liberal Protestants, to organized labor, to progressives, to African Americans, to the University of Chicago, and even to Zionist leaders among the large Jewish immigrant community on Chicago's West Side. The third and last part, consisting of one chapter, traces Sinai's development from 1920 to 1960. Even before Hirsch's passing in 1923, Sinai gradually lost much of the innovative momentum of its earlier years. The congregation moved to the margins of Chicago, literally and symbolically, loosing its role as a controversial trendsetter in the Reform movement. The decision by the board to locate in a neighborhood with limited possibilities for the size and aspiration of a radical Reform congregation exacerbated the crisis.

A final disclaimer: Sinai congregation has not commissioned this book, and the author is not nor has he been a member of the congregation.

Part I.

FOUNDING AND EARLY DEVELOPMENT

1.

JACOB AND HIS SONS

THE HISTORY OF Chicago Sinai congregation begins in central Europe. The founders were recent immigrants who were embedded in social networks that included distant family members, friends, and acquaintances, as well as larger groups of people from the same region. Even a superficial reader of the detailed *History of the Jews of Chicago*, compiled by Hyman Meites in 1924, and similar histories of ethnic communities published in the early twentieth century will note extensive evidence for chain migration.[1] By illuminating a relatively little researched and acknowledged aspect of American Jewish history—the context of out-migration in Europe and the paths and links of migration to and within America—this chapter proposes a differentiated approach to explaining the background of the "German Jews" in the United States. The surprisingly high social mobility and openness to religious change owed much to the conditions Jewish immigrants found in America but also to the cultural baggage they brought with them and put to good use.

EUROPEAN ROOTS AND MIGRATION NETWORKS
In 1850, Jakob Grünebaum was prospering in Eppelsheim, a Hessian village surrounded by agricultural estates, not far from the western bank of the Rhine be-

tween Strasbourg and Mainz. Jakob owned considerable real estate and a farm, and his retail business for farm products was flourishing. In 1852, he left for Chicago, never to return to his ancestral home. He had, as he emphasized a few years later, "no reason whatsoever to emigrate." Economic motives played no role in his decision. Unlike the large majority of German-speaking migrants in Chicago, Jakob was Jewish, but his departure was not connected to anti-Jewish policies. True, his fellow Jewish citizens in the grand duchy of Hesse were not fully emancipated when he wrote his reminiscences in 1859. But Jakob did not mention anti-Jewish discrimination or state repression as a reason for leaving.

Jakob's hometown belonged to the western part of the grand duchy of Hesse, where the liberal policies toward Jews introduced by the French had not been rescinded after 1815. The failure of the 1848–1849 revolution was certainly felt in Eppelsheim but did not concern Jakob either. Unlike most immigrants, he was not young. In 1852, he was fifty-five years old. Why then did Jakob leave for America? He explained, "Although I had there [in Eppelsheim] much of what I don't have here, I did not even for a moment consider returning. The life with my children makes the dear mother and me happy."

Jakob and his wife shared an experience with many Jewish (and Christian) parents in the southwest German states at the time: their sons had gone to America in the 1840s. Michael, then twenty-two, had been the first to leave in 1845; he went straight to Chicago, then a bustling town with a few thousand inhabitants not far from the western frontier, initially with the intention of staying only for a few years. A year later, Elias, their eldest son at twenty-five, followed in Michael's footsteps. Soon Michael changed his mind, deciding to remain in Chicago for good. A short time later, in 1848, Michael and Elias sent for their youngest brother, Heinrich, who was only fifteen years old.

Because of the uncertain political situation—the 1848 revolution was in full swing—Jakob allowed his youngest son to leave. Soon after Heinrich's departure, however, he and his wife realized that they would perhaps never see their sons again, and, as Jakob recalls, the couple spent many a sleepless night. By 1849, they had made up their minds. Jakob dissolved his business and estate. In 1852, he took his wife and their two daughters to Chicago; one son remained in Eppelsheim. In Chicago, he joined the successful plumbing business of his son Michael. Jakob Grünebaum became Jacob Greenebaum.[2]

The Greenebaums were among the more than a hundred thousand Jews from central and eastern Europe who left for North America from the early 1820s through the late 1870s. According to some authors the number was higher and ranged between a hundred and fifty and two hundred thousand.[3] Regardless of the actual number, Jewish migrants from central Europe constitute a small footnote in the story of the huge transatlantic migration. Between 1815 and 1939, approximately fifty to fifty-five million Europeans, roughly 20 percent of Europe's population in 1800, were heading to another continent. About thirty-five million went to North America (the bulk before 1914), eight million to South America, and smaller numbers to Australia and other destinations. At least seven million eventually returned to their home countries.[4] Jews formed a significant part of this migration, but only after 1880. In 1904, more than 10 percent of all immigrants to the United States were Jews from the Russian Empire and the Habsburg monarchy. The more than a hundred thousand Jewish immigrants who arrived in that year alone may well have outnumbered the Jewish arrivals to the United States in the whole period from 1820 to 1880.

It is rarely acknowledged in the literature that, like Jewish migrants from eastern Europe, the earlier Jewish immigrants represented a significant share of the Jewish population in central Europe. In 1816, approximately 260,000 Jews (1.09 percent of the population) lived in states that would form the German Empire after 1871; largely as a result of natural growth, their numbers had almost doubled to 470,000 (1.2 percent) by 1871. This increase was even more impressive than these numbers imply: By 1880, at least 100,000 Jews had departed, overwhelmingly for the United States.[5] Due to insufficient research on Jewish migration from, within, and to central Europe, it is not exactly known how many Jews migrated to America before 1900. Different authors provide widely diverging estimates ranging from 100,000 to well over 200,000 immigrants, and the numbers do not account for natural growth. Most immigrants resembled Jacob Greenebaum's sons and daughters: they were young upon arrival and had established families, often with several children. Therefore, not more than 100,000 Jews from central and eastern Europe may actually have come to America during the period of 1820–1880.[6]

Future research on the micro-context of out-migration may shed more light on the matter. The available data indicates that from 1820 to 1880, Jewish immigrants resembled their Christian counterparts, a view that conflicts with current literature. Until quite recently, the motives of earlier Jewish migrants from central and eastern Europe were not much discussed. Most authors agreed that they departed from the German states and neighboring territories because of anti-Jewish legislation and persecution—just like many Jews from the Russian Empire who ostensibly fled severe government restrictions and the notorious pogroms sweeping across the Pale of Settlement in the early 1880s and again after the turn of the century.[7]

Until the late eighteenth century, Jews across Europe were subjected to various restrictions. They often could not own land, were banned from many cities and territories, and had to live on the margins of feudal societies. The overwhelming majority was poor. But most of their Christian neighbors did not fare much better; they were tied to the land and also lived within a narrowly defined social space. By the late eighteenth century, Jewish and non-Jewish Enlightenment thinkers proposed giving Jews full citizenship rights. Jewish emancipation was part of a larger modernization project whose proponents sought an expansion of individual rights for all members of society. A few years after Jewish emancipation had been seriously debated in the German context, the French Revolution brought liberty to French Jews in 1791. Emancipation was extended in the following years to areas west of the Rhine that came under French rule. Napoleon's *décret infame* reintroduced several restrictions for French Jews in 1808, but it expired in 1815.

Partly under French influence, the various German states lifted some anti-Jewish regulations. Each state designed its own policy, but state bureaucrats shared the view that emancipation should be a gradual process. The granting of rights was tied to proof of Jewish "improvement." With the defeat of Napoleon, Jewish emancipation stalled across central Europe. Jews in the eastern provinces of Prussia and in Bavaria experienced few changes for the better before the mid-1840s. In contrast, several southwest German states continued to pursue liberal policies toward Jewish populations. All German Jews were only fully emancipated in 1871 with the founding of the German nation-state.[8]

Christians generally enjoyed liberties earlier than Jews, but their material situation was frequently precarious. The process of ending feudal rule in the German states echoed the gradual emancipation of Jews. In some territories land reforms dragged on for decades and the situation of many small farmers did not improve. The persistence of traditional regulations and inheritance patterns, coupled with the impact of massive economic transformation, forced large numbers of young Christians in the southwest German countryside to move, especially to nearby cities and, in ever-larger numbers, to America. Most Jews who occupied niches as cattle traders or peddlers in rural economies were affected by economic change, not least by the departure of their Christian customers and employees.

In America, European immigrants found vastly different conditions. No feudal traditions restricted land ownership. Guilds did not exist, so every artisan could open a shop or start a business. Many struggling farmers and artisans from southwest Germany prospered in their new home country. Friends and family members soon joined them, pulling more people from the *Heimat* (home) across the Atlantic. The few hundred Jews living in the United States at the time of the American Revolution were not formally emancipated. Even under British rule, they had been subjected only to limited formal restrictions. The Constitution provided Jewish males, just like all other free whites, with full citizenship rights. Just as Christian farmers left feudalism behind, Jewish immigrants reaching America's shores effectively emancipated themselves as they stepped off the boat.[9]

Emancipation policies did influence Jewish migration from the German states and neighboring regions, but assessing the exact impact in a period of social and economic upheaval, when many Christians were also on the move, is almost impossible. When the formerly French territories west of the Rhine became part of Bavaria, Hesse, and Prussia in 1815, the liberal French laws introduced under the Napoleonic rule were not rescinded. Jews living in these areas, like Jakob Grünebaum, were almost completely emancipated and faced few obstacles in their daily lives. Yet Jews left these areas in significant numbers for American and German cities between the 1820s and the 1870s. This suggests that the lifting of restrictive policies against Jews may not have prevented migration but made it easier because Jews could pursue more options.[10]

Several scholars emphasize the role of anti-Jewish violence as a key factor behind emigration. But apart from two notorious outbursts, in 1819 and in the early stages of the 1848–1849 revolution, when riots against Jews occurred in several communities across central Europe, systematic violence against Jews was rare. A clear link between anti-Jewish violence and Jewish migration to America (or elsewhere) has not been established. The wave of severe anti-Jewish riots in Bohemia and Moravia in the spring of 1848, for instance, had no measurable impact on the strong Jewish migration. Several contemporary Jewish commentators even lamented that Bohemian Jews did not leave because of the violence but were driven purely by material considerations.[11]

Jacob's journey would be of no further significance to this study had his decision only involved his immediate family. Yet every researcher of Chicago Jewish history who briefly glances at his reminiscences will recognize familiar names: Jacob's mother, Miriam, belonged to the Felsenthal family; his wife's maiden name was Sara Herz (anglicized to Hart); and he also mentioned the Rubels and Guthmanns. Members of these families were among the founders and longtime members of Sinai, and they were closely related through marriage decades before the migration to Chicago began in the 1840s—and decades afterwards. Moreover, there were many others whom Jacob knew but did not mention, probably because they were not close relatives. His son Michael was one of the first Jews who settled in Chicago, but he was not the first from the region around Eppelsheim. Indeed, in the first comprehensive history of the Jewish community in Chicago, Rabbi Emil G. Hirsch and his coauthor Herman Eliassof stressed in 1900, "The Chicago Jewish community is indeed deeply indebted to Eppelsheim.... Many of its best and noblest members hail from that distant German place."[12]

EPPELSHEIM TO CHICAGO: CHAIN MIGRATION

The Eppelsheim network reached beyond Jacob and his sons. The Greenebaums came from Eppelsheim, and so did their relatives, the two brothers Abraham and Henry Hart, as did Nathan Schaffner. One of the early immigrants (and another Sinai founder), Leopold Mayer from nearby Abenheim, recalled in 1899, "Fifty years ago ... with my sister and sainted father, I boarded a Rhine steamer." Via Antwerp and New York, the Mayers traveled to Chicago to join Leopold's brother Marx L. Mayer, who was one of the first Jewish settlers in Chicago when he arrived in 1843 and was very likely the pioneer of the Eppelsheim migration network. His friends Elias and Henry Greenebaum helped Leopold Mayer to find a job. In Chicago, Mayer married Regina Schulz from Flomersheim, south of Worms, a relatively short trip from his home village.

Abenheim was also the ancestral home of the Spiegel family. Samuel Strauss came from the nearby town Kirchheimbolanden. Gerhard Foreman and his four brothers, his parents, and a sister grew up in Dirmstein, just across the border in the Palatinate. Several members of the extensive Felsenthal family came from Odenbach and Münchweiler to Chicago. The Rubels from Kaiserslautern, the Mandel brothers from Kerzenheim, Joseph Gatzert (a later president of Sinai) from Hochheim near Worms, and many others belonged to this network. Many of these families were closely related to each other.

Jacob Greenebaum corresponded by mail with his sons before he joined them. These letters formed the links of the migration chain, providing detailed information about the trip and job prospects in the new world. All the persons mentioned, except the pioneer Marx L. Mayer, moved to Chicago between 1845 and 1857. Several married among each other (Greenebaum-Spiegel, Greenebaum-Foreman) and cooperated as business partners, most in the production and retail of various textiles and in banking. Almost all were social climbers; some became wealthy. Several migrants regularly returned to Europe to visit their relatives during the summer months.[13]

Even more Jews moved from the area around Eppelsheim to Chicago. Jeweler Herman Hahn left Eppelsheim with his parents in 1849 but arrived in Chicago only in 1873 after having lived in Pennsylvania and Ohio. In Chicago, he first joined Zion congregation, and, after several years, Sinai. Alfred Decker moved in 1886 from Kirchheimbolanden.[14] Probably, dozens of other families and individuals were somehow related to this network.

One such connection that is not immediately obvious concerns Samuel Adler, the New York rabbi who preached Sinai's dedication sermon in 1861. Superficially, it made sense for Sinai's founders to invite Adler, one of the few university-trained rabbis in America, from Temple Emanu-El in New York. Adler, however, was hardly a stranger, but a *Landsmann*. Between 1842 and 1857, he had served the small Jewish community of Alzey, a short walk from the neighboring village Eppelsheim. Adler was an early advocate of Reform Judaism, just like his close acquaintance Elias Grünebaum, the district rabbi for the southern part of the Palatinate in Landau and a relative of Jacob. Given these links and the geographic proximity, many of the young men and women from the villages surrounding Alzey probably had attended Adler's services at least occasionally and were familiar with the Reform theology he espoused.[15]

One of the more intriguing sources on the Eppelsheim network are the *Reisenotizen* (travel notes) of Bernhard Felsenthal, Sinai's first rabbi.[16] Felsenthal graduated from a higher polytechnic school in Munich in the late 1840s, but as a Jew he could not enter the Bavarian civil service. He returned to his home village in the Palatinate, where he worked as a religious teacher for the local Jewish community. Privately, he studied Jewish history and theology. In 1854, when he was thirty-two years old, Felsenthal left to join his brother in Louisville, Kentucky, on the Ohio River. His exact motives remain unclear, but his job prospects were diminishing as more and more young Jews were departing for cities in central Europe and America. Indeed, especially in smaller villages in South Germany, a whole generation was on the move after 1840. In 1853, the *Allgemeine Zeitung des Judenthums* reported that a small Jewish community just outside of Worms (and close to Eppelsheim) had dissolved because of the strong migration to the United States.[17] The new communities in America, on the other hand, were established and dominated by immigrants of Felsenthal's generation, many of whom had recently married and had children. With his job experience, Felsenthal could expect to find employment relatively easily and start his own family.

The diary provides insight into Felsenthal's journey of the mid-1850s. Felsenthal traveled with a party of relatives and Jewish friends from the same region. The small group left Münchweiler on the morning of June 4, 1854. At a nearby town they boarded a train on the evening of June 6, reaching Paris on the following morning. They had enough time to tour the sights before heading to the port of Le Havre. Here, Felsenthal and most others in his party saw the ocean for the first time in their lives. He wrote, "As I glanced at the open water, that vast, broad, and green plain of water, our home for weeks to come, my heart filled with horror." On June 16, the ship packed with 210 Germans (among them several Jews) left the port and "seasickness came upon [them] soon." Almost a month later, Felsenthal wrote that the ship was still on the open sea. During that period, he was tormented by a severe illness. On June 30, Felsenthal was so sick that several fellow passengers believed him dead. Without access to medication, insufficient care facilities, and lack of drinking water, he must have been in extreme distress. Eventually, his condition improved, against considerable odds. On July 19, when Felsenthal had barely recovered, the ship was rocked by a severe storm; this was followed by days of intense heat and thirst.

On July 23, they saw land. Felsenthal wrote, "Finally, thank God, the American coast lies before us, bathed in golden sunlight! What a joyful excitement." A day later, after a journey of more than five weeks, the ship docked in New York City. Given the anxieties and sufferings of what was actually a fairly typical crossing, most passengers were probably much more relieved to escape the ship than to have reached America. After three exhausting days in America's hectic entrepôt—he complained bitterly about being overcharged and cheated as a "green" immigrant wherever he went in New York—Felsenthal boarded a train to Philadelphia, where he stayed with distant relative Hermann Greenebaum. Perhaps to welcome Felsenthal, another relative of the two men was visiting from Chicago, none other than Jacob Greenebaum.

In the following months and years, Felsenthal wrote only brief entries with long gaps in between, recording the names of his correspondence partners, the places he visited, and the sermons he gave. After a short stay in Philadelphia, he continued his journey to Louisville, Kentucky, his final destination. His brother Marcus Felsenthal had lived there since the previous year (1853). After settling in Louisville, Felsenthal corresponded with Gerhard "Fuhrmann" and (probably Jacob) "Grünebaum" in Chicago and numerous other relatives across the United States and back home. He also got in touch with Cincinnati rabbi Isaac Mayer Wise and contributed at least one article to his weekly, *Israelite*. After temporary jobs as a religious teacher and preacher with Jewish congregations in Dayton, Ohio, and Lawrenceburg, Indiana, Felsenthal moved to Madison, Indiana, on the Ohio River early in 1856, where he served the small Jewish congregation as religious leader and teacher. The diary ends in 1857. The following year, Felsenthal settled in Chicago to work as a clerk in a bank owned by Henry Greenebaum and Gerhard Foreman. After a short time, he emerged as spiritual leader of the nascent Reform movement. He had first met several of its Chicago members long before his move to America.[18]

This individual example illustrates how far the links between immigrants stretched across the Atlantic and the American continent. Felsenthal could rely on precise information on the travel route and knew friends and relatives would provide protection in the first weeks after arrival. The small network ranged in scope from relatives, personal friends, and people from the same village or area to distant acquaintances.

Another interesting aspect of the immigrant story is the duration of the journey. Felsenthal's transatlantic crossing took several weeks and was thoroughly exhausting. By the mid to late 1850s, shortly after Felsenthal's crossing, the use of steam engines began to cut the travel time and increased the safety, making it easier and more affordable for travelers to make the crossing in both directions—and improving the links between different members of migration networks. Soon after the Civil War, steam ships largely supplanted sailing vessels. Already in the mid-1850s, larger towns and cities on both sides of the Atlantic were connected to rapidly expanding railway networks. Leopold Mayer, who had gone from Abenheim to Chicago only a few years earlier, had to rely on more traditional means. He took a Rhine steamer, probably from Mainz, to Antwerp. Once in New York, he could not yet reach Chicago exclusively by train. Steamers covered part of the journey before the mid-1850s, especially the last leg across Lake Michigan. The rapidly improving infrastructure made long-distance migration more feasible and explains in part the rise in migration within and from Europe to America after 1850 and the spectacular growth of booming economic centers like Chicago. Technological innovation facilitated mass migration as more people could cover larger distances faster, more safely, and for much less money.[19]

Felsenthal's frequent correspondence explains how the members of the Jewish immigrant network kept in touch. His move to Chicago was by no means inevitable. Initially, the growing city on Lake Michigan constituted one of several options for him. The Eppelsheim network itself was not limited to Chicago; it stretched across the United States and was quickly connecting with many other smaller networks as immigrants married, established or joined congregations and associations, and founded businesses with partners. Around 1854, members of the related Greenebaum and Felsenthal families lived, according to Felsenthal's notes, in and near Philadelphia (Greenebaum), Louisville (Felsenthal), Sacramento (Greenebaum), and, of course, Chicago. A few years later, several had moved on. But rather than dispersing further across America in the following decades, most Eppelsheimers eventually clustered in a few large cities, especially in Chicago.[20]

THE MIGRATION AFTER THE MIGRATION

Bernhard Felsenthal's story is a case in point that not all Jews belonging to the Eppelsheim network went straight from their home villages to Chicago.[21] Felsenthal's experience was somewhat unusual because he did not go into business; except for his brief job at the bank in Chicago between 1858 and 1861, he was employed as a religious teacher or rabbi. A majority of male Jews worked as peddlers for several years after arriving in America. Jewish immigrants from central and, later, eastern Europe were a prominent group among nineteenth-century American peddlers. The exact numbers are not known, but Jews were certainly overrepresented. Some were indeed "basket peddlers," who took a bundle on their backs and commuted between the larger cities on the East Coast or smaller cities in the West and the surrounding rural areas. Others covered larger distances with small carriages or delivered goods from a centrally located small store owned by a relative or friend.

From the 1820s through the 1870s, when most Jews from central Europe were arriving, the frontier was still open, and huge numbers of settlers, including many German-speaking immigrants, headed west. In the late 1840s, the expansion of a transportation network west of the Alleghenies was in its early stages, the first railroad tracks were laid, and several canals were dug. Communication over longer distances could take many days. As distribution networks were rapidly developing, taking work as itinerant merchants was an obvious choice, especially for those who possessed experience and the necessary skills but lacked capital. For most, peddling provided an entry into America's economy and to upward social mobility. Few immigrants worked longer than a few years as peddlers. Available statistics indicate that peddling was indeed a "universal-male Jewish experience."[22]

Large East Coast port cities and midsized distribution centers further inland, such as Rochester, New York, on Lake Ontario or Cincinnati on the Ohio River, served as bases for distributing wares further inland. Itinerant merchants often preceded the expanding main transport routes and communication lines to the west, south, and north. Along the main corridors, Jews established dozens of communities, especially in the quickly expanding cities of the West: in the 1830s, in the river cities of Cincinnati, Louisville, and St. Louis, and a little later in Cleveland, Columbus, Detroit, Chicago, and Milwaukee. Most peddlers who sold their goods throughout the West settled in these cities after they had accumulated enough capital to open a small store or start a business. Others operated stores in smaller towns such as Lafayette, Indiana, or Peoria, Illinois, or in the South and even California, before moving on to a larger city. Many successful Jewish immigrants had first worked as peddlers. Yet the "legend of peddler to department store owner" that according to one author is a "fact" remained the exception. Many peddlers built small businesses and achieved modest success but did not become rich by default. Some peddlers failed or remained on the economic and social margins, leaving few, if any, traces.[23]

American freedom was not without ambiguities for Jewish peddlers. Few were particularly enthusiastic about the way they made a living. In his diary, Abraham Kohn from Franconia, the first president of Sinai's mother congregation, KAM, complained about peddling. He had been looking for a job as a clerk in New York after his arrival in 1842 but was not lucky. "Whether I wanted it or not, like all the others I had to pack my bundle on my back and walk out to the countryside." For Kohn, a religious Jew, it was hardly possible to observe the *halakha* (Jewish law) while on the road. "We must obey His sacred Torah, the sacred law of Sinai, but with this way of life nobody is able to adhere to even a minimum of it."

The memoirs of Leopold Furth, written in 1855 in several letters, give an impression of the everyday lives of Jewish peddlers. Furth grew up in a small Bohemian village where his father worked as a teacher, most likely for the local Jewish community. Furth described the economic situation as very depressing. He followed his siblings to America, traveling with friends via Bremen to New York, arriving (like Kohn) in 1842. At the inn the Deutscher Ochse (German Ox), he ran into another immigrant who described peddling as a lucrative occupation. For some time, Furth sold vegetables and fruit in New York, primarily to female workers. Most of the other peddlers, he recalled, were Jews from Bavaria. After being wanted for a crime he did not commit (if we believe him), Furth joined a whaling expedition to the Pacific. After safely returning, he moved to Chicago in 1846, where he lodged in a *Bodinghaus* (boarding house) and worked as coachman: "A sailor is like a rabbi; he can also steer." Later, Furth left the city to live in northern Wisconsin, regularly coming back to buy tools.[24] The coachman-rabbi comparison is the only direct hint at Furth's Jewish background. Unlike Kohn, religion did not concern him. Nevertheless, these experiences (apart from Furth's Pacific adventure) were certainly typical. A high degree of flexibility and mobility was required to make it in America.

It is indeed striking how many male Jews worked as peddlers before moving to Chicago. Specific assessments are difficult, because Jewish peddlers often were not registered in address books before settling down. Many of the men involved in establishing Sinai congregation spent several years on the road, often in the region around Chicago, in northern Illinois and Indiana, and in eastern Iowa. During the 1840s, the five Fuhrmann brothers (Foreman in America) and their parents migrated one after the other from Dirmstein in the Palatinate to La Porte, Indiana. The family was part of the above-described network that also included the Greenebaums. From their base in La Porte, they sold clothes and other goods in the surrounding area before moving to nearby Chicago around 1854. Here, the brothers worked alone and as partners in different endeavors: in banking, as insurance agents, as shoe retailers, and in the dry goods business. Joseph Ullmann from Alsace, later a wealthy fur trader, peddled throughout Iowa in the 1850s. Isaac Waixel from Hesse also worked as a peddler after his arrival in 1852. In 1857, he came to Chicago and traded meat products. A year later, he was among the founders of Sinai's predecessor institution, the *Reformverein*. In 1859, Waixel established the first wholesale business for meat in Chicago. His partner was another ex-peddler, Nelson Morris, who was born in Hechingen (Hohenzollern) in 1838. Morris had arrived in Chicago in 1854, finding work as a laborer in the stockyards, where he would make a huge fortune in the following decades. As a small boy, Morris had walked with his father, a cattle dealer, through the villages of the Black Forest. After moving to America in 1851, he first peddled in Massachusetts and, for a short time, worked along the Erie Canal and on boats crossing the Great Lakes.[25]

Most of the early Jewish settlers in Chicago spent years at other places after having arrived in New York or another port. The migration of Maximilian M. Gerstley shows the influence of changing economic conditions and personal circumstances but also the importance of social networks. Gerstley hailed from Fellheim near Ulm in Bavaria. After training as a carpenter, he moved to Vienna in 1840 to work in the business of his half brother. In the early 1840s, Gerstley left Europe for Philadelphia, where another half brother had settled (indeed, with the exception of his brother Heinrich, all of his siblings and half siblings eventually moved abroad). He first peddled goods in eastern Pennsylvania. Near Hagerstown, Maryland, he married a Mennonite woman, but the marriage failed and the couple divorced. In 1848, Gerstley decided to move to Peoria with his son. Although he does not mention it in his memoirs, Peoria was the obvious place for Gerstley to raise his son. According to a history of Jews in Illinois edited by Emil G. Hirsch in 1900, several of the first Jewish settlers in Peoria originated in Fellheim, Gerstley's small home village. Yet Gerstley never made it to Peoria. Once he stepped off the steamer in Chicago, he decided to stay for a while in the rapidly growing city. During the 1850s, he established himself in the clothing sector. When Sinai was founded, the moderate Reformer Gerstley became the president of its mother congregation, KAM.[26]

The story of longtime Sinai member and president Morris Selz also illustrates the correlation between high social mobility and migration. Selz left his home village in Württemberg when he was eighteen years old and started out as a clerk in a dry goods store in Connecticut. He then ran a small clothing store in upstate New York. After it failed, he went to Georgia to work as a traveling salesman for a Rochester-based clothing business. In 1851, he moved—pulled like so many others by the Gold Rush—to California. In 1854, he settled in Chicago, where he made some money in the production and retail of shoes. By the turn of the century, the multimillionaire Selz owned a large shoe factory and directed an "army" of shoe salesmen from his office in Chicago.[27]

A closer examination of the migration paths of Jewish Chicagoans shows that quite a few chose small towns in the wider vicinity of their eventual destination as temporary bases. La Porte, Indiana, was such a gateway town because it was close to Chicago and in a favorable location, straddling the east-west corridor that linked Chicago with the East Coast and close to a north-south route connecting Michigan with the Ohio River Valley. The Indiana town served as a stopover for several Chicago-bound Jews, including the Foreman brothers. At least two of the Eliel brothers from Hesse spent some time in La Porte: the leather trader (and future Sinai president) Gustav between 1853 and 1864 and the tobacco merchant Lambert between 1856 and 1866. In 1857, Lazarus Stern moved from La Porte to Chicago, where he later owned a large furniture retail business. A Ms. J. Florsheim, who managed a small store that sold diamonds and jewels, relocated to Chicago in the mid-1870s. The Liebenstein family in Chicago also had relatives in La Porte. Very likely, many more Jewish migrants went through La Porte, spending only a few weeks or months in the town (and leaving no traces) before moving on to Chicago.

The U.S. census provides additional information about internal migrations. The census takers wrote down the birthdates and the states (or countries) where children of households had been born, but usually not the towns or cities. Therefore, internal migration within Illinois cannot be reconstructed. But the Jewish parents of the sample, most in their mid-30s, who lived in Chicago in 1850, 1860, and 1870 (when the census was taken), had moved from New York or Pennsylvania to Ohio or Indiana and from there to Chicago. Several went straight to Illinois, returned to the East Coast, and then moved back to Chicago. The sample allows for another interesting observation: almost all children were American born. Like many other migrants, young Jewish women and men established families only after arrival and with a sufficient economic basis. For many, it was much more feasible to start a small business in towns relatively close to Chicago to prepare for the move to the large city with its greater opportunities—and risks. While the importance of small towns for American Jewish life has been recognized, apart from Stephen Mostov no author has examined the function of smaller towns and villages as stopover locations for Jewish migrants who were on their way to bigger cities.[28]

JEWISH MIGRATION AND CULTURAL CAPITAL

The founders of Sinai were highly mobile young men and women, often with children, who frequently had lived in smaller towns in America before moving to Chicago. Most belonged to social networks and prospered in their new home city—some spectacularly. Jewish immigrants from central Europe are often associated with high social mobility, but the process remains little understood.

The crossing of Jacob and his family, friends, and acquaintances from the region around Eppelsheim illustrates that Jewish migration resembled the general movement from southwest Germany to North America during the 1840s and 1850s and cannot be separated from it. Most Christians from southwest Germany also migrated in networks, and they, too, were relatively young men and women. Typically, they were small artisans and farmers affected by economic transformation who hoped to improve their prospects in America. The heads of household usually sold their small plots or workshops or were compensated for the expected inheritance. Thus, they could take more capital to America than most Jewish migrants, who usually did not own land or much other property they could sell; the well-to-do Jacob was certainly an exception. Even the suggestion to study Jewish migration within the broader social and economic framework conflicts with the still-dominant view that Jewish migration, even from central Europe, was a distinct phenomenon, a one-way street with no possibility of return.[29]

According to the authors of several recent studies discussing the Jewish migration from central Europe to America, Jews were much more likely to emigrate than Christians. This assertion is based on a comparison of Jews with the "general" movement. Yet, obviously, a very small, clearly defined group comprising less than 1 percent of the general population will a priori differ, if compared with all others. In fact, the only characteristic all "other" migrants from the German states, one of the largest but also most heterogeneous immigrant groups in nineteenth-century America, shared was that they were not Jewish. Moreover, inner-Jewish and regional differences were considerable. Social, ethnic, religious, and other differences between migrants from one region may be more relevant for contemporary historians than they were at the time. Defining one set of people without looking at the larger context and relationships to others can lead to the artificial construction of seemingly cohesive and distinctive groups.[30] Particularly in the context of immigration, Jews did not organize just one clearly defined *Gemeinschaft* but several—small Jewish migration networks almost certainly overlapped with networks of Christians from the same micro-region.

The argument that Jewish migrants were distinct needs to be refined by looking more closely at internal Jewish movement within the German states. Jews certainly had a different economic profile than their Christian neighbors, and, crucially, soon after the middle of the nineteenth century their social mobility as a group was surprisingly high. In early-nineteenth-century central Europe, most Jews (like the Grünebaums) and their Christian counterparts lived side by side in small rural communities. In premodern societies, Jews had been forced into marginal niches such as peddling, selling cattle, dealing with clothes, or lending small amounts of money. Almost all Jews were poor, but unlike their Christian neighbors they were not tied to the land and often were independent mini-entrepreneurs who networked within often extensive family diasporas, for instance, when they bought and sold goods as itinerant peddlers.

Jacob Greenebaum's descriptions of his youth conform to the general trend. As a young boy, he was orphaned, and so was his future wife, Sara Herz. His family lived from hand to mouth, and as a teenager, Jacob, like many other Jewish men, worked as an itinerant peddler. He mentions relatives and friends who carved out niches providing services in the agricultural economy, for instance, as cattle traders or, like his father-in-law, as self-trained veterinarians. After his marriage, Jacob branched out and dealt with agricultural products, tools, and clothes. Before full Jewish emancipation was introduced under French rule in the areas west of the Rhine shortly after 1800, Jews could not own real estate, settle in many larger cities, and join the guilds. Enforced marginality made Jewish males much more mobile than most Christians, and they shifted between different occupations, specializing as peddlers who often traveled over long distances. In the Franconian counties Ansbach and Forchheim, more than 50 percent of the resident male Jews were peddlers in the early 1800s. In rural Alsace, the numbers were probably even higher: In 1846, 78 percent of all Jews in communities studied by Paula Hyman were peddlers.[31]

Within a few years after their immigration, Jacob Greenebaum's sons Michael,

Elias, and Heinrich (who became Henry in America) were well-respected and wealthy citizens of Chicago. Admittedly, the three Greenebaum brothers were more successful than most of their Jewish and Christian counterparts. Yet Jewish immigrants from central and eastern Europe who arrived before the 1870s displayed a remarkably high social mobility. Respected immigration historian John Higham has described mid-century Jewish immigrants from central Europe as the most successful immigrant group in American history.[32] This assessment should certainly be approached with some caution. As mentioned before, Jewish immigrants from central Europe were a small group that can hardly be compared to the millions of Irish or German-speaking immigrants who arrived during the same period. The amazing careers of Joseph Seligman and Simon Guggenheim, who made the transition from poor peddlers to spectacular wealth in a few decades, were the exceptions.

Yet before 1900, Sinai congregation included dozens of the wealthiest citizens of Chicago in its ranks. The files of the main community institutions serving destitute Jews after 1850 prove that there was no Jewish poverty problem to speak of before the late 1870s.[33] The swift economic and social rise of Jewish immigrants as a group may have been without parallel in America—but it shows striking similarities to the mobility of Jews in Germany. This leads to the question of what actually happened to rural Jews in central Europe who did *not* migrate to America.

The migrations of Jews like the Grünebaum family and Christians from southwest Germany to America were linked with internal migrations. Jews who did not leave central Europe had more options than moving to America. The massive economic transformations of the first half of the nineteenth century had an impact on rural economies, forcing young men and women especially to look for new opportunities and, increasingly, to relocate. In 1820, most Jews in the German states were poor, lived in villages, and faced legal and economic restrictions. By 1871, when the last German Jews were fully emancipated, most belonged to the *Bürgertum* (bourgeoisie) and had recently moved to a city. Three decades later, around the turn of the century, German Jews overwhelmingly lived in large cities: Breslau, Hamburg, Frankfurt, Leipzig, and, in particular, in the rapidly growing German metropolis, Berlin.[34] What *is* remarkable about this transition is not the rise of a few Jewish entrepreneurs and bankers to spectacular wealth but the broad *Verbürgerlichung* (embourgoisement) of the large majority of Jews in the German states within one generation. The term *Verbürgerlichung* does not translate directly to English; the concept describes more than the rise from relative poverty or a lower class status to modest wealth and material security. A

CHAPTER ONE

key aspect of *Verbürgerlichung* entails the acquisition of *Bildung* (loosely translated as education, with a strong emphasis on cultural knowledge) and of specific behavioral patterns. Nineteenth-century women and men with *Bildung* either knew how to or aspired to play a musical instrument, were well versed in literature and philosophy, and joined *bürgerlich* associations cultivating the arts and refined sociability.

One author explains this extraordinary social mobility by characterizing rural Jews who went to the German cities as "winners." They were more modern, had enjoyed some education in Germany, and had accumulated capital before they moved. America-bound migrants, on the other hand, were in this view, "losers" of the economic transformation. They were poor, had little, if any, education, overwhelmingly spoke Yiddish, were not "Germanized," and once in America did not "look back" to Germany.[35] But interestingly, Jews in the United States (and to some extent in Britain) also experienced as spectacular a social rise in the nineteenth century as Jews in German states. The successful British and American Jews were of course overwhelmingly the very Jewish "losers" who had left central Europe. These Jewish migrants actually "looked back"—as the following chapters will show—holding German culture in high esteem. And they should not be described as "losers."

The simplistic winners versus losers dichotomy relates to an even older model: very poor Jews left for America, sometimes even with the support of their communities, and thus "helped" to improve the social profile of the remaining Jews. Jewish communities in central Europe did in some cases finance the crossing of impoverished Jews to America after 1815. Christians opted for similar solutions; during the hunger crisis of 1846 and 1847, several villages in Bavaria subsidized the migration of very poor families to America. But these practices were actually much less widespread than contemporaries in America believed.[36] As pointed out above, in Chicago, the number of distressed Jewish immigrants who required support from other Jews remained limited before 1880.

Most Jews bound for German cities or America had few means but certainly enough to migrate. They usually could rely on precise information about the living conditions where they had friends and relatives. And they were young and had skills, often having spent several years in school. Poor Jews without education and skills would not have "made it" in America. The real losers were actually those who did not even have the limited means needed to move. "Poor," like "rich" or "middle class," is a relative term, betraying a rather wide spectrum. Most Jewish migrants were materially poor, but most had accumulated sufficient cultural capital they could invest in the rapidly transforming economies of Chicago, New York, or Berlin in the three decades after 1840: education, skills, and bourgeois values. Jewish migrants to German cities and America carried the key to success in their skills and values, not in their purses.

Jews like Jacob and his sons had better opportunities in the newly emerging capitalist economy than many Christians, because they had experienced forced economic marginalization in the rural economies of central Europe. Intimate knowledge about the mechanics of markets, experience organizing small businesses and pooling capital with trustworthy relatives and close friends, weathering decline and even failure, dealing with arbitrary bureaucratic decisions, and relying on information and deep-rooted and far-reaching family networks quite often proved to be crucial advantages. Jewish entrepreneurs in Germany were trailblazers in many new sectors, notably in the textile industry, retail sector, and, initially, banking.[37] Inherited knowledge and experience alone, however, do not explain the broad rise of a group from relative poverty into the middle class within one generation.

It would be too shortsighted to explain the broad *Verbürgerlichung* of Jews in Germany as a corollary of economic success. In a recent analysis of Jewish social mobility in mid-nineteenth-century central Europe, historian Simone Lässig finds the main cause for the broad and swift *Verbürgerlichung* to be the accumulation of cultural capital as a Jewish response to the prolonged emancipation policies in the German states. State bureaucrats forced *Verbürgerlichung* upon Jews. In France, Britain, and the Netherlands, Jewish emancipation largely followed a laissez-faire approach, leaving Jews with a variety of individual choices, including the refusal to become modern.

In the German states, emancipation was a collective project tied to a quid pro quo: no emancipation without education and proof of civil "improvement." As Lässig shows, *Bildung* was a path quite acceptable for the large majority of Jews because it was broad and tied to a future-oriented, universalistic program. In contrast to the potentially exclusive concept of the nation, the *Bildungsideal* was inclusive. However, and this is the truly intriguing point made by Lässig, Pierre Bourdieu's argument of the conversion of economical into cultural capital was not a one way street: the *Verbürgerlichung* of the German Jews illustrates, almost paradigmatically, that this process also worked in the opposite direction. The accumulation of cultural capital, especially a good and thorough education, was a crucial prerequisite for high social mobility.[38]

Comparisons between the large Irish- and German-speaking immigrant groups in mid-nineteenth-century America indicate higher social mobility of the latter in the first generation, and not only because German speakers owned and brought more economic capital to America than the often almost destitute Irish. German speakers generally were better educated and possessed more skills than Irish immigrants. But as a consequence of emancipation policies, many Jewish immigrants from central Europe had enjoyed an even better education than Christians from the same regions. This subject requires more detailed research on the micro level.[39] Nevertheless, most early Jewish immigrants to Chicago had attended school. Some who arrived in the early 1850s—like Sinai founders Julius Rosenthal, Gerhard Foreman, Leopold Mayer, Bernhard Felsenthal, and others—came from small villages, but they had attended a university or other institution of higher learning before departure. The modestly wealthy Jacob brought his sons into his business during the 1840s, but only after he had sent them to an advanced boarding school, a *gymnasium* in Kaiserslautern for several years. Leopold Mayer worked initially as a teacher in Chicago before establishing a bank. Godfrey Snydacker and Bernhard Felsenthal both taught at religious schools attached to congregations. Glancing over the many dozen biographies of Chicago Jews in a large community history edited by Rabbi Emil G. Hirsch in 1901 it is remarkable how many Jews mentioned their German (and sometimes American) school education. Admittedly, these biographies concentrated on successful men (and a few women active in philanthropic associations). But it is interesting that even around 1900 as many of these men were approaching retirement their German school education continued to be a matter of much pride.[40] And not surprisingly, as we shall see, among various philanthropic projects established Chicago Jews conceived for new immigrants from eastern Europe after 1880 and later for African Americans, schools would figure prominently.

This leads to a somewhat surprising conclusion. The view that gradual emancipation policies in the German states were major factors in driving Jews out is shortsighted. Rather, the pressure of emancipation equipped most Jews with sufficient cultural capital to move up socially and economically, within central European cities and in the United States. The acquisition of cultural capital or *Bildung* reached beyond the economic sphere into the synagogue, as the following chapters covering the early decades of Sinai's history will show.

The backgrounds of migrants and the process of migration influenced social and religious life at the destination. The majority of Jewish Chicagoans from central Europe belonged to a number of networks that can be traced back over many generations. These networks were comprised of family members, relatives, and friends but also of distant acquaintances (and even Christians) from specific places in the *Heimat*. They often moved to several different destinations but kept in close touch and eventually clustered in several places. Although Jewish immigrants did come from small villages in the central European countryside and did not possess much economic capital, they had a solid education. More than a few had been exposed to the teachings of Jewish Reform before departing for America, through local rabbis such as Samuel Adler or Elias Grünebaum. Most immigrants knew what they could expect in Chicago and how they would get there (even if it would take several years). They were well equipped to respond to and prosper in what was a challenging and tough, but also a uniquely promising city.

2.

AT FIRST GLANCE, Chicago in 1861 appeared to be a rather unlikely setting for a radical Reform congregation with considerable intellectual aspirations. By that year, only four other congregations with a similar theological outlook had been established in America, not quite coincidentally in port cities on the East Coast: in Charleston (Beth Elohim), New York (Temple Emanu-El), Philadelphia (Keneseth Israel), and Baltimore (Har Sinai). In stark contrast, Chicago was a bustling but remote western city without much of a history. But it was growing rapidly, attracting thousands of migrants from central Europe, the British Isles, and the American Northeast. In 1840, when the first Jews reached the recently incorporated city, Chicago counted four thousand inhabitants. From 1850 to 1860, the number rose from under thirty thousand to about a hundred and ten thousand, and the city was quickly catching up with its two more established western rivals St. Louis and Cincinnati (each had around a hundred and sixty thousand inhabitants in 1860). Chicago lacked culture, and it was a brutal place. Untreated sewage made life anywhere near the Chicago River or the coast of Lake Michigan intolerable, especially during the blistering summers. Due to the lack of clean water, cholera remained a constant risk, claiming dozens of lives. Most streets were not paved and turned into a morass of mud during the wet season. Hundreds of homeless children lived on the streets; crime and prostitution were rampant. And yet, if the impact of the social and economic transformation that gripped America during the 1850s and 1860s was much more acute in Chicago than elsewhere, the same applied to the possibilities newcomers from Europe and other parts of America found in the city. Newness meant the absence of established elites and of social barriers; and rapid change and technological innovation constantly created new opportunities. Because it was a radical and quickly transforming city, Chicago was well suited for a religious experiment that broke with the century-old religious tradition.[1]

The founding of Chicago's Sinai congregation in 1861 was indeed a radical step. The founders' strong convictions about Reform provided the decisive momentum to launch the congregation—against much opposition. The ideals of the then-fledgling congregation—in many ways reflective of the dynamic, optimistic, and revolutionary city of its origin—were so radical that the Jewish community of the time was thrown into deep divisions on the topic of Reform. In fact, the weekly *Israelite*, edited by influential Cincinnati rabbi Isaac Mayer Wise, summed up the views of many more traditionally inclined American Jews in 1861 with the acerbic criticism that Sinai's split from Chicago's first Jewish congregation was comparable to South Carolina's secession from the Union. To understand the roots of Wise's fury and the betrayal he felt, we must journey back to a cold winter day in early 1860.

A SURPRISE ENCOUNTER

Wise was on his way home from a short visit to Chicago. He was not in a particularly good mood. Initially it had been an amicable visit, like others before. When he had come to Chicago, the leading members of the Chicago Jewish community had treated him in a respectful manner. In 1860, neither of the two Jewish congregations in Chicago had an ordained rabbi; visiting rabbis like Wise partly filled the gap. At the time, having one of the most prominent American rabbis as a guest was a major event for the small Jewish community. As on earlier visits, Wise probably gave a sermon to the larger congregation, Kehilath Anshe Ma'ariv, and a reception was organized in his honor. He also attended a meeting at the local B'nai B'rith lodge, Ramah. The Independent Order of the B'nai B'rith had been founded in 1843 as a fraternal organization to unite Jewish immigrants from all over Europe. Wise was not just a respected rabbi with a national reputation—he also was one of the leading B'nai B'rith members in the Midwest.

But Wise's 1860 Chicago visit quickly took an unpleasant turn. In apparent disgust, he stormed out of the B'nai B'rith meeting. The disturbance had been caused when a man appeared on the scene whom Wise would scornfully depict only a few weeks later as a rather comic figure with a "long hook-nose upon which rest a pair of large silver spectacles, covering a couple of glass-like eyes . . . [like an] elephant . . . the famous . . . Chicago pamphleteer of radicalism."[2] This sarcastic description betrays disappointment, even anger. The memory of this encounter never really faded from Wise's mind. To his last days, Wise and several leading Chicago Jews could not heal the breach that opened up that January.

The reason the appearance of this "radical pamphleteer" triggered the rapid departure and lingering resentment of the respected visitor from Cincinnati went back to the beginnings of the Chicago Sinai congregation. Of course, Sinai had not yet been established when Wise hurriedly left the B'nai B'rith meeting in 1860. But even before the encounter, Wise must have sensed that Reform Judaism was on the rise in Chicago. This raises another question: why did Wise so fiercely oppose the founding of a Reform congregation in Chicago? The Cincinnati rabbi, after all, was the most prominent Reform rabbi in the West. For years he had tirelessly promoted Reform among Chicago Jews. Personal animosity between him and the then-little-known pamphleteer hardly explains Wise's lingering anger.

Much more likely is that the source of Wise's anger was the German-language pamphlet itself. It had appeared in the previous year in Chicago under the title *Kol Kore Bamidbar: Ueber jüdische Reform—Ein Wort an die Freunde derselben* (A voice in the wilderness: on Jewish Reform—a message to its friends). Wise had certainly studied it, but while in Chicago he realized many Jews in the city had also read it and taken its content to heart. As he departed from Chicago, it dawned on him that his vision of Reform (and his personal role in it) faced a serious challenge. The surprise encounter between Wise and the author of the pamphlet and, indeed, the founding of Sinai occurred at a critical juncture in the history of Jewish Reform in America.

ISAAC MAYER WISE: REFORM WITH A SMALL "r"

Like most midwesterners, Isaac Mayer Wise was a European immigrant who had moved to the region only a few years before. In 1846, when he was twenty-seven years old, he departed from his native Bohemia for the New World. Soon after his arrival in New York, Wise moved upstate to serve with Beth El congregation in Albany.

Within months, he had promoted a modernization of the service. A mixed choir was organized, and the congregation sang German and English hymns. Yet several members fiercely opposed these and potential further changes. In 1850, the traditionalists won the upper hand and dismissed their Reform-minded rabbi. Seemingly unfazed, Wise entered the synagogue in full garb a few days later for the Rosh Hashanah service. But as he stepped forward to take out the Torah scroll, Louis Spanier, the president of the congregation rose, stepped up, and knocked the rabbi down in front of the horrified congregation. A large uproar ensued. Only when the Albany sheriff and his men rushed in was order restored. Following this incident, the Reform-minded members walked out and established a new congregation, Anshe Emeth, with Wise as its leader.[3]

Even before his 1854 move to Bene Yeshurun congregation in the bustling Queen City, Cincinnati, Wise set for himself the goal of organizing Judaism in America under one roof—and under his leadership. Having experienced the break-up of his own congregation up close only reinforced his conviction to work towards a common and inclusive religious platform for American Jews. Wise possessed charisma and temperament, seemingly limitless energy, and boundless ambition. Although the extensive travel must have taken an enormous toll before the arrival of the railroad, he frequently was on the road visiting many distant and small Jewish communities to promote his cause. In the year of his arrival in Cincinnati, he began to publish and edit a successful weekly, the *Israelite*. One year later, he launched a German-language weekly for women, *Die Deborah*. Wise saw himself as an enthusiastic Americanizer and modernizer, but reform with a small "r" meant keeping pace with the "present age" and adapting according to American terms, but did not represent a consistent theology.[4] Indeed, as long as other Jewish leaders accepted his leadership role and supported his pet project of uniting American Jewry, he was quite willing to make concessions to more traditionally inclined Jews.[5]

Wise was a *Macher*, a man who could get things done, but occasionally his ambition outpaced his down-to-earth shrewdness. In 1855, he announced a rabbinical conference in Cleveland. A sizable number of Reform and Orthodox rabbis and lay leaders heeded the call. In order to secure wide support for a union based on a synod and a common liturgy (under his leadership), Wise went a long way. For example, he bowed to Orthodox demands by recognizing the absolute authority of the Talmud. This had earned him the criticism of other Reformers. But the formal withdrawal of several Orthodox rabbis from the agreed-upon document after returning to their congregations brought the union project down before it had taken off.[6]

The idea to organize a national institution with a vague similarity to Protestant denominations addressed the increasing disconnectedness among Jews in mid-nineteenth-century America. Until the early decades of the nineteenth century, most Jews in a given place belonged to one synagogue. The arrival of increasing numbers of immigrants challenged this "synagogue community." The arrivals had diverse backgrounds, and they soon outnumbered the established American Jews. During the 1840s and 1850s, thousands were arriving each year from different parts of central and eastern Europe, especially from the South German states, the Prussian province of Posen, Bohemia, Alsace, and Hungary, as well as in smaller numbers from the Polish provinces of the Russian and the Austrian empires. Estimates of their numbers range widely but even so, Jews actually constituted a very small group before the 1880s—less than 1 percent of the U.S. population.[7]

The majority of new Jewish immigrants moved to large cities, initially along the Eastern Seaboard, in particular to New York and Philadelphia, where small Jewish communities had existed since colonial times. But some Jews joined German-speaking immigrants and headed west. They established new communities in Cincinnati, Cleveland, St. Louis, Chicago, Milwaukee, San Francisco, and dozens of smaller towns during the 1830s and 1840s. Some also settled in the South, in Atlanta, Memphis, Natchez, and, in particular, New Orleans.[8]

The new communities frequently differed from the small, cohesive "synagogue communities" on the East Coast. The immigrants did not come together easily in America. In fact, frequently the very characteristic they all shared—their Jewishness—set them apart. Jews prayed according to their own, often deep-rooted, traditions. Jewish immigrants came from far-flung regions and spoke different languages, especially different Yiddish idioms and German dialects. Many got along better with Christian immigrants from their home regions than with "strange" Jews.

Established American Jews did not receive the newcomers with open arms, often refusing to accept them in their congregations and social circles, primarily because they feared for their social status. In 1846, a correspondent of a leading German Jewish weekly described Jewish life in New York as an ethnic-social hierarchy with the established Portuguese (Sephardim) and Germans on top and the Poles on the bottom, with intense hatred dividing the latter two groups.[9]

Moreover, many Jewish migrants were highly mobile, and even small rural communities experienced constant arrivals and departures. The parents of philanthropist Julius Rosenwald are a case in point. Julius's father, Samuel, had left his Westphalian hometown Bünde for Baltimore in 1854. After running a clothing store in Winchester, Virginia he returned to Baltimore to marry Augusta Hammerslough from Bederkesa, near Bremen, in 1857. Within a few years, the couple moved through several small towns in the South and the Midwest: first to Peoria, Illinois, then to Talladega, Alabama, back west to Evansville, Indiana, and finally in 1861 to Springfield, Illinois, where Julius was born in 1862. In each town, Samuel ran small retail stores.[10]

Landsmanshaft (an affiliation to other immigrants from the same home region), diverse cultural backgrounds, status conflicts, and high fluctuation of arriving and departing settlers explain why community building on the local level was cumbersome. All these factors represented formidable obstacles in their own right, but by 1850 religious fissures were turning into divisions. Some Jews were clinging even more strongly to the cherished Old World traditions than at home. Most Jewish immigrants had grown up in small and tight-knit rural communities in central Europe, where traditional Judaism was not questioned from within. But in America—and especially in Chicago—where the rapidly transforming environment was marked by the early beginnings of industrialization and mass migration, others were calling for external changes, partly in an effort promote their integration into American society.

Some obeyed the *halakha* only superficially, trying to map a path between tradition and real-life challenges. And, in significant numbers, "indifferent" Jews were drifting away without formally leaving Judaism, especially younger immigrants. Leopold Mayer, one of the founders of Sinai, recalled in 1899 that around 1850, "the Sabbath was more or less violated. Many stores were already open, and the younger men, engaged as clerks, were invisible in the synagogue."[11]

Wise clearly recognized the impact of the massive social and economic transformation on traditional Judaism. He did see his task as preserving Jewish "synagogue communities" on the basis of moderate reforms. In his view, a unified institution on the national level would provide a pattern for local community building, and vice versa. For this project he did have to seek grassroots support.

It was not surprising, therefore, that in July 1856, soon after his move to Cincinnati, Wise came to Chicago. "A sea of little wooden houses spread over an extended territory, badly paved streets, and wooden sidewalks, with a few handsome buildings in the center—this was Chicago. It looked like an aggregation of a hundred adjoining villages."[12] He encountered a familiar situation—heated arguments over religion and divisions among immigrants from the different home regions. In 1856, Chicago had two Jewish congregations. In 1847, Jews from South Germany had founded the larger congregation, Kehilath Anshe

Ma'ariv (KAM). This name was supposed to mean Congregation of the Men of the West. But the lay founders confused the word Ma'ariv (evening prayer) with the intended word, Ma'arav (West). Embarrassment over the mistake partly explains why the congregation is known under the acronym KAM to this day. The episode also highlights the absence of laity fluent in Hebrew in the late 1840s, when only few trained rabbis had moved to America. The other congregation, B'nai Sholom (Sons of Peace), was established in 1852, partly because immigrants from Posen were not welcome at KAM, and partly because several preferred to pray according to the Polish rite.

Early in the 1850s, a number of younger, better-educated men, some trained at German universities, reached Chicago and called for a modernization of the service at KAM. Lawyer Julius Rosenthal, teacher Leopold Mayer, businessman Gerhard Foreman, and the Greenebaum brothers, Henry, Elias, and Michael, belonged to this group. They explicitly demanded that German be introduced as the language of the service, because nobody could understand Hebrew prayers. The conflict over the language of the service betrayed differing views on Judaism within the congregation: the founders of the congregation valued the tradition, while newer members pushed for change. According to Leopold Mayer, the services at KAM did not appeal to the younger generation, because "religion is for the living and not for the dead." Two problems demanded immediate action: not only did the traditional service seem completely out of place and embarrassing to younger immigrants who had social contacts with Gentiles, but many Jews simply stayed away from services and severed their ties with the community in the making.[13]

In 1856, around the time of Wise's visit, the discussion about reforms began to be felt within KAM. Recent arrivals were especially vocal in calling for more thorough changes in the service. After long debates, a number of external reforms were introduced. Much to the distress of older members, an organ was acquired.[14] Unlike their coreligionists in Albany, KAM members initially avoided a split. However, in 1856, the position of cofounder and longtime president Abraham Kohn became untenable because he resisted any further reforms. Wise openly voiced his support for the Reformers and reprimanded the ultraconservative faction because it risked losing touch with the demands of the time. He summed up his 1856 visit by stressing "no opponent here."[15] Chicago Jewry was safely in Wise's basket, or so he thought.

By the 1850s, only few rabbis had taken up positions in the United States. The first who immigrated during the 1840s and early 1850s, like Wise, often did not have university training, and only a few had been formally ordained. Most did not question the Jewish tradition. By the mid-1850s a new group of rabbis arrived at America's shores: graduates of German universities, often with PhDs in hand, publications to their names, job experience, and firm Reform credentials. One of the best educated was Samuel Adler, who in 1857 joined Temple Emanu-El in New York after having served a *Gemeinde* in the immediate vicinity of the home villages of the young men who were pushing for changes within KAM.

The mid-nineteenth-century German states were the center of the emerging Jewish Reform movement. Through rabbis like Adler, educated lay members like Mayer, and especially the German Jewish press, the movement began to make an impact in America after 1850. From 1855 on, the rising number of Jewish im-migrants, many of them well educated, helped German Reform to establish a foothold beyond New York, Philadelphia, and Baltimore in cities like Chicago. The 1859 pamphlet that incensed Wise so much reiterated in a nutshell the key positions of German Reform. Of course, apart from the Hebrew title, the text was written in German. *Kol Kore Bamidbar* provided the theological underpin-ning for a Reform congregation based on the German model. Sinai's rabbi from 1880 to 1923, Emil G. Hirsch, characterized the text as the "Magna Charta" of Sinai Congregation.[16]

GERMAN REFORM COMES TO CHICAGO

Until recently, scholars have treated Germany as the epicenter of the modern Jewish experience. New research, however, criticizes the German-centered ap-proach (with some justification) for ignoring Jews outside of the German-speaking lands who also developed modern concepts of Jewishness, for example, those living in sixteenth-century Amsterdam or in port cities like eighteenth-century Trieste. In the United States, an indigenous proto-Reform congregation was founded in Charleston, South Carolina, in 1825. Nevertheless, even the crit-ics of the German-centered approach acknowledge the sustained impact of the German-Jewish "response to modernity" on the Jewish world in the nineteenth century.[17]

Jewish Reform emerged during the early 1820s in the German states as a genu-inely Jewish response to the opening of the ghetto and the ideals of the Enlight-enment. Its theology was strongly influenced by the emergence of critical and rational *Wissenschaft* (scholarly study) in Germany. Jewish Reformers opposed external reforms or adaptations without theological foundation, and they did not accept Judaism as a rigid and fixed religion. Therefore, they called for a theo-logical reevaluation based on scholarly analysis of the origins and transforma-tions of Judaism.[18]

Traditional Jews opposed such moves, but even the fiercest critics gradually recognized that traditional Judaism could not be transplanted from the ghetto into the modern world. As a consequence, different theological concepts emerged. Some rabbis attempted to mediate between traditional Judaism and the demands of modern society and scientific progress. Zacharias Frankel, in particular, is considered as an early forerunner of conservative Judaism. Others were more radical. Abraham Geiger, together with Leopold Zunz, one of the founders of the Reform movement, stressed that texts, including the Torah and the Talmud, had no absolute authority but rather, were sources that had to be interpreted and analyzed with the methods of critical, scholarly study.

Geiger and other Reformers also rejected the notion of the reestablishment of a Jewish state and other national aspirations inherent in Judaism. Geiger interpreted Judaism in its specific historical context as a progressive religion. Judaism had changed its forms, but its underlying spirit had persisted—the belief in the one God, a strong emphasis on ethical values, and the vision of peace for mankind. Geiger and other Reformers regarded external changes as necessary if forms, such as parts of the liturgy, did not convey the religious spirit of Judaism in the present age.[19]

On a cultural and social level, the enlightenment ideal of *Bildung* had a crucial impact on German Jews on their way out of the ghetto. Its emphasis on openness and universalism especially exerted a strong influence on Jewish Reformers. The trailblazers and "heroes" of *Bildung* were leading writers like Johann Wolfgang von Goethe, Friedrich Schiller, and Gotthold Ephraim Lessing and composers such as Ludwig van Beethoven.[20] Although Jews living in Germany developed ambitious concepts of modern Judaism, the institutional framework for Jewish life did not change accordingly. The emancipation process gave Jews more individual freedom, but organized Jewish communities faced more state control. In the first decades of the nineteenth century, repressive state authorities closed down early Reform synagogues. Even after 1871, Reformers had to reach compromises with traditional Jews within the state-regulated local community, the so-called *Gemeinde*.

Leaving the umbrella of the established *Gemeinde* was not a realistic option for dissenters, because state authorities would not allow it. It was difficult for openly Reform-minded rabbis to find positions and often frustrating to serve synagogues because of the climate of stagnation within the *Gemeinde*. The one openly Reform congregation in Germany was the Berlin Reform congregation. This pioneering body, founded in 1845, influenced early radical Reform congregations in the United States like Sinai that were founded during the 1850s and

1860s. Yet the members paid a high price for breaking with the Jewish tradition. The Prussian state did not ban services, but it refused to incorporate the congregation. Yet if they did not want to convert to Christianity, Jews were not allowed to leave the *Gemeinde*. Paying for the upkeep of the synagogue in addition to the *Gemeinde* dues limited the growth of the Reform congregation. The corset of the *Gemeinde* and the ever-watchful eye of the authorities partly explain why it remained the only explicit Reform congregation in central Europe at the time.[21]

Younger university graduates with seemingly radical ideas had few prospects of finding a position if they refused to compromise. Kaufmann Kohler, Sinai's rabbi during the 1870s, was such a man. In 1869, shortly before his departure to America, the recent PhD graduate complained in a letter to an American colleague about the dire prospects for Reform in Germany: "For a great and free Judaism I strive. The frail religious life in Germany does not offer any prospects for me."[22] In the United States, on the other hand, the state did not intervene, influential traditional Jewish elites had no real power or did not exist, and Jews could split over religious issues and form separate congregations. However, not all Reform-minded rabbis who had worked in Europe easily adapted to the American congregation. In the German states, especially in large cities with several synagogues under the umbrella of one *Gemeinde*, rabbis had life contracts and enjoyed a high degree of authority over individual members and the community at large—as long as they did not depart from the accepted theological platform. Immigrant rabbis often did not immediately realize that in America individual congregation members had much more influence, that majorities could easily shift, and that unpopular rabbis could find themselves quickly on the street. The behavior of the enraged Albany congregation president Louis Spanier toward Wise remained exceptional. Nevertheless, for German-Jewish Reformers, the conditions in the New World were uniquely favorable, and in the second half of the nineteenth century, America rather than Germany emerged as the land of classical Reform Judaism.[23]

Conflicts over reforms of the service developed in many American-Jewish congregations after 1850. Reform often went hand in hand with bitter power struggles within congregations. Personal animosities also played a part, as the Albany incident shows. The eventual split of a congregation was never an easy matter. In smaller towns, establishing a second congregation was often not even an option. Jews had to compromise, because a synagogue could not exist apart from the community, and vice versa. In big cities with a larger and increasing base of potential followers, splits were much more feasible.

Before the mid-1850s, Jews argued largely over external reforms of the service rather than theology. The shift to a more thorough debate about the justification and extent of reforms owed much to the first leading German-Jewish Reformer who moved to America. Shortly after Wise had taken up his post in Cincinnati, David Einhorn accepted a position at Har Sinai congregation in Baltimore. Einhorn was a highly respected scholar and Reform rabbi who had served with several congregations in central Europe. He would play a crucial role in inspiring the young modernizers in Chicago to set up a Reform congregation.[24]

Einhorn rejected the notion of a return to Palestine and the expectation of a personal Messiah. Rather, he reinterpreted the role of the Jews as a chosen people or, as he put it, as a "priest people." At a rabbinical convention in Frankfurt in 1845, he stressed, "The collapse of Israel's political independence was once regarded as a misfortune, but it really represented progress, not atrophy but an elevation of religion. Henceforth, Israel came closer to its destiny. Holy devotion replaced sacrifices. Israel had the task to spread the word of God into all corners of the world." For the Reformers, the Jewish Diaspora was not a static waiting period that one day would come to an end with the arrival of the Messiah. Rather, the Diaspora represented a phase in the development of the Jews as a messianic people. For Einhorn, universal monotheism had preceded the Jewish people: "It was not a religion, but a religious people, that was *newly* created at Sinai, a priest people called upon, first of all, to impress the ancient divine teaching more deeply upon itself and then bring it to universal dominion."[25] The messianic task or mission of the Jews, chosen at Mount Sinai, was to spread as a "priest people" the original universal message in the world and work toward giving this message universal application.[26] In Einhorn's theology, this task constituted the real spiritual Zion. "We are not concerned with ancient Jewish political life and long *verrotteten* [rotten] institutions, but in penetrating all people with our higher spiritual life. Here [in America], we can look forward to spreading our eternal truths."[27] This quote illustrates the future-oriented direction of Reform theology and the appreciation of the American project that sprang from similar Enlightenment sources as Reform Judaism. America represented freedom and future as opposed to Europe with its "rotten" Jewish institutions, hopelessly stuck in the past.

It is too simplistic to portray early Reform theologians as destroyers of a centuries-old religious tradition. Einhorn and Geiger respected the tradition. Talmud and *halakha* represented significant phases in the development of Judaism. Yet ancient interpretations and laws had largely (but not completely) lost their original meanings for contemporary Jews. For Einhorn, the purpose of ritual was to express "religious reality" for the believer. Extremely specific rules drawn up centuries ago could not be applied rigidly to the modern world, especially if the original intentions were unclear. Einhorn, to give one example, regarded the many rules regulating observance of the Sabbath as outdated and out of place. But the moral message represented by the historical Sabbath was "absolute." Unlike several other Reformers, Einhorn was strictly opposed to performing mixed marriages. He believed Jews could only fulfil their task as a messianic people if they remained conscious of their separateness.[28] Other Reformers took a more relaxed line. But debates over mixed marriages, circumcision, certain rituals, and the importance of keeping the historic Saturday Sabbath betrayed differing concepts of redefining Jewishness and relating to the tradition in the modern world.

By the time he received Har Sinai's offer, Einhorn had repeatedly clashed with the authorities, and his job prospects were diminishing because of his uncompromising stance. Einhorn left Europe with a heavy heart, but he felt he could finally turn his vision into reality without state interference in a congregation with strong Reform credentials and much enthusiasm for its new rabbi. Soon after his arrival in 1855 he was confronted with Wise's union project. A clash between the two men was hardly avoidable. Einhorn did not attend the Cleveland conference, but he criticized it in strong terms, especially Wise's acceptance of the absolute authority of the Talmud. Einhorn also began publishing a German-language monthly, the *Sinai*.[29]

The agenda of his colleague in Cincinnati constituted a gross provocation for Einhorn, who cherished religious pluralism as well as the absence of outside interference and the absolute independence of a congregation in America. A centralized synod presented a grave threat. Surely, such a body would have the authority to define and redefine theological positions, even expelling minorities and so-called heretics and interfering in the affairs of congregations, similar to state authorities in Germany or the British chief rabbi who famously refused to recognize the West London Reform congregation in 1841. A consistent theology was the key to Einhorn's program—political compromises over theological matters were completely out of the question.[30]

KOL KORE BAMIDBAR: DEFINING RADICAL REFORM

The main development leading to the founding of Sinai was a conflict between Wise and Einhorn over the direction of Reform (or reform) in America. Michael A. Meyer and other scholars of the Reform movement have stressed the striking difference between these two personalities. One lacked what the other possessed. Einhorn had thorough *Bildung*, a consistent theology, and deeply held convictions. He was a brilliant but stubborn intellectual who did not easily adapt to life in America and appeared often out of touch. His uncompromising stance forced the outspoken abolitionist to hurriedly leave his home and congregation during the 1861 Baltimore riots.[31]

Wise lacked the necessary *Bildung* credentials; he had not graduated from an institution of higher learning. But if Einhorn appeared as a somewhat remote intellectual, Wise was a pragmatic organizer and a clever politician. He could rally supporters to his cause and quickly adapt to a new environment and situation. Wise's opaque position on slavery in the border town Cincinnati is a case in point. It constitutes a stark contrast to Einhorn's uncompromising stand for abolition. Wise and Einhorn would never get along, but eventually their different talents proved to be crucial for the organization of the Reform movement in America. Einhorn and his supporters (not least at Chicago Sinai) would define Reform theology—Wise would organize the movement. Wise's grudging acceptance of Einhorn and his ilk can be traced back to their first clash in Chicago.

Unlike his antagonist from Cincinnati, Einhorn did not visit Chicago, but he was surprisingly well informed and intimately involved with Reform in the city. In 1856, Einhorn received a letter from another recent arrival, Bernhard Felsenthal, who wished to contribute articles to the *Sinai*. Felsenthal was not an ordained rabbi, but he served a small congregation in Madison, Indiana, as religious leader and teacher.[32] Felsenthal was acquainted with a several Jewish Reform theologians who were also known to Einhorn. Among these was Landau district rabbi Elias Grünebaum, a relative of Felsenthal and the Chicago Greenebaum family. Einhorn was enthusiastic to have found a correspondent for his paper who was in favor of Reform, possessed thorough *Bildung*, and lived in America.[33] Some time before March 1857, Einhorn had also been corresponding with several young Reformers in Chicago. These were the Greenebaum and Foreman brothers, Leopold Mayer, and several others who were pushing for more reforms at KAM.[34] In 1857, Felsenthal himself moved to Chicago. Apart from his Chicago connections, his failure to introduce reforms in Madison explains the decision to move north. Initially, he worked as a clerk at the bank owned by two leading Reformers at KAM, Henry Greenebaum and Gerhard Foreman.[35]

In 1857, shortly before or after Felsenthal's arrival, the Reform-minded members of KAM forced an election and installed their own man, Elias Greenebaum, as president. The traditionally inclined members were upset, fearing marginalization and even eventual expulsion from the congregation they had founded exactly ten years earlier. Former KAM president Abraham Kohn stated in a public letter published in Wise's *Israelite* that the election was "no question of reform" but of *Landsmanshaft*.[36] Kohn had a point. The leading Reformers did indeed originate in or near the Palatinate, as discussed in the previous chapter, and they were closely related through marriage and common business ventures. Kohn's letter illustrates that it would be too shortsighted to reduce the religious debates leading to Sinai's founding to theology. In a period of strong Jewish immigration, power politics between different *Landsmanshaft* factions were very much part of the struggles over the course of congregations. On the other hand, Kohn clearly found it difficult to adjust to the democratic American congregation. In his native Franconia he would have retained his office and probably would have threatened to expel dissidents—but not in Chicago, where he had to accept the will of the majority or leave the congregation himself.

The new president, Elias Greenebaum, had the backing of a majority but still faced the opposition of a vociferous minority. Every step toward further change was difficult, not in the least because the majorities were shifting. The committed Reformers had to compromise with other members to move things their way. And of course since some members occasionally were out of town on business or failed to attend meetings for other reasons, safe majorities were never guaranteed. Shortly before Passover 1858, several KAM members briefly broke away, establishing the Reform congregation Ohabey Or (Friends of Light), but this venture collapsed after a few weeks.[37] None of the Reformers (not even the autodidact Felsenthal) had thorough theological training. To discuss the rationale for reforms and recent publications by Reform scholars, Felsenthal, the Greenebaum brothers, Foreman, and Mayer set up the *Jüdischen Reformverein* (Jewish Reform Association) in June 1858. This discussion forum was the nucleus of Sinai Congregation. Later that year, the Reformers also sought advice from an established Reform figure and a recently arrived *Landsmann*, the new rabbi of New York's Emanu-El congregation, Samuel Adler.[38]

In November 1858, Gerhard Foreman, Leopold Mayer, and Henry Greenebaum inquired from Adler how they could resolve the "*Tohu Wabohu*" (chaos) prevailing at KAM. They asked Adler, "What can they, who keep religion, and Judaism, and the observance—in accordance with contemporary norms—close to their heart, do under such circumstances?" They also wondered whether they should really split and form a separate Reform congregation. Was this even possible, they wanted to know, and if it was, what would be the theological platform for such a congregation?[39] These questions illustrate that even at a relatively late stage a split was not necessarily the obvious step and, on a higher plane, that the adaptation of Jewish immigrants to the congregational and pluralistic model in America was a gradual process.

In an 1859 meeting of the *Reformverein*, Henry Greenebaum, the younger brother of Elias and a rising local politician and banker, brought up the question of Jewish acceptance in Chicago. "He had always been embarrassed by the way the service in the synagogue was conducted. And under all sorts of excuses had he avoided to introduce his [Christian] American friends there [at KAM]." And he called on Chicago Jews to raise their visibility in the city: "While the Christian sects have sent up fifty towers to the sky in Chicago, Judaism had done nothing. It was high time to get moving." As Daniel Bluestone has shown, church towers were important vestiges of social status in antebellum Chicago.[40] For Greenebaum, social status and acceptance were as important as theological principles. This was exactly the kind of thinking Wise attempted to mobilize for his cause. The following passage, printed shortly after *Sinai* had published the proceedings of the *Reformverein* with Greenebaum's remarks, illustrates this point.

In 1859, a Christian visitor reported to a leading Chicago paper: "I understand that the new board of Administration [at KAM] has caused all th[e] change in the mode of service. . . . Some time ago, a stranger, who visited their synagoues [*sic*], would hardly believe that he was among a civilized people . . . [but now the service is] so nice . . . that all prejudice against these, our fellow citizens, must give way." The Chicago Reformers may have been flattered by these remarks, but the passage also indicates that for the Christian observer prejudices against traditional Jews were clearly justified. This did not prevent Wise from reprinting the letter in his *Israelite*, for it supported his criticism of stubborn Reform opponents. He welcomed the turn toward reforms at KAM and saw himself in firm control in Chicago.[41]

Einhorn and Felsenthal discussed the religious conflicts at KAM in several private letters, and in late 1858 and again in early 1859 Einhorn tried to convince Felsenthal that he should take the initiative. "Sie sind der Mann" (you are the man), he told Felsenthal in January 1859. In the *Sinai*, Einhorn covered the events in Chicago in detail. And he reprinted the letters the *Reformverein* members had sent to Adler and his replies, as well as the *Reformverein* minutes from the *Illinois Staatszeitung*.[42] And early in 1859, two years after his arrival, Felsenthal began to move. In mid-1859, he published *Kol Kore Bamidbar*. The title, *Kol Kore Bamidbar* ("A voice [calling] in the wilderness"), referred to the actual location of Chicago on the frontier but also hinted at the theological "wilderness" and confusion at KAM. The text echoed Einhorn's theology and was compiled from a list of essentials Felsenthal had presented to an early *Reformverein* meeting in the summer of 1858. In the religious sphere, Felsenthal, like Einhorn, was a Germanizer. Germany was important to him as a cultural center because the emergence of modern Judaism and the Reform movement in the first half of the nineteenth century had been closely linked with the spiritual revolution and the emergence of critical and rational *Wissenschaft*. Felsenthal emphasized in 1865, after Chicago Sinai's founding, "We must not distance ourselves from German Judaism and its influences. As in medieval times the sun of Jewish *Wissenschaft* was shining on the Spanish sky, this sun is now shining on the German sky, sending out its light to all Jews and Jewish communities, who live among the modern cultured peoples. Germany has replaced Sefard."[43]

In *Kol Kore Bamidbar*, he stressed, "The German people are still the first among the cultured peoples of the world, and we bow our heads in reverence before its spirit, its literature, its language. We American-German Jews want to keep German in our synagogues."[44] For Felsenthal (and even more for Einhorn) America was a cultural desert, a land of spiritual superficiality. This of course was yet another meaning of the title *Kol Kore Bamidbar*—the voice calling in the *American* wilderness. Only a true Reform congregation would turn this wasteland into a blooming landscape of *Kultur* and *Bildung*. Felsenthal praised Germany on a spiritual and cultural level, but politically, he emphasized, Germany was *elend* (miserable).[45]

For Felsenthal, Reform Judaism in Germany had to serve as the model for Reform Judaism in America. The Germanization of Jewish theology was synonymous with the thorough modernization of Judaism. Felsenthal argued that reforms of the service leading to greater decorum, such as the introduction of an organ, were useless unless Judaism was redefined as a modern religion consistent with intellectual progress in the sciences and humanities. For him, Judaism was a progressive religion based on monotheism. Traditional religious practices that did not convey the essential religious truths were to be abandoned, and new elements had to be added, especially a sermon in the German language that would be understood by all congregants. It did not make sense, Felsenthal argued— and Einhorn praised him for it—to introduce copied versions of the Christian service or by turning the Jewish service into a *Schaugepränge* (show) with choirs and music. "Radical Reform" was a matter of spiritual *Bildung* rather than superficial accommodation to the present age as favored by Wise. Felsenthal defined "radical Reform" as a thorough and reflective theology. In other words, "radical Reformers" were guided by theology and not by fashion and ignorance. Felsenthal also rejected unfair accusations: "Some have described 'Radical Reformers' as horrible monsters, as cannibals who eat a few dozen Orthodox for breakfast every morning. But let me assure you, . . . We radical Reformers are very peaceful people who do not want to fight with anybody."[46]

Felsenthal's discussion of Sabbath observance betrays his commitment to *Bildung*. It was wrong to rush from the store to the service on Saturday for one hour or not to attend the service at all, Felsenthal stressed. But it was also wrong for Jews to obey the Talmudic rules without intellectually recognizing the religious truths guiding them. Yes, of course, he stressed in *Kol Kore Bamidbar*, one could smoke a cigar on the Sabbath or, even better, attend a drama by Schiller or walk to the park to listen to a symphony by Beethoven. To educate oneself in this way was better than unthinking obedience to hollow laws without recognition of their inner spirit.[47]

Radical Reformers like Felsenthal characteristically questioned the notion of authority as such: the authority of sacred texts like the Talmud that had regulated religious observance and the daily lives of Jews for centuries, the authority of religious elites who had controlled religious affairs in the old ghetto (or were attempting to do the same in the New World), and the authority of the state that was still meddling in the religious affairs of Jewish communities in Europe. In America, the state did not regulate religious affairs, and Felsenthal often praised religious freedom in the United States. But Wise's union project also threatened to institutionalize a form of authority over congregations.

The Reformers at KAM were still wavering over whether they should form their own Reform congregation. And, while in his reply letters Samuel Adler did not hide his enthusiasm for Reform, he refrained from giving specific advice. He stressed in a letter in December 1858 that he did not want to get "mixed up in internal affairs of a *Gemeinde*."[48] Felsenthal took a clear stand on this question. *Kol Kore Bamidbar* was first and foremost a call for separation on the religious level. In the final paragraphs of the pamphlet, Felsenthal stressed in boldface three (!) times what the "voice calling in the wilderness" had to say: "**Israelite friends of Reform in Chicago, let us join together and form a Reform congregation!**"[49]

The passage justifying why separation was the necessary step to take is perhaps the most intriguing part of the pamphlet. Separation had actually very little to do with Germanization. The hymns Einhorn and Felsenthal sang to Germany can only be understood in their very American context. While Einhorn himself may have never felt at home in America and Felsenthal struggled with the English language for decades, both were well aware that Reforms with a capital "R" could only be realized on American soil.[50] Felsenthal made the convincing argument that in the United States (as opposed to Europe) every individual Jew was free to evaluate Judaism and opt for Reform. The United States Constitution guaranteed the separation of religion and state; there were no old, established religious elites, and religious factions within a congregation could split from each other and form new congregations. In the key passage of *Kol Kore Bamidbar*, Felsenthal directly addressed the Reformers in Chicago. He reminded them that most Reform-minded members had joined the KAM only a few years after it had been established. Expelling the "oldest founders" like Abraham Kohn was not an appropriate solution. "Do you want to expel them [the traditional members]? Do you—and we speak to American Israelites—do you want to dictate to others how they have to pray to their God? Let us not fight, we are brothers! Let us separate!"[51]

This closing statement reads like a paradox, but this call for separation illustrates that at the core, Germanization meant Americanization. Germany was the center of the Reform universe, but Felsenthal and Einhorn had left state intervention, the oppressive *Gemeinde*, and manifold obstacles to Reformers behind. Only in America could Jews split peacefully over religious matters to form their own congregations and yet remain united as Jews outside the synagogue. Wise was still convinced that the synagogue community could somehow be preserved on the basis of reform with a small "r" and a national synod. The incident in Albany, the failure of the Cleveland conference, and the debates in Chicago and many other congregations at the time were, however, pointing in a different direction. Jews were adopting the Protestant pluralist model.

There is, of course, an irony in these developments that has eluded the attention of most historians dealing with nineteenth-century American Jewish history. Traditionally, Wise was (and still is) portrayed as the harbinger of *American* Judaism, highlighted by his opposition to the use of German in the service and his persistent calls for Americanization. Einhorn and Felsenthal, on the other hand, are still described as elitist Germanizers who adhered to the German model of Reform Judaism and called for the Germanization of Judaism in America. A closer look at the sources reveals a more complex picture: Einhorn and Felsenthal, who arrived only in the 1850s, immediately adapted, praised, and defended the specific form of American religious pluralism and the sovereignty of the congregation. Wise wanted to preserve non-American hierarchical structures like the *Gemeinde* (at least on the religious level). Admittedly, Wise's vision of a national union encompassing all Jewish congregations in America under his leadership was inspired by Protestant denominations rather than corporatist European models.[52]

The terminology of Felsenthal's appeal that Jews would remain "brothers" points to an organization that was trying to achieve this goal, the Independent Order of B'nai B'rith. This Jewish fraternal order, founded in October 1843 in New York, was the first secular Jewish association in North America.[53] The very act of founding the B'nai B'rith was an early response to the breakup of traditional Jewish *Gemeinschaft* in America. The B'nai B'rith was secular—but not antireligious. The massive expansion of the order beyond New York occurred during the 1850s and 1860s, not coincidentally when the small established Jewish communities came under intense pressure.

The rise of B'nai B'rith reflected a response to increasing religious conflicts and to the rise in immigration of Jews with diverse backgrounds. Chicago's first B'nai B'rith lodge, Ramah, was established in 1857 by the very same Reformers who eventually would split from KAM. This was, of course, no coincidence. Through Ramah lodge the Reformers embraced their opponents as "brothers" in a social space outside of the synagogue. These activities also explain why Wise felt rather uncomfortable at the B'nai B'rith meeting in January 1860: most of the men he encountered belonged to the circle of the Reformers. In 1857, Wise had joined the Council of Skenim, the leadership council of the B'nai B'rith, when he became president of the Cincinnati-based District Grand Lodge No. 2. This grand lodge comprised all B'nai B'rith lodges in the vast area west of the Alleghenies and east of the Rocky Mountains. After the 1855 Cleveland conference did not lead to the formation of a religious union, Wise hoped the B'nai B'rith would support his union project. But just when Wise gained more influence, the recently arrived David Einhorn and like-minded Reformers made a growing impact on the lodges in the main East Coast cities, which belonged to the District Grand Lodges No. 1 (New York) and No. 3 (Philadelphia). Einhorn never joined the order, but he was well acquainted with several key leaders of the B'nai B'rith, such as Moritz Ellinger. At an 1858 meeting, the order abolished the wearing of regalia and aprons, which had been adapted by the Masons, over the fierce opposition of western lodges led by Wise. The new resolutions were clearly shaped by the universalistic radical Reform ideas Einhorn promoted. Thus the rise of a Reform movement sympathetic to Einhorn in Chicago whose members were also the movers and shakers of the local B'nai B'rith lodge was deeply unsettling for Wise. The Chicago Reformers did not only challenge Wise on the religious level but also threatened his position as leader of the western B'nai B'rith.[54]

On the local level, the existence of the B'nai B'rith lodge helps to explain why Chicago Jews in the midst of the severe conflicts within KAM were striving to create unity outside of the synagogue. The first and, in hindsight, most decisive step was the founding of the United Hebrew Relief Association (UHRA) in 1859. The UHRA was more than an organization devoted to supporting poor Jews; it represented the Jewish community of Chicago. All Jewish congregations, the B'nai B'rith lodge, and existing collective relief societies became corporate members of the UHRA and sent representatives to the annual council. The UHRA was supra-religious and inclusive, and it embodied the B'nai B'rith vision of a "secular *kehillah*." Like in other American cities, overarching organizations built on *tzedakah* (social justice) and devoted to helping poor Jews (and non-Jews) provided the glue for binding diverse Jewish institutions together on a long-term basis.[55]

In a period when traditional Judaism came under intense pressure and the definition of Jewishness in a modern context was contested, Reformers, traditional Jews, and even members of secular Jewish associations could subscribe to the ideals of *tzedakah*, the support of disadvantaged Jews (and others), as a central element of their Jewishness. Helping Jews and non-Jews in need reinforced a feeling of togetherness among Jewish donors and between them and the poor, thus continually recreating Jewish *Gemeinschaft*. And Jewish engagement for social justice and the public good was also a rebuttal of anti-Semitic images of Jews as Shylocks who acted only in their own interest.[56]

From its beginning, Jewish leaders emphasized that the UHRA was more than a charitable organization—it was *the* common platform for most Jews in Chicago. In an 1864 report on Chicago Jewish life for the leading German-Jewish weekly, the *Allgemeine Zeitung des Judenthums*, merchant and Sinai member Raphael Guthmann did not want to focus on differences. Guthmann's remarks echo the ideals of the B'nai B'rith: The UHRA would exist "as long as Jehudim will live in Chicago, be they orthodox or reform, German or Polish or whatever else. Here is the platform where they can unite as *brothers*."[57] Jewish communities in other American cities were also organized on the basis of *tzedakah*. The UHRA and similar Jewish bodies in other cities replaced the all-encompassing European Jewish community. Under American conditions, Jewish communities had to be built and sustained from the bottom up and transcend religion. The UHRA and similar organizations were rooted in the Jewish tradition, but at the same time they served as institutional anchors of loose Jewish community networks in the dynamic American urban context.[58]

Private charity networks assumed such a central role in the United States for another reason. Communal or state-funded welfare was not available in the nineteenth century. Immigrants responded by forming social networks to protect their members against poverty, sickness, and other risks. Membership in the B'nai B'rith, for instance, included life insurance and the obligation to help the widow and children of a deceased brother. Other immigrants in Chicago also organized overreaching benevolent associations, notably immigrants from Scandinavia, Eastern Europe, and Germany. But the professional organization of the UHRA with its corporate membership system was without parallel. The UHRA was rooted in the tradition of the *Gemeinde* and Jewish communal welfare in the ghetto.[59]

THE PATH TOWARD SINAI

Isaac Mayer Wise visited Chicago again in September 1859, after Bernhard Felsenthal had published *Kol Kore Bamidbar*. On this occasion, Wise decided to ignore Felsenthal, whose articles in the *Sinai* he had certainly noticed. He mentioned radical Reform only once in passing. But, always a keen and precise observer, he sensed that change was in the air. Indeed, Chicago appeared increasingly different from other cities, especially Cincinnati. It was quickly expanding and it was *fast*. "Chicago is the old home of the ups and downs. Everybody is in a hurry. Some people have not even time enough to say they have no time. In Chicago people have no time to die. . . . Money business must be excellent here, for people have no time, want no time, give no time, and take no time. . . . [But] some of our brethren are considerably behind the time." While some Chicago Jews ran the risk of falling behind, the Cincinnati visitor did not realize that other Jews were very much in tune with the rapid pace of their home city. In 1859, Cincinnati (160,000 inhabitants) was still significantly larger than Chicago (100,000), but Chicago was growing much more rapidly. Ten years later, Wise remarked, "They move a great deal faster in Chicago. . . . We [in Cincinnati] prefer a quiet life." By 1870, Chicago had grown to 300,000 inhabitants, while Cincinnati had 200,000.[60]

The rise of Reform in Chicago cannot be separated from what happened outside the synagogue. It was no coincidence that the rapidly growing and innovative railroad hub Chicago and not the older and "slower" river cities of St. Louis and Cincinnati emerged as the early western center of radical Reform in the late 1850s. The foundations for Chicago's position as the focal point of the American rail network were already laid in the decade before the Civil War. The city became the epitome of what Wolfgang Schivelbusch has described as the "industrialization of time and space." A fast city without a history provided the climate for radical experiments that would have faced much resistance in German *Gemeinden*, American small-town communities, and even in older American cities with established elites and a higher degree of social control.[61]

When Wise announced his January 1860 visit after having gone to Chicago only a few months earlier, Einhorn was alarmed. It is quite likely that this time Wise decided to take on the radical Reformers. Einhorn suspected such a move and warned Felsenthal that the Cincinnati rabbi would try to interfere in Chicago,[62] but his worries were unfounded. Wise again promoted his vision of Judaism in America: "Judaism changes not, but its forms, its outside, has changed very often and must change again to suit our age and land, our taste, views, demands, and wants." On his earlier visits, he had not mentioned Felsenthal and the other Reformers, but now he could not ignore them any longer. He alleged that those he termed radicals had no significant following: "There is nothing in existence of it [radical Reform] except a pamphlet which starts with rationalism and ends in kitchen and stomach, with the extreme nonsense between." He emphasized, "This party will never succeed in Chicago." He described Felsenthal scornfully as a "pedantic and fantastic man" and a "ship-wrecked egoist." Eventually he encountered Felsenthal at the B'nai B'rith lodge meeting. Apparently, Felsenthal asked Wise for a debate, but Wise would have nothing of it: "This gave my pedantic spectacled and ship-wrecked opponent an opportunity to criticize, scold, lament, decry, laugh, cry, and practicing German grammar, of course when I was gone."[63]

Wise's scorn and sarcasm were indications of Felsenthal's success. Throughout 1860, the *Jüdische Reformverein* attracted new recruits. Not surprisingly, Einhorn was in a jubilant mood. Enthusiastically, he referred to Felsenthal as "unser Felsenthal" (our Felsenthal).[64] The rise of the *Reformverein* was a severe defeat for Wise's union project. Until this point, he had faced opposition from orthodox opponents of reforms, but now he had to deal with a determined opposition within his own camp and—an even more troubling prospect—in his own western backyard.

Just before reaching the finish line in early 1860, however, it appeared as if the Reformers were ignoring Felsenthal's advice not to force the traditionally inclined founders out. Under a new president, Benjamin Schönemann, KAM was embarking on a clear course toward radical Reform. In April, KAM employed a known German Reformer, Dr. Salomon Friedländer, as new rabbi. Friedländer had briefly served as assistant of the famous Reform theologian (and friend of Einhorn) Samuel Holdheim at the Berlin Reform Temple. Shortly after his arrival, the promising young rabbi died of blood poisoning. After this tragic event and renewed arguments over the future of KAM, the committed Reformers finally decided to separate.[65]

Wise's attempts to save the union had ended in failure; now, with secession looming, he portrayed the radical "German" Reformers in Chicago as rebels who were about to torpedo the Union. "South Carolina is not alone to secede," declared the *Israelite* late in 1860, when the Reformers entered into negotiations over the formal split from KAM. Wise could not resist taking a cheap shot at the "shrewd brokers and shavers among the 'R. R.' [Radical Reformers]." Several leading Reformers were indeed bankers and insurance agents. But the conditions of the split were fair. KAM kept most of its property including the synagogue; the Reformers took the organ, much to the relief of several traditionally minded KAM members.[66] On April 7, 1861, the "secessionists" ratified the constitution and bylaws. The new congregation, named after Einhorn's journal *Sinai*, and, of course, the very foundation of Reform theology, was established.[67] Five days later, on April 12, the Confederates attacked Fort Sumter.

3.

FIGHTING FOR EMANCIPATION

SINAI'S FOUNDING IN April 1861 occurred on the eve of the Civil War. Internal Jewish arguments over union projects and the terms of secession from a congregation cannot be separated from much more far-reaching debates outside of the small Jewish communities in Chicago and other American cities. In this period of rapid socioeconomic change and national crisis, one question loomed ever larger: how much union could be achieved (or preserved) in the face of growing diversity and change in America, and at what cost? The loss of *Gemeinschaft* in the religious sphere was hardly a distinctively Jewish experience.

After the American Revolution, the so-called comprehensive congregation that embraced all Protestants and, thus, almost every inhabitant of smaller towns and villages was gradually replaced by congregations affiliated with different denominations. The strong immigration from northwestern Europe before 1850 led to the formation of new and to the diversification of existing Protestant denominations. Even Catholics, united by a common liturgy, were dividing—at least on the local level—into different ethnic and linguistic parishes. Unlike native-born Americans, Jewish and Christian immigrants hailing from long-established and often state-regulated religious communities in Europe experienced the transition to the dynamic American style congregational model in fast-forward. Class also became a divisive force, even within small religious subgroups. Indeed, Sinai's founding occurred during a veritable congregation boom. In 1820, more than ten thousand congregations existed in the United States, and by 1860 the number had risen to more than fifty thousand. This was only secondarily a consequence of strong immigration. Unlike the comprehensive old European church or synagogue community or the eighteenth-century American comprehensive congregation, the new congregations were organized around the service. And congregations, divided from others along social, ethnic, and religious lines, now covered only a part of people's lives. Congregations had to compete not only for members but also with leisure time, family life, longer work hours, and increasing mobility.[1]

Apart from contested visions over the relationship between the states and the Union, and the transformation of religious life, striking a balance between diversity and unity most obviously concerned the rapidly growing American cities. After 1850, the ever-faster pace of industrialization, along with westward expansion and mass immigration, changed American society beyond recognition. Nowhere was this change more visible than in the expanding northern cities. An increasing part of the new urban population hailed from Europe, especially Ireland, England, and the German states. And unlike their predecessors, a growing proportion of these new immigrants were not Protestant but Catholic and—in very small numbers—Jewish.

According to social historian Mary Ryan, widespread violence in American cities prefigured the Civil War. In the cities, migrants from different parts of North America and Europe lived in close proximity, often in primitive slums with horrific hygienic conditions. Economic crises, as well as social and cultural differences between immigrants and "natives" (most of whom were immigrants or the children of immigrants), triggered strife and violence—even within seemingly homogeneous immigrant groups. Mass immigration, the growing rift between North and South, and economic change were the main factors behind the rise and electoral success of the nativist movement of the 1850s.[2]

JEWISH REFORMERS AND THE CIVIL WAR

In its early days, the war sidelined and even transcended many real and imagined divisions, north and south of the frontline. The national crisis was a chance for immigrants to prove their loyalty. Tens of thousands volunteered for hundreds of newly formed units. Even in the South ethnic units were established. The largest of these units were Irish and German. Many smaller groups also raised their own units, even two Northern Jewish communities, one in Syracuse, New York, and the other in Chicago.[3]

Early on, Bernhard Felsenthal emerged as a public voice calling for the abolition of slavery in the South and full equality for free African Americans living in the North. Sinai's rabbi hinted at similarities between the situation of slaves in the South and of Jews in Europe. In his article "The Jews and Slavery," printed by the *Staatszeitung*, he pointed especially at the enduring second-class status of most Jews in the German states and the widespread belief, even in America, that Jews were being "condemned to eternal slavery." Given their historic experience, he concluded, American Jews had a special obligation to fight for the liberation of slaves. The article was reprinted by Einhorn in his *Sinai* and by the German-Jewish *Allgemeine Zeitung*. In a second article, "The Law for Negroes and Jews," he explicitly criticized the treatment of African Americans in the Union. He drew a parallel between the treatment of Jews in the German states and Russia and a law in the District of Columbia excluding African Americans as witnesses.[4] Repeatedly, free African Americans and runaway slaves were attacked in Chicago. In July 1862, just when Felsenthal's articles were printed, Jewish lawyer and alderman Edward Salomon intervened when a mob attacked a runaway slave and saved his life.[5] This was not the first time Jews had helped African Americans. In 1853, Michael Greenebaum went a step further when he mobilized a mob and successfully liberated a runaway slave from the hands of a U.S. marshal (decades later, Leopold Mayer, another founder of Sinai, recalled this dramatic incident).[6] The opposition of Jews and leading German immigrants in Chicago to slavery was genuine. Unlike many native-born Americans, educated German immigrants, especially Jews and Forty-Eighters (German liberals who had fought in the 1848–1849 revolution in the German states and found asylum in the United States), perceived slavery as an inhuman anomaly, a stark violation of the democratic and republican ideals that had drawn them to America. Indeed, slavery was the antithesis of the *Bildung* ideals they held in such high esteem. For Jews, of course, the experience of slavery had a special resonance. Apart from the history of the Exodus, the actual meaning of the term "emancipation," in its original Roman context, refers to the liberation of slaves. Some Jewish contemporaries described the fate of unemancipated Jews in Europe in terms of slavery. This specific Jewish experience was another strong motivation to fight an injustice that contradicted the universal ideals formulated in America's founding documents.[7]

Two examples illustrate how even during the war Jews were not fully accepted and their presence was not officially acknowledged in America. Felsenthal joined other American Jews in protesting a law that defined army chaplains as "ministers of some Christian denomination." He sent a protest letter to Senator Henry Wilson of Massachusetts, who sponsored a successful bill changing the passage on army chaplains. Wilson responded to Felsenthal in a personal letter informing him about the change of the law. The definition "ministers of some religious denomination" opened the door for Jewish (and later other non-Christian) army chaplains.[8] In this case, non-Christians had perhaps been ignored rather than consciously excluded. The same can hardly be said of General Ulysses Grant's infamous General Order #11. In December 1862, Grant expelled Jews "as a class" from the military department under his command in Tennessee, because "these people" were allegedly involved in illegal smuggling across the front line. Anti-Jewish prejudice was pervasive in midcentury America, but the backing by one of the highest-ranking military officials in the land for a discriminatory and unproven accusation against Jews constituted a worrying and dangerous shift. Again, Sinai's rabbi was one of many Jews who successfully demanded that President Lincoln immediately lift the order.[9] These two events were setbacks for American Jews, but their outcomes also offered encouragement. Small, seemingly powerless groups could successfully claim rights guaranteed in the Constitution, acting in the interest of future Americans.

Sinai's rabbi used his pen and, very likely, the pulpit to call for action.[10] Congregation member Henry Greenebaum took action. When the war entered a difficult phase and President Lincoln called for urgently needed troop reinforcements in the early summer of 1862, Greenebaum sent out invitations for a Jewish mass meeting. On August 13, 1862, hundreds assembled, and within minutes $6,000 was raised to furnish an all-Jewish company. The *Chicago Tribune* and the *Staatszeitung* praised "our patriotic Israelite fellow citizens" for their determined action.[11] A second meeting on the following night proved to be decisive, because many more Jews attended. Before the meeting, Greenebaum had reached out to Maximilian M. Gerstley, the new president of KAM. Gerstley also presided over the UHRA and was, thus, the symbolic representative of the organized Chicago Jewish community. On August 14, almost all Jews in Chicago came together for the first time as Jews under one roof. They formally resolved to put aside their numerous differences for the time being, particularly with regard to religion. This resolution was a powerful rejection of Wise's accusation that the Sinai Congregation destroyed rather than fostered Jewish *Gemeinschaft* but also an indication that inner-Jewish divisions ran deep. Tellingly, in New York City, with its much larger and more diverse Jewish population, attempts to organize a similar unit failed.[12]

During the August 14 meeting, Greenebaum addressed the Jewish crowd in German and reminded them, "they owe the Union loyalty, because it gave them social and political freedom, freedom they did not enjoy in Europe." And his call was heeded: all Jews present agreed in their resolution that they felt "compelled—driven by . . . deep patriotic feelings, and by our commitment and love to the fatherland of [their] choice—to undertake as a community an effort for [the] fatherland." The donations collected on that evening were enough to fund a company of 101 Jewish volunteers, fully equipped. The size of the company is remarkable, because there were only 2,000 Jews living in Chicago in 1862. The Jewish Company C became part of the 82nd Illinois Volunteers Regiment. This unit was led by the famous German Forty-Eighter Friedrich Hecker and mostly was composed of German immigrants.[13]

The readiness of Chicago's Jews to volunteer for the war represented a definitive turning point. The symbolism of recent immigrants defending the Union as American citizens and explicitly as Jews in an effort to liberate and emancipate an enslaved population can hardly be overestimated. On August 18, another meeting took place to celebrate the formal entry of the Jewish company into Hecker's regiment. The Jewish women of Chicago donated the regiment's flag to Colonel Hecker, who attended the meeting with Lorenz Brentano and other prominent Chicago Germans, the Chicago mayor, and the deputy governor of Illinois. Apart from the Jewish immigrants, the small but influential group of the Forty-Eighters were the only other German speakers in Chicago who owed their freedom to their new home country. In hindsight, another relationship is even more intriguing. Like several Jews, such as Julius Rosenthal, Hecker and Brentano both hailed from the German state of Baden, where they had been proponents of Jewish emancipation during the 1840s. In a remarkable speech on that evening, Hecker connected the struggle for Jewish emancipation in the German states with the fight for the emancipation of the black slaves in the South: "What I could do in my former home-country to defend the [civil] rights of Jews against intolerance and race-hatred is being repaid today [by you]. Just as emancipation was inscribed on our flags then, this flag will be the symbol of emancipation."[14] Jews and liberals had struggled unsuccessfully against oppression and for freedom, equality, and democracy in the 1848–1849 revolution. By immigrating to the United States, Jews literally had emancipated themselves. Now many viewed it as their duty as new Americans to repay this symbolic debt and fight together for the emancipation of the black slaves in the South. A few months later, on January 1, 1863, President Lincoln issued the Emancipation Proclamation, making the liberation of all slaves an official war goal. Regardless of the complex background and motives behind the declaration, for many participants in the Chicago meetings, their calls and action on behalf of the Southern slaves appeared fully vindicated.

Not all Jews in northern cities took such determined action. In Baltimore, radical Reformer David Einhorn was isolated as a resolute proponent of abolition. His orthodox colleague Bernhard Illowy even defended slavery based on scripture, while the more moderate rabbi Benjamin Szold argued for cautious changes. The differing attitudes of these rabbis reflected their positions towards reforms in the religious sphere. Isaac Mayer Wise, who had denounced slavery before the war, took a position in "the middle of the road" during the first years of the war. When the war began, half of the subscribers of his *Israelite* lived in the South. And unlike Chicago's economy, which benefited enormously from the war, Cincinnati depended on the southern trade and many Jews and their gentile neighbors sympathized with the South.[15]

Chicago Jews were praised for their quick response, and they were proud of themselves. Later in 1862, the directors of the UHRA declared in their annual report:

> The very existence of that good Government, to which the Israelite especially is indebted for the enjoyment of political equality, and religious liberty, is threatened. . . . The Stars and Stripes, that emblem of justice and free institutions, have been trampled under foot by traitors at home, while the act, if not openly commended, is secretly cheered by Despots and Crowned heads of tyrannical Europe. . . . And nobly, yes thrice noble, and patriotically did the Israelites of Chicago respond in the emergency. With a burning love for country and freedom did they arise . . . and praise resounded throughout the land for their support of the war.[16]

The Jewish company and its soldiers did well in the war, although it suffered casualties. Many soldiers were decorated and returned as officers. When Hecker was wounded at Gettysburg, Edward Salomon replaced him until he recovered. Following Hecker's resignation in early 1864, Salomon assumed command of the regiment. At the end of the war, he was brevetted a brigadier general.[17] Even though this was an honorary promotion, such careers were not even imaginable for Jews in central Europe. When Salomon led the regiment back to Chicago, Mayor John Wentworth recalled the nativism of the 1850s and the betrayal of the Union by the Confederates: "A few years since, there was a cry raised that 'foreigners' could not be trusted, and an attempt was made to disenfranchise you, but when at last the time came that tried men's souls—when native-born Americans proved false to their allegiance . . . you 'foreigners' came forward and showed yourselves true men . . . you have proved that this country owes its existence to foreign immigrants."[18]

Jewish civic and political engagement in Chicago was not limited to the Civil War period. Several Jews had been active in Chicago and Illinois politics in the years before the war. Henry Greenebaum was elected to the city council during the mid-1850s as a Democrat. Edward Salomon too served as a Democrat alderman at the beginning of the war, and as clerk of Cook County after the war. Greenebaum and Abraham Kohn were well acquainted with Abraham Lincoln.[19] The longtime Sinai leaders Leopold Mayer, Julius Rosenthal, and Charles Kozminski (as well as Kohn) were among the founders of the Republican Party in Chicago during the mid-1850s.[20]

The early participation of Jews in politics (even in different parties) distinguished Chicago from other western cities like St. Louis or Detroit and even Cincinnati, the city with the largest Jewish population in the West before the Civil War.[21] Keeping close ties to the large German community, especially to the influential Forty-Eighters, was vital for Jewish politicians because the Jewish constituency was far too small to get them elected. Sinai members Julius Rosenthal and businessman Hermann Felsenthal represented the Republican Party on the Chicago Board of Education during the 1860s. In 1865, board chairman and Forty-Eighter Lorenz Brentano in tandem with Felsenthal garnered support to introduce German as second language of instruction in Chicago public schools.[22] The representation of Jews on the Board of Education was a safeguard against repeated attempts to Christianize the secular public school. In this respect, Jewish elected officials acted also in the interest of Germans and other immigrants who were freethinkers or socialists, and even Catholics who faced widespread discrimination in Chicago and across the country. Political engagement owed as much to as it reinforced the radical Reform convictions of these Jewish politicians.

Civic action raised the profile of Jews and earned them much respect in the Chicago public, at a time when most Americans had never met a Jew and were still strongly influenced by stereotypical images of Jews. In Chicago, as in other western cities, anti-Jewish stereotypes were more subdued than on the East Coast. Jews had been among the pioneers and were involved in establishing many Chicago institutions; their prominent role during and after the war helped to dispel existing anti-Jewish sentiments. The persistence of anti-Jewish stereotypes, however, should not be underestimated. And Chicago was not an island. Early in 1867, several New York insurance companies publicly announced they would only accept Jewish businessmen as clients if they fulfilled special obligations. Between the lines of this announcement lurked again the image of Jews as treacherous Shylocks who allegedly could not be trusted. Due to frequent fires and other hazards, property insurance was crucial. Farsighted businessmen bought insurance from different out-of-town companies because—as many Chicagoans would find out in 1871—local insurance companies too could be wiped out by natural disasters. Much more dangerous was the accusation of lacking trust, in a booming economy built on trust. When Julius Rosenthal and other Chicago Jews publicly protested this measure, Chicago's most prominent businessmen, led by Jonathan Young Scammon, Mayor Rice and several other politicians joined them. Rosenthal, Henry Greenebaum, and Abraham Kohn organized a public protest meeting. Prominent Gentiles led by Scammon and other influential businessmen and politicians attended. The meeting passed its own boycott resolution toward the insurance companies. Several prominent speakers stressed the trustworthiness of Jews, emphasizing their solidarity with Jewish Chicagoans. The *Chicago Tribune* carried an extensive report of the meeting. This was a serious matter for the integrity of Chicago as a place of business, hardly an internal problem of a marginal group.[23]

Was the impressive action of the Jews of Chicago during and after the Civil War simply a consequence of the national crisis and rising anti-Jewish discrimination as well as exceptional personalities such as Greenebaum and Felsenthal? Or was Sinai's radical Reform agenda the driving force? No doubt, the combination of circumstances, participants, and their specific convictions was crucial. Yet it was hardly a coincidence that the most visible and committed Jewish speakers in Chicago belonged to Sinai. They had taken on the activist message of Reform. Felsenthal, Greenebaum, Rosenthal, and several others had a very clear sense of what they were trying to achieve—and why. Before 1858, the Reform-minded members of KAM had only a vague idea of the rationale for changes, as their questions to Samuel Adler illustrate. The *Reformverein* discussions, the debate over *Kol Kore Bamidbar*, the first steps of Sinai congregation, and Felsenthal's sermons had given them a clear idea of *their* place in the modern world. As modern Jews, they could not remain passive when the war entered a critical phase in the summer of 1862. KAM leaders Gerstley and Kohn, their erstwhile opponents, did not stand back. Instead of reverting back to orthodoxy, KAM was explicitly committing itself to Reform (albeit not of the radical kind) only months after the formal split in early 1861. Gerstley, the new KAM president, kept in touch with events in the Reform sphere; Einhorn mentioned him as a subscriber of the

Sinai in June 1861. Most KAM members realized quickly that Sinai congregation had found its place in Chicago and in America.[24]

KAM's altered position is remarkable because few Christians traveled this far, certainly not the Catholic and Lutheran fellow immigrants from central Europe. Even decades later, German immigrant clergy preached a rigid and conservative message that did not resonate well with bold civic action and social bridge building, let alone with openness to modernity and social change. In the 1860s, most Protestant and Catholic congregations in Chicago drew a sharp line between the church and the world outside. This conservative position was also a reaction to the rise of Socialism. By the late 1860s German immigrants who found work in Chicago's new industries organized under the flag of Socialism and even anarchism rather than going to church.

Even though the Christian response to modernity was largely pessimistic, Christians did not remain passive. Much valuable work was done on behalf of poorer Chicagoans. But the growing misery and violence in American cities provided the Christian pulpit with a strong case against change. Sinai members and leaders, on the other hand, recognized that rejection was not a sufficient response. Spreading the universal truths and interpreting Judaism as a progressive religion resonated well with the fundamental American values springing from similar Enlightenment sources.

Apart from several leading Germans, agnostic liberals, such as Brentano, or socialists, like physician Ernst Schmidt, only a few native-born liberal Protestants emerged as fellow travelers of radical Reform Jews during the 1860s. Unitarian minister Robert Collyer was among the first liberal Protestants who joined hands with Chicago Jewish Reformers. The Unitarian Unity Church had employed the former Methodist in 1863.[25] Sinai's second rabbi, Isaac Loeb Chronik, stressed in 1869, "Unitarianism here in North America stands close to us. It proves how the religious rigidity of English-Americans has become fluid."[26]

FINDING A RABBI

Even after the Civil War started, the prospects for Sinai looked more than favorable. The progressive congregation had a loyal membership base in a booming city. In a period of relatively low immigration with rising numbers of people arriving in and departing from Chicago, Sinai increased its membership from the sixty founding members to approximately a hundred by 1863. KAM had a hundred and twenty, and B'nai Sholom had eighty members.[27] Sinai's members were excited and ready for new challenges.

In April 1861, Sinai purchased a former church on Monroe between Clark and

La Salle Streets and converted it into a synagogue. It is labeled on an 1862 map as "Jewish Church." Samuel Adler came from New York to conduct the dedication service on June 22, 1861. According to Felsenthal, on this occasion the "first public divine service was held by the young congregation, and a new ritual, the Einhorn ritual, was for the first time used in a western congregation."[28] The congregation adhered to the *Reformverein* platform. A German sermon and German songs dominated the service, and men and women sat next to each other in family pews. Interestingly, the men covered their heads during the first two years. Only when Sinai relocated to a new building in 1863 did they remove their hats during the service. These reforms might not have appeared spectacular to Christians of the time, but each one was groundbreaking for Jews. Only a handful of Jewish congregations in and beyond the United States had dared to step into this territory in the early 1860s.[29]

Mixed seating highlights how in the American context theological reforms were intertwined with pragmatic considerations. When the Berlin Reform congregation was founded in 1845, men and women sat on separate sides of the sanctuary but on the same floor. This constituted a radical departure from the traditional arrangement whereby women sat on galleries behind a *mechitsa* (partition). In the United States, newly founded Jewish congregations frequently acquired former churches without balconies. This background partly explains why Isaac Mayer Wise's Albany congregation, Anshe Emeth, was probably the first to introduce mixed seating when it was founded in 1851 and acquired a former church. Temple Emanu-El in New York adapted the practice in 1854 when the congregation moved to a new building, also a former church without balconies but with family pews. When David Einhorn began his tenure at Har Sinai in Baltimore in 1855, he abolished the galleries for women. But for several years, following the Berlin model, men and women sat separately on the same floor. In typical fashion, Einhorn justified the introduction of mixed seating at Har Sinai by tracing the separation of the sexes to an ancient practice that had lost its original meaning in contemporary America. The Chicago *Reformverein* accepted Einhorn's rationale, and Sinai opted for mixed seating from the beginning.[30]

Sinai also adopted Einhorn's German-language prayer book, *Olath Thamid, Gebetbuch für Reformgemeinden* (Prayer book for Reform congregations). Membership entailed the right to a burial and a pew in the synagogue. In November 1861, Sinai rented rooms for a religious school. The members were recent immigrants who were relatively young. Most had several children who attended the religious school for a small fee. Due to the Illinois incorporation law, the board minutes were kept in English. In 1863, the congregation relocated to a former church with more seating capacity, on the corner of Van Buren Street and Third Avenue (today, Plymouth Court).[31]

Yet who was going to preach those German sermons and serve as religious leader of the congregation? Sinai struggled for almost ten years to find an inspiring personality. This was hardly surprising. The Reform movement was still in its infancy. Convincing a qualified rabbi with the necessary Reform credentials to move to what was still considered a distant western city must have been difficult, especially for board members who had little hands-on experience in managing a congregation.

In spring 1861, Sinai almost succeeded in recruiting a rabbi with perfect credentials. This man was not Bernhard Felsenthal. His limited job experience was not even the main stumbling block; he simply lacked the obvious qualifications required for the position: a doctorate from a German university and rabbinical ordination. Sinai's favorite candidate had both. Indeed, he was the spiritual founder of the congregation. Of course, nobody was better qualified to lead the bold Reform experiment in Chicago than David Einhorn. He had relentlessly rallied support for the project of a radical Reform congregation in Chicago. His theology had inspired the founders of Sinai, and he (assisted by Felsenthal) had shaped the outlook of the new congregation. Einhorn was also a prominent member of a still-small circle of leading Reform rabbi-scholars. He was a younger member of the founding generation of the movement and acquainted with the most prominent German Reform theologians, Abraham Geiger and Samuel Holdheim. The latter, who served the Berlin Reform congregation until his untimely death in 1860, shared Einhorn's radical views more than any other Jewish theologian. In 1861, Einhorn was the only leading Reformer of this first generation of rabbi-scholars who had left central Europe. Others, such as Samuel Hirsch, would only arrive in America a few years later.

Einhorn's monthly *Sinai* had inspired the name of the new congregation.[32] The naming of the congregation certainly flattered Einhorn; it may even have been an attempt to lure him to Chicago. Sinai's negotiations with Einhorn were hardly a secret. The *Staatszeitung* strongly backed his appointment. Attracting an intellectual of such stature, it claimed, would be an "immeasurable gain" for German spiritual life in Chicago.[33] Fate seemed to deal Sinai a helping hand. Just when the congregation was established in April 1861, pro-slavery vigilantes suddenly confronted the outspoken abolitionist Einhorn. In mid-April, shortly after the Confederate attack on Fort Sumter, civil order in Baltimore broke down, rumors about threats to Einhorn's life were circulating, and several close friends began to guard the rabbi's house. After wavering for several days, he fled to nearby

Philadelphia on April 22. Returning to Baltimore was out of the question. On May 16, he announced his resignation. Three days earlier, he had received a letter from Har Sinai pleading him to return. The congregation president assured Einhorn that order had been restored. But in the interest of his personal safety and that of his congregation members, he asked him "to avoid anything from the pulpit which touches upon the stirring daily questions."

He should have known better than to make such a request. Einhorn printed the German letter in the *Sinai*, describing his journey to Philadelphia, and explaining his decision to resign. The message certainly was not lost upon Sinai's founders. A completely free pulpit would become one of the essentials of the new congregation, even if some members found it sometimes hard to accept. On May 16, the day of his formal resignation, Einhorn announced the receipt of a telegram from "a virtuous congregation" that had elected him as its new minister; very likely he was referring to Sinai.[34] Two weeks later, he confided to Felsenthal that he had received offers from Sinai, Anshe Emeth in Albany, and Philadelphia's Keneseth Israel.[35]

Indeed, why not go west to serve a group of committed followers deeply influenced by his theology? Einhorn was certainly tempted. Yet times were uncertain. Moreover, Chicago was—certainly from a Philadelphia perspective—still uncomfortably close to the frontier. Einhorn must have dreaded the complete lack of cultural and intellectual life. The position in Chicago would have been yet another experiment with an uncertain outcome for a man who had been through a fair share of such ventures and disappointments. He probably still vividly recalled his unhappy days in remote Mecklenburg-Schwerin in northern Germany. Moving into Isaac Mayer Wise's backyard would almost certainly have led to difficult and unpleasant encounters. At the age of fifty-two, Einhorn could hardly pass as a young man, and his doctor strongly advised against the long journey and the intense heat in Chicago.[36]

After the dangerous escape from Baltimore, he, his wife, and his daughters were craving security. Keneseth Israel congregation in Philadelphia was more than eager to guarantee him just that. After toying with the idea to go west, he turned Sinai's offer down. On May 19, three days after receiving the telegram, Keneseth Israel elected Einhorn rabbi, and he accepted. Probably on his recommendation, Sinai offered the position to Felsenthal who, according to Einhorn, needed some persuading to take the job. In June, Felsenthal signed his contract.[37] By late 1861, Einhorn and Samuel Adler formally declared him a rabbi.[38] But this was not to be the end of the story.

Through their regular correspondence, a close and cordial relationship formed between Einhorn and Felsenthal. Sinai's leaders, however, continued to woo the Philadelphia rabbi. They underestimated Einhorn's growing commitment to Felsenthal. At least once between 1861 and 1864, Sinai made Einhorn a new offer. At the same time, Felsenthal's contract was extended only annually. Einhorn's letters to Felsenthal shed light on this unfolding story. In his characteristic, hard-to-decipher, jagged German handwriting, Einhorn kept his friend in Chicago closely informed about the steps taken by Sinai congregation. "Do you really think I am capable of forcing you from your position?" he asked Felsenthal on April 24, 1864. Some time before, he freely admitted, he had given some thought to a renewed offer from Sinai, but no longer. No—and this he stressed in no uncertain terms—he would stand on Felsenthal's side rather than accepting any further offers from Chicago.[39]

In this light, it is hardly surprising that Felsenthal's tenure at Sinai was a brief—and not particularly happy—one. Einhorn's sympathetic attitude may also have been influenced by the personal tragedy that befell Felsenthal. In early 1864, his young wife Caroline died, leaving him with a one-year-old daughter, Ida. A few weeks later, facing yet another one-year extension and knowing Einhorn on his side, Felsenthal asked for a long-term contract, expecting a firm commitment from the congregation. In response, the board raised the rabbi's annual salary from $1,200 to $1,500. This was approximately the annual salary of an established lawyer or doctor and sufficient to raise a family. In 1860, an unskilled worker made about $100 a year, while a white-collar employee could earn about $200.[40]

But a raise was not what Felsenthal really wanted. He reiterated his demand. Recognizing the importance of this matter, the board called a meeting of all members. The majority rejected a long-term contract, and Felsenthal promptly announced his departure. In June 1864, he delivered his last sermon as Sinai's rabbi. Soon, many would regret this outcome. Within days of his official departure, a small delegation was dispatched to Philadelphia. Yet it returned empty-handed. The dogged pursuit of Einhorn had been in vain. Now, the young congregation faced a prolonged period without a rabbi. In the mid-1860s, a pool of potential candidates hardly existed. Apart from Einhorn and Felsenthal, only a handful of Reform-minded rabbis had immigrated to America in 1864. All had good jobs, were hardly inclined to settle in Chicago, and (with the exception of Samuel Adler and Einhorn) did not share the radical "German" agenda of Sinai's members. In other words, Sinai could not expect to recruit a radical Reform rabbi with *Bildung*. As long as the war was continuing, finding a rabbi in Europe was out of the question.[41]

Felsenthal's sudden departure caused another severe crisis. Some Sinai members were displeased by the way Felsenthal had been treated. Sinai, these members felt, had not shown its rabbi due respect. More than a few of these men and women had long-standing personal links with him and his family in the German Palatinate. Many of these members lived not in the Loop but on the West Side. Because of the distance from the lake and the Chicago River—years before a sewage system had even been proposed—the West Side was Chicago's upscale neighborhood. Walking to the Loop took time, especially for the children who attended Sinai's school. The Chicago River, parents complained, "is a very prominent highway of marine commerce steamers . . . constantly passing and repassing, necessitating the opening of the various bridges, making it dangerous in fact for children crossing the same unsupported."[42]

In the summer of 1864, in the midst of a period of rapid economic growth, the business fortunes of most Sinai members looked more than favorable. These developments explain why a small faction, led by Henry Greenebaum, left the congregation in July 1864 on amicable terms. Thus, after a few weeks, Felsenthal reemerged as the rabbi of Chicago's second radical Reform congregation, Zion, on the city's West Side (initially on the corner of Des Plaines and Madison Streets). The annual reelection, "the sword of Damocles," as Felsenthal characterized it, was removed. Zion gave its rabbi a life contract. This was an unusual commitment on behalf of the congregation. Even in the mid-1870s, Felsenthal was the only minister of any denomination in Chicago who had a life contract.[43] In hindsight, this proved to be a blessing for Sinai—and for scholars of Chicago Jewish history. Felsenthal quickly put his bad feelings about Sinai to rest and remained close to his erstwhile congregation and many of its members. Even before his departure from Sinai, he had shown an interest in the history of the Chicago Jewish community. The pencil-written notes of a talk he gave to the Chicago Historical Society in 1863 on Chicago Jewish history are the oldest extant history of the Chicago Jewish community (and of Sinai) and one of few such documents that was not consumed by the 1871 fire.[44]

Nevertheless, the efforts to recruit Einhorn had severely shaken the prospering congregation. Within a few weeks, Felsenthal had left disappointed, followed by a faction of key members. One unintended but welcome consequence was that Sinai and KAM officially healed the rift that had opened between them in 1861. On Yom Kippur 1864, KAM's new rabbi, Liebmann Adler, officiated at Sinai. Adler was not a radical Reformer, but he encountered little resistance when he suggested reforms that only months earlier had provoked Sinai's split. From the start, Adler insisted on preaching in German. This was symbolically important but had a practical reason: Adler would never fully master the English language.

To find a qualified rabbi, Sinai's leaders now had to turn to the motherland of Reform. Several surviving founders recalled fifty years later that they were looking for a university graduate "and a regular acknowledged rabbi." For Jewish Reformers, Germany—in a cultural more than in a geographical or political sense—represented the point of reference.[45] A highly German-trained rabbi-scholar in the pulpit added to the status and prestige of urban congregations such as Sinai.

During the 1860s, America was a growing but still insignificant outpost of the Jewish Diaspora. Jewish life in the German lands was blossoming, and large Jewish communities were expanding and flourishing. Indeed, while thousands of rural Jews from central Europe were crossing the Atlantic, many more settled in the growing cities in the wider vicinity of their home villages such as Frankfurt, Munich, Breslau, Hamburg, Königsberg, Leipzig, and especially Berlin. In 1865, Sinai president Benjamin Schönemann ventured to Germany to find a rabbi for Sinai.[46]

The systematic digitization of newspapers in recent years allows for an intriguing find. During the second half of the nineteenth century, New York newspapers daily published the names of departing and arriving steamship passengers who traveled first or second class (and not in steerage). According to such a list a "B. Schoonemann" from Chicago was one of 463 passengers on the ship *America* that departed New York for Southampton and Bremen on July 15, 1865. It is more than likely that "B. Schoonemann" was Sinai's president, for he was hardly the only member of Sinai on the *America*. Among his fellow passengers were Michael Greenebaum, Raphael Guthmann, Julius Rosenthal and Nelson Morris, all with their wives and children.[47] These members did not assist Schönemann but very likely went to their former home villages for family visits during the summer—another indication for the close ties between network migrants many years after their own move to America.

In Frankfurt, Schönemann met with the leading Reform theologian Abraham Geiger, who recommended a rabbi in the Baltic port of Königsberg. This man, Dr. Isaac Loeb Chronik, seemed to be a good fit: a true radical who was looking for new pastures. Schönemann immediately undertook the long train journey to meet this man. On the way from Frankfurt to the distant Baltic port and on the return journey, Sinai's president passed through Berlin. It is not known whether he interrupted his journey there. Few places in the German lands were more symbolic for Jewish Reformers than the rapidly growing Prussian capital. Berlin was the city of the great Jewish philosopher Moses Mendelssohn, in whose circle the idea of Jewish Emancipation had first been formulated. In Berlin, Jews in significant numbers had "left the Ghetto" on their own terms. Here stood the cradle of the Jewish Reform movement, and it was the city with the most Jewish scholars. Yet in contrast to the United States, Reform was only gradually making an impact. One striking exception, of course, was the Berlin Reform congregation, the only explicitly radical Reform congregation in central Europe during the 1860s. It was the first Jewish congregation that conducted Sunday services and abolished Saturday services. If he stopped in the city, Schönemann probably visited the construction site of the Neue Synagoge (new synagogue). After its dedication in the following year, 1866, it was for decades Germany's largest and most splendid synagogue. This impressive building demonstrated what Henry Greenebaum had demanded during the late 1850s, it was a proud and optimistic display of Jewish pride and belonging within a strongly transforming and opening society. Its distinctive Moorish architecture and golden cupola also expressed an acceptable degree of difference at the very center of a large central European capital. Unlike most Reform synagogues in America, however, the Neue Synagoge had balconies for women.[48]

By the mid-1860s, American Reform congregations were diverging from the German model. That more traditionally inclined German Jews were shocked by some of the reforms implemented in America is hardly astonishing. In 1861, a German-Jewish traveler passing through Chicago joked about the *Reformwuth* (Reform madness) at Sinai. Yet even leading Reformers in Germany watched with some unease what was happening in American Reform synagogues. Abraham Geiger did not approve of certain reforms introduced by Sinai and several other congregations, notably mixed seating.[49] But he was not unsympathetic, for he knew that the American Reformers held him in the highest esteem. The movement of young Reform rabbis from Germany to America also seemed to ensure a degree of control over American congregations.

In Königsberg, Chronik and Schönemann quickly settled on a five-year contract and an annual salary of $3,000. Even if the inflation after the Civil War is taken into account, that was much more than Sinai had offered Felsenthal. Chronik, however, was *gebildet*. He had a doctorate under his belt, an academic reputation, and job experience in different congregations. Sinai's new rabbi probably was not fluent in English. Yet that was not a barrier. Sinai wanted him to preach in German, and not just for symbolic reasons. German was still the native language of all members. And Chronik was moving to one of the largest "German" cities outside of central Europe. In 1870, the census takers counted more than fifty thousand German-speaking immigrants in Chicago. If one adds the American-born children, Germans constituted more than a quarter of the Chicago population.[50]

In Chicago, readers of the *Sinai* and the German-Jewish press probably recalled Chronik's name from a notorious incident. Sinai's new rabbi was a known political radical and an uncompromising Reformer. His involvement in the 1848–1849 revolution had forced him into Dutch exile. Like Einhorn, he was not a man who could easily be intimidated. In June 1860, Chronik began to conduct Reform services in the Amsterdam Jewish quarter. The services triggered an immediate and violent response from traditional Jews. On July 14, 1860, several broke into the meeting hall, interrupted his sermon, and surrounded him, screaming: "Stone him, stone him!" Under a hail of stones thrown from windows and protected by several policemen, Chronik managed to leave the premises and the Jewish quarter unharmed. The mayor of Amsterdam guaranteed Chronik full police protection. Unimpressed by further threats to his life, the rabbi returned to the quarter two weeks later to conduct services. Dozens of policemen, some with swords drawn and several on horseback, held a hostile Jewish crowd in check while accompanying the rabbi to the synagogue. The leaders of the Amsterdam Jewish community, while not sympathetic to Reform, were embarrassed and accused the rioters of desecrating the Sabbath. Fearing further disturbances, the Reform society located outside of the Jewish quarter. This constituted an acknowledgement of defeat for the Reform project. The Dutch king incorporated the society a few weeks later, confirming its position, yet apart from the existing (Orthodox) community. The incident briefly captured the attention of the Jewish press across Europe. Ludwig Philippson, a moderate Reform rabbi and editor of the influential *Allgemeine Zeitung*, Einhorn, and other Reformers were outraged. Open violence from within Jewish communities against Reformers remained the exception, but these incidents highlighted the divisiveness of Reform.[51]

Chronik is rarely mentioned in Sinai documents. Quite soon after his arrival, most Sinai's members realized they had employed the wrong man. Ironically, Chronik was too academic, too German, and too radical. Even members versed in the more challenging sources of *Bildung* had trouble understanding Chronik's densely intellectual sermons. It is hard to assess his position within the congregation, because the members were understandably reluctant to make their true opinion about the rabbi public. A revealing clue as to why Chronik was out of touch with his congregation can be found in the short-lived monthly *Zeichen der Zeit* (Signs of the times), which he edited and Sinai funded. It was launched

CHAPTER THREE

in January 1869 after a significant delay. Chronik covered many interesting topics years ahead of time, such as the theology of Buddhism or women's suffrage, but he tended to lose himself in dense philosophical treatises.[52] Admittedly, publishing a monthly or weekly demanded some talent and shrewdness Chronik did not possess. He also lacked the sharpness of Einhorn's pen. Even the *Sinai* folded in 1863 due to a lack of subscribers. The highbrow *Bildung* message, reprinted sermons, and news from other Reform-minded congregations alone did not attract readers. In this field, Wise had a much better developed sense of what most Jews of the period wanted to read—and what they did not.

Another factor was Chronik's firm and often repeated conviction that Germany was the leading *Kulturnation*, the "beloved German fatherland," "the Zion of the religious idea."[53] No doubt, Reformers like Felsenthal and Einhorn subscribed to this view, but they also stressed in the same breath the unique potential of Reform in America and the need to spread *Bildung*. But Chicago in 1866 was not Chicago in 1860. Chronik arrived after the transformative experience of the Civil War. Einhorn's escape from Baltimore, Felsenthal's articles against slavery, the Chicago war meetings, the successful fight against anti-Jewish discrimination and slavery, the death of brothers, fathers, and sons in battle, Lincoln's assassination—all of these experiences and others had transformed Jewish immigrants into patriotic Americans. Promoting German superiority raised Chronik's profile among many Chicago Germans and some Jews. Yet Chronik failed to understand that America, for all its flaws, had a much more concrete meaning for many of his congregants than it had only a few years earlier.

Sinai's new rabbi was not a reclusive scholar. Soon after his arrival, he gave a series of public talks on biblical themes (in German) and regularly wrote for the *Staatszeitung* on Jewish theology and literary issues. According to the *Staatszeitung*, his work was proof "for the spiritual superiority of Germandom in the United States." Chronik could not have put it more succinctly.[54] It would, however, be unfair to sketch Chronik's tenure in an entirely negative light. He did not hesitate to get involved in Chicago politics. In December 1867, he brought Jewish and German leaders together in his home to form a Comite gegen Temperenz und Sabbath-Zwangsgesetze (Committee against temperance and enforced Sabbath laws).[55] Renewed demands to regulate the public consumption of alcohol and Sunday laws threatened the cultural habits of Germans as much as the right of Jews to keep their businesses open. Nevertheless, Chronik could not match the public standing of Felsenthal or Greenebaum or even that of leading members of Sinai such as Godfrey Snydacker or Julius Rosenthal.

More interesting is Chronik's theological radicalism. In the late 1860s, most

Sinai members seemed unprepared for Chronik's radical agenda, or, unlike his predecessor and successors, Chronik was not able to convince his congregants of the theological rationale for radical Reform. Apparently, Chronik inspired the movement for the Sunday Sabbath at Sinai. His attempt to introduce Sunday services at Sinai failed. But a minority strongly supported it—and continued to do so.[56] In 1867, Sinai did radically break with another Jewish tradition. Over the fierce objections of several members, a majority voted against buying land for a separate Jewish cemetery and for the acquisition of a large plot in the nondenominational Rosehill Cemetery on the Far North Side.[57]

In 1869, Chronik participated with Felsenthal in the first meeting of Reform rabbis in America, held at the Philadelphia home of Samuel Hirsch, who had succeeded Einhorn at Keneseth Israel in 1866. Einhorn came from his new congregation, Beth El in New York. Among the participants were the recently arrived Solomon Sonneschein (St. Louis), Kaufmann Kohler (Detroit), and none other than Isaac Mayer Wise. Anyone who expected a clash between Einhorn and Wise at their first personal meeting was sorely disappointed. Wise kept a low profile. Being a part of the circle of leading Reformers was all that mattered for him, even though he had to sit for hours in the same room with Einhorn and Felsenthal and listen to longwinded theological discussions in German.

From the perspective of Sinai's history, it is noteworthy that on this occasion Chronik and Felsenthal met with two future Sinai rabbis, Kohler and the son of the host, eighteen-year-old Emil Gustav Hirsch. Chronik tried to set the agenda, visibly upsetting Einhorn and the other rabbis. His proposal for the complete abolition of Hebrew in the liturgy and the religious schools was firmly rejected, and his call for the introduction of Sunday services by all Reform congregations in America was tabled for another meeting.[58] Apart from Wise, none of the other rabbis attended the follow-up meetings in Cleveland and Cincinnati in the following two years. These meetings and the Philadelphia conference had no lasting impact. In America, the congregations, not the rabbis, had the last word over reforms. In 1870, Sinai decided not to renew Chronik's contract beyond 1871 and offered the position to the young Kaufmann Kohler. Kohler accepted, and it was agreed he would begin his tenure in Chicago on November 1, 1871. Nobody, of course, could know that large parts of Chicago, including Sinai's Temple, would be reduced to a smoldering wasteland by this day.[59]

REFORMING THE B'NAI B'RITH

When in 1860 he hurriedly left the B'nai B'rith reception in Chicago after encountering Felsenthal, Isaac Mayer Wise probably anticipated that the founding of a radical Reform congregation would have repercussions beyond the synagogue, especially in the B'nai B'rith order. The conflict between the Chicago B'nai B'rith lodge and its western fellow lodges is surprisingly well documented and provides an intriguing perspective on Sinai's bold vision in its early years. The debates demonstrate that the opposition of the radical Reformers in Chicago to traditional ritual was not limited to the synagogue. Behind the conflict loomed the large question how to define Jewish identity in a rapidly transforming society.[60]

Most of the members of Chicago's first B'nai B'rith lodge, Ramah, belonged to the radical Reform faction that became Sinai in 1861. As discussed in the preceding chapter, when the radical Reformers recognized the divisiveness of their theological agenda, Ramah became the platform for safeguarding the union of Chicago Jews outside of the synagogue. This hedging strategy on behalf of preserving Jewish community paid off, as the establishment of the UHRA in 1859 and the 1862 war meetings illustrated impressively. Yet, within the B'nai B'rith, Ramah's close relationship with Sinai congregation constituted a challenge to the leadership of for Isaac Mayer Wise. As president of B'nai B'rith District Grand Lodge (DGL) No. 2 for the western states, Wise had already clashed with East Coast lodges sympathetic to the universalistic ideas of radical Reform. In 1858, the eastern lodges had successfully pushed through a reform of the B'nai B'rith ritual, abolishing the wearing of aprons and regalia. But the western lodges, led by Wise continued to argue for restoring the old ritual. Once Sinai had been founded, Ramah—led by Felsenthal and Henry Greenebaum—did not waste much time and joined the debate over the ritual question.

At the annual DGL No. 2 convention in Chicago, held July 13–14, 1862, Felsenthal outlined Ramah's case. He fiercely criticized the case for restoring the old ritual, stressing it contradicted the spirit of modern Judaism and reinforced anti-Jewish stereotypes: "What is there in Judaism that it has to hide itself before the world?" The symbols and uniforms were "empty forms without meaning . . . playthings for big children." The conclusion of the speech was vintage Felsenthal: "If the brothers, however, insist upon having regalias, let them wear at least Tefillin in their meetings and processions, instead of the ridiculous aprons, for which there is not the shadow of an apology."[61] The representatives of the other western lodges voted down Ramah's move. Felsenthal had predicted such an outcome, but he reminded the brothers to rethink the essential cause of the B'nai B'rith. Was it just a "mutual benefit society" with a hollow ritual, or did it have a higher mission? Most western B'nai B'rith members simply could not grasp the justification for Felsenthal's radical case. They lived in smaller towns and cities like Evansville, Indiana or Louisville, Kentucky, and favored limited external reforms, very much along the lines of Wise's agenda. These western Jews, who were much more committed to the Jewish tradition, did not understand why they should drop the ritual that defined fraternal relations within the lodges.[62]

After recognizing the degree of opposition within DGL No. 2, the Chicago brethren decided to take the bull by its horns by bringing Wise to their side. To achieve this bold plan, they worked out a clever strategy. In 1863, a great project was taking shape: the B'nai B'rith sponsorship of a Jewish orphans' home in Cleveland. The members of Ramah opposed the orphans' home, because it would divert urgently needed donations from the fund for a Jewish hospital in Chicago. In 1863, only New York and Cincinnati had Jewish hospitals. Ramah, therefore, proposed two alternatives: a scheme to adopt Jewish orphans in families rather than place them in a cold (and costly) home and a less expensive and much-needed institution that would be a shining monument of B'nai B'rith generosity for generations to come: a rabbinical seminary in Cincinnati. Wise was flattered by this suggestion. He joined the Chicago brethren in support of this—his—pet project. The other brethren were rather unimpressed by such stratagems and passed the motion in favor of the orphans' home, which duly opened its doors in 1868. As it would turn out, Ramah had been sadly prophetic. In the orphanage's first decade, the children suffered under a dictatorial and cruel headmaster; only after his departure in the late 1870s did the home live up to its promise.[63]

The rise of Sinai and the growing respect Jews enjoyed in Chicago explain why Ramah persisted with its reform agenda in the face of strong opposition. Ramah envisioned a new fraternal organization that would transcend all ethnic, religious and political divisions. But its western fellow lodges in the DGL No. 2 refused to cooperate, accusing Ramah of undermining the order. The conflict highlights the widening gulf between metropolitan Reform Jews in Chicago and the more traditional, down-to-earth lodge members from smaller Jewish communities throughout the Midwest who did not want to yield to a radical minority from one city.

Finally, in 1867, Ramah moved again to abolish the secret ritual and the aprons, which the Constitutional Grand Lodge had reintroduced over the objections of eastern lodges in 1863. Now, the DGL No. 2 leadership voiced cautious support but decided to do nothing.[64] Much more problematic from Ramah's perspective was the decision by DGL No. 2 in 1867 to deny membership to candidates who were married to gentile women. As a result, the Chicago lodges formally demanded the installation of a new DGL, but the majority of the other lodges voted against this motion. The relationship between Chicago and the other towns and cities in DGL No. 2 had now deteriorated to such a low point that most Chicago Jews anticipated their formal exclusion from the order. The struggle resonated well beyond the confines of the meeting halls. The *Staatszeitung* openly backed the Chicago brethren against "the narrow-minded orthodoxy . . . the apparatus of medieval inquisition" in Cincinnati, the seat of DGL No. 2.[65]

At this point, the postwar boom in Chicago and the rising Jewish migration to its city provided Ramah with a strong case for a new DGL. A second Chicago lodge, Hillel, joined Ramah in 1866. A third lodge, named after a recently deceased B'nai B'rith leader and rabbi, Maurice Mayer, was installed in February 1868; a fourth lodge was on the way; and a fifth was only a matter of time. The internal politics of the B'nai B'rith also betray the changing fortunes of Chicago and Cincinnati. The Civil War had propelled Chicago into the dominant position in the Midwest. The older centers of St. Louis and Cincinnati were now visibly falling behind. More and more Jewish immigrants were streaming to Chicago, and even established Cincinnatians and their businesses were heading north.

At the same time, more lodges were being installed across the Midwest, and a reorganization of DGL No. 2 was inevitable. The Constitutional Grand Lodge in New York solved the simmering conflict within DGL No. 2 by installing a new DGL (No. 6) in Chicago in 1868. This meant a setback for Cincinnati. DGL No. 2 lost a significant number of member lodges and much of its influence.[66] DGL No. 6 included all lodges in the states of Illinois, Wisconsin, Iowa, and Minnesota. The installation of DGL No. 7 in 1873, which comprised the southern states, reduced the influence of DGL No. 2 further.[67]

The first DGL No. 6 convention, which met in Chicago in 1868, overwhelmingly voted Henry Greenebaum into the president's chair. Greenebaum had invited members of the Gentile elite of Chicago, including leading businessmen and Unitarian minister Robert Collyer—an indication not only for the high degree of acceptance Jews enjoyed on an official level in Chicago but also for the inclusive, universal vision of the new DGL. Greenebaum sketched his agenda for the order at large that closely echoes the theology of radical Reform movement: "We do not regret the past. We do not regret all the misfortunes of our race. We do not regret all the prosecutions under which we have suffered. . . . In return for all this which we have suffered, we will teach the whole Jewish world, love, forgiveness, fraternal feeling, charity, benevolence and peace." In the long run, all divisions that separated people from each other should be overcome, divisions "between one race and another, and one nationality and another, and . . . those social barriers." These statements echo the radical Reform theology and the *Bildung* ideal. Yet it was a surprise that Greenebaum demanded to open the order as soon as possible for every man (albeit not for women), regardless of his religion. In the *Staatszeitung*, Felsenthal, an ardent supporter of this project, pointed out that "der großartige deutsche Geist der Universalität" (that grand German spirit of universality) precluded exclusion as such. The B'nai B'rith should be open to every man.[68]

By accepting Gentiles, the DGL No. 6 would have solved a fiercely debated issue that had already occupied the B'nai B'rith for years. The B'nai B'rith was an order for Jewish males, yet it was not a religious organization. But how could the order determine whether an applicant was a Jew? Were children of mixed marriages Jewish? Could a brother take a Gentile woman as wife? Could the B'nai B'rith base its access rules on traditional Jewish law, and, if not, which criteria should be the basis for accepting somebody as Jewish? Greenebaum's radical plan would have immediately solved this conundrum, but it never came to pass. Voting for the affable and energetic Greenebaum as president was one thing; voting for his revolutionary agenda was quite another.[69]

Although Chicago was in a stronger position in the new and smaller DGL, a decisive majority voted against Greenebaum's and Felsenthal's plan. The Chicago brethren had gained much political clout within the order with the installation of the new DGL, but they could not take their ambitious agenda beyond Chicago. Why did the bold reform project of Sinai's and Zion's members for the B'nai B'rith fail? The Chicago Reformers would have dragged an organization committed explicitly (and with good reason) to religious neutrality into the religious sphere. Even sympathetic observers could not deny that the order would have become a vehicle of the radical Reform cause. In hindsight, Felsenthal's diagnosis that the order was not more than a mutual benefit society if it did not boldly pursue universalistic ideals, was visionary. The B'nai B'rith continued to expand impressively and did much to support distressed Jews, but it was losing its initial momentum. The B'nai B'rith episode was hardly the last time Sinai members would try to push the fluid boundary between religious and secular Jewish identity and, indeed, the limits of Jewish identity itself.

GERMANS OR JEWS?

An organized community representing German-speaking immigrants in Chicago existed only for a limited period of time. Interestingly, efforts to bring the many German-speaking immigrants in Chicago under one roof were often led by Jews. But Jewish activities in German associations took place on an individual basis. Although Jews, among them most of Sinai's leaders and rabbis, belonged to Chicago's ethnic leadership of "Germans" into the 1870s and beyond, Jewish associations and congregations did not consider themselves as part of the German community. No Christian congregation was as committed to German *Kultur* as Sinai and Zion were, but the two Reform congregations never publicly participated in the German community project. The numerous parades Chicagoans organized during the 1850s and 1860s illustrate this subtle division. Jews participated in most German parades (or in the German cohort), often as leaders and main organizers—but as individuals. While Christian congregations marched, Jewish congregations did not, although many of their members (including rabbis like Felsenthal and Chronik) certainly did. After a large parade in 1871 celebrating German unification, led by Henry Greenebaum and organized in the office of Julius Rosenthal, the vision of one organized community of most German-speaking immigrants in Chicago collapsed because of many deep-seated differences, especially between the growing group of left-wing, working-class Germans and the more established earlier immigrants who opposed Socialism.[70]

While the German community remained more of a vision than tangible reality, the UHRA strengthened its position during the Civil War by pushing ahead with the hospital project. Jewish hospitals are indicators for the presence of an organized Jewish community. Hospitals required then (as today) large investments and long-term funding that only an organized community could provide. Sinai and Zion congregations never participated in a German parade, but they did march in Chicago's first Jewish parade. On September 2, 1867, all five Jewish congregations of Chicago (Sinai, KAM, Zion, B'nai Sholom, and newly founded North Side Hebrew Congregation), the Jewish fraternal lodges, and the philanthropic societies formed a parade, led by the Civil War hero General Salomon, Chicago's mayor, and the Great Western Light Guard Band. The parade, made up of carriages and marching columns, moved from the business district up to the North Side toward the building site of the future Jewish hospital that was to open its doors to every distressed person "without distinction of nationality, race, religion or color."

Businessman Godfrey Snydacker, who would assume the presidency of Sinai in 1868, addressed the large crowd in German. He pointed out that this event reminded him of his "theure alte Heimath" (beloved old home country), where Jews used to live in close-knit communities. In America, however, Jews formed separate groups, driven apart by religious orientations, conflicting political affiliations, and social differences. One platform remained where Jews "from the North-Sea, the Baltic, from the Rhine and Danube" could meet and unite as "true brothers and sisters": *Wohlthätigkeit* (benevolence). Benevolence was the "true" source of *Einigkeit* (unity) for all Jews in Chicago, and, he concluded, "unity makes us strong."

In his speech, delivered in English, Henry Greenebaum described the importance of the Jewish tradition of helping the poor. He then shifted to a taboo topic, anti-Jewish stereotypes. He picked a classic stereotype of his day, the Rothschild family, to prove that anti-Jewish stereotypes were useless and wrong. In the middle of the nineteenth century, the spectacular rise of the Rothschild banking empire had provoked countless anti-Jewish attacks. The Rothschilds, Greenebaum emphasized, were extremely wealthy, but they were also among the most active benefactors for charitable and philanthropic endeavors worldwide. He concluded his speech by reminding his Jewish listeners to contribute generously to Catholic charities in Chicago and to attend the upcoming German Turner-Fair, a big fund-raiser for the German Aid Society.[71]

The parade and the *Festreden* (festivity speeches) highlight the attempt of Jewish leaders to foster a collective identity and build a community centered around benevolence—in order to unite the participating Jews of diverse backgrounds and, at the same time, to demonstrate to Chicagoans that Jews were not a marginal group but that a civic-minded and patriotic Jewish community existed in their midst and contributed to the city's well-being, putting civic action over discrimination and exclusion. In this light, Greenebaum's call to support the charities of the much-despised Catholics is indeed remarkable.

The vision of a strong Jewish community and of a larger community of all Chicagoans—both committed (like the nation) to pluralism—cannot be separated from each other. Snydacker spoke in German to most Jews, highlighting Jewish *Gemeinschaft*. Greenebaum spoke in English to the other Chicagoans, emphasizing the themes of civic responsibility and inclusion.

As this chapter has shown, it was hardly a coincidence that both speakers were committed radical Reform Jews. The impressive actions of Sinai's leaders and members in the public arena and in American Jewish life betrayed their Reform convictions. Yet Sinai congregation itself did not live up to its initial promise during the 1860s and was rarely mentioned in public. The members struggled finding the right spiritual leader who would rally them around the Reform cause. This would change during the 1870s with the arrival of the promising scholar-rabbi Kaufmann Kohler. But under Kohler's tenure, Sinai's members faced the challenging question whether radical Reform would eventually transcend Judaism.

4.

A STEP TOO FAR?

The Introduction of Sunday Services

IN SINAI'S FIRST DECADE, its members were more active outside of the synagogue than inside. As Sinai forcefully promoted the universal message of Reform in the local community as well as within Jewish circles in Chicago and beyond, the congregation itself became a matter of secondary importance. This was partly related to the Civil War, but lacking inspiration from the pulpit also played a part. Neither Felsenthal nor Chronik could engage the congregation, let alone attract a wider public to the temple. As congregation, Sinai was hardly visible in the city; the members continued to worship in a small, relatively unobtrusive former church building. Apart from the *Reformverein* agenda, only the purchase of lots in a nondenominational cemetery represented a radical step, and even that was hardly noticed outside the Jewish community.

During its second decade, Sinai's members began to focus more on the congregation itself and on the radical Reform agenda and its wider implications. In 1870, before the arrival of Kaufmann Kohler, Sinai was a young radical Reform congregation in a growing yet still peripheral city. Sinai could not match the influence of more established congregations committed to radical Reform, such as Keneseth Israel in Philadelphia and Beth El and Temple Emanu-El in New York, all three with renowned German scholar-rabbis in the pulpit. But by 1880,

79

Sinai had become a prominent and distinctive Reform congregation with a large temple—in a city miraculously transformed into America's new metropolis. Sinai's rise was in large part due to the efforts of its third rabbi, Kaufmann Kohler. Yet the match between the recently immigrated theologian and a young congregation was hardly a perfect union. By the end of the 1870s, Sinai faced a severe crisis when Kohler and influential members clashed over the destiny of radical Reform theology.

THE CHICAGO FIRE

Fire disasters were quite common in nineteenth-century American cities, because buildings were largely built from wood. Security precautions tended to be lax, and fire was used for many purposes, often carelessly. Most Chicagoans were not particularly alarmed when a fire erupted on the Near West Side on the evening of October 8, 1871. Yet once the fire, fanned by a strong and persistent wind, jumped across the Chicago River into the business district, it was clear the damage would be considerable. The firestorm raged on for two days, destroying almost everything in its path. The extent of the destruction was impossible to grasp. The city center, with the courthouse, most offices, and countless businesses and retail stores, and large parts of the densely settled North Side were almost completely wiped out. More than a hundred thousand people—a third of the city's population—lost everything. No contemporary city had ever experienced such massive and swift destruction. People looked back to biblical catastrophes to make sense of the disaster that had consumed their blossoming city, yet the Chicago fire differed from many earlier and later such disasters in one crucial respect: the casualties were limited. Not more than three hundred people lost their lives.[1]

Most of the several thousand Jews in Chicago were relatively lucky. The Jewish neighborhood on the southern edge of the Loop was only partly destroyed. Prosperous Jews had been leaving this area for the Near South Side since before 1871. KAM had located its synagogue further south. Sinai too was in the process of selling its synagogue in the Loop. The West Side, home to the members of Zion congregation, was mostly spared. Only the few Jewish families living on the North Side were hit hard. For Jewish congregations and institutions, the picture was less rosy. Sinai, B'nai Sholom, and the North Side Hebrew Congregation lost their synagogues. The pride of the community, the recently erected Jewish Hospital, was completely destroyed.[2]

Initially, the desperation was great. Henry Greenebaum telegraphed the *Jewish Times*: "God grant that further collections come in rapidly; the distress of hundreds of our co-religionists is appalling." According to the *Israelite*, most Chicago Jews were working in the Loop, but flames had consumed the business district. Thus, Jews were hit harder than other Chicagoans. Initially (and understandably), more than a few Jews left Chicago. The KAM synagogue became the makeshift center of the Jewish community and the meeting place for the UHRA, which was in charge of distributing aid to the worst hit members of the community. The daughter of a KAM member remembered the scene in the 1930s: "The pews were filled, man high, with bedding, food, shoes, hats, utensils, and all sorts of things."[3]

No Jewish Chicagoan was killed in the blaze. Some apparently had barely escaped: the Seligman family managed to jump onto a boat just before the flames reached the lakeshore. A Jewish businessman noticed a woman with a baby in a house engulfed by flames. He rushed in, pulled them out, and, wielding his gun, stopped the driver of a carriage, forcing him to take the woman and her child to safety. These are only two of countless fire stories that quickly found their way into print. Soon, myth and memory overshadowed history. Historian Karen Sawislak has shifted the focus back to the untold history and the real victims of the fire: working-class immigrants, mostly Irish and German, who lost whatever little they possessed, received hardly any aid, and lacked a voice.[4]

Less than two weeks after the fire, on the morning of October 21, many Chicago Jews were stunned when they opened the *Chicago Tribune*. According to the paper, only one man could be trusted to "bring order out of confusion": Henry Greenebaum. The paper demanded he should immediately be elected to the mayor's office. Although not native born, as the *Tribune* pointed out, Greenebaum had lived in Chicago longer than most inhabitants. More important, he was a capable and trustworthy politician who steered clear of corruption. Greenebaum was one of the "few men fit to be entrusted with the office of Mayor at a junction like the present." Greenebaum politely declined. Apart from his countless obligations to the community, he had to tend to his business affairs. Greenebaum wisely judged the broader social climate. His close ties to insurance companies on the East Coast had certainly influenced the *Tribune*'s move. In this critical and charged situation he would have unnecessarily exposed himself—and indirectly the Jewish community—to anti-Jewish attacks.[5] Nevertheless, the episode illustrates the degree of acceptance Jews enjoyed in Chicago after the Civil War. The *Tribune*'s call was a far cry from descriptions found in its pages in the early 1850s, when Chicago Jews were portrayed as peculiar strangers. In addition, Greenebaum did not hide his Jewishness. He was not just a well-connected ethnic powerbroker—he was a modern Jew.

Although visibly shaken by the fire, Sinai's existence was never threatened. Most members were businessmen who carried enough insurance or had sufficient capital invested outside of the city to carry on. Sinai had lost its home but soon found temporary shelter. The critical situation produced admirable displays of solidarity and cooperation across religious lines. KAM graciously offered to share its schoolrooms with Sinai and a Protestant congregation; a Presbyterian congregation invited Sinai to use its church free of charge for Saturday services.[6]

The most pressing matter for the board concerned the new rabbi. While there were calls to suspend the activities of the congregation for several months, it was this question that kept Sinai going. Kaufmann Kohler was scheduled to arrive on November 1. When news of the fire reached Detroit, his congregation, Beth El, loath to see him go, offered Kohler a new contract. Not surprisingly, Kohler himself wondered whether he should move to a city that seemed to have been more or less destroyed to serve a congregation with an uncertain outlook. On October 22, less than two weeks after the fire, Sinai's board met to reach a decision. Although it would prove to be difficult to raise enough cash in the short term, a suspension of activities for several months was now out of the question.

Sinai's future was inextricably tied to Kohler's appointment. Another prolonged period without a rabbi would have threatened the existence of the congregation. Due to the exceptional circumstances and time pressure, a vote of all members on this crucial question could not be called. The board unanimously extended an invitation to Kohler to move to Chicago, guaranteeing his salary and an apartment for him and his family with an attractive ten-year contract. Less than a month after the fire, on November 2, several board members welcomed the new rabbi and his family at the train depot. A few days later and after a four-week hiatus, services resumed with Kohler's inaugural sermon. One Mr. Baiersdorfer was so impressed by the new rabbi that he joined Sinai on the spot. The board saved his enthusiastic letter (written in German).[7]

Kohler was a good fit for Sinai. The twenty-eight-year-old rabbi was one of the most gifted young Reform theologians of his generation. Having grown up in a staunch orthodox family in the old Jewish community of Fürth, near Nuremberg, Kohler had first attended Talmudic schools in Mainz and Hamburg before studying with Rabbi Samson Raphael Hirsch in Frankfurt am Main. Hirsch opposed Reform theology but recognized that traditional Judaism could not withdraw from the great social and cultural changes affecting European societies. As Kohler entered the secular university system, he continued his intellectual journey and became a Reformer. Kohler's doctoral thesis, submitted at

Erlangen University, was considered so radical that he could not hope to secure a position with a Jewish community in central Europe. With the help of Abraham Geiger and Bernhard Felsenthal, Kohler managed to land the job in Detroit. Beth El was a traditional congregation but open to modest reforms, comparable to KAM in the mid-1850s. With the move to a much larger city and to a congregation deeply committed to the teachings of radical Reform, Kohler hoped to embark on a career appropriate to his impressive *Bildung* credentials.[8]

The bizarre landscape of charred ruins and shocking cases of poverty, with federal troops patrolling the streets, must have been a surreal sight to the young rabbi. For several months, the de facto city government was the Chicago Relief and Aid Society. It collected and distributed donations coming to the city. The only immigrant on its board was Sinai member Julius Rosenthal, one of the city's most respected lawyers. The main purpose of the Chicago Relief and Aid Society was to support the most "deserving" victims, primarily established Chicagoans of the same class as the board members. The real victims, thousands of poor, working-class immigrants who could not rely on a social safety net, received little support. In early 1872, when its coffers were bursting with cash, the Chicago Relief and Aid Society terminated the support of eight hundred destitute families because they were "chronically poor." Judged with a businessman's practical logic, their support was considered a waste of funds.[9]

By November 1871, rumors had been circulating that the Chicago Relief and Aid Society discriminated against Jews and Germans in particular. Rosenthal, who was also active in German circles, emphatically refuted this allegation. In the case of the Jewish victims, this was probably accurate. The United Hebrew Relief Association largely succeeded in supporting destitute Jews.[10] But Rosenthal's ambiguous role clearly showed that Sinai had become very much a part of the city's establishment. Preserving class divisions justified even gross social injustices. Jewish leaders were soon reminded of clearly drawn limits dividing them from most Protestant members of the upper echelons of Chicago society. Soon after the fire, Protestant business leaders renewed previous demands for introducing Sunday laws prohibiting the sale and consumption of alcohol. Many proponents of this "reform" saw the fire as God's punishment for years of vice and sin in the wicked city of Chicago. In one of his most decisive political moves, Henry Greenebaum managed to bury this project by putting together a short-lived coalition of Irish and German immigrants across all party lines in 1873.[11]

Sinai's files provide a glimpse of the many small tragedies that followed in the wake of the disaster. In November 1871, merchant Raphael Guthmann, one of the founders of the congregation, informed the board, "[The fire] swept away my entire capital.... My loss is a total one. I ... cannot afford to remain a member of your congregation.... The time may come, I hope, when I shall again be able to knock at Sinai's door for readmission." Guthmann asked for permission to take part in the weekly service in return for a modest contribution, and his request was granted. When Benedict Schlossman, another founder, did not pay his dues for a several months, the board withdrew his voting rights and threatened to expel him. A distraught Schlossman wrote almost a year after the fire:

> I am one of the 29 or 30, who started this congregation.... I worked dili-
> gently with you, to bring this Reform about. ... I am very sensitive. ...
> Never [will I] forget the Humiliation of the last Meeting, when the Ayes
> and Nays were called about the Sabbath question my name was omitted....
> [You] should not make a person an outcast.[12]

These two examples hint at the loss of social status associated with expulsion and the sharpness of class boundaries. Names disappeared from membership rosters and were quickly forgotten. Although former friends and business associates continued to live in the same city, their paths rarely crossed. Schlossman's case is a telling example; he never recovered from the fire. In the 1890s, he and his wife were admitted by the Chicago Home for Aged Jews with "no means whatever." One can only speculate as to how difficult it was for him to face the board of the home, composed of other Sinai founders, such as banker Berthold Loewenthal. Schlossman died a poor man.[13]

For Chicago's fortunes and its fortunate citizens, the fire was a blessing. After the first shock, Chicago's business leaders found much hope for optimism. The city's economic nerve centers were largely intact: the Union Stock Yards, most of the huge grain elevators, the giant lumberyards, and most factories. New rails were in place in a matter of days, streets were cleared of rubble, and damaged harbor facilities were quickly repaired. Chicago's key function as a distribution center was hardly affected. Crucially—from the detached and rational perspective of outside investors—the congested business district of a booming city with homes, small stores, churches, and even synagogues had been cleared overnight for new development. Chicago became the first large American city with a central district devoted almost exclusively to business.[14]

Not surprisingly, investors reaped huge profits from real estate speculation. The fire accelerated Chicago's transition from a city developing along an east-west to a north-south corridor. Initially, Chicagoans with some means moved west to escape the polluted river and the foul-smelling lake. Every new inhabitant added more sewage, and, indirectly, industrial waste. The unusable remains of slaughtered animals were either burned or dumped into the Chicago River and Lake Michigan. A contemporary remembered, "The Chicago River was the source of all the most detestably filthy smells that the breezes of heaven possibly float to disgusted olfactories." The most destitute huddled near the river in primitive buildings and sheds; one was Irish immigrant Kate O'Leary, who was blamed for having triggered the Great Chicago Fire. The North Side was largely working class and German. Before the fire, some speculators had began promoting the South Side; wealthier Chicagoans started relocating there in the late 1860s. In the immediate aftermath of the fire, many homeless victims found shelter on the unharmed West Side; the spread of temporary slum settlements housing homeless victims of the fire further reduced its attraction to speculators.[15]

By 1870, it was clear that Sinai's future for the coming decades lay on the South Side. After 1871, the north-south State Street replaced the east-west Lake Street as the city's main business artery. State Street attracted the prime department stores and served as the city's gateway for the wealthy residents from the nearby South Side. The innovative idea, put forth just before the fire, to turn the flow of the Chicago River away from Lake Michigan and export the sewage and industrial waste toward the Illinois River boosted the reorientation of Chicago's internal geography. Areas along the lake on the South and North Sides became more attractive for speculators. A city ordinance designed to prevent the rapid spreading of future fires made it impossible for most working class Germans to rebuild their North Side homes because all new buildings erected within city limits had to be built from the more costly stone. The new building codes literally priced poorer Chicagoans out of the city, pushing them beyond North Avenue, or, in the case of Germans, toward the northwest along Milwaukee Avenue. The unaffected West Side, with its cheaper traditional housing, also pulled in people with limited means.[16]

FORTUNES AND FAILURES

For many contemporaries during the 1870s and beyond, the story of Chicago began with the rebuilding. In hindsight, the fire signified the rebirth of a city. Within a few years after the event, the largely untold human misery quickly faded into the background.[17] The catastrophe struck at the very moment Chicago had become the hub of the continental transportation network, with its prime position between the wheat fields, cattle, forests, and mines to the west and the markets to the east and in Europe. The Civil War had boosted Chicago's growth and led to a diversification of its business sector. Food processing, tool production, and the clothing industry especially prospered. Due to its function as railroad hub, its homegrown industrial production, rising settlement of the West, and steadily decreasing delivery times, Chicago became a perfect location for wholesale businesses: textiles, shoes, tools, even luxury goods, were distributed to smaller retailers across the continent. Chicago developed, in the words of William Cronon, into "a shopkeeper for shopkeepers, a market for other markets."[18]

Jewish immigrants could be found in all innovative sectors of Chicago's economy, not least in wholesaling. In a history of post-fire Chicago, Bernhard Felsenthal described the economic profile of the Jewish community:

> Commerce in dry goods, clothing, hardware, boots and shoes, tobacco—in short, in every imaginable branch—is largely shared in by Jewish houses. So are many banking institutions owned and successfully conducted by Jewish firms. So is the manufacturing of clothing, cutlery, chemical preparations, cigars, furniture; so are printing and lithographic institutions, bookbinderies, tanneries, beef packaging houses etc., etc., conducted by Jewish owners and energetic Jewish minds and hands.[19]

Almost all of Sinai's members thrived, some far beyond their own expectations. According to an 1872 overview of religious life among the German-speaking Chicagoans in the *Tribune*, "the wealthiest Hebrews in the city" belonged to Sinai. They were by no means representative of the Jewish community at large. With the economic boom, a gulf opened between a few successful and increasingly wealthy business owners and many small storeowners, clerks, workers, and even peddlers.

Sinai was not representative of American Jewish life more generally, either in terms of social mobility or of theology. Jewish immigrants from central Europe were a very small group. This skews comparisons with Irish or German immigrants. Relatively few individual Jews made spectacular journeys from rags to riches. Quite a few were among the members of Sinai. One was Nelson Morris. In the early 1850s, he tried his luck as a simple hand on the Chicago Stock Yards, earning $5 a month. With his savings, Morris established a small wholesale business for meat in 1859. The Civil War provided a boost to his enterprise. In 1870, he possessed $100,000—a substantial fortune. The fire hardly affected his business, and by 1890 he owned and managed one of the Big Four Chicago meatpacking businesses and was one of the wealthiest men in America. The *Chicago Tribune* estimated that he was easily worth $10,000,000.[20]

CHAPTER FOUR

Making and administering such huge fortunes required good judgment and a thorough knowledge of transforming markets. In the rapidly expanding Chicago markets, fortunes could be easily made—and lost. One of the most spectacular business failures of the 1870s was that of Henry Greenebaum, who had misjudged the full impact of the changing topography on the real estate market in the early 1870s. Apart from his activities in Chicago politics, along with Jewish and German ethnic life, Greenebaum owned and ran two of Chicago's leading financial businesses, the German National Bank and the German Savings Bank. He weathered the 1873 recession, but excessive investments in real estate on the West Side proved to be his undoing in the 1877 economic decline. Unable to pay his creditors in cash, his banks collapsed, and he was briefly arrested. Greenebaum eventually recovered, paying back every cent he owed to his creditors. Although he was still in his prime during the late 1870s, he lost his position as mighty ethnic broker in Chicago politics.[21]

Relatively few Jewish immigrants went through such dynamic rises and falls. Much more remarkable is another less notable story: a surprisingly high num-

ORIGIN OF THE MEMBERS OF SINAI CONGREGATION (1870)

Origin	Number (%) of congregants
Unknown	25 (31.25)
Bavaria	12 (15)
Prussia	12 (15)
Hesse	11 (13.75)
Germany*	9 (10.25)
Baden	4 (5)
France	3 (3.75)
Württemberg	2 (2.5)
Hungary	1 (1.25)
United States	1 (1.25)

Sources: Handwritten list of eighty members of Sinai Congregation, 1875, box 1, folder 5, Sinai Papers, MS-56, AJA; *Chicago Census Report and Statistical Review embracing a Complete Directory of the City of Chicago* (Chicago: Richard Edwards, 1871); U.S. Census 1870, Illinois, Cook County, Chicago.
*It is unclear how the census takers defined "Germany" in 1870.

ber of Jewish immigrants who arrived before the 1870s established themselves in relative material security, providing their American-born children with a decent education and careers in business and the professions. Their modest successes are loosely connected with the unparalleled rise of almost all Jews in the German states into the middle class—in only one generation.

An analysis of an 1875 membership list on the basis of the 1870 U.S. census shows that Sinai was indeed a "German" congregation; most members hailed from the German states. Jewish immigrants, who began arriving in Chicago in the late 1860s from Latvia and Lithuania in the Russian Empire, as well as from Galicia, came from different social and political contexts. Unlike villages in the German states, rural communities in eastern Europe were only superficially affected by modernization. These migrants often lacked the solid school education central European Jews had enjoyed. By the time they reached America in rising numbers after 1870, the moment of economic opportunity had passed. After boom of the 1860s, it was much more difficult for new immigrants to accumulate enough capital to set up small businesses, and many lucrative niches were occupied. The rocky economic climate of the 1870s did not help. The new arrivals worked as peddlers and, in increasing numbers, as workers, especially in the textile industry, often in businesses set up and managed by their central European co-religionists. In Chicago, they established their own small, traditional congregations and prayer rooms on the Near West Side in a residential area described by the mid-1870s as one of the poorest in the city. A correspondent of the *American Israelite* wrote, "[These immigrants live] in such disreputable parts of the city that I did not wish to be seen in their neighborhood."[22]

Sinai's members were socially and spatially far removed from these Jewish arrivals. Thirty years earlier, they too had come to America with little more than their clothes. However, by the late 1860s, most lived on the Near South Side, far from the working-class areas near the stock yards on Chicago's West and North Sides. Only three of Sinai's eighty members were employees; the others were self-employed entrepreneurs, with more than half in retail of some kind and a third in the garment trade. Gerhard Foreman and Berthold Loewenthal were bankers; several were producers and wholesalers in the textile business. Others, like Morris Selz and Isaac Greensfelder, made and sold shoes. A few were in the lumber business. The Mandel brothers established one of Chicago's leading department stores on the city's new showcase State Street during the 1870s, and Nelson Morris was a big player at the Union Stock Yards. The three "others" were lawyer and notary Julius Rosenthal, an insurance broker, and a saloon owner. Some members were among the wealthiest Chicagoans. Foreman became a millionaire by the mid-1870s, and Morris Selz, Sinai's president between 1880 and 1883, may have been even wealthier. Some of the clothing entrepreneurs had invested capital of several hundred thousand dollars each in various businesses, and Josef Ullmann was one of the leading fur traders in the United States. By the late 1870s, he too approached millionaire status. He split his time between Chicago and the German city of Leipzig, the uncontested hub of the world fur trade until 1933.[23]

The exact causes for the concentration and the success of Jewish immigrant entrepreneurs in the textile business have not been researched sufficiently. The similarities to Europe, however, are striking. In Germany, and to a lesser extent in western and eastern Europe, Jewish entrepreneurs also played key roles in the production and retail of textiles and related products. One obvious cause was the economic and social marginalization of Jews until the mid-nineteenth century. Across central Europe, male Jews traveled the countryside as itinerant peddlers selling used clothes, in a period when only wealthy people could afford

FIELDS OF BUSINESS OF MEMBERS OF SINAI CONGREGATION (1870–1871)

Business type	Number of congregants
Textile (retail and/or production)	28
Dry goods (retail)	8
Unknown	8
Leather	6
Banking	4
Tobacco	3
Meat packing	3
Jewelry	3
Real estate	3
Lumber	2
Furniture	2
Other	3

Sources: Handwritten list of eighty members of Sinai Congregation, 1875, box 1, folder 5, Sinai Papers, MS-56, AJA; *Chicago Census Report and Statistical Review embracing a Complete Directory of the City of Chicago* (Chicago: Richard Edwards, 1871); U.S. Census 1870, Illinois, Cook County, Chicago.

new (and hand-tailored) attire. In eastern Europe, many Jews worked as tailors, repairing and designing clothes for sale. Detailed knowledge about styles, production, changing tastes, and the volatility of markets went back for generations. With the industrialization and urbanization, textile production and retail were obvious routes for many Jewish immigrants. The machinery for the mass production of various textiles required relatively little starting capital and space. Therefore, sweatshops were often located in the inner city, close to retailers and immigrant neighborhoods.[24]

Was significant wealth a precondition for membership in the congregation and perhaps even a factor behind the radical Reform agenda? Sinai's mother congregation, KAM, also had several very wealthy members but was not as radical as Sinai. Wealth and high social mobility, per se, were by no means a precondition for Reform. In Baltimore, many well-to-do Jewish immigrants from central Europe belonged to a traditional congregation opposed to Reform. But, unlike Chicago, Baltimore was a more established city that did not experience Chicago's extreme boom and bust cycles.[25] Sinai's membership dues of $70 in 1874 and $100 in 1877 were affordable for successful businessmen but not for a typical doctor or lawyer who made about $1,000 per year in this period, let alone for recent working-class immigrants. Indeed, Kaufmann Kohler's starting salary of $3,000 (the equivalent of US$55,000 in 2011) allowed him and his family a lifestyle comparable to the average member, as Sinai provided free housing for its rabbi near the synagogue in Chicago's best neighborhood.[26]

Members often had to contribute additional sums to balance the budget and to raise funds for ambitious projects like a new synagogue. Sinai's 1874–1875 annual budget of $11,800 was a case in point. The largest single expenditure was Kohler's annual salary. The dues of the approximately one hundred members covered only $7,000, leaving an additional $4,800 to be raised from the members. In 1874, plans for the new temple were taking shape. The overall cost was estimated to reach $40,000. In September 1874, the board called on all members to donate generously; members with limited means were expected to give at least $300–$500. Half a year later, in June 1875, the expected overall bill for the temple had climbed to $75,000; the final sum was even higher.

Thus, poorer immigrant Jews could not even think of applying for membership at Sinai. Additional evidence of the air of social exclusivity is the close relationship between Sinai and the Standard Club. After its founding in 1869, Sinai's members socialized at the Standard Club, and occasionally events were held at the club's quarters. Membership was limited to successful Jewish businessmen. Unfortunately, no sources shine a light on the reasons for establishing a separate

Jewish club. The founding may be an indication that the public support for Jewish businessmen was not matched on the private level.[27]

But why did Sinai plan for a building with a thousand seats when only a hundred members used at most three hundred and fifty to four hundred seats with their families? Obviously, the congregation expected to boost its membership. Another factor was status; the building of a splendid new temple, located in the heart of Chicago's leading residential neighborhood, was a public symbol for the success of and self-confidence of Jewish Reform in Chicago. A larger temple provided room for nonmembers who attended services. As a radical Reform congregation, Sinai put much emphasis on keeping its doors open to the wider community. The major reason for joining or belonging to Sinai was the radical Reform agenda. But class and status should not be discounted.

THE INTRODUCTION OF SUNDAY SERVICES

As Sinai's male members participated so successfully in their city's spectacular growth, they had less and less time to attend weekly services—unlike their wives, mothers, and daughters. And Sinai still was homeless in 1874. After using the First Presbyterian Church for a year and sharing a church with an Episcopalian congregation, Sinai rented temporary quarters at different locations on the Near South Side.[28]

In the meantime, after two years in the pulpit, Kaufmann Kohler was frustrated. Countless businesses had collapsed in the serious economic downturn of 1873. Several members left Chicago to seek better opportunities elsewhere. The plans for a new synagogue seemed to go nowhere. In late 1873, the exasperated rabbi sat down and penned a letter to Sinai's president, Gustav Eliel. In typical fashion, he did not mince his words. An established New York congregation, Anshe Chesed, had made him an almost irresistible offer. He was indeed wondering what still kept him in Chicago. He deemed the "indifference" of most members to be without parallel. "Hardly another Jewish congregation in the world neglects and despises the Sabbath service so much." Yet he saw a glimmer of hope. He might be persuaded to stay in Chicago if most members attended the service more regularly and even the "most conservative members" ended their opposition to the planned introduction of a Sunday service, "which consists of a learned religious lecture accompanied by songs and prayers." These were designed for members whose business obligations made it impossible to attend on Saturdays. Introducing Sunday services, Kohler argued, would also be in "the interest" of the younger generation. In a longwinded fashion, Kohler demanded that all members should unanimously vote for Sunday services. The

FIGURE 2. Kaufmann Kohler, circa 1900. Courtesy of the American Jewish Archives, Cincinnati, Ohio.

letter ended on a positive note, much to Eliel's relief—although he must have wondered about the implications of the last sentence. "The material of the Sinai Congregation . . . is good and it ensures that one day . . . it will become a leading congregation in the West. I am convinced to have not a single opponent in the congregation."[29]

Sunday services would become Sinai's signature reform, and the change did, in hindsight, redefine Sinai as a leading congregation, just as Kohler had envisaged in his letter. But why and how did this particular reform become so emblematic, and what was the rationale behind it? Sinai was only the second Jewish congregation in the United States to experiment with Sunday services. The model was the Berlin Reform congregation, where Sunday services had been conducted since 1845. By 1848, the congregation had even abolished Saturday services. That constituted a truly radical step. But all members also belonged to the Berlin Jewish *Gemeinde* and thus had the option to attend regular Sabbath services. In America, the short-lived Hebrew Reformed Association in Baltimore briefly offered Sunday services in 1854, but once David Einhorn arrived, it dissolved and most members joined Har Sinai.[30]

An additional service on Sunday did not automatically constitute a violation of the Jewish tradition, as long as the congregation continued to recognize and observe the biblical Sabbath. Even traditional Jews conducted additional services on days other than the Sabbath. At first glance, Kohler's (and later Emil G. Hirsch's) rationale for Sunday services seems sensible. Most members did not attend Saturday services, so why not hold a service on a more suitable day to attract a sizeable group of members? For more traditionally minded Reform Jews within Sinai, this went too far. From their perspective, Sunday services sidelined the Saturday Sabbath service, constituting a sacrifice of a powerful symbol of Jewish difference in an overwhelmingly Christian environment. Indeed, Jewish critics wondered what would distinguish radical Reform Judaism from liberal Protestantism except for the recognition of Jesus as the Messiah. While the introduction of Sunday services as such did not represent a gross violation of the Jewish tradition, this particular reform stirred up Jewish emotions more than debates over the abolition or preservation of kosher butchering or circumcision. One obvious reason was the public nature of religious worship.

Early on, the Sunday service became a symbolic pivot for the destiny of Reform in America. For its supporters, the Sunday Sabbath was a pragmatic adaptation to the demands of daily life to make it easier for modern Jews to join congregations and attend services. Jews were, after all, a small group in American society that could not afford to rest on Saturdays and Sundays. Even well-to-do entrepreneurs could not take more than one day away from their offices or close stores and factories for two days. For the opponents, Sunday services were a voluntary surrender to the Christian majority and a tacit admission that Reform would lead to the dissolution of Judaism as a religion.

In August 1873, Kohler published a lengthy article in one of Chicago's leading dailies explaining the theological rationale for Jewish Sunday services. In his opinion, Jews should go with the times rather than stick with dead "letter-worship." The Jewish Sabbath had "withered" and was not observed by most Jews. But the Christian Sunday too was in a crisis. Kohler pointed to working-class German Chicagoans for whom Sunday was a day of excess and drinking. In the new and anonymous city, immigrants could leave behind the religious and social constraints of the ancestral villages. The traditional power of religious elites and rituals was greatly reduced. For Kohler, the move toward Sunday services represented not a Christianization of the Jewish Sabbath but an attempt to revive the religious and spiritual message behind the day of rest more generally by reaching out to non-Jews:

> This is the Jewish Sabbath in its character. This, our notions and habits, we will preserve and propagate even when we shall, in a time not very far off, adopt the Sunday as our Sabbath. We transfer all the blessings, and all the rich seed of moral and spiritual elevation, all our dear remembrances from the old historical Sabbath day to the public Sabbath, which we are in fact already celebrating, with our young, with our employees, with our [non-Jewish] fellow-citizens.[31]

With this public article, Kohler increased the pressure on Sinai's board to act. The rabbi's appeal to the wider public regarding a controversial debate within the congregation was hardly welcomed by the board, even by members in favor of Sunday services.

A closer look at the available sources helps to explain why Kohler, after his departure from Chicago, would become a prominent opponent of Sunday services. When Kohler arrived at Sinai, the members had been debating the merits of a Sunday Sabbath for several years. Kohler's predecessor, Isaac Loeb Chronik, who had tried to introduce the Sunday services in the late 1860s without success, was still a member of Sinai. Chronik apparently tried to use the controversy to his advantage, setting himself up as the rabbi of a breakaway Sunday faction. At a meeting in September 1872, some members moved to strike the words "Biblical Sabbath" from the constitution; the motion failed 26–16 (not all members attended). Several letters from David Einhorn to Kohler provide even more intriguing clues. In 1870 Kohler had married Einhorn's daughter Johanna. The few remaining letters from his father-in-law hint at a close and cordial relationship. According to rumors that reached Einhorn in 1872, Chronik was planning to establish a Jewish Sunday congregation in New York. In August 1873, several leading Sinai members visited Einhorn in New York to seek his opinion on the Sunday issue—an indication of Einhorn's continued influence in Chicago. Einhorn made no secret of his skepticism about this "dangerous" reform. He also warned Kohler not to pursue a policy of "brinkmanship" by opting for Sunday services. In a letter from January 23, 1874, five days after the first Sunday service at Sinai, Einhorn credited Chronik with being the main force behind the change.[32] Chronik's role, regardless of his true intentions, indicates that congregation politics heavily influenced theological debates. Kohler seized the opportunity to strengthen his position within the congregation. Instead of siding with the conservative skeptics, he decided to take the lead and establish Sunday services while attacking the truly radical Chronik on his own turf. The demand for Sunday services was a defensive move by a rabbi worried about his standing within the congregation. Other letters Kohler sent to the Sinai board support this thesis. In December 1873, Kohler wrote (in German):

> In regard to the intended Sunday-Service, I find that there is a silent, but strong and determined opposition existing against a Sunday forenoon Service, especially on the part of the Ladies, which will have the most damaging influence on the whole movement and make it a perfect failure. I therefore declare myself, without reserve in favor of Sunday evening lectures by which our Congregation would, most assuredly, gain many sympathies, and lose none! . . . [I want] to have the signature of 50 members of our congregation, pledging themselves to attend the Sunday-Service with their Ladies and children for a whole year. . . . Neither the congregation nor myself can afford to risk a failure.[33]

Only two days later, on December 3, 1873, Kohler had sixty-four signatures on his desk and a declaration in German: "The undersigned hereby promise to attend the same [Sunday forenoon service] with their families on time."[34] Two weeks later, some of the same members sent a second list of forty-eight signatures to the rabbi with the pledge that the undersigned would "not object" to the introduction of Sunday services. However, they continued, "We deem it our duty to protect against any measure that may serve to lessen among our members the interest heretofore manifested in the historical Jewish Sabbath."[35] This grudging declaration of support demonstrates that Kohler's move, at least initially, was a success; a split of the congregation was avoided. The supporters of establishing a Sunday Sabbath made the concession not to abolish Saturday services and to respect the historic Sabbath. Chronik left Chicago soon afterwards and moved back to Germany. He revived his *Zeichen der Zeit* weekly in Berlin, where he died in 1884. Having received formal support from the board, Kohler declined the offer from Anshe Chesed. The New York congregation then offered the position to none other than Isaac Mayer Wise. The Cincinnati rabbi could also make good use of the offer: to retain his services, the board of Bene Yeshurun gave Wise a significant pay raise, from $4,000 to $6,000, twice as much as Sinai paid Kohler.[36]

Kohler's remark regarding the "determined opposition" of the "Ladies" and the signatures of some members under both letters, one strongly in favor of Sunday services, the other much more skeptical, hint at the impact of Sinai's women. Unfortunately, no memoir or private letters provides information about the role of women, but it is hardly surprising that the wives and mothers of Sinai members were hardly as enthusiastic about Sunday services as their husbands and sons. Established women lived in an enclosed and more exclusively Jewish sphere than men did. Jewish wives, especially those of well-to-do bourgeois businessmen, mostly stayed at home as guardians of Jewish tradition and managers of the household, and they were more likely to attend services. According to the few available sources, Jewish women in Chicago tended to socialize with other Jewish women rather than with Christians, even after 1880. In Chicago's Protestant churches too, women were more likely to attend services. In fact, historian Daniel Bluestone even traces the gradual move of Chicago's leading Protestant congregations from the business district along Washington Street to a more residential area several blocks southeast during the 1850s and 1860s to the "feminization of urban religion."

Women are not mentioned as participants at the *Reformverein* meetings or the long discussions leading to the establishment of Sinai. We can only guess at the arguments exchanged at Chicago breakfast and dinner tables and after High Holiday and Sabbath services before and after 1861. Sinai's women certainly had strong opinions and were as well informed about Reform theology as their husbands and sons, if not better. More than a few women of the immigrant generation had enjoyed a solid education in the German states, and the younger daughters of Sinai's members attended the congregation's school. The male members, on the other hand, spent their days outside of the home and had frequent exchanges with Christians.[37]

The first Sunday service at Sinai was conducted on January 18, 1874.[38] Many members honored their promise and attended in the following weeks. According to Sinai president Berthold Loewenthal, the new service was "a success beyond the expectation of its most ardent supporters." The Saturday services, on the other hand, did attract fewer members than before—according to Kohler, mostly women and elderly men. Indeed, women dominated Saturday services at many American synagogues at the time, because their husbands, adult sons, and fathers were occupied by their professional lives. Loewenthal, an advocate

　　　　　CHAPTER FOUR

of Sunday services, could not resist reminding "especially the adherents of our historical Sabbath" in the congregation to live up to their earlier promise. Without a doubt, he was specifically addressing the male supporters of the Saturday Sabbath.[39]

The German Jewish press ignored the introduction of Sunday services, perhaps an indication of Chicago's remoteness. Closer to Chicago, the *American Israelite* did not hide its disapproval. Solomon Sonneschein, a Reform rabbi who had recently moved from Europe to the Shaare Emeth congregation in St. Louis, accused Sinai in strong terms of watering down the essence of Reform Judaism by adopting a Christian practice. "What right has such a congregation to remain a distinctly Jewish one! Why not drop the Jewish denomination entirely?"[40] It was beneath Kohler's dignity to reply to this attack in the pages of Wise's *American Israelite*. Instead, he chose the *Jewish Times*. This weekly, edited by Moritz Ellinger in New York since 1869, provided radical Reformers like Einhorn, Samuel Adler, Samuel Hirsch, and Felsenthal with a new forum following the demise of Einhorn's *Sinai* in 1863. Kohler rejected Sonneschein's "malicious article." Sinai's regular Sabbath service was "as well attended as before, and as I am informed, a great deal better than for instance that of Dr. Sonneschein of St. Louis."[41] The move toward Sunday services also constituted an attempt to reach out to Chicago's educated public. In his response to Sonneschein, Kohler mentioned in passing that Sinai's Sunday services were attracting Christians, indicating that the religious message was now reaching beyond the Jewish community. For several years, Sinai remained the only radical Reform congregation in America with regular Sunday services. Other Reform congregations responded to the declining attendance on Saturdays by offering Friday evening services. The greatest proponent of this reform was Isaac Mayer Wise, who conducted the first Friday evening service in 1869. The success of Friday evening services across the country increased Sinai's isolation but also explains why early on this particular reform became the keystone of Sinai's identity.[42]

One episode illustrates this point. In the fall of 1874, several members of KAM and Sinai suggested a merger of the two congregations. Earlier in 1874, KAM had lost its synagogue in a smaller fire that destroyed parts of the Near South Side. Pooling resources could have made it financially viable to build a new house of worship for one rather than two congregations. In the early 1870s, KAM had taken another major step toward Sinai's Reform agenda by voting for the introduction of Einhorn's prayer book.[43] Influential and respected KAM founder Abraham Kohn, who certainly would have resisted further reforms, had died in 1871. In an August 1874 report, KAM president Maximilian M. Gerstley attacked "superstition" and "antiquated habits . . . which have become untenable for the condition of our social lives . . . and repugnant to the practical ways of our modes of living." He called for overhauling the weekly service according to the tenets of the Reform movement.[44] Nevertheless, the merger discussions with Sinai quickly hit a stumbling block. KAM's negotiating team, according to the Sinai board, refused to make a "concession for the instruction of those unable to participate in the Sabbath service," opposing "the Sunday service under all circumstances." When KAM became aware of Sinai's strong commitment to Sunday services, the merger was called off.[45]

Just how far Sinai, KAM, and Zion had transcended their German origins is illustrated in the reaction of leading Chicago Reformers when news of Abraham Geiger's death reached Chicago. Liebmann Adler and Kohler had known the famous German rabbi personally, and Felsenthal had regularly exchanged letters with him. While his colleagues praised Geiger's role as founding father of the Reform movement, Kohler politely (albeit somewhat bluntly) reminded the audience of Geiger's opposition to radical Reform in America. The Geiger memorial was conducted (and printed) in German, but this should not be taken as a proof of a continuing importance of close ties to Germany. Rather, Kohler's comments highlight the distancing of the radical Reformers from spiritual Germany.[46] This, however, was a gradual process; the contours of an explicitly American Reform agenda were not yet fully recognizable.

A stronger pledge for America did not mean a break with Germany or a rapprochement with Wise's union project. Just as Sinai was embarking on the path toward Sunday services, the union Wise had worked for finally came to fruition. Several leading members of Wise's Cincinnati congregation, Bene Yeshurun, suggested founding a Union of American Hebrew Congregations. The organization was founded on July 8, 1873, in Cincinnati. To bring a wide spectrum of congregations under its wings, the UAHC constitution explicitly guaranteed the sovereignty of the congregation; the union would not interfere "in any manner whatsoever with the affairs and management of any congregation." This distinguished the UAHC from Protestant denominations, which demanded stricter adherence to a common platform and liturgy.

Two Chicago congregations joined the union relatively early: KAM sent delegates to the constitutional convention and became a member in 1874, while the more traditional congregation B'nai Sholom followed in 1875. The UAHC started with twenty-eight member congregations and quickly expanded. By 1879, more than one hundred congregations were members.[47] Sinai and Zion both received an invitation to attend the 1873 constitutional convention in

Cincinnati. In a coauthored public letter, the boards of Sinai and Zion declined the invitation, expressing particular criticism of the plan to establish a rabbinical seminary in Cincinnati. It was too early to educate rabbis in America. Only German universities, they claimed, could offer would-be rabbis a comprehensive scholarly education.[48]

The gap dividing radical Reformers from the majority of moderate Reform congregations was still wide. Radical Reform congregations in New York, Philadelphia, and Baltimore also did not join. Yet the UAHC continued to woo the "German" congregations. By 1874, Moritz Loth, the Cincinnati businessman who had been the main force behind establishing the union, politely asked Sinai to join, but Sinai refused. The animosity toward Wise and his projects was still strong, and after the attacks against its Sunday services in the pages of the *American Israelite* earlier in 1874, Sinai's leaders felt the gap between their vision of Reform and the mainstream represented by the UAHC had widened rather than narrowed.[49]

In June 1875, in its fourteenth year, Sinai's board presented the first historical overview to the members, reflecting on key dates and events in the congregation's history: Samuel Adler's dedication sermon of June 22, 1861, the commitment to Einhorn's theology, the abolition of "everything that seemed objectionable in the light of modern civilization," the purchase of lots at a nondenominational cemetery, and, finally, the introduction of Sunday services in 1874.[50] The main reason for this report was to rally the congregation behind an ambitious building project that required a strong financial commitment. While the members did donate generously, the attendance for Saturday and Sunday services again lagged in early 1875. In a report to the congregation, President Loewenthal complained about "indifference and lack of interest in congregational matters." He hoped the completion of Sinai's new temple would boost attendance.[51]

5.

FELIX ADLER COMES TO CHICAGO

IN HINDSIGHT, the introduction of Sunday services betrays a serious theological and spiritual crisis. Instead of attracting new members and increasing attendance, the new services seemed to have little effect on the congregation after the initial excitement subsided. It appeared as if the radical Reformers at Sinai had overreached. Introducing bold reforms alone was not enough to overcome "indifference" and attract younger Jews to the services. During the mid-1870s, most members of Sinai belonged to the founding generation, men who had been in their late twenties and early thirties when Sinai was established and who now were contemplating how to arrange a smooth handover to the younger, mostly American-born generation. Yet younger Jews preferred social activities on Sundays and Saturdays to listening to long-winded academic German sermons. A public clash between Kaufmann Kohler and a charismatic young Jew who represented a competing vision to radical Reform exacerbated the conflict within Sinai Congregation over its identity as a Jewish congregation, forcing Kohler to rethink his theological agenda.

INTERNAL CRISIS

Until the mid-1870s, radical Reform theologians often looked back to explain the need for more reforms, addressing men and women who had grown up in traditional Jewish homes in Europe and could appreciate the Reform message. Now they faced increasingly younger members who did not know much about the Jewish tradition and wondered why Reform Judaism mattered for them. Maximilian M. Gerstley, president of Sinai's moderate Reform mother congregation, KAM, expressed this sentiment in 1874 when he appealed to his more traditionally inclined members not to resist reforms, lest the younger generation drift away: "What good can we accomplish in upholding a system . . . which our children are neither able to comprehend, nor willing to accept as their own? Is our cause to be advanced by keeping up a Chinese wall . . . in order to keep separated the present from the rising generation? Is it prudent to swim against the tide?"[1] Sinai and other congregations certainly recognized the importance of language. In 1872, KAM hired a second rabbi who could preach in English. After 1874, Kohler occasionally delivered some sermons in English instead of German.[2] Yet younger Jews did not seem interested in joining either congregation.

When Sinai dedicated its new temple on April 8, 1876, the final price tag had risen to a substantial $125,000. The impressive edifice, designed by Dankmar Adler (the son of KAM's Liebmann Adler) was Chicago's first major new synagogue. It offered seating for 1,200 persons. The large cupola at the front visibly distinguished the synagogue from churches, and the interior of the building betrayed oriental influences. Sinai's synagogue was located on one of the main arteries of the South Side residential neighborhood, the corner of Indiana Avenue and 21st Street. The splendid temple was a proud symbol of Jewish life in Chicago—just as Henry Greenebaum had envisaged it in 1859. Although Sinai struggled for a few years to pay off the debt, the members could afford to cover the significant sums necessary for the construction. KAM, on the other hand, postponed the planned construction of a new synagogue and remodeled a former church a few blocks from Sinai's temple. During the 1870s, a number of Christian congregations in Chicago also commissioned large and representative houses of worship. Unlike Sinai, however, several congregations collapsed, because they could not afford the costs of construction.[3]

Just as Sinai's new temple opened its doors, members were less and less interested in spending time inside. On some days, especially Saturdays, there were not even enough men for a minyan, the minimum number (ten) of Jewish males required to conduct a service. Women attended these services, but even at Sinai they did not count toward the minyan. In October 1877, Kohler complained to Sinai president Godfrey Snydacker about the "disgraceful indifference," especially during the Sabbath service, and asked Snydacker to guarantee "the presence of at least ten gentlemen of the Congregation at the commencement of the sermon."[4]

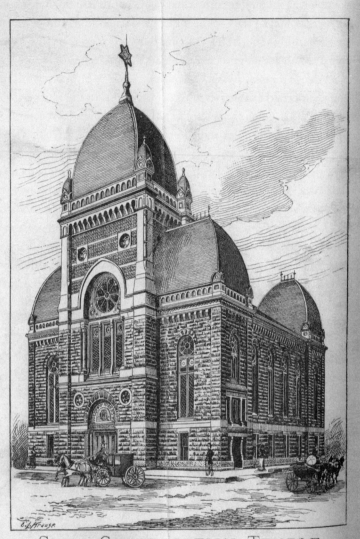

SINAI CONGREGATION TEMPLE.
S. W. Corner Indiana Ave. and 21st Street.

J. L. GATZERT,	President.		DIRECTORS:
JOSEPH SPIEGEL,	Vice-President.	E. MANDEL.	JOSEPH CAHN,
B LOWENTHAL,	Treasurer.	HARRY HART.	B. ARNHEIM,
ADOLPH LOEB,	Recording-Sec'ary.	L. E. FRANK,	H. E GREENEBAUM,
B. MERGENTHEIM,	Financial-Secretary.	ISAAC MEYER,	PHILLIP OPPER.

RABBI: DR. E. HIRSH

Services are held every Sunday at 10:30 A. M.

Engraved and Printed by "THE OCCIDENT" Publishing Co., Chicago,

FIGURE 3. Engraving of Sinai Temple, 1888. Reprinted from Emil G. Hirsch, *Tolerance: A Discourse before the Sinai Congregation and Repeated before Zion Congregation–West Side* (Chicago: Chicago Sinai Congregation, 1888). Courtesy of the Newberry Library, Chicago.

The *Allgemeine Zeitung des Judenthums* discussed the crisis of the established American Reform congregations at some length in 1879, picking Chicago as an exemplary case. The magnificent Reform synagogues stood empty, while the "dirty and desolate prayer houses with their appalling disorder . . . are filled." The paper advised Chicago Reformers to avoid "splendor and inappropriate decorations," pay more respect to the Jewish tradition, turn away from radical Reform, and lower the annual membership dues to attract eastern European immigrants interested in the Reform message. The high membership dues, the author observed quite correctly, were designed to keep less wealthy Jews out.[5]

For German Jewish readers, the article seemed to confirm the appeal of liberal Judaism, the peculiar German compromise between Reform and tradition, brought about by the state-regulated *Einheitsgemeinde*. American Reform Judaism, it appeared, had overreached. By concentrating on representation and social status, the religious message itself had been lost, and the temples stood empty. The article betrayed distance and arrogance toward recent immigrants from eastern Europe—at least on the part of the German Jewish author. Yet the contrast between the attraction of traditional Judaism for recent immigrants and the crisis of radical Reform was undeniable. Other Reform congregations in America faced similar challenges; attendance at services was disappointing, membership stagnated or even declined, German-trained rabbi-scholars often struggled to connect with the younger generation, and the future seemed uncertain. According to historian Leon A. Jick, by 1880, the service in most Reform temples "had been substantially Protestantized." Specifically Jewish elements of the service were either abolished or accommodated: like most other Reform congregations, Sinai had no cantor but a choir, and the Torah portion was read and not chanted. Although Einhorn and his followers associated external changes without theological underpinning with Isaac Mayer Wise, Sinai with its Sunday services not only resembled a Protestant church, it appeared to be losing touch with its specific theological cause and its own membership.[6]

In 1879, a reporter recorded his observations of a typical Sunday service conducted by Kohler in the new temple. The correspondent of the *Inter Ocean*, a Chicago daily that regularly and objectively covered religious life in the city, was impressed by the beautiful interior and went on to characterize the service:

The student-like, antique face of Dr. Kohler, his dry, rattling way of speaking, and the extreme quietness of his restrained manner in the pulpit, are elements that add to the picturesqueness. The service on Sunday is extremely simple. As a rule, there are more persons in the choir than there are in the congregation, and Dr. Kohler has preached many a Sunday to not more than a score of people. The spectacle of this learned rabbi talking scholarly German to empty benches was always suggestive, but never more so than in the present complications.[7]

This description again hints at the contrast of the beautiful building and the choir with the religious message. Kohler could not reach his congregation. A closer look at his sermons provides some clues as to why young members were not inclined to attend. Several of Kohler's English-language sermons were printed in the *Chicago Tribune*, indicating the degree of acceptance Jews enjoyed in the city as well as genuine interest in the community among more than a few Christian readers. A sermon Kohler preached on Jewish and Christian concepts of morality in mid-February 1877 illustrates why many congregants stayed away: only well educated members up to date on theological and philosophical literature could truly appreciate Kohler's finer points. The rather dense sermon was really an academic lecture. Sinai's rabbi did not once connect his subject, morality, with the social reality outside the temple.[8]

In 1877, thousands of Chicagoans were suffering from poverty and living in unspeakable conditions. Immigrant Jews were also in great need, as the annual reports of the UHRA prove forcefully. The social distance between Sinai's well-to-do members and working-class Chicagoans was great. In June 1877, the *Inter Ocean* covered the wedding of Emma Einstein, daughter of Sinai member Arthur Einstein, to Sigismund Beir of Rochester, New York—"one of the most gorgeous weddings that has ever taken place among the Jewish elite of this city." After Kohler performed the wedding at the temple, a "brilliant reception" was held at the Standard Club. The paper described the dresses of the women present. The headline, "A Dazzling of Oriental Beauty and Oriental Magnificence," hinted at the boundary separating this Jewish affair from similar weddings by well-to-do Christians.[9] The well-stocked Klau Library of Hebrew Union College in Cincinnati holds another clue why Kohler was not eager to confront Sinai's members more forcefully with the social question. Even a quick search in the catalog under Kohler's name shows an impressive record of publications for the 1870s. Some are printed sermons, but Kohler published widely in academic venues. Indeed, Kohler was emerging as the spiritual heir of his father-in-law, David Einhorn.

The June 1879 service in a largely empty temple was one of the last Kohler ever conducted in Chicago. The disappointing attendance on this occasion, however, was not related to indifference alone but rather what the *Inter Ocean* reporter cautiously circumscribed as "present complications." In 1879, the climate between Kohler and the congregation had deteriorated to such a degree that the rabbi was not even on speaking terms with several leading members. A few weeks later, Kohler moved to the New York congregation Beth El to succeed Einhorn upon his retirement. Kohler had gradually been drifting away from Sinai, and he was certainly keen to move to America's cultural metropolis. Chicago, after all, was a very significant economic center, but it was still a newcomer city, lacking the cultural and intellectual pedigree of the large cities on the East Coast. The main cause for Kohler's decision to leave Chicago, however, was a severe conflict over the future of Sinai, and, more generally, Reform Judaism in America.

FELIX ADLER'S VISIT TO THE SINAI LITERARY SOCIETY

At the center of the controversy stood a young man from New York, Felix Adler. The nineteenth- and early-twentieth-century histories of Sinai and the Jews in Chicago are silent on the controversy within the congregation regarding the visit of Felix Adler. Even the otherwise-detailed board minutes do not mention the clash. But there is no doubt that the Felix Adler affair constituted an embarrassing low point in Sinai's short history.[10]

The conflict highlighted the growing gap between the congregation founders and the younger generation. Kohler and most other Chicago rabbis did not confront a burning question that engaged a growing number of young Chicagoans from established families, Jewish and Christian: how to deal with the consequences of dramatic economic growth and mass immigration. During the 1877 recession, thousands of working-class Chicagoans lost their jobs, leading to an outbreak of riots across the city. Again, National Guard units were brought in to restore order. But repression did nothing to solve the underlying causes of urban misery. For younger Jewish men and women who grew up in the relative safety of bourgeois Chicago households during the 1860s and early 1870s, the large Reform congregations offered little. The B'nai B'rith, once the vehicle of Jewish community building across America, had lost its initial momentum. Businessmen of all ages joined primarily to take advantage of the life insurance, and lodge meetings were dominated by long-winded discussions about the order's statutes and the relationships between individual lodges.

Why Chicago's rabbis did not speak to the fate of the distressed masses is open to interpretation. Most of Sinai's members were self-made men. They felt little compassion for destitute workers who sympathized with Socialism or even more radical causes. Some members reasoned that generous donations to the

UHRA were sufficient. But in the late 1870s the UHRA, for the first time in its short history, admitted that it could not support all Jews in need due to insufficient funds.[11]

A new Jewish association partly filled the spiritual and social void during the 1870s. The Young Men's Hebrew Association (YMHA) combined social activities with academic lectures and philanthropic endeavors, and the meetings were open to young Jewish women. The first YMHA chapters formed during the 1850s and 1860s, but only in the 1870s did the YMHA expand in a significant way. Unlike the B'nai B'rith, the YMHA embraced religion and stood close to congregations. Frequently, the rabbi of a congregation would provide spiritual guidance.[12] The literary association of Zion congregation was an early forerunner of the YMHA in Chicago. Its membership included both men and women. A visitor described the first monthly meeting in 1866: Henry Greenebaum discussed a poem of the German writer Ludwig Uhland. Miss Mayer followed him; she "sang in Italian. It sounded . . . like German." After a few musical performances and recitations, Greenebaum explained the purpose of the new association: for young Jewish men and women from Chicago's West Side to practice *Bildung*. Refined socializing would protect the younger generation from "idling away their time and wasting health, mind and body, by playing poker or similar games."[13]

Not coincidentally, YMHA gained favor in Chicago when the Reform congregations were losing appeal. The rabbi of the North Side Hebrew Congregation, Aaron Norden, founded the first chapter in May 1877. By November, fifty young Jews had joined the all-male chapter. At a typical event a few months later, the young people dressed up. Unlike those of the 1860s, the recitations were in English. Retired KAM rabbi Liebmann Adler, who gave a short address in German, appeared to belong to a bygone era. An observer concluded, "It is a new way to get up social affairs in Chicago, indeed." In June, a YMHA chapter was organized on the West Side, probably as the successor of the Zion Literary Association; half of its members were women. Since May 1877, a similar society was active on the Near South Side, the literary society of Sinai congregation. The association boosted its membership within a few weeks from ten to more than thirty young men and women. Many nonmembers also participated in its regular meetings and were thus drawn into Sinai's circle. In addition to musical performances and recitations, the participants staged fierce debates over current political and religious issues.[14]

Debates continued over several sessions and had to be settled by arbitration. Very contentious was the discussion of whether American women should have the right to vote. Only after the third session in early October 1877 did a majority decide against extending suffrage to women, perhaps because young males were slightly in the majority. But the debate seems to have continued, because two months later the composition of the all-male board changed. In December 1877, Rosa Rice was elected vice president, and Leah Felsenthal joined the board. A controversial topic was scheduled for October 24, 1877: whether Sunday services in Jewish synagogues should be abolished. A majority voted in favor on November 7. This was an undisguised attack on Sinai's board and its rabbi, because no other American Jewish congregation had introduced Sunday services.

The Sinai Literary Society quickly built links to the other YMHA chapters in Chicago, and the members launched a small philanthropic network for poor Jews. Kohler, himself only thirty-four years old in 1877, participated occasionally as honorary member. The society met in the rooms of the new temple. [15] In the spring of 1878, these promising developments came to a sudden end. On March 21, Kohler read in the *Chicago Tribune* that the group would host Felix Adler at the Standard Club on March 26. He immediately sat down and wrote a public letter to the Sinai Literary Society. Kohler expressed his strong disagreement with the "infidel" Adler, and he threatened to ban the association from "his temple" following rumors that Adler originally had been scheduled to speak at Sinai.[16]

Who was this man, Felix Adler, and how can Kohler's outrage be explained? Felix Adler was one of the most talked-about figures among Jewish Reform circles during the late 1870s and the 1880s. Adler was born in Alzey near Worms in 1851 and had come to New York as a child when his father Samuel Adler became the rabbi at Temple Emanu-El. The older Adler was acquainted with several Sinai founders who hailed from the vicinity of Alzey. In June 1861. he had preached the dedication sermon when Sinai was formally established. In the late 1860s, Samuel Adler and many congregants of Temple Emanu-El expected Felix to become the new rabbi. Initially, everything went according to plan. The younger Adler graduated from Columbia and pursued graduate studies at the universities of Berlin and Heidelberg during the early 1870s. He was among Abraham Geiger's first students at his recently established Hochschule für die Wissenschaft des Judenthums (University for the Scholarly Study of Judaism) in Berlin, which was the first rabbinical seminary of the Reform movement. Another student at the Hochschule was the son of the Philadelphia rabbi Samuel Hirsch, Emil Gustav Hirsch, who struck up a friendship with Felix. After returning to New York, Adler decided, much to the disappointment of his father, not to become a rabbi. But this decision alone hardly constituted a scandal.

Adler's decision against pursuing the rabbinate had deeper spiritual roots. Adler was the first Jewish Reform theologian who openly raised the question whether the movement was viable in the long run. Adler criticized Reformers for not addressing the contradiction between the continuous evolution of Judaism and its universal destiny. In his view, the time for an all-encompassing religion with a universal agenda had come. The logical conclusion was to break free by overcoming the artificial separation between Jews and others. Adler also expressed doubts whether God had inspired biblical texts, and he rejected the special covenant between God and the Jewish people. Adler was no atheist, but openly described himself as agnostic, anathema even to most Reform Jews.[17]

Adler made a case for replacing the scholarly German Reform theology with an inclusive and nondogmatic religious movement that concentrated on social action. This new religion would take inspiration from all world religions. In 1876, Adler established the Society for Ethical Culture in New York. Anyone could join, regardless of religious background or gender. The motto of this pragmatist and humanist religion, very much in the tradition of the universal ideal of *Bildung*, was "Diversity in the creed, unanimity in the deed. This is practical religion from which none dissents." The members met every Sunday in a rented hall to listen to lectures by Adler and guest speakers.

Under Adler's guidance, members developed a number of groundbreaking philanthropic projects, such as a school for poor immigrant children on the Lower East Side. The society was an early response to social problems of many urban dwellers, especially immigrants, whose situation worsened during the 1873 and 1877 recessions. It connected the lofty, universal message of *Bildung* with social action on behalf of disadvantaged Americans. Adler was a forerunner of the Progressives, and he is regarded as seminal in the elevation of sociology as an academic discipline.[18]

The Society for Ethical Culture cannot be analyzed separately from the rise of liberal and conservative Protestantism in American cities. Adler's emphasis on "practical religion" and large lecture events on Sundays were hardly unique. Several Protestant ministers in large American cities also addressed the spiritual crisis felt by many young middle-class Americans. During the 1870s, Chicago preacher Dwight Lyman Moody became known nationally for his revival services. He appealed to the emotions of his congregants, attracting more than a thousand people to his services every Sunday. Moody also supported a number of projects for the urban poor. While Moody adapted to the rapidly changing urban environment, finding new ways of rallying people behind his religious cause, he remained a deeply conservative evangelical. Liberal Protestants also

CHAPTER FIVE

responded to the massive transformation of American urban society. Some were genuinely interested in the message of Jewish Reform and ethical culture. Liberal Protestants too wanted to overcome rigid traditions; they accepted scientific progress, valued biblical criticism, and stressed the importance of ethical practice and helping the poor. However, liberal and conservative Protestant ministers (like most leading Reform rabbis) did not identify with protesting workers in Chicago. Compassion for the urban poor must not be confused with attempts to break down class barriers.[19]

Two Chicago ministers, David Swing and Hiram W. Thomas, who had both departed their denominations over accusations of heresy (Presbyterianism and Methodism respectively), began to offer Sunday lectures in 1875. Both called on their listeners to act on behalf of poor Chicagoans. Their theological openness, combined with engagement with social reforms, attracted the urban middle classes, especially young men and women, and even Jews. According to the *American Israelite*, younger Jews in Chicago sympathized with Thomas's supradenominational Philosophical Society, a forerunner of the People's Church he established in 1880.[20] Just as many Protestant and Jewish congregations like Sinai were following their members from the inner city to residential neighborhoods, Swing and Thomas returned to the heart of the city, eschewing expensive and prestigious churches and renting public halls and theaters instead, selling tickets for every Sunday lecture service.

In 1876, Adler launched a successful Sunday lecture series in a rented hall in Manhattan. In particular, he attracted the younger members of the city's leading Reform congregation, Temple Emanu-El, still led by his father. Since Adler had not formally severed his ties with Judaism, Reform-minded Jews considered participating in his lecture events to be acceptable. Unlike Sinai, Emanu-El offered no Sunday services, so there was no direct competition between father and son. Adler also began to lecture outside of New York. To radical Reformers, Adler represented a serious challenge, not least because he initially did not distance himself from Judaism. Adler accused Reform rabbis—not without reason—of refusing to acknowledge their closeness to his own positions.

Adler was a highly educated and articulate thinker who could not be easily sidelined or ignored. Most Reform rabbis were not particularly alarmed by Adler's message. In fact, rabbis like Isaac Mayer Wise lived in cities smaller than New York and knew their members would perhaps listen to Adler but not join his movement. A big and hustling center of radical Reform with growing social tensions, Chicago was different. Understandably, Rabbi Kohler, whose congregation had gone further than any other in departing from the Jewish tradition, was worried. The young Jews who attended the lectures of Thomas's Philosophical Society obviously did not attend Kohler's Sunday services. Now an even more persuasive speaker might even establish a chapter of his society in Chicago. Long before March 1878, Kohler had emerged as one of Adler's fiercest critics.[21]

The invitation of this man, by members of his own congregation without his knowing, constituted a serious transgression in Kohler's eyes. The dwindling attendance at his services had eroded his position. Now, it appeared members were in open rebellion against him. The anger and disappointment of the proud rabbi are certainly understandable. Kohler concluded his public letter by expressing regret "that my weekly lectures before your Association have not fallen on a more fertile soil." He also accused Sinai member Julius Rosenthal of involvement in the affair. And he dispatched a copy of the letter to the *Tribune*.[22] Kohler's public letter threatening to ban the Sinai Literary Society and his personal attack against Rosenthal put the members of Sinai's board in a difficult position. Several had children who belonged to the literary association.

In the days leading up to Adler's March 26 visit, a theological controversy transformed into a dramatic and very public clash between Kohler and Rosenthal. Both exchanged increasingly insulting letters in the pages of the *Tribune* and the *Staatszeitung*. Kohler portrayed Adler as an atheist and concluded a letter in the March 23 edition of the *Staatszeitung*, "Kling Klang! Kling Klang! All Jewish men and women in Chicago and others . . . who have pledged allegiance to the banner of atheism, make sure to attend Standard [Club's] hall on the 26th to listen to Professor Felix Adler."[23] The American Jewish press eagerly followed the conflict between the prominent Reform rabbi and his well-known congregant. Wise's *American Israelite*, for years a critical observer of radical Reform in Chicago, reprinted the letters.[24]

The highly educated and respected lawyer Julius Rosenthal was not easily intimidated. In true lawyerly fashion, he assembled a number of quotes from Kohler's articles and sermons to prove an obvious point: no other American Reform rabbi held positions as close to Adler's as Kohler, whose statements describing God as an "ideal" rather than a "reality" appeared similar to Adler's agnostic teachings. Rosenthal also reminded Kohler that the board of Sinai—not the rabbi—would have the last word over banning their "children" from the temple. He deplored Kohler's overly academic sermons, because they did not address social realities. Adler, on the other hand, offered a welcome change from "Dr. Kohler's brain-religion." For Adler, Rosenthal emphasized, religion was not only a spiritual matter but also closely tied to ethical life and social action.[25]

This devastating letter only confirmed Kohler's suspicion of a brewing conspiracy against him. In his response, Kohler condemned Rosenthal's "coarse and ungentlemanlike conduct . . . perhaps without parallel in the annals of Jewish and American society."[26] Rosenthal, increasingly frustrated and probably under some pressure from the board to end this "debate," called on Kohler not to behave like a "Pastor, Bishop, or Pope" but to concentrate on his job. Kohler was now so enraged that he could not resist abusing Rosenthal from the pulpit.[27]

This public row, of course, drew a large crowd to the premises of the Standard Club on the evening of March 26, 1878. More than five hundred Chicagoans attended Adler's lecture, among them, rabbis Liebmann Adler and Bernhard Felsenthal. Neither agreed with Adler, but they deplored Kohler's polemical reaction and wanted to exchange arguments with the lecturer and the audience. Adler began by expressing his deep regret over the whole affair, stating that Kohler deserved "respect" as scholar and rabbi. Nevertheless, after rebuffing the various accusations against him, Adler asked Kohler to abide by the accepted rules of "fair play" so "deeply rooted in the American character."

The large audience represented not an a priori "endorsement" of Adler's positions (as Kohler had claimed) but rather indicated the great interest in religion and ethics. In his lecture, Adler reiterated his well-known positions, emphasizing that action, not "dogma," was decisive. He rejected the notion of an "omniscient and omnipotent" God "because events [in human history] do not prove it." Interestingly, Adler primarily criticized Christianity, expressing doubts in the existence of a God who created "men for a miserable existence on earth [and] a world of punishment thereafter." In Adler's view, men should act ethically in this world without expecting compensation in another.[28]

Bernhard Felsenthal took a markedly different approach to confronting Felix Adler. Almost a year later, he reflected on the public affair in one of the first issues of a new Chicago Jewish weekly, the Jewish Advance. Sinai's former rabbi wanted to bring Adler and his followers back into the fold of Reform Judaism. While Kohler had chosen antagonism, Felsenthal wanted to learn and embrace. He saw in Adler's ideas and his movement the critical inspiration for Reform Judaism. Adler's critics among Jewish reformers had apparently forgotten what Felsenthal vividly recalled: traditional Jews had attacked the reformers as "atheists" twenty years earlier. Indeed, Adler called on Reformers to look into the mirror. He wanted them to see that they had gone too far by abolishing almost all ritual practices and traditions, save the High Holidays. In reality, the radical Reformers stood uncomfortably close to Adler because they had cut the last ties that still bound them to Judaism: "Now we are all *gebildet*.... And we prove this our *Bildung*, etc., by our fine dinners on Yom-Kippur down town in fashionable restaurants, and by other such acts. Yes, we Reformers! ... We were not satisfied that the innocent Christmas tree found silently its way into a number of Jewish houses; we agitated and worked for its introduction."[29]

In 1879, Adler formally broke with Judaism. However, Felsenthal did identify a crucial point about Adler's appeal. The rise of the Society for Ethical Culture in New York triggered a reflection among leading radical Reformers about the significance of ritual and tradition. This eventually opened the way to a compromise with Isaac Mayer Wise and the organized Reform movement around the UAHC. Interestingly, in 1885, Kohler would take the lead in reaching out to Wise by defining the core positions or common "platform" of Reform. Felsenthal responded differently. There can be no doubt that Adler's decision disappointed him. The roots of Felsenthal's engagement for Zionism can be traced to the 1870s, when he increasingly worried about the dissolution of Judaism.[30]

The clash over Adler's lecture led Kohler to rethink his position. A debate with Felsenthal a few months after Adler's visit in the pages of the *Staatszeitung* titled "Religion and Race" illustrates his change of heart. In a small pamphlet, Felsenthal made a case for accepting mixed marriages, writing that the "happiness of the family" mattered more than dogmatism. Felsenthal recommended that converts be interviewed to examine their motives. Male converts who married a Jewish woman would not be required to be circumcised, but Felsenthal warned against abolishing circumcision as such (as some radical Reformers had demanded), because it was still "sacred" to many Jews. Felsenthal was not opposed to radical changes but felt that such steps should only be taken when Jews did not connect any "religious feelings" with a ritual. Months earlier, Kohler had shared Felsenthal's liberal position on mixed marriages; he had even called for the complete abolition of circumcision. Now, he rejected Felsenthal's arguments. He agreed to perform mixed marriages but insisted that any male convert would have to undergo circumcision.[31]

KOHLER'S DEPARTURE

After the dust over Adler's controversial visit had settled, the literary society formally apologized to Kohler. But it was too late; the relationship between Sinai and its rabbi had soured irreparably. The society did not return to the temple and dissolved in early 1879.[32] In June 1879, Kohler informed the board that he had not been able to engage the members of Sinai to attend the services. He hoped Sinai would find "a leader more successful" than he had been."[33]

Why did Kohler fail in Chicago? He was never able to establish a mutually close relationship with his congregants, nor did he reach out to the wider community in Chicago, Jewish or otherwise. The UHRA struggled during the late 1870s as more Jewish immigrants who required support moved to Chicago. Although the 1877 recession affected even well-to-do businessmen, the widely respected rabbi of a congregation with many wealthy members could have done much to help. But the social question did not concern Kohler.

With the banning of the Sinai Literary Society, Kohler ousted the one promising project from the temple that could have reenergized the congregation. His tendency to publicize internal conflicts weakened his position considerably and undermined whatever trust may have existed between rabbi and board. Underneath all this lay a deeper conflict. Kohler, after all, was a recent immigrant and a scholar who struggled to adjust to the politics of the American congregation. At Sinai, Kohler faced a number of educated and proud self-made businessmen. Instead of socializing with the members and involving himself with other Chicagoans, Kohler preferred to work in his study. His letters to Sinai's presidents and to the press give historians revealing insights, but they hint at a lack and (eventually) a breakdown of communication. In his first decade in America, Kohler preferred direct and public confrontation to compromise and negotiation.

Kohler's departure left a void. In the last report to the congregation in spring 1879, before Kohler submitted his resignation, outgoing president Berthold Loewenthal pointed to the wide gap between Sinai's high expectations and the rather depressing reality. Sinai, he began, "claims to be and is looked upon as the leading Jewish institution in the west." And indeed it possessed a beautiful temple and had a famous scholar-rabbi in the pulpit. Yet the members did not attend services, several had left the congregation, others were not paying their dues, and indifference threatened to destroy the link between the parents and the children of the founding generation and, eventually, the congregation.[34]

But that was not even the main problem. Shortly after the resignation of Sinai's rabbi was announced, the *Chicago Tribune* published an interview with Kohler and Rosenthal under the headline "Two Sundays." Both interviewees confirmed that the congregation was divided into Sunday and Saturday factions. According to Kohler, members were fighting over this issue when he arrived in 1871, and he had barely managed to hold the congregation together. Most of the businessmen who rarely attended services were not in favor of Sunday services. The Sunday faction was a vociferous minority, composed of several educated members like Rosenthal. Against this backdrop, Kohler claimed, he had negotiated a compromise to avert a split: Sunday services were introduced without giving up Saturday services. Kohler predicted the congregation would split after his departure. His assessment was that of a disappointed man looking back on eight difficult years, and he certainly overstated his role as a unifying figure.

Rosenthal tried to play down Kohler's expectation of a split and especially his role in holding the congregation together. Kohler really was a "man without a backbone." Rosenthal probably suspected Kohler of having supported Sunday services for opportunistic reasons rather than out of true conviction. Although Rosenthal had little sympathy for Kohler, he largely confirmed Kohler's diagnosis. The introduction of Sunday services had been an amicable agreement between the two Sabbath factions and the prerequisite for building the temple. The Saturday group was mostly composed of the "ladies"—a group with limited influence in Rosenthal's eyes. And while a split was not imminent, he did not deny that the factions did not "interfere" with each other. In other words, Sinai comprised two alienated groups, each with its own service.

Lately, Rosenthal admitted, new Sinai president Morris Selz had "stirred up a fight" between the two factions. Rosenthal, a respected figure in Chicago, knew his attack against Selz would be in print the following morning. The *Tribune* reporter even tried to get Selz's opinion, "but the truthful housemaid at Mr. Selz's residence remarked, after making enough noise up-stairs to wake the dead, that Mr. Selz had gone to bed, not feeling very well. Truly, he must have slept the sleep of the sound."[35]

Sinai advertised the vacant position for rabbi. The ideal candidate would have graduated from a German university and would be a good speaker with some experience who could preach in German and English. In essence, the congregation needed a man larger than life who could fill the spiritual and social void—a radical Reformer who could heal the wide rift between radicals and more traditionally inclined members, a gifted speaker who could rally proud and educated businessmen and their wives but also the disaffected younger generation and would convince new members to join. He needed to be a highly qualified spiritual leader with a vision who would speak for Sinai and radical Reform in Chicago and perhaps even on the national stage, and perhaps even a man who would contemplate on the impact of the massive social and economic changes that were affecting Chicago and American society—and make a difference. Indeed, Sinai was looking for a leader in the mold of a Felix Adler, but a Jewish Felix Adler. That Sinai managed to find this man against considerable odds would open the most fascinating chapter yet in the still-short history of Sinai congregation.

The credentials of the new rabbi, Emil Gustav Hirsch, were impressive. He was the scion of a distinguished rabbinical family with close ties to the beginnings of Reform theology in Germany. His father was Samuel Hirsch, a revered German Reformer of David Einhorn's generation who had been an early proponent of Sunday services during the 1840s. Emil was closely related to Sinai's spiritual founder and his predecessor, having married Einhorn's daughter Mathilde in 1878. Her sister Johanna was the wife of Kaufmann Kohler.

Hirsch was born in Luxembourg in 1851, during his father's tenure as Grand Rabbi of Luxembourg. The family settled in Philadelphia in 1866 when the older Hirsch accepted an offer from Keneseth Israel congregation to replace Einhorn, who had moved to New York. Even in America, German culture continued to make a strong impact on Emil as he grew up. German was spoken in the home, by many close acquaintances of the family, and of course in the synagogue. Philadelphia also had a large German immigrant community. Hirsch went to the Episcopal Academy of Philadelphia, and after graduating, he attended the University of Pennsylvania, where he played for the football team. His education helps to explain why Sinai's new rabbi was much more in tune with American culture and society than his predecessors. Early on Hirsch seems to have decided to become a rabbi. Together with Felix Adler, he was among the first students of the Berlin Hochschule in 1873, where he studied with Abraham Geiger. He heard lectures at Berlin's prestigious Friedrich-Wilhelms University and probably at the University of Leipzig, a famous center of Semitic studies at the time. Leipzig was the alma mater of his father Samuel, and his brother-in-law Kohler spent his last year before his emigration at the university. According to the entry on Hirsch in the *Jewish Encyclopedia* that was edited under his auspices between 1901 and 1906, he obtained a doctoral degree at Leipzig in 1876. Strangely, the entry provides the wrong date of birth for Hirsch (1852 instead of the correct 1851). The Leipzig University archive has no records on Hirsch, not even proof of enrollment, and no thesis was ever published under his name. Hirsch's son-in-law, Gerson B. Levi, did not mention a PhD degree in an otherwise detailed overview of Hirsch's life compiled in 1925. After returning to the United States in 1876, Hirsch first preached at Rodeph Shalom congregation in his hometown before moving to a position at Har Sinai, the former Baltimore congregation of Einhorn. In 1878, he accepted a call from Adath Israel congregation in Louisville, Kentucky.[36]

Like Adler, Hirsch belonged to a small but influential intermediary generation whose members followed in the footsteps of German-born and bred immigrant rabbis and preceded rabbis fully educated in America. Hirsch and several men of his age went to college in America but received their rabbinic ordination and graduate education in Germany. The decision to go to Germany may appear as a logical step for young men with Hirsch's background who wanted to become rabbis. Indeed, in its job advertisement, Sinai explicitly demanded a German university education: the board would only consider "Jewish theologians of modern Reform principles and of good repute, who have graduated at a German University with honor, [and] are excellent—also in all those branches of study which characterize the learned Rabbi of our day and who are good orators and able to preach in the German and English vernacular." Hebrew Union College (HUC), the first American rabbinical seminary, had opened its doors in 1875. But Sinai and several other congregations close to the teachings of Einhorn did not approve of Isaac Mayer Wise's role as president or the affiliation of HUC with the Union of American Hebrew Congregations; they openly ridiculed the college. Only in the early 1880s, after overcoming initial problems to recruit faculty, could HUC establish itself as a serious and respected institution. Therefore, before 1880, Germany was the obvious place to go for men seeking serious rabbinical training. The legal obligation for future rabbis to attend university or a similar institution of higher learning and the availability of a large pool of well-trained Jewish academics explain why the first seminaries were founded in the German states. In the early 1870s, Geiger's Hochschule (founded in 1872) and the Berlin neo-Orthodox Rabbinerseminar (1873) joined the older and more traditional Jüdisch-Theologisches Seminar (1854) in Breslau, an institution that mediated between Reform and Orthodoxy and was a forerunner of Conservative Judaism in America.[37]

The few young Jewish men from America who attended rabbinical seminaries and universities in Germany were part of a larger movement. In the last three decades of the nineteenth century, many American college graduates headed to Germany for their graduate education in the humanities and arts as well as in medicine and the sciences, especially if they were embarking on an academic career. During the first half of the nineteenth century, German universities, in particular those in Heidelberg, Göttingen, Berlin, and Leipzig, had emerged as groundbreaking research institutions. The farsighted reforms of the higher education system in several German states owed much to the *Bildung* ideal held in such high esteem by many Jews in America. After 1870, Harvard, Columbia, the University of Pennsylvania, and several other universities adapted the model of the German research university by nurturing graduate schools. The Johns Hopkins University (founded in 1876) and the University of Chicago (1892) combined the German-style research university with an Anglo-American college. Returning graduates and imported German academics helped to transplant the German model to America.[38]

Among the Jewish returnees, four sons of immigrant rabbis stand out: Felix Adler, Richard Gottheil, Morris Jastrow Jr., and Emil G. Hirsch. After college, they graduated from the Berlin Hochschule (except for Jastrow, who graduated from the Breslau Jüdisch-Theologisches Seminar) and attended German universities, like their fathers. Only Hirsch eventually lived up to the expectations of his father and stuck with the rabbinical career after returning to America. The Leipzig graduates Gottheil and Jastrow were appointed to chairs in Semitics at Columbia and the University of Pennsylvania, respectively; both helped to institute Semitic studies as an academic discipline in the United States. Adler initially concentrated on expanding his ethical culture movement. From 1902, he taught political and social ethics at Columbia. Hirsch, who was proud of his German education, was appointed to a professorship in Semitics at the newly founded University of Chicago in 1892. Following an invitation by Kohler, he joined the editorial board of the *Jewish Encyclopedia* around the turn of the century and contributed several articles but otherwise did not publish on academic subjects. Hirsch may have regretted his choice for the rabbinate, especially when he struggled with the more mundane obligations of his job. But a university appointment, even at Columbia or the University of Pennsylvania, was not nearly as prestigious then as it is today. Unlike Jastrow and Gottheil, Hirsch was a famous public figure whose sermons were widely distributed and discussed. Sinai provided Hirsch with a very substantial income and additional benefits, such as free housing, life insurance, and a pension. Even today, few universities could afford to offer even their most prestigious professors comparable conditions.[39]

For Sinai, Hirsch was an attractive candidate. Apart from his academic track record, he was young but not without experience. He was an articulate speaker who could engage an audience and could be expected to attract new members, especially men and women of his generation. From the letters Hirsch exchanged with the search committee, one German sentence stands out: "Ich bin noch ein sehr junger und unerfahrener Mann!" (I am a still a very young and inexperienced man!)[40] This was certainly an understatement but it increased Hirsch's chances. The older board members could hope to exert some control over the new rabbi in his first years at Sinai.

Another much more pressing issue explains why the board and many members placed high expectations on the shoulders of the young candidate. The job advertisement clearly limited the search to rabbis willing to preach on Sundays but also Saturdays:

> Circumstances over which we have no control prevent a large member of our members and young Israel especially from attending public worship on the biblical Sabbath, this congregation considers it an imperative duty to continue to hold services on the common day of rest—and to this end it shall be the duty of the incoming minister to attend to all functions of his station on Sabbaths and Festivals and to deliver lectures before this congregation on every Sunday.

To the uninformed reader, this hints at a heavy workload. At no other American Jewish congregation did a rabbi have to preach on Saturdays and Sundays. But much more was at stake. The matter-of-fact-job description betrays a deep division within the congregation over the Sunday issue. Under Kohler, Sinai had failed to reach out to the younger generation and appeared to have lost touch with the broader social transformation. A minority of Sinai's members, among them founders Berthold Loewenthal and Julius Rosenthal, and the erstwhile members of the Sinai Literary Society, was willing to move ahead with the Reform project and make modern Judaism more inclusive, perhaps even for Gentiles. Some of these members expressed strong sympathies for ethical culture. Many married women and several older members, a larger albeit less articulate group, opposed this radical agenda. They valued the Jewish tradition, notably the historical Sabbath. This left a not clearly defined majority, represented by Sinai president Morris Selz. These members were middle-aged businessmen who were less involved in the congregation than some of the older members and struggled to accommodate the two factions.[41]

Occident, the local Jewish weekly, mused in November 1879 whether any figure could "successfully minister" the divided congregation. Although Sinai had distanced itself from the Jewish tradition, "they cannot wipe out the fact that they are yet Jews." The author advised the congregation to make a truly "radical move" and join Felix Adler's ethical culture movement.[42] In late 1879, Sinai did not have a figure with the necessary intellectual authority to dismiss such critics and explain the theological position of the congregation to a wider Jewish (and Chicago) public. Not only in hindsight was the young Hirsch the ideal and rare figure to bridge the deep chasm that had opened up between the visions of Felix Adler and more traditionally inclined members—and to put the congregation on a firm course again.[43]

It was no secret that Hirsch stood closer to Felix Adler than any other rabbi of his generation. He sympathized with Adler's ideas, but instead of following in Adler's steps he chose the rabbinical career. As Adler moved away from Judaism, Hirsch took the opposite route. He left a radical Reform congregation in Baltimore for a mainstream Reform congregation in a midsized city far from the East Coast. This was certainly not lost on Sinai's board members. If Hirsch was successfully serving a congregation more in tune with the Jewish tradition, he would certainly be able to heal the divisions within Sinai. Moreover, through his wife Hirsch was related to Kohler, a leading critic of Adler.

Most members of Sinai must have wondered where Hirsch would lead the congregation. A compromise between Adler's course and core elements of the Jewish tradition such as the historic Sabbath appeared unachievable. As a radical Reform congregation Sinai faced the crucial question about its future even more acutely than the Reform movement at large. Should Sinai follow Adler on his path towards universalism, stopping just short of formally severing its ties with Judaism, or should the congregation emphasize the importance of the tradition and reach out to the mainstream represented by Isaac Mayer Wise? Against considerable odds, Hirsch could accomplish the remarkable feat of squaring both of these seemingly contradictory goals.

Part II.

SOCIAL JUSTICE AND CIVIC ACTION

6.

TURNING POINTS

Emil G. Hirsch and the Transformation of Sinai

IN THE SUMMER of 1880, Sinai stood at a crossroads. Not for the first time in its short history, the existence of the congregation hinged on the appointment of a new rabbi. As it turned out, in Emil G. Hirsch the board had picked a young man who would emerge as one of the most influential and eccentric figures in the history of Jewish Reform in America. The arrival of Sinai's new rabbi coincided with a momentous event in modern Jewish history: the beginnings of the Jewish mass migration from eastern Europe. The immigrants overwhelmingly settled in a few large urban centers. Apart from the uncontested center of New York, Chicago and Philadelphia were the principal destinations. In 1880, the Jewish population of Chicago numbered about ten thousand. By 1920, the number had risen to a staggering three hundred thousand—more than in any other city, except New York and Warsaw.[1] The immigration of hundreds of thousands who closely identified with the Jewish tradition or Socialism, exacerbated the pressure on the Reform movement in America to define its agenda. By 1880, Reform had established a firm foothold, especially in the growing cities. On the other hand, in Germany, the motherland of Reform, Reformers had been locked into a compromise with traditional Jews in the state-regulated communities, blocking any progress in the foreseeable future. Thus on the eve of the mass migration from eastern Europe, America had become the uncontested center of the Reform movement.[2]

As older and much-respected immigrant scholar-rabbis like Samuel Adler and Samuel Hirsch retired around 1880, and Germany as a point reference was fading, the pressure for American Reformers to assert themselves was growing. The indifference of the younger generation, contested issues like intermarriage or Sunday services, the rise of ethical culture, and above all, the mass immigration of traditionally minded Jews from eastern Europe raised the possibility of a complete dissolution of Reform Judaism in America. Before long, Reformers had to settle their differences and agree on a common theological response to these challenges.[3]

The mass immigration of Jews to America and the internal debates about the visions for Reform Judaism cannot be separated from America's social and economic transformation at that time. Most American cities underwent a striking makeover in the last three decades of the nineteenth century, but Chicago was in a league of its own. It became the fastest-growing large city in the world. In 1880, the city counted about five hundred thousand inhabitants, ten years later, in 1890, the number had doubled to a million, and by 1905, two million people lived in the metropolis on Lake Michigan. Only four other cities in the world were larger. These net numbers give only a vague idea of the dramatic events on the ground. The urban infrastructure could hardly cope with the massive influx. Almost 80 percent of the one million Chicagoans in 1890 were immigrants and their American-born children. Even for a booming American city this was an unusually high proportion. Eastern and southern Europeans—Jews, Poles, Greeks, Czechs, Italians, and others—settled in central neighborhoods, often in appalling circumstances. Many started work at a young age as unskilled workers, in the stockyards, in the steel industry, on the railroads that converged in Chicago, or—as many Jewish men, women, and children did—in the garment sector. Uneven business cycles caused massive suffering; thousands were laid off and frequently became homeless. No public welfare system to speak of existed. Private, often Christian charities cared for the most destitute. Chicago became the place of some of America's most violent social conflicts between 1870 and 1900. The socially engaged members of Chicago's better classes, represented not least by the members of established religious congregations like Sinai, were under some pressure to respond. Withdrawing into heavily fortified homes and relying on repression to uphold social order offered no longtime solution to the social question.[4]

The members and leaders of Sinai took an active part in dealing with these immense challenges on the local, national, and even international stages. At the same time, Sinai transformed into one of the largest and most respected Jewish congregations in America. In no small part, this astonishing makeover was the achievement of the congregation's new rabbi. Emil G. Hirsch helped to redefine the American rabbinate by taking a proactive role in Jewish community matters and beyond, quickly earning respect as a public intellectual and social reformer in Chicago and nationally among Jews and Christians. Sinai's rabbi was an exceptional figure who thrived in the radical environment of Chicago in a way he could not have in smaller cities or even in the older East Coast centers.[5]

CROSSING THE JORDAN

In his inaugural sermon, "The Crossing of the Jordan," delivered on September 5, 1880, Hirsch gave a hint of what was to come. He addressed two related issues, the future of the Reform movement (and indirectly Sinai congregation) and the great changes affecting American society. The founders of Reform, he claimed, had concentrated their efforts, understandably, on reexamining and critiquing the tradition. But now a turning point had been reached; Reformers had to do constructive work:

> The times are charged with volcanic energy; social upheavals multiply in number . . . and the whole fabric of our boasted culture seems out of joint. . . . To-day it becomes the sacred duty of Judaism, to construct on the eternal principles of Judaism, an all-embracing philosophy of life, to study man in his ethical relations, to listen to his doubts, and to confirm him in his hopes, to brace him for the struggle of life, and show him the palm of victory to be striven after.

Even this short passage illustrates why Hirsch offered an unambiguous departure from Kohler's academic sermons. He touched on the social question stressing the ethical dimension of religion and the mission of (Reform) Judaism to heal the world. The verbs he used here (construct, study, listen, confirm, brace, show) hint at an activist message, close to the concept of ethical culture. Unlike Adler, however, Hirsch was not ready to break with Judaism. He took a clear stand on the issue of agnosticism by brushing aside questions raised by modern science and philosophy about the existence of a personal God. God was not "an abstract idea" but "a living reality." Atheism meant destruction; only with God could constructive work be completed. "For the thoughtful, history points out one lesson: Atheism has ever been the grave-digger, never the architect of civilization." Hirsch warned against delaying action and getting stuck in a for-est of dogmas. Memory was not an "end in itself" but a "means." The new rabbi preached a forward looking message; the Jewish tradition mattered—man could not break with or escape history—but Reform Jews should not argue about the past and turn their backs to the future, but rather step forward and act. Almost as an aside, Hirsch expressed strong support for Sunday services. But he also de-clared his respect for the historical Sabbath.[6]

In the first annual report after Hirsch's arrival, the board expressed satisfac-tion. The congregation had come out of the "gloomy" void left by Kohler's de-parture. Hirsch was an engaging and articulate speaker who was "attracting a steadily growing attendance." Sinai had made progress and was on a financially stable footing after having paid off most of the remaining debt for the new tem-ple. Hirsch received a ten-year contract with a starting salary of $3,600. Almost annually the board gave him a raise, broadly in line with the growth of the con-gregation. Sinai's membership almost doubled between 1881 and 1886, from 86 to 157, and it became the Jewish congregation with most members in Chicago. By 1886, Hirsch's salary had risen to $6,000.[7] These increases illustrate the ap-proval of the board and the congregation. An annual income of several thou-sand dollars was considerable. For the congregation, composed of some of the wealthiest citizens of Chicago, the (publicly known) salary constituted a vestige of its social status. In 1886, Hirsch was already one of the highest-paid rabbis in America, as a brief comparison illustrates. The rabbi of the Jewish congregation in Fort Wayne, Indiana, a typical small city congregation, earned $1,200 in 1881. Rabbis in rural towns and of small immigrant congregations received much less. In contrast, Gustav Gottheil, who had succeeded Samuel Adler at New York's Temple Emanu-El in the mid-1870s, made $10,000 in 1884.[8] Like Gottheil and other rabbis and ministers of large urban congregations, Hirsch had to negotiate a considerable workload. He was the main employee of the congregation. He acted as superintendent of the Sinai school, had to conduct the routine tasks of any minister like weddings and funerals, and (at least in his first years in Chi-cago) preached on Saturdays and Sundays. In addition, he joined the board of the United Hebrew Relief Association. A highly educated theologian and ar-ticulate speaker, Hirsch was Sinai's public face. The spiritual leader of a large urban congregation was expected to attend various social functions, not just in the Jewish community. Hirsch often gave interviews to Chicago's newspapers explaining Sinai's and his theological position and Judaism more generally.

Two events in 1881–1882 highlighted Sinai's theological and social isolation, and the challenges the new rabbi faced. In mid-July the UAHC convened its annual meeting in Chicago. The president of KAM, Maximilian M. Gerstley, welcomed the guests "on behalf of the Hebrew congregations of Chicago." Most of the larger American congregations and their rabbis were represented. Even Temple Emanu-El and Kohler's new congregation, Beth El, both close to Einhorn's theology, had now joined the UAHC. Among the large urban radical Reform congregations only Sinai, its daughter congregation, Zion, and the Philadelphia congregation of the older Hirsch, Keneseth Israel, remained on the sidelines.[9] Six months later, in January 1882, Felix Adler gave a lecture at the First Methodist Church in Chicago titled "Future of Judaism." His host was one of the Chicago B'nai B'rith lodges; several of its members also belonged to Sinai. Adler was introduced by Eli B. Felsenthal, the son of influential Sinai member Herman Felsenthal. The young lawyer had been one of the founders of the Sinai Literary Society, which had hosted Adler's controversial 1878 visit. Many Sinai members attended. In his lecture, Adler argued as a separate people and religion Jews had no future. Their mission had been fulfilled and "the new age" had arrived. Jews were not "faithless" when they embraced "humanity."[10] Identifying with ethical culture did not require a renunciation of Judaism or a formal conversion. In Adler's view, Jews already belonged to the religion of humanity. But this religion was open to every woman or man regardless of their background—it was not Judaism.

In a public letter, a J. L. Stone, who spoke for the "Polish and Russian Jews in Chicago," questioned Adler's "remedy" to Judaism by referring to a well-known Talmudic story: when the fox advised the fish fearing the fisherman's net to leave the water, the fish replied to the fox:

> "The beasts say that you are the wisest of the whole of them, but we must call you the biggest fool of the whole of them, because you advise us to come out of our natural environment, in which we were born and raised, and in which we have nothing to fear but the net, to which we are already accustomed, and on the dry land we cannot live even one day." Professor [Adler] tell us where are the millions of Jews who have during the past went out of the Biblical Lake?[11]

All of this left Sinai in a precarious spot, indeed, almost like a fish on dry land. The congregation had clearly isolated itself from the Reform movement, and thus from the Jewish mainstream. In fact, many Jews in Chicago and beyond wondered whether Sinai was still a Jewish congregation. Hosting the UAHC convention in 1881 as the city's leading Reform congregation would have been a symbolic recognition, but this did not come to pass. On the other side beaconed Felix Adler and his message. In October 1882, events came to a head when several adherents of Felix Adler founded a chapter of the Ethical Culture Society in Chicago.[12] With this move, a split of Sinai congregation became a real possibility.

Hirsch's sermon, "Reformed Judaism," was a direct response to Adler and in particular to Adler's followers within Sinai. Adler, Hirsch explained, "as so many before him, in perfect honesty doubtlessly, *utterly* and *absolutely* misconceived of Judaism." Adler's Judaism was lifeless "dogma," not a living religion capable of adapting its forms to its respective environment. Hirsch emphatically rejected the motto of ethical culture, "By the Deed, not By the Creed," making an impressive case for a seemingly similar albeit strikingly different agenda: no (constructive) deed without a creed. For Hirsch, humanity and moral action sprang from and were intrinsically connected to a religious source. Contemporary *and* historic Judaism proved the importance of the combination between creed and deed. Judaism, Hirsch underlined, could hardly be "accused of having done nothing in the direction of practical good." Jews had a long tradition of providing welfare to the poor (regardless of their religion, as he could have mentioned). Numerous Jewish hospitals, orphan asylums, and similar institutions were visible testaments of this ongoing work. An obvious example was the Jewish hospital in Chicago, one of the largest and most advanced of its kind. After a ten-year hiatus, the Michael Reese Hospital (named after the main donor) reopened in 1881. According to the record book, many Christians were treated free of charge.

Hirsch wondered why some Jews had left congregations and identified with ethical culture but still belonged to B'nai B'rith lodges and Jewish association such as the prestigious Standard Club. The membership in exclusively Jewish societies appeared to contradict the tenets of ethical culture and was rather a sign for the continuing impact of anti-Jewish prejudice or the continuing attraction of Jewish sociability. Another development that Hirsch did not even mention but most of his listeners were acutely aware of concerned the rise of modern anti-Semitism in Germany and the wave of pogroms against Jews in the Russian Empire in 1881. Clearly, the time for exchanging Judaism for a universal ethical religion had not yet come.[13]

In hindsight, Hirsch's difficult early years in Chicago are easily ignored. Many Sinai members did not take part in the Sunday or Saturday services. And even the ones who attended frequently came late or left early, creating some noise and disorder. Hirsch had to plead with the board to make sure the doors to the temple remained closed "during the delivery of lectures on Sundays and Holidays." In a more extended letter he sent to the board a few weeks later in March

1883, Hirsch depicted Sinai as a very "peculiar" congregation and deplored the "utter absence of enthusiasm." Especially the Sunday services remained behind his expectations. At most two hundred people would come, enough to sustain the services but much less than the "600–1000" who had participated in his services in Louisville and Baltimore. Hirsch may have exaggerated, but even the low number (in Hirsch's eyes) of two hundred attendees is remarkable compared to the almost empty temple in Kohler's last years.

In passing, Hirsch mentioned he was preaching in German. Obviously, English-language sermons—Hirsch hinted between the lines—would attract a much bigger and younger crowd. In the interest of financial stability and to increase the attendance on Sunday and especially Saturday ("for the older men and ladies") he even recommended a merger with KAM. Such strategic decisions were not for the rabbi to make, as Hirsch knew very well. But he concluded the letter with an implicit warning. He had turned down offers from two well-known congregations. Whether true or not, like Kohler, Hirsch knew to make use of such offers in order to expand his influence within the congregation.[14]

A few months later rumors about a merger of Sinai and KAM were flaring up in the local press. KAM's longtime rabbi, Liebmann Adler, had recently retired, and KAM faced a difficult decision: should it remain a vaguely mainstream Reform congregation with both Reformers and traditional Jews in its ranks, or should it perhaps merge with its daughter? Hirsch (after seeking permission from Sinai's board) preached Saturday sermons at KAM in June 1883, an indication for KAM's openness to more radical Reform ideas. The *Occident* interviewed leading members of both congregations. The Sinai members were open-minded but not enthusiastic. None of the interviewees wanted to sacrifice the Sunday service. Julius Rosenthal was skeptical. He considered the merger "women's gossip." In his opinion the "Saturday-Sabbath" was doomed in Chicago. KAM could not expect Sinai to nurse its "old sick man, called Shabbes." A merger might have financial advantages but, as he frankly admitted would "strengthen our few Saturday-Sabbath members." The KAM interviewees overwhelmingly supported the merger. President Gerstley strongly argued in favor of a merger. The "younger element" of KAM would attend only High Holiday services—and Sinai's Sunday services. Gerstley himself, as he freely admitted, was a regular guest at Sinai's temple on Sundays. He hoped a merger might engage a considerable number of young Jews who were drifting away from KAM. Only banker Lazarus Silverman, a traditionally minded longtime member, was "strenuously opposed"—to a merger and to Reform more generally; he felt KAM should not sacrifice the "Jewish Sabbath."[15]

The balance of power, as the interviews demonstrate, had clearly shifted. Sinai was now Chicago's leading Jewish congregation, drawing an audience far beyond its actual membership to its Sunday services, while KAM was struggling. KAM rather than Sinai was pushing for a merger, but no formal talks took place. Later in 1883, KAM employed Samuel Sale, an American-born radical Reformer who had studied with Hirsch at the Berlin Hochschule and moved from Baltimore's radical Reform Har Sinai Congregation to Chicago. KAM's decision for

FIGURE 4. Emil G. Hirsch, circa 1880. Courtesy of the American Jewish Archives, Cincinnati, Ohio.

a radical Reformer was clearly driven by the interests of the younger generation rather than the sensibilities of the traditionally minded founder generation. Sinai's success with its energetic young rabbi certainly was not lost on the leaders of KAM.[16]

Hirsch was endowed with a brilliant mind. As a speaker he could move audiences to tears. But he was also a proud, thin-skinned, and eccentric man. Only two years after his arrival, the thirty-year-old rabbi was accused of "popish manner" following a meeting of the Russian Refugee Committee. More than once Hirsch had to apologize in public for his behavior. The papers of the congregation contain several complaints by members about Hirsch's arrogant behavior. There is little evidence that Hirsch fostered closer personal relationships beyond his family, not even with men and women who did not cease to express their admiration for him. In contrast to his brother-in-law Kohler, who repaired the relationships with his former congregants and repeatedly returned to Sinai as a guest, Hirsch was extremely vulnerable to personal attacks and incapable of embracing his (perceived) enemies. In his memoirs, David Philipson recalls Hirsch's sarcasm and wounding irony when the recent HUC graduate and young rabbi spoke at Sinai in 1893. There can be little doubt that Hirsch's overbearing attitude betrayed deep insecurities and anxieties. In the 1880s, Hirsch did admit to his "faults"; later, as we shall see, he thought it beneath his dignity to publicly reflect on his conduct.[17]

In the fall of 1883, Hirsch provoked the first public scandal. On the occasion of Martin Luther's four hundredth birthday he was invited to deliver a memorial lecture at the Central Music Hall. At Sinai, he preached a Sunday sermon on the same topic. Hirsch praised Luther as a role model for the Reform movement. Here was a man who had almost single-handedly changed the religious landscape of Europe. Luther as a reformer had exposed and publicly condemned the abuse and open violation of the Bible's original teachings by the corrupt church apparatus and its representatives. He went beyond criticizing the church by translating the Bible into German and taking it—almost literally—to the people. Luther was a man of action. In Hirsch's words, he was "the greatest in that constellation of stars." Hirsch played down Luther's role in the Peasants' War (he had supported the princes), as well as his notorious anti-Jewish writings. The sermon met with widespread disapproval.[18]

THEOLOGY

In 1892, Hirsch characterized the theology of Sinai congregation in a German-language history of Chicago, published on the occasion of the 1893 World's Columbian Exposition. The text was addressed to Christians with little knowledge of Judaism and its history. At the outset Hirsch stated, "[Sinai] is more radical *than any other Jewish congregation in the world.*" This statement was followed by a concise definition:

> Modern Jewish Reform theology fully recognizes [the findings of] modern science, it accepts the results of biblical criticism but also in the field of natural sciences. It rejects national Jewish pretensions and defines Judaism as a historic and at the same time progressive religion which as been chosen by history to preach the highest morality as the true service to God, and to spread the belief in a moral destiny and moral freedom of man, as an exemplary model, among all mankind. It regards Judaism as a precursor, as a means to achieving the eventual unification of all mankind in *one* religion of brotherly love and virtue. This is the creed of Sinai Congregation and of *all* Reform congregations. Sinai Congregation is exceptional because it is free from romanticism and emotional confusion in pursuing this goal.[19]

Most American Reform rabbis could have underwritten this relatively general statement (except perhaps the last sentence). They regarded Judaism as a progressive religion with the mission to eventually unify all people under the wings of one overarching religion. Most Reformers opposed (proto-) Zionism, because it did not resonate well with the universal aspirations of Reform. Yet even more traditionally oriented rabbis agreed with Hirsch in one respect: Sinai Congregation was indeed the most radical Jewish congregation in America and beyond. Admittedly, for some traditional Jews, Sinai could not be considered as a Jewish congregation anymore.

Hirsch's public statements were frequently provocative. This was calculated but more than once Hirsch misjudged the reaction to his comments. Nevertheless, Hirsch intentionally promoted an image of himself as a Jewish theologian who was pushing the limits of Reform beyond what was generally regarded as acceptable. One example was frank support for cremation, a touchy issue, even for radical Reformers in the early 1880s.[20]

The most distinctive element of Hirsch's theology was the strong emphasis he placed on social action. He was very much in tune with the social gospel movement and was exchanging ideas with like-minded liberal Protestants. Hirsch often spoke about the importance of social action in the Jewish and larger community, and he constantly reminded his listeners of their moral obligation toward the weak and poor members of society. His early work for the Chicago UHRA must be seen against this background. Around 1890, Hirsch began to work with other social reformers in Chicago, especially Jane Addams, who repeatedly spoke at Sinai. He also persuaded the UHRA to adapt to the latest standards in the massively changing field of social work. For Hirsch, talk alone was not sufficient. He believed in the free will of the individual and the moral responsibility of every person to take action on behalf of people in need. This activist message helps to explain why more and more Christians began to attend Sinai on Sundays. The concepts "moral destiny," "social justice," and "duty" stood at the center of his theology and appear in most of his sermons: "Would I comprehend God in my own life and in the life of society, I should spell his name Duty." Hirsch's social theology did resonate with the teachings of ethical culture, but the lack of a religious "creed" precluded a closer cooperation. More obvious was the overlap with liberal Protestants, who had a creed and common roots. On the pulpit, Hirsch often discussed Christian theology, in particular the role of Jesus, whose ethical teachings betrayed his Jewish origins: "the Christianity of Jesus, if we grant all the gospels claim for him, is Judaism pure and simple."[21]

Quite early, Hirsch began to reach out to local Unitarians. In June 1883 he preached a Sunday sermon at the Church of the Messiah, the Unitarian congregation of Robert Collyer. In the sermon, he condemned the "fallacious theories of the modern agnosticism" (i.e., ethical culture).[22] Like ethical culture, Unitarianism was a potential competitor of radical Reform. Younger Jews, especially, if they intended to marry Protestants, were likely recruits. Sinai could look back on a long tradition of cordial and close relations with local Unitarian congregations and ministers, not least with Collyer. In fact, Hirsch was not a guest speaker in June 1883, but he preached on the occasion of a joint service of the Church of the Messiah and Sinai Congregation. The case of the St. Louis Reform rabbi Solomon Sonneschein proves why the 1883 interfaith service was truly exceptional in this period.

Repeatedly, Rabbi Sonneschein, an erstwhile critic of Kohler's Sunday services, flirted with Unitarianism and ethical culture. In 1885, the board of his Shaare Emeth congregation rebuked him because he had invited a Christian minister to the congregation's pulpit. On a Sunday in 1886, Sonneschein himself preached at a leading Unitarian congregation in Boston and met with leading Unitarians. His "apostasy" created a huge, albeit short-lived, scandal in the Jewish public. Sonneschein, a difficult man, was forced to leave Shaare Emeth, serving with a number of smaller Jewish congregations in the following years. His influence was greatly diminished. Close contacts with Unitarians were a difficult matter not only in St. Louis. Rabbi David Philipson invited a Unitarian minister to his Bene Israel pulpit in Cincinnati only a few months after his appointment in 1888. He did seek permission, but the board was hardly enthusiastic, supporting him only with a narrow margin. Sinai's board encouraged interfaith contacts much earlier than most other Reform congregations.[23]

In the early 1880s, Reformers faced not just a rising number of traditionally Jewish immigrants and ethical culture but a nascent religious movement that would position itself between traditional Judaism and Reform. The early adherents of Conservative Judaism hailed from the moderate wing of the organized Reform movement. Conservative Jews were not willing to reject Talmudic law, the traditional liturgy, Kashrut, and the observance of the Sabbath and the High Holidays. Its early leaders, the respected Philadelphia rabbi Marcus Mordecai Jastrow, Alexander Kohut of New York, and Benjamin Szold in Baltimore were attracting a growing following. The rise of Conservative Judaism was a response to radical Reform but also to the rising immigration of more traditionally minded Jews. Several Reform rabbis from the East Coast reexamined radical Reform and gave up some of their former positions. In Hirsch's view, this reaction constituted a serious error, even a betrayal of the Reform agenda.[24]

At a particularly critical moment, in early June 1885, Hirsch spoke on the occasion of his father's seventieth birthday at Keneseth Israel congregation in Philadelphia. He used the occasion for a sharp attack on Conservative and moderate Reform Jews. Hirsch's lecture was a direct response to Alexander Kohut, one of the most forceful speakers of what was then still considered the traditional wing of Reform. Kohut, a German-educated and highly articulate rabbi, had only arrived in America from his native Hungary a few weeks earlier in May 1885. Immediately after New York's Ahavath Chesed congregation, a member of the UAHC, had appointed Kohut, he launched a sharp attack against radical Reformers, accusing them of having severed the ties to historical Judaism. Kohut insisted Jewish law was divine and could not be tossed aside. Radical Reform was nothing but "Deformity." Kohler, the most prominent Reform theologian in New York, felt he had to respond to this attack and defend Einhorn's theology. Throughout May and early June, the two men indirectly debated each other from their respective pulpits, drawing large audiences. Hirsch's Philadelphia lecture echoed Kohler but, as could be expected, he was more antagonistic.

Like Einhorn (and his father) Hirsch insisted radical Reform engaged with the core principles of Judaism, while "Conservative Reformers" like Kohut (whose name he did not mention) were preoccupied with formal aspects of Judaism. Judaism, Hirsch stressed, was not rigid "law" but progressive "life," a developing religion in harmony, not in conflict with society at large. For inspiration Hirsch quoted a guiding principle of the older Hirsch, "Doings and doctrines must be harmonized!" Therefore, accusations that Reform was "destructive" missed the point. Radical Reformers were not really interested in "hats off or hats on." Rather, radical Reform was "in the highest sense *constructive*," because its followers seriously engaged with the original sources of Judaism. Conservative Reformers and Orthodox Jews, on the other hand, defined their theology on the basis of *halakha* (Jewish law) and thus risked losing touch with real Judaism. Hirsch, in typical fashion, could not resist attacking his opponents. He mocked "Conservative Reform," describing its cautious approach as "a knife without a blade and handle." His lecture culminated in a sharp rebuke: "Show your colors; and if Orthodoxy and Conservatism cannot follow, lead on, march on! Not *we* are the apostates; rather they are! apostates [*sic*] from the progressive spirit of prophetism."[25]

This rather forceful promotion of his radical Reform theology provoked widespread criticism. But Hirsch angrily dismissed "timid" critics from within the Reform movement. Congregations in the west and "Western men" like him, he declared, now represented the future of radical Reform. Unlike Kohler, Emanu-El's rabbi Gustav Gottheil, or the Conservative leaders Jastrow, Szold, and Kohut, several younger rabbis who served with midwestern congregations were open to Hirsch's message. Most of these men were immigrants, but some were native-born or had come to America at a relatively young age. A few were early graduates of Hebrew Union College. Particularly sympathetic were Joseph Krauskopf, who joined B'nai Jehudah Congregation in Kansas City in 1883, and Joseph Stolz, who succeeded Felsenthal at Zion congregation in 1887. Stolz was one of the first American-born and educated rabbis. Another native-born fellow traveler was Samuel Sale, who had studied with Hirsch in Berlin. Sale left KAM for St. Louis in 1887 to replace Sonneschein. At Shaare Emeth, Sale found a membership much more receptive to radical Reform than at KAM. Hirsch also closely worked with the brothers Isaac S. and Adolph Moses, who served Reform congregations in Milwaukee, Chicago, and Louisville. Adolph Moses replaced Hirsch at Adath Israel in Louisville while his brother Isaac was Sale's successor at KAM. The Moses brothers and Hirsch edited a German-language weekly *Der Zeitgeist* (The contemporary spirit) in the early 1880s.[26]

Hirsch's sermon, "The Antithesis between Race and Religion," preached in late 1885, was another vigorous dismissal of the views held by moderate Reform and Conservative Jews—and even by the late Einhorn. According to Hirsch, Judaism was a religion and Jews were not a race. Einhorn had opposed intermarriage, because Jews would have to remain separate as a group to complete their specific mission. Hirsch did not agree; he especially questioned the exact connection between racial exclusiveness and religion: "To maintain, that race and blood are the sponsors of Judaism, is . . . to my mind rank materialism!" He then argued on the basis of biblical and Talmudic texts that since the earliest days, Jews had married and openly accepted non-Jews into their fold: "We know that Moses—hold up your hands in horror! married a non-Hebrew woman." In his view, present Judaism was not threatened by intermarriage because it had occurred on a constant basis throughout history. For Hirsch anti-Semitism was in part a "punishment" for Jewish exclusiveness. Jews should understand and constantly redefine Judaism as a living religion rather than stick with the deterministic concept of a separate race.

The printed sermon betrays a sarcastic and confrontational tone towards his opponents but it also provides some insight into why Hirsch was effective as a speaker. He switched repeatedly between descriptive-analytical sections and sharp attacks. In one of the key parts of the sermon he did not mince any words: "For all that, we are no longer a nation and cannot be a nation. . . . We are of the purest blood! To allow any one not of that blood to enter into our families is an outrage! We are the most exclusive people on the earth! . . . What in all the world have all these things to do with Judaism! Jewish Spencer Clubs and Jewish Literary Clubs and Jewish—heaven knows what else in the shape of clubs! Everything Jewish!"[27] Many Jews, not least Reform rabbis like Kohler, described themselves in racial terms at the time, but frequently without reflecting the deeper meaning and implication of the concept. This partly explains Hirsch's opposition. With the rise of Zionism during the 1890s the debate about race entered a new phase and, as we will see, Hirsch would reexamine his earlier position.[28]

Hirsch remained true to his word. Like several other rabbis he occasionally performed marriages between Jews and Christian converts to Judaism. In 1888, he traveled all the way to New Orleans to marry a mixed couple in a Jewish ceremony. Although mixed marriages between Jews and Christians did occur regularly, it was clearly national news, as the short article in the *New York Times* indicates. The local rabbis had refused to perform the ceremony but apparently the congregation did not oppose the ceremony taking place in its temple. The *Times* summed up Hirsch's rationale. Liturgy should not stand in the way of love. "Judaism was more than a religion or a creed. . . . Judaism is a mission and a message of love and righteousness."[29] In these words, the strong ethical aspect of Hirsch's theology is expressed. The episode highlights his unequivocal position against formal obstacles and for an inclusive ethical Judaism.

Hirsch was one of its most radical and visible trailblazers of the new American

Reform rabbinate. In Chicago he developed an innovative concept of the Reform rabbinate, even of the ministry more generally. Like the evangelical preacher Dwight L. Moody or the liberal Protestant minister Hiram Thomas Hirsch, he was not interested in organized denominations. Rather, he carefully polished his image as an independent and provocative outsider in the Jewish sphere and as an intellectual pundit and social critic in the general public. To reach a wider audience, Hirsch made sure his sermons and articles were published. After *Der Zeitgeist* ceased publication in 1883, the *Occident* reprinted many of his sermons in English translation. Sinai too printed and distributed several sermons during the 1880s. Together with Kohler and Adolph Moses, Hirsch also edited the short-lived *Jewish Reformer* in the mid-1880s. Early on, Hirsch made himself a name as commentator on various topics in the general press, ranging from international politics to Jewish issues and in particular social problems. Hirsch was often the first port of call for Chicago journalists who were reporting on developments in the Jewish world. In 1889, for instance, he gave an extensive interview to the *Chicago Tribune* and the *Chicago Times* (reprinted by the *Occident*), discussing the transformation of Judaism and the meaning of Orthodox rituals. Interestingly, in this public forum he did not condemn Orthodoxy. He objectively described and explained the rituals and their meaning for Orthodox Jews.[30]

Unlike Kohler and many other Christian ministers, Hirsch could present intriguing answers to the massive changes that so visibly affected the world at large and Chicago in particular. Hirsch could explain social and cultural transformations and their complex implications in plain words. He combined sharp analysis with a theological message that resonated far beyond the actual audience, pulling in more people. Especially his calls for social responsibility and the proximity to the Christian social gospel movement met with much approval beyond Sinai. Hirsch condemned materialistic egoism. Only concerted action of like-minded individuals could bring about change for the better: "Not selfishness, but self-development is the cardinal precept of our ethics. . . . One God certainly may be translated into the phrase: One Humanity. . . . Judaism is not a philosophy of the strong, it is a philosophy of the weak."[31] Rather than discussing obscure theological subjects, Hirsch discussed the works of leading philosophers, writers, and scientists of his day—the men who interpreted and imagined the modern world. One was the contemporary German philosopher Friedrich Nietzsche. While keenly aware of the shortcomings of Nietzsche's philosophy, or rather, the different interpretations of Nietzsche's works, Hirsch clearly believed—as did many other intellectuals at the time—in the great influence of a few exceptionally talented (male) leaders on the fate of humanity. Indeed, Hirsch—not a modest man—saw himself as such an *Übermensch* who would throw open a new chapter in the history of religion and social reform in America.

Another inspiration for Hirsch's activist Reform theology was Darwinism. Older Reform theologians, notably Abraham Geiger, David Einhorn, and Isaac Mayer Wise, had rejected Darwinism, emphasizing that this theory could not be applied to humans. Kohler, recognizing the importance of Charles Darwin's *Evolution of Species* in the early 1870s, argued that Darwin's concept of evolution resonated well with the idea of Judaism as a progressive religion that adapted to its specific environment but continued to change. Hirsch took a similar approach. Of course, Hirsch perceived Darwin as an influential strongman: like Jewish Reformers, Darwin was an outsider who had convincingly crushed the "ossified belief in dogma." And, "his method taught us [Reformers] to explore new paths in the field of religion." Darwin's concept of evolution should serve as a paradigm. "Reform theology is based on the idea that religion is *constantly developing, it is for man and not for God.*" However, Hirsch knew not to take such analogies too far. In fact, it would be too short-sighted to describe Hirsch as an uncritical follower of Nietzsche. Applying Darwin's theory to human life, Hirsch clearly recognized, was dangerous. Among human beings not the physically stronger but the "morally stronger" men and women would excel.[32]

On certain key issues Hirsch remained surprisingly vague and inconsistent. He had publicly rejected atheism and agnosticism in the early 1880s, but sometimes he came rather close to Adler. In 1882, he declared God was "impersonal." But, as he explained, God was "impersonal" because he was "more than personal." Until his death, Hirsch did not clearly define his position in this matter. He never made a secret out of his conviction that humans and their actions and mutual relations mattered more than God.[33] Of course, there is a great irony in this. Hirsch, as he admitted in a private letter to Adler in 1918, actually had considered following in Adler's footsteps: "I believe the gulf between your position and mine is neither wide nor deep. Sometime[s] I regret that I did not take the step which you have. At other times I feel that you ought to have staid [*sic*] with us."[34]

ABOLISHING SATURDAY SERVICES

The long shadow of ethical culture was still looming over Sinai congregation during the mid-1880s. The Sunday issue remained unresolved—until March 1885. On the morning of March 27 of that year, the day after Sinai's annual meeting, Hirsch opened the pages of the *Occident*. He had not attended the meeting and was probably eager to learn the paper's opinion on several new reform measures discussed at the gathering. To his utter surprise, as he glanced over the various articles, Hirsch noticed a public letter by Sinai president Berthold Loewenthal to all members of the congregation. Loewenthal, known for his radical views, had recently been reelected to the presidency. The letter threw Hirsch, if we believe him, into a deep depression. Loewenthal apparently went beyond what had been discussed at the meeting and in the weeks previously. He demanded major changes to Sinai's service and liturgy that, once more, echoed the ideas of Felix Adler. The content was truly explosive, betraying the strong antiritualistic beliefs of Sinai's more radically minded members. But this was not the cause for Hirsch's irritation and disappointment. Rather, Loewenthal had never discussed these plans with the rabbi. Loewenthal wrote:

> Our prosperous condition, financial as well as otherwise, may lead many of you to think that we have reached the climax of modern reform .... To be sure, we have discarded many obsolete rites ... [and] have succeeded in convincing at least some of our orthodox brethren that we have not done this ... for the purpose of hiding our identity as Jews. ... Our work will not be completed until we have removed every unnecessary vestige, until we have built upon the old foundation a new structure, in keeping with the modern style of religious architecture, in the creation of which science has assisted.

For Loewenthal, prayers had become a hollow ritual, reminiscent of "Chinese prayer machines." "All Hebrew readings and prayers" should be abolished. Likewise, Sinai should reject circumcision, that "*disgusting relic of barbarism*," as prerequisite for membership in Sinai. According to Sinai's founding documents, circumcision was not a formal requirement for membership, but Loewenthal aimed for an explicit rejection of this ritual. He went even further by touching on the sensitive Sunday question. Not only did he call for the transfer of Saturday services to Sunday, provoking the ire of some Sinai members, he also wanted to transfer all High Holiday services to the following Sunday. Loewenthal was fully aware of the implications of his letter: "The influence of Sinai Congregation in creating and fostering a progressive and enlightened Judaism reaches far beyond the walls of our Temple. Our every step is watched."[35]

After several days, Hirsch wrote Loewenthal, hinting at a serious communication problem: "The right inherent in my position to be consulted on such measure—a right guaranteed by the constitution—might, <u>unintentionally</u>, be overlooked. I must say that I am surprised." He then commented on Loewenthal's suggestions, supporting some, rejecting others. On the following day, Hirsch sent two more letters to Loewenthal. In the first he tried to appease the president, but in the second letter he did not hide his anger and disappointment. "I do not remember of ever having spent days of greater mental misery, than the last were." It would have been better to exchange "an open word." On the following day, Loewenthal apologized. He was not happy about Hirsch's criticism but had "no personal feelings."[36] None of this became public. Sinai did however publish the proceedings of a special meeting of the congregation on April 9, 1885. Hirsch approved Loewenthal's agenda with one exception. He agreed to disregard circumcision, abolish Hebrew prayers, and discontinue Saturday services: "The old Jewish Sabbath is dead. To successfully revive it, seclusion on the part of the Jews from the outer world in a new Ghetto would be the price. We cannot afford to pay that price." While the Sabbath was universal, the High Holidays were Jewish. These days were crucial "symbols of historical associations" that still "appeal with old fervor." Hirsch was *unequivocally opposed* to a transfer of the High Holidays. With this step, the congregation would break with Judaism.

The congregation and board accepted Hirsch's position in a seemingly subservient manner. At least symbolically, Hirsch's authority was restored: "Resolved as follows: Owing to the arduous labors devolving on our Worthy Minister, Dr. E. G. Hirsch, this Congregation hereby resolves to relieve him from preaching on Saturdays."[37] In reality, as the confidential minutes of this meeting show, intense discussions preceded this decision. Initially, a majority of the forty-three participating members voted against abolishing Saturday services. Only after Loewenthal intervened did the motion pass with twenty-eight to fifteen votes.[38] The long-term impact of this incident should not be underestimated. Hirsch must have decided not to allow similar digressions by the board in the future.

Perhaps to avoid an open row with the supporters of the Saturday Sabbath, Saturday services were not immediately discontinued. But attendance was lagging. Finally, in December 1885, Hirsch stopped preaching on Saturdays. In his report for the annual meeting in 1886 he stated his position quite bluntly: "The rabbi, Sexton and choir and Janitor never failed to be in attendance ready to perform their duties. But—no one came. . . . Those that wish to have a Saturday service must attend personally to have it. I cannot keep *their* Sabbath for them. . . . My salary warrants no hiring of a Minyan to keep up a pretense."[39]

Hirsch is widely portrayed as the most radical (Reform) rabbi of his time, and as a man who was the driving force behind Sinai's extremely radical Reform agenda. In reality, as the internal discussion about Saturday services proves, it was Hirsch who acted as a restraining force within the congregation. He was holding back the president and very likely a majority within the congregation from pursuing an even more radical course. Even though he regarded the Saturday Sabbath as "dead," he continued to preach on Saturdays, until even its supporters stopped attending. In fact, as Kohler points out in his obituary of Hirsch, after 1885, Sinai's rabbi still regularly preached on Saturdays at other Chicago congregations. Hirsch's emphasis on his personal beliefs and his willingness to tolerate members with differing views, ranging from supporters of the Saturday Sabbath to atheists, strengthened his position. Later in 1885, Hirsch emphasized Sinai was inclusive but still not where he wanted the congregation to be: "We have people here in this congregation, I presume—I have never inquired into any member's belief—who call themselves agnostics—also we have *perhaps* . . . atheists. We have pantheists, and theists, and others. Whoever objects to their coming?—We have a crazy quilt[,] beliefs and unbeliefs [*sic*], and still held together by one common purpose, but *no creed*!" Hirsch called on the members not to accept Judaism as a fixed entity but to actively shape Judaism through ethical action and thus grasp its meaning as a progressive religion.[40]

The reforms Hirsch sanctioned still constituted radical steps. With the exception of the Berlin Reform congregation, no other Jewish congregation had abolished Saturday services. Instead of moving toward the mainstream, Sinai was pushing the limits of Reform even further. But Hirsch's public refusal to transfer the High Holidays illustrates that at least with him in the pulpit, Sinai would remain a Jewish congregation.

Hirsch's rising star and his social agenda explain why the influence of ethical culture in Chicago remained limited. According to the remaining files of the Chicago Ethical Humanist Society, only few members had Jewish backgrounds, unlike in New York. Julius Rosenthal, who had made no secret of his support for Adler, joined in 1883 but did not relinquish his Sinai membership. Adler came repeatedly to Chicago during the 1880s, mobilizing many younger Jews across the city. But this had no effect on the membership of the local society. The lack of an engaging leader of like Adler and the presence of Hirsch doomed what might have become a serious challenge for Sinai congregation. Not more than a hundred members and their families listened to the Sunday lectures of its preacher, William Mackintire Salter. As a speaker, he was no match for Hirsch, and it appears after the mid-1880s many more Christians and Jews went to Sinai's temple to listen to Hirsch's sermons.[41]

Counter to expectations, the increasingly radical agenda of Sinai's board and rabbi did not add to the relative isolation of the congregation. The rise of the second generation changed the outlook of many Jewish congregations in America. New board members and rabbis were more open to radical Reform than their predecessors. Especially in other western cities, as mentioned above, Sinai's message did not fall on deaf ears after 1880. Western Jews had been open-minded about Reform early on, partly because the influence—indeed, the presence—of more traditional Jews was limited. And before the 1890s, the rising immigration of Jews from eastern Europe affected New York and Philadelphia much more strongly than it did western cities. In the mid-1880s, a number of Jewish congregations were discussing and even experimenting with Sunday services or lectures. Tifereth Israel (known as the Temple) in Cleveland, Shaare Emeth in St. Louis, Adath Israel in Louisville, Beth El in Detroit, but also, further east, Keneseth Israel in Philadelphia, Har Sinai in Baltimore, and Adath Israel in Boston introduced Sunday services or lectures before 1890, as did Zion congregation and the North Side Hebrew congregation in Chicago. Emanu-El in San Francisco experimented with Sunday services in the mid-1880s. At some congregations members opposed Sunday services. HUC graduate David Philipson, who joined Cincinnati Reform congregation Bene Israel in 1888, was in favor of Sunday services. Yet before the turn of the century, the members foiled Philipson's repeated attempts to introduce Sunday services. A powerful force behind the scenes was Isaac Mayer Wise, who enjoyed much respect among the members of Bene Israel and was a strong opponent of Sunday services. Only after Wise passed away in 1900 and when Philipson had gained the respect of his congregants could he introduce Sunday lectures in 1909. Sinai, as the board minutes indicate, followed these developments. When Rabbi Aaron Hahn introduced Sunday services at Tifereth Israel in 1888, critics and supporters both referred to Hirsch and Sinai in the rather heated discussion.[42]

Michael A. Meyer has characterized the period between the 1880s and 1920s as "Classical Reform Judaism." Leading Reformers were mapping a path between universalism and even indifference on one side and the traditional Judaism of the immigrants from Eastern Europe on the other.[43] The decisive founding event, characterized by Isaac Mayer Wise poignantly as Reform's "Declaration of Independence," was the Pittsburgh Platform. In the early fall of 1885, several leading Reform rabbis received a call by Kaufmann Kohler to agree on a constitution of the Reform movement at a meeting in Pittsburgh in mid-November. The clash with Alexander Kohut in May and June 1885 had been the last straw for Kohler. Before sending out invitations, he discussed his plan with Samuel Hirsch and Isaac Mayer Wise. At this point, the conflict between the followers of Einhorn and Wise had died down. The passing of Einhorn in 1879 eased the simmering tensions, and most radical Reformers began to accept the UAHC as the loose umbrella institution under Wise's formal leadership. In return, Wise yielded the theological platform almost literally to Kohler—and Hirsch. The Cincinnati rabbi formally chaired the Pittsburgh meeting, but the eventual text owed much to the theology of his erstwhile antagonist Einhorn. "Western" rabbis who were more open to radical Reforms such as Sunday services were over-represented among the participants. At Pittsburgh, Einhorn's two sons-in-law formally claimed the mantle as theologians of the American Reform movement. Kohler was the convener and he had written the first outline of the platform. His first draft reiterated, in a nutshell, the key positions of Einhorn's theology. Emil G. Hirsch contributed the eighth and last paragraph of the Pittsburgh Platform: "We deem it our duty to participate in the great task of modern times, to solve, on the basis of justice and righteousness, the problems presented by the contrasts and evils of the present organization of society."[44] In Hirsch's view, the social tradition of Judaism constituted a great potential to address the burning social question in America. The strengthening of Jewish *Gemeinschaft* and of social bonds more generally, especially on the basis of a (privately run) professional and progressive welfare system, would be a powerful repudiation of anti-Semitic stereotypes. "It was high time, he [Hirsch] said, for the Hebrews to take a stand against the prevailing sentiment that the Hebrews as a class were merely migratory in disposition and were money-makers, possessing neither moral nor social influence in the community. It was time to correct that impression."[45]

Shortly after the conference, Julius Rosenthal emphasized in a newspaper interview that Hirsch cared primarily about the eighth paragraph; the rest was trivial in his eyes. Sinai congregation was far too radical to bow to the constitution.[46] The proceedings of the conference lend support to this view. During the meeting Hirsch argued (unsuccessfully) to open Judaism for proselytes and openly compete with ethical culture and Unitarianism: "Let us remove that barrier! There are many beyond the lines nearer to us than others born within the lines, men who share our ethical monotheism and would gladly join us in the fulfillment of our historic mission." Calling for the acceptance of proselytes was a far-reaching demand. It clearly proves how close he stood to Felix Adler. As could be expected, Hirsch promoted Sunday services and defended Sinai against the many critics among more moderate Reformers: "Are we in Chicago Christians for our Sunday services?" Only Samuel Sale, who did not preach on Sundays at KAM, defended Hirsch in this matter, declaring the usefulness of Sunday services in this "irreligious age." The rabbis eventually reached a compromise, a partial victory for Hirsch and Sinai. All rabbis recognized the historical Sabbath, but they did not formally reject Sunday services. As all were preparing to leave Pittsburgh, Hirsch could not resist a provocative parting shot, "Uniformity and unity are to my mind two different things." Even though the Conservative Reformers broke away from Reform after Pittsburgh, Sinai was one of very few Reform congregations that did not join the UAHC. Sinai was committed to the unity of Reform Judaism, but it considered itself as a fully sovereign congregation that would not bow to any theological regulations or constraints from outside institutions, a conviction that owed much to the origins of the congregation.[47]

HAYMARKET

On May 16, 1886, Sinai celebrated the twenty-fifth anniversary of its founding with a special service. The guest of honor was Samuel Hirsch. He was joined by Kaufmann Kohler, Bernhard Felsenthal, Liebmann Adler, and Samuel Sale. During a splendid banquet in the halls of the Standard Club, prominent founding members of Sinai gave short speeches followed by a toast. Sinai's first president, Benjamin Schönemann, presented reminiscences of the early days of the congregation. Berthold Loewenthal's brief address illustrated the confidence and pride of Sinai's lay leaders: "Sinai Congregation is today recognized and usually denounced as the most radical reform congregation in America, if not on the face of the globe. We are proud of the distinction of being the best abused congregation on this continent, that of itself would be sufficient cause for celebration." Kohler, in contrast, was an isolated voice of caution, representing the Reform mainstream; he warned the congregation not to go "too far" with its Reform project. Joseph Gatzert, the new president, stressed the theme of unity. He paid special tribute to Emil G. Hirsch for the wide appeal of his Sunday lectures. Thanks to him, Sinai had become a truly "*United*" Congregation." Most of the persons present recalled only too vividly the struggles over the Sunday issue in the past decade.[48]

The celebration of Sinai's radical legacy occurred in one of the most critical moments in Chicago's history. As Sinai's members and their guests were raising their glasses and exchanging toasts on the evening of May 16, the Chicago police conducted a notorious witch hunt on the streets outside of the Standard Club quarters. The report of Sinai's anniversary in the *Occident* makes no mention of the dramatic events, and the minutes of Sinai's board are also silent, although most participants were deeply worried about the future and their personal safety.

On May 1, two weeks before Sinai's celebration, a violent clash with the police at one of Chicago's biggest employers, McCormick Reaper Works, had claimed the lives of several striking workers. On the evening of May 4, workers held a large protest meeting at Haymarket Square. It has never been established who threw a bomb that claimed the lives of several policemen who were dispersing the crowd. Although the police shot and killed dozens of workers in the immediate aftermath, the press and public opinion were outraged over the actions of radical anarchists. A specific issue was the foreign background of several of the leading activists. On the day after the fatal Haymarket riots, groups of Jewish immigrant protesters calling for better working conditions in the sweatshops clashed with the police in the center of Chicago. The response of the city and the federal government was ferocious. Hundreds were arrested. Eight men (six were German-born immigrants) were indicted and subjected to a hastily organized and grossly unfair trial. Seven alleged ringleaders were sentenced to death.

Fears over the rising power of organized labor and xenophobia were the major driving forces behind the strong reaction by the public and the authorities to the Haymarket events. In the early 1880s, America was in the midst of a massive and uneven transformation to an urban industrial society. Haymarket seemed to prove widely held fears that the mass immigration of poor foreigners was undermining America. Not quite coincidentally, several of the most aggressive anti-immigrant commentators and police officials (notably cartoonist Thomas Nast and Chicago police officer Michael Schaack) were themselves immigrants from central Europe. Shortly before the scheduled execution in November 1887, only few voices apart from organized labor questioned the fairness of the trial and called for clemency, at least a commutation of the death sentence. In the pulpit of Beth El in New York, Kaufmann Kohler urged to fight anarchism with all necessary means; the anarchists had to be "hanged for the good of society," as the *Inter Ocean* summarized his sermon. Kohler did not just speak for his well-to-do congregants but expressed the views of the urban American middle class at large who feared a socialist revolution. From many other pulpits in Chicago, a similar message was preached. The execution symbolized the last line of control; the anarchists had to be executed to set a sign against the rising urban chaos. Even religious leaders who had expressed sincere concern about of the depressing situation of the working classes supported the executions. A prominent example was the moderate Unitarian minister Robert Collyer, who had moved to a New York pulpit shortly after Kohler. He refused to sign a petition asking for clemency for the convicted anarchists. Emil G. Hirsch, however, was no conformist.

On a first glance it appears as if Sinai's leaders and its rabbi ignored the Haymarket events. But Hirsch differed from Kohler and many older rabbis, as well as Christian ministers, by taking a clear stand on the social question. His response to the Haymarket affair is a remarkable example of his serious commitment to his social agenda. Together with Julius Rosenthal, Hirsch drew up an influential petition asking the governor of Illinois for clemency for the convicted anarchists. A prominent signer was the publicly minded Chicago banker Lyman Gage. Speaking up against the execution of the Haymarket anarchists—in an extremely frenzied situation—required courage, especially in Chicago, and especially if the petitioners were Jewish and known to be prominent Germans. Rosenthal had long been one of the most active members in various German associations. And Hirsch had quickly been accepted as a leading intellectual representative of the large and heterogeneous German community. Admittedly, more than a few prominent Chicago businessmen signed clemency petitions only because they worried the executions would spark riots across the nation and turn the executed anarchists into martyrs of a still heterogeneous and actually weak movement.[49]

Unfortunately, the exact motives of Hirsch and Rosenthal remain unclear. But Hirsch must have realized early on that the execution would not solve but exacerbate the divisions and would do nothing to address the obvious plight of the working class. Hirsch and Rosenthal were on good personal terms with Ernst Schmidt, a renowned Chicago socialist who publicly spoke up for the Chicago anarchists in 1886–1887. After coming to America as a political refugee from Germany following the failed 1848–1849 revolution, Schmidt had been appointed as head physician at the first Jewish hospital in Chicago in the late 1860s. In these days, perhaps even earlier, he befriended Julius Rosenthal and several other members of the Jewish community. During the 1870s and 1880s, Schmidt became a powerful voice on the left-wing spectrum in Chicago. In 1886, he organized a fundraising drive for the defense of the accused anarchists and condemned the apparent injustice. This truly Nietzschean figure must have immediately impressed Hirsch when he first met him. Schmidt was a sincere and fearless social critic, an excellent physician, a highly educated German, and most importantly, a charismatic man of action who knowingly risked arrest or worse in his support for the anarchists and the urban underclass. Suffice to say, Schmidt (like Hirsch) was opposed to violence and anarchism. He did not condone the actions the anarchists were accused of. When he died in 1900,

Hirsch paid respect to his brave and uncompromising stance on behalf of the weak. This compassionate and "noble man" disproved Nietzsche's concept of the egoistic *Übermensch*: "Dr. Ernst Schmidt was the living refutation of the theory that selfishness is necessarily the keynote to strongmen's lives. . . . He defended the 'anarchists' and befriended their families at a time when passions ran high and even the kindest of men were afraid to act in behalf of innocent victims."[50] Hirsch's courageous engagement for the anarchists and indirectly for disadvantaged masses must have deeply unsettled some Sinai members but it certainly won him many sympathies among the Jewish immigrant workers and critics of the social divisions in the city.

7.

ON OCTOBER 9, 1897, Emil Hirsch gave one of his widely noticed public addresses. The *Chicago Tribune* article carried the eponymous headline, "Dr. Emil G. Hirsch speaks." On this day, Hirsch, in his role as outgoing head of the Chicago Public Library board, oversaw the dedication of a splendid new library building on the corner of Michigan Avenue and Randolph Street. In 1897, Sinai congregation could look back on a particularly close relationship to the library. From its founding in 1872, at least one member of the library board belonged to Sinai congregation. Julius Rosenthal was a member of the founding board. Sinai's longtime president, Berthold Loewenthal, was a board member throughout the 1870s and early 1880s. The Chicago Public Library symbolized *Bildung* more than any other public institution in the city and thus deserved special support. The dedication of the new building was a special moment for most Sinai members.[1]

Hundreds of official guests filled the room. Outside a crowd of thousands had assembled. The *Tribune* noted, "The people who will derive most good from the building . . . were on the outside importuning for admittance." As Sinai's rabbi stepped to the rostrum, he faced the city's establishment in the front rows, the leading local politicians, the governor, and businessmen, such as Philipp D.

Armour. Several close collaborators of Hirsch were present: Jane Addams, Unitarian minister Jenkin Lloyd Jones, and William Rainey Harper, the president of the newly founded University of Chicago. Another attendee was John Dewey. The young philosopher had come to the University of Chicago as head of the philosophy department in 1894. Like Hirsch and Jones, he belonged to the circle of Jane Addams at Hull House.

Even in print the power of Hirsch's speech still resonates: "Chicago, synonym of energy and industries, push and ambition—Chicago, swarming hive of restless millions, of many languages and many hearts, but one loyalty and love, owns no title of distinction more legitimate or lustrous than its possession of this grand, its own, public library." This civilizing institution would create unity in the diverse metropolis and offer every citizen, young or old, the possibility of self-education. In short, the library was, as he put it, the "People's University." The Chicago Public Library was a powerful expression of the universal and optimistic message so dear to Sinai congregation and so well in tune with the American ideals.[2]

Hirsch's address was impressive, as was his enthusiasm for social causes in Chicago and his desire to engage Sinai Congregation and the many men and women present at the 1897 celebration in those causes. Yet, in hindsight, the scenery appears odd. As the promoters and donors celebrated inside, the mostly blue-collar Chicagoans for whom the library was designed remained outside. This chapter will examine the causes and implications of the divisions between the established and the disadvantaged in Chicago. Sinai showed an impressive engagement for Chicagoans in need, especially for recently arrived Jewish immigrants. Yet even though genuine and remarkable in its reach, this engagement had much more to do with the visions and self-perception of the sponsors than with the actual needs and circumstances of the recipients.

SINAI AND THE ORGANIZED JEWISH COMMUNITY

At no time did the increasingly radical Reform agenda loosen Sinai's ties to the organized Jewish community in Chicago. Since its earliest days, Sinai and the other larger Jewish congregations in Chicago were affiliated with the United Hebrew Relief Association, the institutional anchor of the Jewish community. Sinai's leaders and members took the commitment for the Jewish community seriously, in large part because they felt responsible for the split in the religious sphere. Even before its delegate count surpassed that of KAM during the 1880s, Sinai was the single most influential member of the UHRA. Most of Sinai's board members and presidents served on UHRA committees between 1861 and the 1920s. In some years, for instance, in 1867, the UHRA board was made up exclusively of Sinai members. The first rabbi who joined the UHRA board in the mid-1880s was Emil G. Hirsch. No other Jewish congregation in Chicago showed a similar level of dedication. Sinai founder Henry Greenebaum served as first UHRA president in 1859–1860. Of his nine successors until 1900, five were members of Sinai (Godfrey Snydacker, Isaac Greensfelder, Berthold Loewenthal, Abraham Hart, and Charles Kozminski); three belonged to KAM, and one to the North Side Hebrew congregation (the forerunner of Temple Sholom). None served longer than the "Dean of Jewish Charities," Isaac Greensfelder. The longtime Sinai board member occupied the UHRA president's chair for seven years (with interruptions) in the 1860s and again for a remarkable twenty-two years from 1877 to 1899. The self-made owner of a large wholesale shoe business (the mother business of the Florsheim Shoe Company) spent much time and his personal money on the UHRA.[3]

Hirsch provided Sinai with the theological justification for social action. He tirelessly promoted the centrality of "duty" toward society, especially to its weakest members, urging Sinai's members and the listeners and readers of his

FIGURE 5. Isaac Greensfelder, circa 1900. From the Michael Reese Hospital Collection, Chicago Jewish Archives. Courtesy of the Spertus Institute of Jewish Studies.

CHAPTER SEVEN

sermons to become actively involved and help people in need. Indeed, individual members of Sinai not only raised funds for the UHRA, but several designed and managed innovative projects for recently arrived Jewish immigrants from eastern Europe. Frequently, non-Jewish social reformers like Jane Addams participated during the planning stages. Yet in contrast to Hull House, Sinai targeted primarily Jews.

How can the combination between a universal theology and the engagement for other Jews after 1880 be explained? Obviously, sharply increasing Jewish immigration forced established Jews to respond. Most feared what would happen to their hard-won social status if poor Jews became a public charge or accepted Christian aid. But another aspect should not be overlooked. Apart from contacts in the workplace and civic forums, the members of Sinai still lived in an almost exclusively Jewish sphere. This also applied to married women, who were not employed and stayed at home. Intermarriage and conversion to Christianity remained rare. Yaakov Ariel has drawn attention to the social "paradox" of Reform Judaism, the seeming contradiction between the universal rhetoric of radical Reform Judaism and the tribal "reality of Reform life" before the 1950s. Jewish communities, especially in large cities, offered so many opportunities to socialize that few Jews felt the need to fully "assimilate" to a Protestant environment. A conversion would have entailed a more or less complete departure from the Jewish social sphere.[4]

The appeal of Jewish sociability, rather than anti-Jewish discrimination, also explains the role of the Standard Club. Since its founding in 1869, the club served as informal social space for most Sinai members. Family celebrations, especially weddings, usually took place in the club quarters. Before the 1890s, Jewish businessmen seem to have experienced little informal, let alone explicit discrimination in Chicago. Several leading Sinai members like Julius Rosenthal belonged to other private clubs in Chicago, such as the Union League Club.[5]

The rise of the Young Men's Hebrew Association is another indicator of a vibrant Jewish life. After 1880, the YMHA continued to attract more members and, along with Sinai, increased its influence within the UHRA. In addition to organizing smaller social events, the Chicago YMHA chapters regularly staged spectacular fundraisers. The grand 1882 annual charity ball attracted almost three thousand Chicago Jews and netted a considerable $25,000 for the UHRA. The description of the fine-looking dresses worn by the female attendees covered almost a whole page of the *Occident*. It was indeed a splendid affair: "In front of the main door was a miniature lawn, in the centre of which was an immense pink azalea tree. Around this were the letters forming the word 'Charity' in pink flowers. . . . At the east end of the hall . . . were 'Rebeccas', dressed in fanciful costumes, who served out lemonade to the thirsty. . . . In the corners were statues of Göthe [*sic*] and Schiller."[6] This display combined the Jewish tradition of *tzedakah* with sociability and fun. The statues of the two famous German writers—at an explicitly *Jewish*, not German event—illustrate the lingering importance of the universal *Bildung* ideal, even among younger American-born Jews. The expansion of the YMHA—this was certainly not lost on the leaders of Sinai and the other congregations—exposed the inability of congregations to offer social activities for younger women and men under the roofs of synagogues and temples.

Sinai expanded its influence over the Jewish community in another sphere. In 1891, the congregation provided the funds for a weekly newspaper. As the editor, Hirsch could address a much larger audience in and beyond Chicago. The *Reform Advocate* soon emerged as the quasi-official community paper as well as an influential voice of the radical Reform movement in America. Other Reform rabbis, such as Jacob Voorsanger in San Francisco or Max Heller in New Orleans, also edited weekly papers, which combined articles on their respective theological agenda with news about their local Jewish communities and the Jewish world. This illustrates a shift. The scholar-rabbis of the 1860s and 1870s, whose sphere of influence did not really extend beyond their respective congregations and an international academic Diaspora were replaced by men who acted as brokers within and between Jewish communities and society. Early role models were *Occident* editor Isaac Leeser and, of course, Isaac Mayer Wise. Hirsch, however, explicitly addressed non-Jewish readers by opening the *Advocate* (and Sinai's pulpit) for Progressive reformers and liberal Protestants. Indeed, Hirsch became the widely accepted informal speaker of the established Jewish community in Chicago. Nevertheless, the *Reform Advocate* primarily represented the views of the Jewish establishment. Even before 1890, several Yiddish papers began to serve the new Jewish immigrants in Chicago. One of the most influential papers, *Der Taeglicher Idisher Kuryer* (Daily Jewish Courier), had been appearing daily since 1887—a powerful demonstration of the scale of the immigration to Chicago.[7]

SINAI AND OTHER PROGRESSIVES

Hirsch and several younger members of Sinai were among the pioneering and most influential spokesmen of the Progressive movement in Chicago. The Progressives comprised semiprofessional, initially frequently self-taught social workers (women and men), investigative journalists, reform-oriented politicians, academics, and religious leaders. Most were Protestants, but their primary goal transcended religion in a narrow sense. The advocates of this broad and diverse movement demanded more social justice for all Americans. Christian Progressives happily embraced members of Adler's Ethical Culture Society and Reform Jews whose universal agenda resonated with their broader cause.[8]

The projects Sinai's members developed echoed these ideas. Progressives relied strongly on expert knowledge. Highly trained professionals were put in charge, rather than wealthy donors and inexperienced volunteers. They conducted detailed research into the causes of poverty and other social ills, stressing the need for prevention. The emphasis on self-help and education also appealed to Reform Jews. And finally, Progressive reformers favored decentralization. Rather than asking them to come to a central office, the poor were targeted in their neighborhoods, even in their homes.[9]

Jews made significant contributions to the Progressive movement throughout America. This was hardly a coincidence. Welfare organizations formed the backbone of Jewish communities and were affected by rising Jewish immigration already in the early 1870s. Earlier than other Americans, Jewish community leaders began to rethink traditional approaches to helping poor Jews. In 1882, Sinai congregation opened an innovative school for Jewish immigrant girls. In 1884, the UHRA set up an employment agency to help immigrants find work, and it coordinated its activities with its sister societies in other American cities. The UHRA workers began to visit applicants for aid, providing advice and collecting and assessing information in order to improve the living conditions of poor Jews. Traditional paternalism often went hand in hand with genuine concern, for instance, for immigrant women who had been deserted by their husbands. The UHRA also managed the Jewish hospital, which had reopened its doors in 1881. The new hospital was named after Michael Reese, a San Francisco Jew who left his Chicago relatives a large sum for philanthropic causes. Michael Reese Hospital quickly became one of the most advanced in Chicago. In 1890, a ward for children and a training school for nurses were added. In 1888, the UHRA changed its name to United Hebrew Charities (UHC), in part to express the more professional and "scientific" approach to overcoming poverty.[10]

In the early 1890s, the number of Jewish immigrants in Chicago increased significantly. In 1893, a recession hit the UHC hard. Its expenditures reached record levels just as donations were drying up. A crucial figure in this critical period was its main manager, Julian Mack. Together with Julius Rosenwald, Hannah Solomon, and Sadie American, the Harvard Law School graduate belonged to a group of younger Sinai members who were influenced by Hirsch during the 1880s and became advocates of social justice in their own right. In 1894, Mack helped to steer the UHC through the most difficult period in its history. The rise of several competing philanthropic institutions—the Jewish Training School, the Maxwell Street Settlement, and the Home for Aged Jews—drained the UHC of urgently needed funds. In 1898–1899, Mack, Greensfelder, Hirsch, and other UHC leaders engineered a massive reorganization of Jewish philanthropy by bringing these new institutions under the umbrella of the new Associated Jewish Charities. They secured a donation of $75,000 from the Young Men's Hebrew Charity Association to overcome another budget shortfall.[11]

Hirsch was an influential driving force behind the modernization of the UHC during the 1880s and 1890s. He encouraged younger Sinai members to participate in social projects, and he convinced wealthier congregants like department store owner Leon Mandel to make generous donations to projects administered by experts. His sermons attracted new recruits. He and several Sinai members helped to build bridges to other philanthropic organizations, notably to the Hull House settlement, which was founded in 1889 and soon gained wide recognition throughout America and beyond. Hull House was an obvious partner for the established Jews, because it was secular. Well-educated younger women and men moved to the Hull House building in the heart of the West Side immigrant neighborhood. The settlement residents were available day and night, serving as bourgeois role models for their neighbors. The settlements offered a variety of evening classes, as well as social entertainment. Hull House was designed as a socio-cultural neighborhood center to educate children, women, and men and to contain threatening immoral influences and vice. Like Hirsch and other likeminded reformers, Hull House founder Jane Addams uneasily watched the growing division between rich and poor and the rise of unrestrained individualism and capitalism in the rapidly expanding American cities. What she called "the better element"—men and women like her, educated and materially secure—had the obligation to overcome these divisions, improve the lives of the poor, and bring about social justice. Hull House also served as a gateway to research the causes of poverty in inner-city neighborhoods. The settlement cooperated with the sociology department at the University of Chicago. Hirsch, Mack, and later Julius Rosenwald—this is ignored by most biographers of Jane Addams—belonged to a circle of Progressive reformers who often met with Addams and Hull House residents.

Hull House constituted a departure from rigid moralistic concepts, which blamed the poor for their own misery. Addams frequently acknowledged the limited opportunities for the urban working class, but her approach (and that of many other Progressive reformers) suffered from a blind spot: most inhabitants of the West Side were indeed working class and poor, but they were also recently arrived immigrants. Addams had spent several months at the pioneering Toyn-bee Hall settlement in London's East End in 1887, an area overflowing with Irish and Jewish immigrants, but she and her coworkers were not sufficiently prepared for the diverse cultural (and religious) backgrounds of the women and men they encountered in Chicago.[12]

In its first years, Hull House struggled to connect with the immigrants who showed little interest in its highbrow cultural programs, which owed more to the aspirations of the rather elevated American sponsors rather than to the social needs and interests of hardworking blue-collar immigrants who spoke little or no English and hailed from rural areas in different parts of Europe. The short-comings of the Hull House agenda in its early years are illustrated by a settlement that was managed by Jewish community leaders. In November 1893, Hirsch and other Jewish social reformers, advised by Addams, launched the Maxwell Street Settlement. Several young Jewish women and men, led by Sinai members Jacob Abt and Sadie American, moved to the heart of the Jewish immigrant neighbor-hood to "uplift" their new neighbors. Yet only individual immigrants showed serious interest in the archetypical *Bildung* canon offered by the settlement: Ger-man and Latin classes and courses about the English novel found few takers. Only the programs for children seem to have been successful. A young Jewish immigrant later depicted the settlement as "extremely unpopular" and "patron-izing . . . to an extent which bordered on insult." Progressive "experts" frequently were constrained by a stereotypical perception of the people they wanted to support.[13]

Like Hull House, Sinai bonded with another institution with Progressive cre-dentials: the University of Chicago. After a predecessor institution had folded during the 1880s, several donations by John D. Rockefeller relaunched the uni-versity in 1891–1892. Rockefeller was initially drawn to the university project be-cause of its Baptist credentials. Early on, the support by non-Baptist Protestants and Jews helped to give the private institution a nondenominational outlook. In the critical founding phase, members of Sinai donated generously. At an 1890 meeting at the Standard Club, Hirsch and former Sinai president Loewenthal led a fundraising drive that netted $27,000. Following the successful model of The Johns Hopkins University, the University of Chicago was conceived as a combination between an American liberal arts college and a cutting-edge Ger-man research university.

In 1893, Sinai congregation raised $5,000 for a Semitic library, named Sinai Library. Individual Sinai members later gave thousands of books to the library, which became part of the university's Oriental Institute in 1931. Several members, especially Leon Mandel and, after the turn of century, Julius Rosenwald, contributed large sums to the University of Chicago. To protect the interests of its Jewish donors, the university appointed Sinai member Eli B. Felsenthal to its first board of trustees. In 1902, president William Rainey Harper praised the "Jews of Chicago" for their generosity in the difficult founding phase. Emil Hirsch's appointment as professor of Semitics in 1892, however, should not be seen as a reward for Jewish generosity. His thorough academic training at a German research university—he was fluent in several Semitic languages—and his rising reputation as public intellectual and reformer in Chicago made him an ideal candidate to help building a Semitics department. Hirsch happily accepted the position because it added to his cachet. Through the appointment Hirsch established a close relationship with several professors, notably with Harper who also served as the first head of the Department of Semitic Languages and Literatures.[14]

In 1901, Hirsch summed up the intention and broader implication of Jewish engagement for social causes in Chicago:

> In certain ways the Jews of Chicago may claim the credit of having been among the first to inaugurate the better methods according to the truer standard of the new philanthropy in the dispensation of relief or the provision for the education of the young. . . . The Jews of this city can proudly point to the fact that they were the first to bring about systematic co-operation among the various agencies for the administration of the charities.[15]

Hirsch claimed, convincingly, that the federated structure of the UHRA served as a model for coordinating the work of various social institutions in Chicago. An institution that was organized along similar lines was the Chicago Civic Federation. At the height of the severe 1893 recession, Hirsch, Jane Addams, the publicly minded banker Lyman Gage, the University of Chicago sociologist Albion Small, and one of the wealthiest Chicagoans, philanthropist Mrs. Potter Palmer, formed the Committee of Fifteen to establish the federation. Gage, who had risen from a clerk in a lumberyard to the chief executive of the First National Bank of Chicago, was elected as president. This exemplary Progressive body addressed social and economic problems in Chicago. It partly echoed the moral crusades of earlier decades by supporting drives against drinking and gambling as well as cleaning the streets of trash. But the Chicago Civic Federation aimed at coordinating the work of various privately run social institutions, and to find quick solutions in times of crisis. Hirsch and Addams wielded great influence within the federation, acting as mediators between wealthy and publicly committed businessmen and people or institutions in need of support. The federation was particularly critical of political corruption and bad government. In 1894, Hirsch gave a forceful address calling for a separation of the police force from the corrupt political apparatus. When Gage accepted an appointment as secretary of the treasury in the McKinley administration in 1897, businessman and Sinai board member Adolph Nathan became his successor.[16]

Progressive institutions like the Chicago Civic Federation and Hull House had worthy goals and some notable achievements to their name. Yet they were also elitist, reflecting underlying fears of social chaos and the big city, associated with immigration and proletarian masses. It was of course an irony that the very same people whose wealth depended in no small part on cheap immigrant labor were uneasy about the consequences of mass immigration and urban growth. Neither Jane Addams, Emil G. Hirsch, nor business leaders like Lyman Gage favored immigration restrictions. But in their eyes, immigrants resembled children who had to be educated and protected against the dangers of the city. Paternalistic Americanization schemes were an attempt to shape the new immigrants according to the self-image of their sponsors. Like Hull House, the established Jewish community struggled to come to terms with the Jewish immigration from eastern Europe.[17]

THE GHETTO

The mass immigration of Jews forced radical Reformers to rethink their own identities, as well as their ties to other Jews. Unlike New York, Philadelphia, and other East Coast cities, Chicago lacked larger numbers of traditional or even Conservative Jews among the Jewish establishment who could have mediated between radical Reformers and traditionally minded newcomers. Two examples illustrate the huge social distance dividing established Jews from new immigrants. In 1893, Hannah Solomon, one of the most active young women at Sinai, overheard the conversation of several women on a Chicago street. Only later, as she freely admits in her memoirs, did she realize the women had been talking in Yiddish. The young Rose H. Alschuler, who had grown up in a city with a large Jewish immigrant population, first encountered orthodox Jews from eastern Europe in the early 1900s—as a tourist in Vienna.[18]

Most Jews in Chicago expressed genuine compassion with the Jewish victims of the 1881 pogroms in Russia. But they reacted with disbelief when larger groups of eastern European Jews arrived in their city in the summer of 1882. Hirsch expressed a widely shared sentiment when he lamented the effects of the "rapid flood": "In Chicago dozens of families show up every day, coming straight from Liverpool . . . the small city of Milwaukee is surprised by half a thousand on a beautiful summer morning." He accused Jews in western Europe of forwarding indigent Jews from eastern Europe to Chicago. America was no "dumping ground" for poor Jews from Russia. In 1882, the UHRA even sent back several immigrants: "We had to rid our community of their presence as speedily as possible. Self-protection demanded it." Before long, most established Jews in Chicago and elsewhere understood they could neither stop the immigration nor refuse aid. But much of the initial support, or the sending back of immigrants, was driven by deep-seated fears.[19]

Jewish immigration to Chicago increased substantially starting in 1891. Only then did the community leaders fully grasp the enormous scale of the new immigration—and the potential consequences. For years they had proudly promoted America as the destiny for modern Jews, as the new "promised land" where Jews from different parts of backward Europe would push open the door to a new universal future, eventually transcending Judaism. Sinai congregation saw itself as the vanguard of this movement. Admittedly, Jewish immigrants from eastern Europe had come to America in increasing numbers since the late 1860s. But until the 1880s it could be expected that they, or at least their children, would sooner rather than later join the institutions of the established Jews. But the sheer size of the immigration threw this prospect into doubt. It appeared to the established Jews as if the European past was suddenly being transplanted to the very heart of America, almost literally pulling Reform Jews back in time and space to a world they had left behind. The immigrants moved to inner-city Jewish neighborhoods, where they seemed to cling to a traditional way of life, just like the members of other large immigrant groups arriving at the same time. Soon after the turn of the twentieth century, Hirsch expressed the bewilderment established Jews felt: "Darkest Russia transplanted to light flooded America. . . . We have Russia at our very doors, we have the pale [of settlement] across the [Chicago] river."[20]

Mass immigration was hardly a Jewish "problem," Yet Jewish leaders feared that just as they were entering the American mainstream, the presence of traditional "ghetto Jews" strengthened a resurgent anti-Semitic movement. The visibility of the immigrants was a matter of great concern. In February 1891, the *Chicago Tribune* demanded eastern European Jews be sent to Palestine. There was enough space for them. The paper repeatedly published unsettling reports from the "ghetto." In the summer of 1891, just when the number of Jewish immigrants was increasing, a reporter summed up his impressions: "On the West

Side . . . one can walk the streets for blocks and see none but Semitic features and hear nothing but the Hebrew patois of Russian Poland." Only 8 percent of the ghetto's denizens, according to the reporter, were "normal" (productive) workers or artisans; all others were working in some kind of (supposedly unproductive) commerce. While some young women appealed to the reporter, he depicted the older women as "ugly." All Jews in the ghetto were "dirty." In marked contrast, an 1896 article was sympathetic, but the author concluded, "this unique people in our midst, and yet no more of us than are the people of the South Sea islands." Reform Jews—and in particular, Sinai congregation—had discarded almost all symbols traditionally associated with Judaism. But the ghetto epitomized Jewish visibility. Many Reformers feared the presence of traditional Jews would provoke other Americans.[21]

In several European countries, traditional Christian and social stereotypes of Jews were superseded by a new phenomenon during the 1870s. The ideologues of

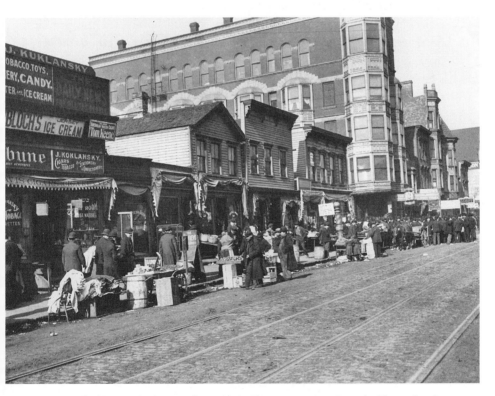

FIGURE 6. Bloch's Jersey Ice Cream, Jefferson Street, Chicago, circa 1900. From the Chicago Jewish Archives. Courtesy of the Spertus Institute of Jewish Studies.

modern anti-Semitism borrowed heavily from the contemporary scientific and popular discourse promoting distorted images of Jews and portraying them primarily in racial terms. For many of its followers, modern anti-Semitism constituted a quasi-religious belief system. Jews were identified as agents or modernity and blamed at the same time for such contradictory developments as radical anarchism and cutthroat capitalism. In Austria, Germany, and France, politicians and parties campaigned successfully on explicitly anti-Semitic platforms.[22]

One did not have to be a pessimist to expect a similar development in America, especially against the background of great social inequality and strong immigration from countries where Jews faced massive discrimination and even persecution. On the eve of the 1893 World's Columbian Exposition, an anonymous author, referring to the Chicago ghetto (and the Dreyfus Affair), warned in the *Reform Advocate*, "anti-Semitism again looms on the European horizon. There are some who think they see the storm cloud brewing even in our own free, progressive America. Who shall stem the tide?"[23] Established American Jews began to encounter informal exclusion more frequently after the mid-1870s: at private clubs and resorts, but also at some of the new research universities. Anti-Semitic prejudice was yet another reaction of socially established Americans to the dramatic social transformation. Jews were caricatured as nouveau riche parvenus who lacked the appropriate forms of behavior. Other outsiders—Catholics, Chinese and Japanese immigrants, and African Americans—encountered much more open discrimination, even violent attacks. But low social mobility and, in the case of former slaves or Asian immigrants, strictly enforced racial segregation, excluded them from social spaces established Jews, as whites, could enter. Whiteness and high social mobility made Jews particularly suspicious in the eyes of self-declared defenders of the old order.[24]

Against this background, most established Jews in Chicago were deeply concerned about the rise of the ghetto. Even though, as in most other western cities, the established Jews in Chicago faced only limited informal discrimination, the enormous scale of the immigration caused alarm. The UHC directors declared in 1897, "If you could give to your board $50,000, they would expend it well. They could take a first step toward clearing out the ghetto and preventing our applicants from huddling together in one corner of the city." Hull House also took a strong line against the ghetto. Settlement worker Charles Zeublin emphasized the redeeming features of the ghetto, not least the absence of saloons. But he condemned the omnipresent Talmud schools for boys: "young boys ruin their eyesight over Hebrew characters, distort their minds with rabbinical casuistry . . . and defer the hopes of American citizenship by the substitution of Jüdisch

[Yiddish] for English." The "annihilation" of the ghetto, he concluded, was its "greatest need."[25]

As thousands of Jewish immigrants were settling on Chicago's West Side, Hirsch, in typical fashion, did not mince his words. In an 1894 editorial for the *Reform Advocate*, he ridiculed the "perverted religion among these people." The ghetto, "this new *Judengasse* west of the river" was a "heavy burden on our communal institutions." He even denied the existence of a religious and racial bond between established Jews and new immigrants:

> We cannot take care of new accessions to the swarming hives of our ghetto! ... We have made too much also of the *unity* and *identity* of Judaism as a religion.... There is not a single religious idea which they have in common with us.... The bond which binds us to these unfortunates is *not* identity of religion; it is not identity of race. It is sympathy of and a sense of duty springing from the community of historical memories.[26]

In 1895, he described the ghetto as a "great danger," characterizing its inhabitants as "our half-Asiatic co-religionists." Hirsch was repelled by "the men and families now huddled together in these streets plastered all over with Hebrew lettered signs." Most had not come to Chicago "by their own free choice" and would, he was convinced, happily return if they had the means. He pointed to a great irony: in Russia the Jews "were harassed and persecuted without mercy," but in America, Jewish immigrants had become the "slaves of sweat-shops." In his view the "Ghetto in itself ... is the root of the trouble ... this piece of Russia and Medieval Germany here on the soil of America." Hirsch associated with the ghetto with one particular "danger," the rise of a Jewish "nationality" in America.[27]

These unsettling comments should not be taken out of context. Hirsch often (and intentionally) used inflammatory language. Only a few years later, he began to reexamine his position and many immigrant Jews would hold him in high respect as leader and as trusted protector against capitalist exploitation. Hirsch's strong reaction in the first half of the 1890s is not very surprising. When he moved to Chicago, Reform Judaism had become the dominant force in the Jewish religious landscape in America. Now, only a few years later, Reform Jews were a minority whose influence decreased as more and more immigrants were arriving from Europe. It is hardly surprising that Hirsch, who had grown up with the Reform movement, could not easily come to terms with this rapid transformation. For him and Sinai congregation, the mass immigration meant a severe setback. Instead of a post-ethnic universal Judaism in America, the ghetto raised the specter of the dark European past, of a closed traditional Judaism and of a Jewish "nationality." Soon after the turn of the century, Hirsch publicly acknowledged defeat: "These hordes from the East of Europe will determine the character of the Judaism of tomorrow in the United States. We have ceased to be the dominant factor. We are now in the minority."[28] Hirsch's emphatic rejection of a religious and "national" bond between established Jews and immigrants demonstrates his difficulties of accepting the undeniable implications of the new immigration: radical Reform Jews, of course, shared much more than a "community of historical memories" with the new immigrants.

Some Sinai members reacted rather differently to the immigration. Not surprisingly, they personally knew immigrants and recognized the gap between perception and reality. Earlier than most established Jews, Julian Mack took issue with the widespread arrogance towards the immigrants. "The caste feeling is strong amongst us, even in the younger generations. Wealth and culture are too apt to beget a sense of superiority and, all-forgetful of the moral truth that character, not wealth or birth, is the criterion of rank, we, who have had the greater opportunity and have too often abused it, look down upon the struggling foreigner because, forsooth, he was reared in a wretched hovel of a Russian ghetto."[29] This self-critical assessment reflected the beginnings of a wider shift and gradual opening to the immigrants. Even Hirsch became aware of the potential pitfalls of his hostile rhetoric. Only a few years after his sharp comments about the new immigrants Hirsch rebuked the *Tribune* for spreading negative stereotypes: "The current prejudice against him [the Russian Jew] is based on the hasty conclusion that he is a bundle of vices without redeeming virtues." He demanded, "Give him a chance and he will rise to an equal height with his more favored fellowmen."[30]

THE JEWISH TRAINING SCHOOL

One institution, located since 1890 at the very heart of the ghetto, symbolized Sinai's strong commitment to new Jewish immigrants and the social question in all its complexities. The Jewish Training School was the epitome of what Hirsch circumscribed in 1901 as "new philanthropy" and one of the most intriguing aid projects designed for immigrants in America. The school was conceived, managed, and largely funded by Sinai members. More than any other modernization scheme, the school symbolized a combination between the *Bildung* legacy of Sinai (and the Reform movement) and the social activism Hirsch preached from the pulpit. The school relied on a strikingly modern concept and demonstrated

Sinai's dedication to the Jewish community, society at large, and the new immigrants. Yet beneath the modern veneer lurked a distorted and ill-informed perception of Jewish immigrants.

The life experience and vision of the participating Sinai members explain why a nonparochial school was the obvious choice for a cutting-edge social project. The sponsors were social climbers who owed their economic success in no small part to a solid German school education. Their deep commitment to *Bildung* defined their vision as modern Jews and shaped their response to the Jewish mass immigration. In their eyes, the immigrants were traditional Jews who came straight from the eastern European *Shtetl* to an industrial city and were clinging to a traditional way of life rather than integrating in American society. Educating the immigrants, especially the children, appeared to be the most promising path to turning them into self-supporting Americans. The links to the emerging Progressive agenda are obvious; indeed, the school became quickly known as a hallmark reform project beyond Chicago. In addition to the standard subjects the Jewish Training School offered gender-specific manual training to equip the children with practical skills and thus advance their social mobility. Rabbi Joseph Stolz, the head of the school's board in its early years, explained the basic philosophy in the first annual report:

> It is barely possible to do much for the permanent social improvement of the adults . . . but the children we can influence. Those saplings can still be bent. Of them we can still make clean, honest, useful, educated Americans. Of them we can still make men who will follow honorable pursuits, and women who will become good mothers and good housekeepers. Of them we can still make independent men who will not have to beg for our charity, but will add dignity to labor by becoming skilled artisans.[31]

These words reflect the elitist paternalism characteristic for many Progressive projects, and they betray an arrogant view of the immigrants. Indeed, in 1893 economist Richard T. Ely would make very similar statement, praising the education provided for working-class children in George Pullman's model town south of Chicago.[32] Yet Stolz's statement also hints at the far-reaching impact of the so-called productivization idea. In the early 1880s, manual training was a relatively recent innovation in America but it had deeper roots. The concept was familiar to many established Jews who had grown up in the German states. In the late eighteenth century, bureaucrats in charge of Jewish emancipation reasoned Jews should only become full citizens when they did not differ from the rest of the population. To further the "normalization" of Jews as they left the ghetto, German state governments promoted systematic education and productivization as part of a massive social engineering project. After graduating from school, young Jewish men were to be trained in the two fields hitherto restricted to them: farming and crafts. Jewish community leaders in favor of emancipation eagerly embraced this idea. In many small towns across southern Germany, Jews formed dozens of associations to support Jewish artisans and farmers. Hundreds, if not thousands, of younger Jews were trained as artisans or farmers during the first half of the nineteenth century. In a period of rapid economic change, neither farming nor most crafts were promising fields. Jewish apprentices faced much discrimination by struggling Christian farmers and artisans; low-level bureaucrats put up many obstacles. This was another reason why especially young male Jews left for America. Several founders of Sinai had started out as artisans, for instance, Michael Greenebaum (plumber) and Isaac Greensfelder (shoemaker). Like other Jewish immigrants, the two men made good use of their training. Greenebaum established a successful plumbing business in Chicago and Greensfelder made a fortune in the wholesale of shoes.[33]

Like the *Bildung* ideal, many Jewish immigrants from central Europe took the productivization ideal to heart—and to America. The best-known Jewish social engineering projects for other Jews in America, agricultural colonies for recent immigrants, epitomized the productivization ideal—and its pitfalls. In the early 1840s, Jewish leaders in New York, themselves recent immigrants, had established agricultural colonies to productivize Jewish peddlers from Bavaria. These early colonies were influenced by similar schemes in the German states. The embryonic Jewish community in Chicago owes its existence partly to a failed agricultural colony. The farm colony, set up in 1842–1843 in Schaumburg, near Chicago, was the brainchild of B'nai B'rith cofounder William Renau. Like the other early colonies, it dissolved within a few years. In a period of rising anti-Semitic discrimination and Jewish mass immigration after 1881 the colony idea reappeared on the agenda. In 1881, Sinai cofounder Leopold Mayer, who had come to Chicago shortly after the demise of the Schaumburg colony, rejected agricultural colonies as a futile exercise. But he was ignored. The prospects for traditional subsistence farming were dire, but for the sponsors of the colonies (not least Hirsch) the image of a few sturdy Jewish immigrant farmers on the American Frontier was a powerful rejection of widely held anti-Semitic stereotypes which alleged Jews could not be "normal."[34]

The productivization of poor Jews had much more to do with the self-image and the internalization of the emancipation process by the sponsors, and even with a genuine belief in social justice, than with concrete needs of the Jewish immigrants. Most Progressive reform projects, not least Hull House, suffered from a paternalistic approach and a stereotypical perception of the men and women for whom they were designed. Nevertheless, it should also be stressed that the overwhelming majority of Jewish immigrants did not require, ask for, or receive support from established Jews, although they lived on very low incomes, often under challenging circumstances. In the late 1860s, Jewish immigrants from eastern Europe began building up their own social safety networks in Chicago. At the grassroots level, immigrants organized *Landsmanshaftn*, which were made up of families from the same *Shtetl* and surrounding region. These were sometimes linked with small congregations. After 1900, the new immigrants, like their earlier predecessors, created a federated system similar to the UHRA/UHC and thus laid the groundwork for a second Jewish community.[35]

The Jewish Training School developed out of a teaching program several Sinai women planned and funded in 1882 for recently arrived Jewish immigrant girls. The Jewish Industrial School, according to its founding charter, would "teach reading, writing, sewing and cleanliness to girls of poor parents." The traditional curriculum was coupled with training in household duties expected from young (middle-class) women. Teaching lessons were scheduled on a weekly basis, usually after the public school on Monday afternoons. During the summer break, the girls received daily instruction at different South Side locations, including Sinai's temple. Admitted were several dozen daughters of indigent immigrants—many applicants were turned away because of lack of space. The girls had to walk a considerable distance from the West to the South Side. Religion was not taught, but the highlight of each school year was the Chanukah celebration—the only time when the sponsors and the parents met in person. The girls received presents and recited poems.[36]

In 1886, Hirsch called for expanding the small-scale teaching program and proposed a training school for the children living in the ghetto. In his opinion the American public school education was deeply flawed, because it was based on mindless repetition and instruction but not learning. Children should not become followers but be raised as independent and critically minded individuals. In October 1886, a school committee was formed in Hirsch's house. Initially it was planned to erect the building for the Jewish Training School of Chicago next to Sinai's temple. The concept of a work or training school was relatively new. The combination of learning and manual training in various crafts can be traced to the German and Swiss educators Julius Fröbel and Johann Heinrich Pestalozzi. Their approach focused on developing the creative faculties of young children through object lessons and manual work. Creative work with objects, they argued, would enhance the learning of traditional subjects. In America, Felix Adler helped to popularize Fröbel and Pestalozzi. Hirsch and leading Sinai members were familiar with his publications on the two educators. Moreover, in 1878, Adler had launched the Free Kindergarten in New York, an innovative preschool inspired by Fröbel's concepts. In addition, three pioneering schools influenced the Jewish Training School; all were inspired by European models: the St. Louis Manual Training School (opened in 1879), the Chicago Manual Training School (1883), and the New York Workingmen's School (1883), the second ambitious project of Adler's Ethical Culture Society. Several Chicago businessmen set up the Chicago Manual Training School as a model institution. Many of its graduates became engineers and displayed high social mobility.[37]

Hirsch, Joseph Stolz, Julius Rosenthal, and Henry Greenebaum led the fundraising for the new school. In 1888, they decided to locate the school in the ghetto. A $20,000 donation by Sinai member Leon Mandel made the project feasible. An even bigger check—more than $40,000—came from the YMHA. In 1889 architects Louis Sullivan and Dankmar Adler received the commission to design an advanced multipurpose building with facilities for training workshops. During the construction, Sinai's parsonage served as a provisional home for the small school. As director the founding committee poached Gabriel Bamberger, the head of Adler's Workingman's School. The German-born and trained educator was the ideal expert to manage this ambitious project. Bamberger who joined Sinai had been recruited by Adler as an early proponent of the work school idea from Germany in 1883. Most of the leading board members and supporters of the Jewish Training School belonged to Sinai; the one prominent exception was Stolz.[38]

The founders recognized the challenges faced by public schools in inner city neighborhoods to educate children of different backgrounds, who often did not speak English. Like the Chicago Manual Training School, the Jewish Training School was explicitly designed as a model for reforming the public school in a period of mass immigration. It appears almost as a paradox that a religious congregation promoted a non-parochial school. But for Jewish (social) Reformers, the engagement for poor Jews was part and parcel of a wider civic effort to bring about more social justice for Americans. The explicit goal, providing a model for reforming the public school, was one reason why the school was secular. Religion was also sidelined to avoid inner-Jewish conflicts. Like other Progressive projects, the school pursued a broader social agenda transcending ethnic and religious boundaries. Even though the school targeted primarily Jewish immigrant children, the board made sure that a few non-Jewish children were also admitted.

After moving to the new building in 1890, the school enrolled boys and girls in eight grades. In 1890 a thousand children were admitted, in the following years about six hundred children attended annually. From the beginning the school had a kindergarten: To "bring the children . . . under our sway before evil home influences have taken root in them, we determined to enroll them at the tender age of three when their faculties, in their more plastic state, readily mold themselves to the will of the teacher." The school also offered evening classes; in 1891–1892, more than two hundred young men and women took English classes and a course on American geography and history. The school was so successful that a branch opened on the South Side in 1893 for the children of the established Jews. Here the parents had to pay tuition, not least to fund the mother school.[39]

The purpose of the Jewish Training School was to turn Jewish immigrant children into *gebildet*, patriotic and self-sufficient men and women worthy of

FIGURE 7. Rooftop dance class at the Jewish Training School, circa 1911. From the Jewish Training School Collection, Chicago Jewish Archives. Courtesy of the Spertus Institute of Jewish Studies.

American citizenship. The annual reports of the school betray a distorted view of the immigrants, especially with regard to religion and ethnicity. Orthodox Judaism and Yiddish were seen as epitome of the ghetto "spirit." The teachers dissuaded the boys from attending the Orthodox cheder. In the 1892 report, the board commended children who "do not want to go to the Cheder and dislike the 'Rebbi' who curses and strikes." Yiddish, the "corrupted" language of the ghetto, was the other major obstacle to Americanization, because it was regarded as defining aspect of a Jewish "nationality." According to the report, "a training school is needed that will go to the root of the disease and work towards a systematic but tolerant extirpation of the Jargon that transplants to this free and hospitable country the baneful seeds of intolerance and oppression." Much emphasis was put on hygiene. The established Jews (and as we have seen, the *Chicago Tribune*) associated the ghetto with dirt and disease. The children "must be thoroughly imbued with the lesson of cleanliness. . . . [T]hey must with special emphasis be taught to practice the laws of hygiene." The children's health was a matter of great concern and was closely watched. A physician and dentist belonged to the school's permanent staff. Each morning the children had to clean themselves under supervision in the school bathrooms. Photographs of the Jewish Training School depicting the teachers and children are noteworthy for their absence of Jewish symbols in a neighborhood defined by visible Jewish symbols. The school was the antithesis of the traditional ghetto, and of course, a model for reforming the public school.[40]

Even in hindsight, the Jewish Training School was a success. The agricultural colonies failed, because the urban sponsors had little knowledge of farming, the colonists were not sufficiently trained, and the colonies were located far away from Chicago.[41] The teaching in the traditional subjects in this private and well-endowed showcase school was much more advanced than in the neighborhood public schools. The advanced education provided the children with skills they could use in the urban industrial environment, even if they did not become housewives or artisans as envisaged by the founders and donors. In addition to the traditional subjects and the gender specific manual training, all children attended mandatory physical education classes and took music lessons. German lessons were obligatory from first grade—yet another indication of the lingering impact of the *Bildung* ideal. However, cultural arrogance alone does not explain the choice of German. In the 1890s, German was the leading international academic language. The school leaders recognized the relative ease with which Yiddish speakers could learn German and reasoned it might serve as a useful skill.

In 1893, director Bamberger stressed, "Education is the one radical remedy which will solve all these terrible problems. . . . We not only instruct, we educate our pupils." The school frequently received visitors from all over the country, and was regarded as one of the most advanced Progressive projects of its kind in Chicago, alongside Hull House and the Abraham Lincoln Center, an innovative cultural center managed by the Unitarian All Souls Congregation on Chicago's South Side.[42]

The immediate impact of the school certainly was limited. Six hundred children was only a tiny fraction. According to a 1912 school handbook, a mere twenty to thirty children graduated from the school annually. Most children transferred to public schools or dropped out before graduating. Many graduates ended up in white-collar occupations. Nevertheless, the indirect impact of this showcase school should not be underestimated. Since the 1860s, Sinai members had served regularly on the Chicago Board of Education. In the late 1860s, Herman Felsenthal, the father of longtime University of Chicago trustee Eli Felsenthal, was instrumental in introducing German as language of instruction in Chicago's public schools. Several other Sinai members followed him, notably Charles Kozminski and Emanuel Frankenthal. Joseph Stolz, one of the main forces behind the Jewish Training School, was elected to the Chicago Board of Education in 1899 (he served until 1905).[43]

Indeed, if there was one thread running through Sinai's various activities on behalf of Jewish immigrants and civic institutions in Chicago, it was the promotion of *Bildung*. Most Sinai members had enjoyed a thorough school education; *Bildung* defined Sinai's theology; education and instilling the virtues of social mobility shaped the response to Jewish mass immigration; and most important, education drove the civic projects funded or managed by Sinai's members. These ranged from the University of Chicago to the Jewish Training School, the Chicago Civic Federation, and the city's board of education, and, as highlighted at the beginning of this chapter, the Chicago Public Library. But the impact of *Bildung* reached even further. As a member of Sinai in the 1880s and 1890s Julius Rosenwald witnessed the launch of the Jewish Training School. Was it a mere coincidence that one of his most groundbreaking projects was the construction of almost five thousand schools for disadvantaged African American children across the South?[44]

8.

SPIRITUAL LEADER AND EMPLOYEE?

BY THE LATE 1880s, Sinai as a congregation was hardly recognizable to outside visitors who had attended services before Kohler's departure. A typical urban Reform congregation with a relatively close-knit membership known for its distinctive Sunday services had transformed into a grand weekly lecture event. Every Sunday, hundreds of Chicagoans of different faiths flocked to Sinai's temple to listen to one of America's "greatest pulpit orators," Hirsch's "discourses," his sophisticated and often sharp takes on the social and political affairs of the day, were much discussed throughout the city. In addition to the *Occident* and the *Reform Advocate*, the *Chicago Tribune* began covering Hirsch's sermons and activities regularly and extensively.[1] This unexpected success was not without drawbacks. Sinai's reputation was enviable: representatives of the congregation, Hirsch in particular, were prominent civic leaders and closely involved in some of the most ambitious social and cultural projects in Chicago. But the charismatic rabbi had eclipsed the actual congregation. The crowd Hirsch attracted was composed overwhelmingly of persons who did not belong to the congregation. And some observers wondered whether Sinai was still a congregation—or still Jewish.[2]

In 1893, Hirsch himself addressed the pitfalls of Sinai's transformation, calling "for a more extended and aggressive participation in our congregational and religious affairs." Most Jewish Reform congregations had been reduced to "lecture associations," defined largely by the "personality of the lecturer." Some congregations were in an even more sorry state: "The center of their interest is the cemetery. . . . [I]t is by the solemn certainty of death that the living profit to erect temples." But he pointed to a silver lining on the horizon. The women, whose considerable efforts were frequently overlooked, should be given more formal influence within congregations and assume leadership positions. Hirsch even suggested ordaining women as rabbis.[3]

During the 1890s, several large Reform temples in other American cities began to tackle the much-discussed crisis by organizing a diverse range of social activities to involve members of all age ranges in different ways with the congregation and draw more people into their orbit. Gradually, many larger American Jewish Reform congregations adapted the social center model, or elements of it. Sinai's leaders, however, initially decided against going down this road. They did not have to worry how to fill the temple on Sundays, and theirs was one of the most respected congregations in the land. But there was a catch: Sinai's success largely depended on just one man. In 1898–1899, a long simmering conflict between rabbi and board erupted in an ugly and public row. As Hirsch tendered his resignation, the members faced the question whether Sinai as a congregation was viable without its illustrious rabbi.

"NOT A JEWISH CONGREGATION IN THE NARROW SENSE"

In March 1890, Sinai Congregation had 232 members and continued to grow. The Sunday services—"free from rite and practices, both impractical and almost meaningless in our day"—often pulled in over 1,000 people. Sinai's temple had become too small. Without any formal announcement, Hirsch had switched to delivering his sermons in English a few years previously. This and his growing appeal as a preacher help to explain why the attendance grew at a much faster rate than the actual membership. It is important to distinguish between the two numbers; Sinai's actual membership in 1890 says little about the impact the congregation was making in Chicago. In 1889, Hirsch suggested a major extension of the temple to add more seating. He even toyed with the idea of building a much larger temple further south. In his estimate, only half of the members regularly attended services, while more and more people from outside were coming, many "of non-Jewish origin." Apart from Christians, many of the Jewish listeners were unaffiliated; they could not afford or did not want to join a congregation.

Unaffiliated Jews remain the least studied and most obscure group in American Jewish history, because they left hardly any traces as Jews in the historical record. Their number, so much is clear, exceeded those of formally affiliated Jews by far. As an "open" congregation, Sinai managed to pull growing numbers of these women and men, along with affiliated and unaffiliated Christians, into its temple on Sunday. But initially, only a few joined. Especially for younger men, the relatively high membership dues constituted an obstacle. This issue had to be resolved if the congregation aimed to expand its membership.[4]

After lengthy discussions, the board decided against a move. In 1891–1892, architect Dankmar Adler oversaw an ambitious refurbishing and extension project. Adler's partner, Louis Sullivan, beautifully redecorated the interior. Almost 1,000 new seats were added to the original 1,260, providing space for 2,210 people. The building received state-of-the-art electric lighting, an advanced air-conditioning and heating system, a large kitchen, and an extended space for social gatherings in the basement, as well as classrooms for children. The organ, as the *Chicago Tribune* put it in its detailed description of the interior, was "made over and greatly enlarged." Jewish visitors immediately noticed a rather drastic change as they entered the sanctuary. The Sepher Torah was gone. A sympathetic observer explained in 1901, "the ark has been omitted, the scrolls of the law not being used in Sinai Temple." Hirsch had dispensed with the liturgical reading of the Torah. What became of Sinai's Torah scrolls, the most sacred object of almost any Jewish congregation? The board minutes of May 1894 tell the story bluntly: "Whereas, the Congregation is the owner of a Sepher Torah, the use of which in the service has been dispensed with; Therefore, Resolved, that said Sepher Torah be donated to the University of Chicago, as part of the Semitic Library, donated by the Congregation." For Sinai and its rabbi, the sacredness attached to the Torah scroll had lost its religious meaning; what mattered was the text, or rather, the universal spirit contained in it. The attitude behind this act was deeply unsettling for almost every observant Jew.[5]

Thus an uninformed visitor entering through the open doors of Sinai's refurbished temple would not have immediately recognized the interior as a Jewish house of worship. Indeed, the Star of David on the cupola was the only remaining Jewish symbol—and there was no explicit reason to preserve it. Some time after 1890, Sinai occasionally shifted the High Holiday Services to the following Sunday—although Hirsch had strongly condemned this practice in 1885.[6]

At least one other congregation, the Temple (Tifereth Israel) in Cleveland, Ohio, pursued a similar course. In 1892, HUC graduate Moses J. Gries joined the Temple. He considered Emil G. Hirsch as his spiritual role model. After introducing Sunday services in 1893, Gries ceased reading the Torah during the service

FIGURE 8. Temple of Chicago Sinai congregation, located on Indiana Avenue, after the renovation in 1891–1892, circa 1900. Courtesy of the Chicago Sinai congregation.

some time before 1898. In that year, Orthodox rabbi Zvi Hirsch Masliansky visited Chicago, Cleveland, and Cincinnati. In his memoirs, he expresses his "outrage" over Gries's removal of the Torah, apparently over the objections of many members. According to Masliansky, the Torah was "put away in the cellar and an English bible was placed inside the Ark." He also recorded a conversation with

Isaac Mayer Wise in Cincinnati a few days later. Wise condemned "the deceitful action" of his former student Gries. But he emphasized (as Masliansky puts it), "I am not to blame—this doctrine was given from the 'Sinai' of Chicago." Not surprisingly, Masliansky, a devout Jew, had little positive to say about radical Reformers in Chicago: "Grey temples with no devotees to pray in them; learned Rabbis with no true sense of the Torah; 'Prayer Books' without prayers, music without a Jewish tone—Jews devoid of Judaism." He characterized a Sunday service conducted by Hirsch as "quiet, cold, monotonous, and moribund from beginning to end, frozen, cold, dead." Masliansky describes Hirsch, with whom he conversed in Hebrew after the service, as highly educated and charming, yet also as inconsistent.[7]

Of course, Sinai was criticized for these moves by many other Jews, formally and informally. But this had been the case throughout the existence of the congregation and only reinforced the board's conviction to move ahead. An 1892 board meeting devoted to widespread criticism illustrates this attitude. Sinai had been accused of being devoted to "the head rather than the heart." And allegedly, the congregation "lacked that sentimentality of spirit which is characteristic of the truly religious element in human life." For many Jews, Sinai had forsaken the "right" to call itself a Jewish congregation. But Sinai was unfazed: "We admit that ours is a religion of the mind. . . . We do not and have not forsaken the past, its recollections, . . . its history, we nurture and cherish and its traditions we respect . . . but we believe that . . . progress in Art, in science and in every other branch of human activity, so too may it advance in the domain of religion and therefore have we replaced the cherished ceremonies of the past with usages more in consonance with present thought."[8]

But what was still Jewish about Sinai Congregation after these (at least symbolically) far-reaching changes? In an 1893 "discourse" titled "Universal Religion and Judaism," Hirsch openly declared Sinai to be standing on the border between Judaism and universal religion:

Six years ago, as urged by the president of the congregation, we declared that we are not a Jewish congregation in the narrow sense, that Jews by the accident of birth can join us; we are a society of men and women banded together for the spread of the ideas, proclaimed by our prophets. . . . I verily believe this Sinai Congregation, as a Jewish congregation, could become the nucleus for a wider movement to embrace all that are unchurched, but that are not ready to hold that God has been dethroned and this world is the purposeless product of chance. We could father a genuine "ethical culture" movement, but from the inclusive side. . . . And therefore our Judaism may welcome every movement looking toward a universal religion. We cling to the word Jew, because the world for eighteen centuries hath made it synonym with all that is evil. . . . May God speed that day when Judaism is no longer needed![9]

These were truly radical words. Eight years earlier at the Pittsburgh Platform meeting in 1885, Sinai's rabbi had made a similar case when he argued to open Judaism for proselytes. Admittedly, Hirsch's concept of "ethical culture" was anti-materialistic and monotheist. But he wanted to offer full membership in the congregation to individuals and groups who believed in one God. Obviously if the test for membership was professing one's belief in one God and a renunciation of materialism, a formal conversion was not required for Christians or Muslims, let alone the "Abrahamic rite" for male converts, discarded years earlier. But even if Sinai remained a Jewish congregation only in a *broad* sense, Hirsch was not (yet) ready to sacrifice Judaism for universalism. Sinai was still strongly committed to its radical legacy as an independent and fully sovereign congregation. Yet it had a dialectical relationship to the breakup of the "synagogue community." Sinai was fiercely proud of its theological radicalism, but the congregation also was the strongest supporter of the organized Jewish community in Chicago.

THE RISE OF THE INSTITUTIONAL CONGREGATION

Sinai's social engagement owed as much to Hirsch as to Chicago's massive growth, the pressing social question, and the impact of Jewish mass immigration. Yet in this, Sinai was hardly exceptional. Other Reform rabbis, notably Joseph Krauskopf (of Kansas City and Philadelphia), Jacob Voorsanger (San Francisco), Moses Gries (Cleveland), and Henry Berkowitz (Kansas City), also reinvented the congregations they joined between 1880 and 1892. With the exception of Voorsanger, they were recently ordained HUC graduates. Like Hirsch, these young rabbis reached out to the wider community, promoting social reform projects for Jews and non-Jews, establishing contacts with liberal Protestants, and working with Progressive reformers, often with the support of lay members. Their temples were comparable to Sinai: established urban Reform congregations comprising leading Jewish businessmen and supporters of civic causes. However, earlier than others—as David Kaufman has shown in his detailed study on the synagogue center—these rabbis in particular began to reorganize their strongly growing congregations, developing and testing models later adapted by other congregations, not least Sinai.

Krauskopf and his brother-in-law Berkowitz both made a case for reinventing the Jewish congregation as a social center. In 1887, Krauskopf left his pulpit at B'nai Jehuda in Kansas City to become the successor of Hirsch's father at Keneseth Israel in Philadelphia. A few months later, in 1888, B'nai Jehuda appointed Berkowitz as its new rabbi. He first suggested bringing traditional Jewish associations with a social purpose under the roof of the congregation. Berkowitz cultivated personal relationships with his congregants. He visited the members in their homes and he launched an "auxiliary." This body, in a nutshell, incorporated the synagogue center of the early twentieth century: after a few years, the auxiliary comprised committees in charge of physical culture, public entertainments, and "charity and aid." Krauskopf transformed Keneseth Israel in a similar fashion, successfully boosting its membership. B'nai Jehuda and several smaller congregations also formed literary associations, which closely resembled the short-lived Sinai Literary Society of the late 1870s. These pulled younger Jews into the orbit of the temple and served as incubators for a wide range of activities. In fact, the Jewish Publication Society in Philadelphia grew out of the literary society at Keneseth Israel.

At Temple Emanu-El in New York, Rabbi Gustav Gottheil organized the first sisterhood in 1889, inspiring several other congregations in the city. However, the early sisterhoods differ from their contemporary namesakes. These "sisterhoods of personal service," as Felicia Herman has defined them, focused on social problems outside of the congregation, following the model of Protestant women's organizations. They were primarily involved in helping needy Jewish immigrants, especially in the entrepôt New York. The erosion of the Victorian ideals of the caring woman in the early 1920s led to a reorientation. The new sisterhoods provided support within rather than outside of the respective congregation. Another pioneer was Moses Gries, who introduced one of the first lecture series at his Cleveland congregation in the early 1890s, inviting the Unitarian minister Jenkin Lloyd Jones from Chicago and Felix Adler, two figures close to Hirsch. Krauskopf and Gries supported and successfully introduced Sunday services and were invited as guests of honor when Sinai celebrated the twenty-fifth anniversary of its Sunday services in 1899.

The social congregation put additional demands on the shoulders of the respective rabbis. Although congregations created positions for administrators, one rabbi alone often could not handle the increasing workload. In 1893, Keneseth Israel employed J. Leonard Levy as "associate minister" to assist Senior

Rabbi Krauskopf in the religious school and various activities under the roof of the congregation. An assistant rabbi had supported Gustav Gottheil at Temple Emanu-El since the mid-1880s. Hirsch certainly could have asked Sinai's board to create such a position to relieve him of his heavy workload. According to the board minutes, he did not raise this issue. In all likelihood, Hirsch would not have tolerated another rabbi permanently in or even near "his" pulpit.[10]

The social or institutional congregation, often with hundreds of members participating on several levels and generations in different societies and special events under the auspices of the congregation, was of course not a Jewish invention. As he himself put it, Berkowitz had "studied the methods of other religious bodies." Catholic parishes in particular served as an early model for Protestant and Jewish "social center" congregations. Unlike Protestants and Jews, Roman Catholics opted against the pluralist denominational model. Even before 1850, immigrant Catholics from Ireland and the German states formed large parishes that resembled the European *Einheitsgemeinde* and encompassed various associations for philanthropic and other causes under their wings. In large cities, however, the Catholic hierarchy struggled to keep an ethnically diverse and fluctuating membership under one institutional roof. Many immigrants did not understand English and did not want to discard centuries-old customs. In Chicago, German-speaking and Irish immigrants organized parishes along ethnic lines. Yet soon after the turn of the twentieth century, ethnicity gradually lost its drawing power. English, in addition to Latin, became the dominant language of worship, and territorial superseded ethnic parishes. Some groups, especially Polish immigrants, continued to resist Catholic integration for decades. For all its shortcomings, the overarching Catholic parish model impressed some Protestant and Jewish congregation leaders. By dividing over religious issues into congregations and denominations, Protestants and Jews had yielded most of the traditional social tasks of the premodern *Gemeinde* to the secular sphere. Catholic parishes, on the other hand, covered a broad spectrum of nonreligious activities: sports teams, sewing societies, reading groups, kindergartens, and old people's homes, to name just a few. By the 1880s a growing number of Protestant congregations began to offer activities for all age groups not just on weekends but during the week. Some congregations even organized basic medical services and employment agencies. Most acquired libraries and erected gymnasiums near (or even as part of) their respective houses of worship. Institutional congregations boosted their memberships, a development midsized congregations struggling to retain members could not ignore.[11]

Although Sinai raised its social profile outside of its temple, the congregation and its leaders watched the social center movement uneasily. Sinai regarded itself as a leader and not a follower. Why should the congregation copy other congregations when it was so successful pursuing its own agenda? The membership continued to grow, although hardly spectacularly. Sinai's distinctive theology was outward oriented. For Hirsch, it was crucial to spread the universal Reform message as widely as possible. He certainly sympathized with the idea of the institutional (or social) congregation. But an inward-oriented Jewish profile would have diluted Sinai's open theological message, increasing the isolation from the liberal mainstream. Nobody could accuse Sinai of ignoring the Chicago Jewish community. But the social congregation symbolized ghettoization and Jewish ethnicity in the religious sphere, two developments that were anathema to Hirsch and were associated with the new Jewish immigrants. For Hirsch, "closed" institutions and universal religion could not go together; in 1899, he stressed in a sermon that "institutionalism means nothing. Free Judaism cannot be an institutionalized Judaism."[12]

RABBI VERSUS BOARD

In reality, the remarkable transition of Sinai under Hirsch was deeply ambiguous. Hirsch, it is true, bore a large responsibility for reinventing the congregation. Every Sunday, he attracted hundreds of Chicagoans to his sermons—when he actually preached them. In the early 1890s, Hirsch emerged as a much-sought-after public speaker on the national lecture circuit. He accepted a growing number of invitations from congregations, civic institutions, and universities, especially on the East Coast. Usually other Chicago ministers or rabbis, Sinai members, or prominent local figures filled his pulpit. His growing national reputation was a matter of great pride for Sinai. Yet his frequent absences produced some discontentment among the board members. It did not help that Hirsch repeatedly suffered from longer periods of illness after 1890 and had to be replaced by guest speakers.

A close reading of the board minutes for the mid-1890s hints at an increasingly antagonistic relationship between Hirsch and several members. Hirsch's growing reputation and influence as a public intellectual brought a larger question to the fore: could Sinai afford to lose Hirsch, and if not, what would be the price to keep him? Hirsch was an employee of Sinai, but he was also the spiritual leader of the congregation. Sinai's board had to strike a new balance between these two potentially conflicting roles. Raising his salary and granting additional benefits—so much was clear—was not enough. Hirsch wanted more formal power and influence.

In Germany, most rabbis received life contracts and were independent from their flock. Quite often, they did not know more than a few of the men and women attending their services. Apart from a few independent, mostly Orthodox congregations, rabbis were employed by the state-regulated Jewish *Gemeinde* at a certain city or town. Only men who fulfilled certain formal qualifications—they were graduates of a university who had been ordained as rabbis—could apply for a vacant position. Rabbis received fixed salaries, comparable to civil servants. In America, rabbis were employed by voluntary associations, which could dissolve or merge at any time. A rabbi's position depended on good relations with the congregation's members and the executive board. Large urban congregations like Sinai did insist on university training. Yet formal qualifications, though certainly a big plus, could be waived. Neither Isaac Mayer Wise nor Jacob Voorsanger, the respected rabbi of Emanu-El in San Francisco, had graduated from a university or college. American rabbis served as spiritual leaders of their congregation, but legally, they were employees and often were treated as such. Around 1880, most rabbis received fixed-term contracts, which were usually extended but not by default, as Sinai's second rabbi, Isaac Loeb Chronik, discovered in 1870. The lifetime contract Bernhard Felsenthal had been offered by Zion congregation in 1864 or Isaac Mayer Wise by Cincinnati's Bene Yeshurun in 1854 remained the exception.[13]

Boards often made strategic decisions, sometimes even in the theological domain, without consulting the rabbi. In 1885, Hirsch first learned of the president's far-reaching reform program when he opened the newspaper. However, as Sinai's board knew only to well, a few successful and popular rabbis were well placed in the American system. Other congregations tried to poach them, and rabbis could negotiate lucrative arrangements at their existing or future congregation. It was quite common for respected rabbis to move more than once during their career. Hirsch's significant pay raise in 1888 was as much a sign of reverence as a precautionary measure to prevent him from departing. That was certainly a shrewd move. The generous salary and the great respect Hirsch enjoyed in America's second largest city took most other positions out of the running. In fact, by leaving Louisville, Hirsch moved to a top-tier congregation. Even in larger cities, only a handful of congregations could match the salary Sinai paid him. The relatively young Joseph Krauskopf assumed the Philadelphia pulpit of Samuel Hirsch in early 1888 after a protracted struggle with his Kansas City congregation over his departure.[14] Hirsch's generous 1888 contract may have been influenced by fears that he might become his father's successor in Philadelphia. That left New York, and really only one congregation, Temple Emanu-El. This highly respected old

Reform congregation counted investment banker Jacob Schiff and other leading members of the American Jewish establishment among its members. In comparison to this aristocratic congregation, Sinai—very much like Chicago—appeared as a radical newcomer, admittedly with a brilliant leader and an intriguing concept, but lacking the appropriate pedigree.

Not just for a prominent Reform rabbi from the Midwest, New York was in a league of its own. For educated Americans devoted to the arts and European culture, the city had much to offer. Chicago, in comparison, appeared as a young upstart and a rough and uncultured place. But it would be too shortsighted to describe Chicago as an apocalyptic urban abyss rocked by almost constant social conflict. Within a few years after the 1871 fire, the Loop had been rebuilt impressively as America's first modern business district. In the last decades of the nineteenth century, Chicago was growing faster than New York, and it had become one of the largest industrial centers in the world. An increasing share of the huge profits pocketed by successful businessmen was invested in social and cultural causes. During the 1880s, a growing number of Chicagoans discovered cultural philanthropy, donating some of their wealth to cultural institutions— and of course also to social reform institutions, such as hospitals and settlement homes. The Art Institute was founded in 1879, and the Chicago Public Library continued to expand under Hirsch's leadership. The Chicago Symphony Orchestra was formed in 1890. Two years later, the University of Chicago enrolled its first students. These and other influential institutions were innovative at the time but initially they could not compete with their older counterparts on the East Coast. The World's Columbian Exposition in 1893 gave Chicago's cultural life a decisive boost, and it helped to put the city on the map. But the event lasted only a few months; the notorious Pullman Strike and a severe recession overshadowed the closing stages. As the quintessential American city without a history, Chicago competed with New York primarily in the economic domain. New York's role as America's traditional gateway remained uncontested. Around the turn of the twentieth century, New York was the only city in the Western Hemisphere that could seriously aspire to close the gap to Europe's leading cultural centers, London, Paris, Vienna, and Berlin. Daily, dozens of large ocean liners and hundreds of trains moved an endless stream of people from all over the world to and through the city. Many immigrants settled down for shorter or longer periods in a city with more than four million inhabitants (compared to Chicago's less than two million). Successful businessmen, writers, and artists from across America and Europe were drawn to New York. Its elites wielded enormous economic and political clout in the nation's capital and beyond. And, of course, in the late 1890s, New York was the city with the largest Jewish population in the world.[15]

As it happened, Temple Emanu-El's rabbi, Gustav Gottheil, a moderate Reformer and (much to the embarrassment of the congregation) a Zionist, was approaching his seventieth birthday in 1897, and the board was looking for a successor. Hirsch, a regular visitor to New York and Temple Emanu-El and a known critic of Zionism, belonged to a small circle of serious contenders for the job. In 1896, Hirsch received an initial offer. The New Yorkers were willing and could clearly afford to lure him to the Upper East Side by offering a longer contract and a higher annual salary (the figure of $15,000 was mentioned). Hirsch was flattered, and he seriously considered the move. Apparently he had also received offers from other New York congregations. In the same year, Sinai's board extended Hirsch's contract for another ten years, at the same salary of $12,000 (the equivalent of more than $320,000 in 2011) and with substantial benefits—and Hirsch decided to stay.[16] But he continued to play with the idea to move, especially since Temple Emanu-El seemed to be fixated on him. Moreover, in his view, a simple extension of his earlier contract without any changes did not reflect his rising role and importance.

Things were amiss at Sinai. During a special board meeting in June 1897, several members discussed their concerns about the rabbi's awkward behavior. Hirsch was visibly unhappy and had "complained"—on the pulpit—about specific members whom he considered "hostile." To cheer up the rabbi on the eve of a summer trip to Europe, the board organized a splendid farewell celebration. "The temple was befittingly and tastefully adorned. Over the pulpit a row of lanterns bore the greeting, 'Bon Voyage,' and higher still appeared the Doctor's portrait wreathed in laurel and festooned with flags." In hindsight this can easily be misinterpreted as a hint for Hirsch to leave for good, but that was clearly not the intention. The board and the members were genuinely worried that Hirsch might not return to Chicago. Board member Adolph Loeb, the first speaker, explained the purpose of the celebration. The congregation wanted to "dispel" any "doubts" Hirsch might have in regard to the "loyalty and love of Sinai's members." As the main speaker the board had recruited the Unitarian minister (and friend of Hirsch) Jenkin Lloyd Jones. He praised the rabbi as bold spiritual leader, widely recognized as the minister of Sinai—and of Chicago. After this address several leading members expressed their gratitude to Hirsch. With the words, "God may spare him many years to serve his loving congregation," President Fishell stepped forth and presented Hirsch with a "magnificent silver loving cup." Hirsch rose and thanked the congregation for this sign of affection. He admitted to "doubts" about lacking "sympathies" of Sinai's members, but the celebration clearly showed he was mistaken. Hirsch apologized to some members for his "impatient" behavior, pointing to the heavy burden on his shoulders. He had been very moved by many letters written by "prominent Chicagoans" who had asked him not to accept "a tempting call to a New York congregation." Three years earlier, in September 1894, Sinai had feted Hirsch similarly upon his return from a summer trip to Europe. Almost six hundred turned out and expressed their gratitude to the famous minister whose huge portrait was displayed in the main hall of the synagogue. "He had been glad to get away on his vacation," Hirsch frankly admitted, "but was equally glad to get back."[17]

But this was not the end of the story. Hirsch really aimed for a far-reaching renegotiation of his relationship with the congregation. The recording secretary, August Binswanger, took verbatim minutes of the board meetings in 1898–1899, when events took a dramatic turn. Thus it is possible to take a close look at the discussions among the board members about the rabbi. Who were the leaders of the congregation facing Hirsch at this critical juncture in 1898?[18]

Albert Fishell (born in Blowitz, Bohemia, and fifty-four years old in 1898) occupied in the president's chair since 1896. After attending Charles University in Prague and working for various businesses, he left for in America in 1866. After some difficult years, his business fortunes improved considerably during the 1880s. Fishell settled in Chicago only in 1890. Four other board members had also immigrated as young men. The treasurer Bernhard Mergentheim (seventy-three, from Lübbecke, Westphalia) was the only founder of Sinai who still sat on the board. He had worked in the leather business before retiring and devoting more time to the UHRA/UHC and Sinai. Adolph Loeb (fifty-nine, from Bingen, Hesse) had lived for several years in Memphis before coming to Chicago in 1873, where he made his living in the insurance business. He joined several Jewish associations and served for almost a decade as president of the B'nai B'rith District Grand Lodge No. 6. Leo Fox (fifty-four, from Oettingen, Bavaria) was a former banker. After moving to Chicago from Oregon in 1887, he had soon retired to devote his time to various philanthropic causes. Two board members had immigrated as children: Conrad Witkowsky (fifty-nine, from Posen) had lived in Chicago since 1852 and worked in the insurance business, and Adolph Nathan (fifty-four, from Prussia) was a Civil War veteran and a successful businessman who for many years had been a railroad executive before moving into the retail sector. In 1897, he became president of the Chicago Civic Federation. The vice president of the congregation, Leon Mandel (fifty-seven, from Kerzenheim, Palatinate), was another longtime member. His family belonged to the Palatinate network whose members had founded Sinai. He had arrived in Chicago as a ten-year-old with his mother and brothers following the death of his father. Mandel was a self-made businessman. Together with his two brothers, he owned and managed one of Chicago's most successful department stores, Mandel Brothers on State Street. Mandel was a respected philanthropist who supported especially institutions devoted to education, notably the Jewish Training School and the University of Chicago.

Four board members were native born: Martin Barbe (fifty-seven, from Cincinnati) had moved to Chicago with his parents in 1845; they were among the earliest Jewish settlers in the city. As a boy, Martin had been a pupil of Sinai founder Leopold Mayer. In 1898, he was associated with a wholesale clothing firm. Edwin G. Foreman (thirty-six, from Chicago) was a child of Sinai. His father was founder Gerhard Foreman, who had died the previous year. Edwin presided over the successful bank his father had founded, which was incorporated as a state bank under the name Foreman Bros. Banking Co. in 1897. Moses Bensinger (fifty-nine, from Louisville) was the president of America's largest billiard table company, which had been founded by his close relative John Moses Brunswick and was a prominent Chicago business. Recording secretary August Binswanger (fifty-four, from Baltimore), a member of Yale's first law school class, had moved to Chicago from St. Louis in the previous decade to work as legal council for the giant meatpacking business of Sinai member Nelson Morris. As we will see, he had the courage to stand up to Hirsch more than once—and was willing to pay the price in the end. A possible explanation for Binswanger's unfazed position (apart, perhaps, from courtroom experience) may be traced to his time at Shaare Emeth congregation in St. Louis. As a board member, Binswanger had found himself in the midst of the controversy over Solomon Sonneschein's alleged apostasy in 1886. Like Hirsch, Sonneschein was a difficult rabbi prone to provoking public scandals. After Shaare Emeth's board replaced Sonneschein with Samuel Sale, the congregation quickly recovered.[19]

The composition of Sinai's board was similar to that of other large urban Reform congregations in this period. With the exception of the lawyer Binswanger, Hirsch had to deal with self-employed executives. The board members managed large businesses with hundreds of employees. Several had retired, but with the exception of Mergentheim and the younger Foreman, they were all in their fifties. The seven immigrants still outnumbered four native-born members, but three had immigrated at a young age. No woman had yet been elected to the board.

These men did respect—even admire—Hirsch as a rabbi and public intellectual. But the board and the rabbi represented two strikingly different worlds. On one side sat a group of rationally thinking and self-confidant businessmen who were used to taking difficult decisions and weighing the balance between input and output. Most of their working lives were spent in various boardrooms, and several had (as we will see) some difficulty to adapt to the boardroom of a congregation. On the other side stood one man, a highly educated and articulate thinker who was proud and egocentric—and an employee. Judged with a cold businessman's logic, some board members may have reasoned that Hirsch was paid rather generously for giving beautiful sermons and representing the congregation.

EMPLOYEE AND SPIRITUAL LEADER?

On April 25, 1898, a regular board meeting took a surprising turn. Somewhat unusually, Hirsch had asked the board to participate in the meeting. Apart from two minor issues, Hirsch announced he had been invited to speak from the pulpit of a New York congregation in May. He suggested asking Jane Addams or William Rainey Harper, the president of the University of Chicago, to replace him. Instead of formally granting his wish, as in the past, several board members objected to Hirsch's frequent absences. Adolph Nathan, the former railroad executive, addressed Hirsch: "Doctor, the members of your congregation prefer to have you in the pulpit, and they do not like to have you go away so often; they prefer to listen to you. But if you go away, they desire to have men of some standing fill the pulpit, and not mere boys." The forty-two-year-old Harper, a widely respected university administrator and a remarkable scholar, was indeed relatively young; but Hirsch was only four years older.

In the years leading up to this meeting, Hirsch had repeatedly taken short leaves of absence, usually for out-of-town speaking engagements. He had always sought (and received) formal permission by the board or president but was clearly unhappy about submitting himself to this formal procedure. In June 1891, for instance, he informed Sinai's president, Joseph Gatzert, that "one of the most advanced Unitarian ministers in this city," would preach during his absence. To his knowledge, he added, most Protestant congregations in America did not require their ministers to seek formal permission if they were occasionally preaching out of town. But Sinai's board refused to yield to Hirsch in this matter, expecting him to formally seek approval for accepting outside invitations.[20] For Hirsch this particular issue highlighted the contradiction between his role as a leader and his actual status as an employee of a congregation run by businessmen. Now in 1898, instead of dismissing the critical board members or arguing his case objectively, Hirsch talked himself into a rage. He bitterly complained about not being invited to board meetings and having been abused by certain members. He then stated his position in no uncertain terms:

"I am not an employee of your congregation, working for a salary like other employees. I am co-ordinate with this Executive Board, and I do not need to ask for leave of absence. . . . I am not like a book-keeper and paid employe[e]. I am a man who has a national reputation . . . I am tired of hearing about this matter of my salary, my $12,000 a year. I won't tolerate it!" and with this Dr. Hirsch jumped out of his chair and said, "I am sorry I did not accept the call to New York, where they offered me $15,000, $3,000 more than you are paying me."

The board members were shocked. "Mr. Mandel said, 'If such scenes are to go on here, I want to tender my resignation . . . right now. I do not want to be an officer of a Congregation where there is such feeling expressed by the Rabbi.'" At this point, Binswanger rose and seconded Mandel—"I see no reason why he [the rabbi] should be invited to attend the Executive Board meetings. These are business meetings, with which the Rabbi has no concern." Now, since the cards were on the table, Binswanger raised several other points, which apparently nobody had dared to openly discuss with Hirsch in the preceding years. He criticized especially one change, "usage has grown up that our holiday services are to be held on the next Sunday immediately succeeding or preceding that holiday." In other words, Hirsch had yielded to the more radically minded members and shifted the High Holiday services, at least occasionally, to the following Sunday. This radical change is indeed remarkable in light of Hirsch's rather emphatic defense of the High Holidays in 1885. Binswanger then explicitly asked Hirsch to end his public attacks on Sinai's board. He should have known better. Hirsch was angry; now he could not control himself:

The Doctor then jumped out of his chair in a violent rage, tearing his hair, and said "I want that issue made up, and I will resign!" and taking up his chair, which was a heavy one, he struck it down twice, and showed that he was in an ungovernable rage, and he leaned up against the mantle, whereupon someone said, "For heaven's sake, Doctor, don't make such an exhibition of yourself. Be a man." Mr. Fox got up and said, "The Doctor ought to be ashamed of himself for making such an exhibition, it is a disgrace to himself and to the members of the Board. There is no necessity of such a scene as this. You ought to keep cool and calm and not act like a mad man."

A few minutes later, Hirsch apologized, and the board granted him leave to go to New York in mid-May.[21] Yet after these dramatic scenes, the relations between Hirsch and the board had deteriorated almost beyond repair. Hirsch immediately resigned from the Sinai school and ritual and choir committees, reducing his commitments to the absolute minimum. A few days after the meeting, he tested the waters when he asked the board whether he could accept another invitation by the University of Iowa in mid-June. In a friendly reply letter, President Fishell refused to make a decision (unlike in earlier instances) and referred the matter to the board. The board unanimously (!) turned Hirsch's request down. In early May, after learning about this decision, Hirsch informed the board that Albion Small, the head of the University of Chicago Sociology Department, had agreed to replace him during his New York absence in mid-May. "He has kindly consented to occupy my—or must I say your?—pulpit during my absence on May 15th."[22]

CELEBRATING SUNDAY SERVICES

After the 1898 summer recess, the conflict moved to the sidelines for several months as Sinai prepared for the large "silver" celebration of Sunday services scheduled for January 1899. In the fall, Hirsch and the board members corresponded with potential guests and collectively organized the celebration. Among the guests of honor were several of the younger rabbis who were openly sympathetic to Hirsch: Max Landsberg from Rochester, Moses Griess from Cleveland, and J. Leonard Levy, from Philadelphia. Krauskopf could not attend but congratulated Sinai in a public letter. Kaufmann Kohler accepted the invitation, although he now openly opposed Sunday services. In a letter to Hirsch, he stressed he had "become more careful and emphatic in insisting on the maintenance of the traditional Sabbath." But he would "never . . . fail to recognize the great impetus given . . . by that movement with which I was for many years identified."[23] Isaac Mayer Wise was not invited, but he was almost eighty years old. Although the hostility of earlier days had faded, he and the *American Israelite* were prominent critics of Sunday services—and Sinai still had not joined the UAHC.

The *Reform Advocate* devoted a special issue to the celebration. The event reflected the enormous pride of the congregation in its ultimate success and leadership. But the unclear situation regarding Hirsch's future at Sinai hung like a dark cloud over the celebration. Sinai's members were not the only ones who speculated who of the younger rabbis among the guests might become Hirsch's successor. The speeches by Kohler and Hirsch—now the unrivaled leaders of the Reform movement—defined the event, albeit in very different ways. Kohler spoke as the representative of the Reform mainstream to an audience overwhelmingly composed of radical Reformers. He refused to condemn Sinai (and his own legacy) but freely acknowledged his change of opinion: "Our ways have parted. We walked in different directions. You, under the powerful sway of your peerless leader, have persistently and consistently moved on, unconcerned about the rest, on the road of radical reform, scoring triumphant success for the Sunday-service, while dropping the ancient Sabbath and the Torah scroll from sight." Sinai blazed its own trail but, in his view, it was still very much a Jewish congregation. Yet—as on earlier visits to his former congregation—Kohler warned Sinai not to storm ahead and lose touch with the Reform mainstream. This was more than an implicit call to join the UAHC. American Reform Jews, he urged, had to preserve "unity" and prevent a "schism" at any cost; especially at this moment. Judaism in Europe remained trapped "in the Ghetto" and was incapable of facing up to the challenge of modernity. The main task American Jews faced was to Americanize the Jewish immigrants from eastern Europe and win them for the Reform movement.[24] From a theological perspective, Kohler's concern seemed justified. Only a hairbreadth seemed to divide Sinai from ethical culture.

Kohler had little reason to worry, as he could convince himself at the celebration. Almost all guests invited to the splendid banquet belonged to the Jewish community. This was an exclusively Jewish event. During the evening banquet, Hirsch replied to Kohler, stating emphatically: "We are a *Jewish* congregation. This first, second, third, this last and all the time." But Hirsch had his own agenda, trying to convince Temple Emanu-El that he was no Felix Adler. And indeed, the board and many members must have rather uneasily looked forward to Hirsch's evening address. At the close of the speeches by the invited guests earlier in the afternoon, President Fishell had symbolically bowed to Hirsch, "our captain, our chieftain." Rumors about Hirsch's move to Temple Emanu-El were now openly circulating. The formal evening event at this symbolic celebration presented an ideal opportunity for Hirsch to draw a line under almost twenty years in Chicago and announce his decision to follow Kohler to New York. He was forty-seven years old and had achieved more than anybody could have hoped for. He had saved and redefined Sunday services and reinvented Sinai congregation. The dramatic nineteenth century was drawing to a close, and he more than so many of his contemporaries seemed ready to step into a new era. If there was an opportune moment to move on, now it had arrived.

Much to everybody's relief, Hirsch did not take this dramatic step—at least not yet. But his address betrayed anger and disappointment. The rabbi launched a sharp and unprecedented attack on the board. "I have grown old in your service—older than my years should make me." He extensively praised Sinai for the freedoms it supposedly allowed its rabbi, but in reality these words were full of sarcastic irony. He and the board, Hirsch emphasized, were "perfectly on a level as co-equals." That was, of course, not the case, at least as far as most board members were concerned. He continued, "Sinai congregation has a message to the Jewish congregations of this land. Sinai's pulpit has always been absolutely free. There was never a trace of bossism in our congregation. This has been the glory of our position." Never had a rabbi of Sinai been forced to ask the board like a "beggar" for a leave of absence. Again, most members of the audience knew Hirsch was implying the exact opposite. Therefore, his next point constituted an implicit warning, even a threat. "Make your pulpits free. Do not interfere with them." Only after these words could the board members take a deep breath of relief, as Hirsch switched to his prepared address and praised the founders and legacy of Sunday services at the congregation. But not only the board members were wondering what to make of this sentence: "Whatever the future may bring forth, I am grateful to Sinai congregation."[25]

The press reaction was mixed, as could be expected. Although by now Sunday services were expanding and more than a dozen large urban congregations had introduced them, the overwhelming majority of American Reform Jews remained opposed, not to mention Jews abroad. The *American Israelite* covered the event objectively without taking a position. The *Hebrew Union College Journal* was surprisingly sympathetic. Whatever critics made of Sinai, the congregation and its radical Reform agenda had to be taken seriously, and its "influence on the future of American Judaism" was "far-reaching." Papers opposed to the Reform movement like the *London Jewish World* or the *American Hebrew* were critical, but that had been expected. The London *Jewish Chronicle*, however, pointed out that a weekly attendance of two thousand constituted an impressive achievement. The *Jewish Spectator* from Memphis congratulated Hirsch—but not Sinai congregation:

Sinai Congregation has the good fortune to sit at the feet of a rabbi who, by virtue of his eloquence, scholarship and personal magnetic attractions, could make a Monday-Sabbath or a Wednesday-Sabbath as much of a signal success as he did make the Sunday-Sabbath. Moreover, Chicago has an immense Jewish population, hundreds of men and women are not affiliated with any congregation. . . . Chicago can always have "full houses."[26]

This comment in particular raised the question what future Sinai would have without Hirsch, if any.

Only days after the celebration, Temple Emanu-El made Hirsch an official offer (which included a higher salary of $14,000). The *Chicago Tribune* published the news in its January 19 edition as part of a longer interview conducted with Hirsch on the previous evening. Emanu-El, Hirsch pointed out, was larger than Sinai and would offer him more possibilities. But he would have to weigh his decision with his family and Chicago friends. He did not mention Sinai congregation. The *New York Times* stressed that Emanu-El was more "orthodox" than Sinai, but apparently Hirsch had promised he would hold services on Saturday, as long as these were attended. In the *Reform Advocate* special issue covering the celebration of the Sunday services anniversary, which was published on January 21, Hirsch printed a congratulatory letter by none other than Emanu-El's rabbi, Gustav Gottheil. The older rabbi stressed that Sunday services "have come to stay." This reform had brought many indifferent Jews back to the synagogue. He praised Sinai and extended his best wishes to Hirsch, the "eloquent and energetic guide and instructor of that ardent body of Israelites." This letter, regardless of its intentions, could be read as an expression of support by the senior rabbi for his potential successor. On February 10, the *New York Times* reported Hirsch was "seriously considering the call."[27]

A week later, on February 17, Sinai's board came together for a special meeting. Each member was asked to state his position. Most were in favor of retaining Hirsch, even if his salary had to be raised to match Emanu-El's offer, but they also wanted to hear Hirsch's opinion. According to Adolph Nathan, 95 percent of the members did not want to lose Hirsch. "We know his many faults, but we also know his wonderful genius." Adolph Loeb advised the board to offer Hirsch, in a unanimous vote, a life contract. Only such a demonstration of trust would appease Hirsch. Edwin Foreman supported Loeb, although he warned, "In our own business, as careful and prudent business men we would not make any such contract." Sinai, however, was different, because "the Doctor" really had "given us all his life." This is an interesting remark, Foreman clearly distinguished between the two boardrooms: Sinai was no business, and the conditions Hirsch enjoyed could not be measured with a businessman's logic.

Only President Fishell openly called for letting Hirsch go. The congregation was "on fire." In his opinion no member would resign if Hirsch moved to New York. Before the vote Nathan made a surprising statement that is touching in its honesty:

> He [Hirsch] has grievous faults . . . with all his sarcasm and his cynical expressions [he] drives the young men out. If he were a modest man and not so full of the ego and vanity, he would not do it . . . [he] would increase our membership more than thirty-three per cent. . . . sometimes I feel like going out and staying out, because we are denounced from the pulpit. We are called fools and ignoramuses; I believe we are such, but I do not want him to tell it to me it is true.

The board then voted unanimously to keep Hirsch as a rabbi. Three days later, on February 20, Hirsch met with the board. The moment of truth had arrived. For once the roles were reversed, and Hirsch relished the situation. Now, the board came "begging" to him and he was in a position to decide. A few days earlier, a board member had been honest enough to admit his own shortcomings. The same cannot be said about Hirsch.

Time and again, Hirsch declared as he addressed the board, he had suffered when he had to go to the board as a "petitioner" to ask for short leaves of absence. Sinai had never treated him in the respectful manner he as a great scholar rabbi deserved. Not so Emanu-El: "Three years ago I preached at Temple Emanu-El; they gave me a banquet and presented me with a silver service . . . they will care for me, when I am old." In New York, he would introduce Sunday services. And within a few years he would emerge as the new leader of American Judaism. Kohler had never been able to fill the void left by Einhorn. And Isaac Mayer Wise was an old man. "His successorship will fall on me. It will probably be but a few years when he will no longer be the head of that College, and I have no doubt that with the money influence behind me in New York I can have that college removed to New York and I [will] be the head professor of that College. You stand alone. You will belong to nothing." And he had enough of the frontier-town Chicago: "A man who lives at the frontier a long time feels as though he wants to go back to civilization again." All of this was hard to swallow for the board members, but suddenly Hirsch changed his tune. The public appeals and not least letters by several leading Christians had moved him. Yes, he was willing to stay in Chicago, if Sinai gave him a life contract. He concluded with a couple of petty attacks on several senior members of Sinai who allegedly had talked during the service and spread negative rumors about him. A brief discussion followed. Binswanger (again) voiced his opposition to a life contract and asked Hirsch how he could go to an "orthodox" congregation and hold Saturday services. Given the circumstances, it was brave to even ask Hirsch a question. Another furious reaction could be expected. Even braver was the actual question, for Binswanger really suggested Hirsch was an opportunist who was willing to sacrifice his theological positions for an attractive job and more money. But Hirsch politely dismissed Binswanger; Emanu-El was not "orthodox" and, of course (and that was true), he had never renounced the historic Sabbath. The board then voted to give Hirsch a life contract and raise his salary to $13,000 per annum. "Whereupon Dr. Hirsch suddenly arose and said: 'Well, gentlemen, I will tender my resignation.' He seemed to be angry but none of the members knew the cause. He left the room, and about three minutes thereafter the meeting adjourned, at 10:40 o'clock." On the following day the board members met again—they were clueless. Fishell presented Hirsch's formal resignation letter, written and signed by Hirsch only a few hours earlier. Nothing was decided.

Although the board meetings were not open to the public, these stirring events were not taking place behind closed doors, which only increased the pressure on Sinai's board to act. The Chicago and New York papers and the *American Israelite* covered the developments at Sinai extensively. On February 24, the board called a meeting of the congregation for February 27. In the days leading up to the meeting, seventy young men joined Sinai to express their support for Hirsch; the local papers and leading personalities called on Hirsch not to leave the city.[28]

Hirsch, of course, continued to preach his weekly sermons. It may not have been purely coincidental that some of his most outspoken attacks on big business fell into these weeks. Fishell recalled in 1921 how Hirsch had constantly called on entrepreneurs and shop owners to treat their employees "more humanely."[29] That was a somewhat euphemistic description. In reality, Hirsch went much further. On New Year's Day 1899, Hirsch sharply condemned trusts and corporations accusing them of ruthless practices—even murder—and the undermining of American society. "Competition is looked upon as its own justification." As an example he pointed to the distribution of meat to American soldiers; in a recent case, several soldiers had been poisoned after consuming contaminated meat. Although the person responsible in this case appeared to be a high-ranking military official, this was a thinly veiled attack against big meat

Characteristic attitudes sketched during his sermon yesterday morning.

FIGURE 9. Rabbi Emil G. Hirsch, as depicted by Will Koerner in "Popular Preachers of Chicago No. 4," *Chicago Daily Tribune*, September 18, 1899.

producers in America. The center of the American meat trade was Chicago, and one of the "Big Four" packinghouse owners happened to be a founding member of Sinai congregation. He was also one of the richest men in America: Nelson Morris.[30]

Even more revealing was the sermon, "Jewish Reform," Hirsch preached in late January. On this occasion he attacked the wealthy members of Sinai head on, publicly and more aggressively than ever before, lambasting their "materialism": "Was it for this that you craved equality with others? If it were for this you came out of the night of medæivalism, then you are merely the parasites of civilization." Wealth did carry ethical obligations. Jews—especially wealthy Jews—had "more duties than the non-Jew." A strong commitment on their behalf to general society was required not simply to fight anti-Semitism but rather to pursue the ethical mission, which defined Reform. Hirsch called on Sinai (and really all wealthy Jews) to donate generously for "the larger life of the people":

> Nothing would redound more to the honor of Chicago and the Jews than if the names of some of our wealthy Jews were written on the campus of our universities as patrons of the gentle arts and the classics. I say for the cause of Judaism it were far better if this method were adopted than by endowing old people's homes and orphan asylums.

Jewish philanthropists should not only direct their funds toward Jewish causes (however worthy) but to general society as well. Behind this stood the fear that Jews were withdrawing into a social ghetto, instead of increasing their involvement with society at large.[31] Several members of Sinai had already donated generously to the University of Chicago and other civic institutions. In hindsight, this sermon appears as a wakeup call for a little-known member of the congregation who would soon emerge as one of the leading American philanthropists. Julius Rosenwald, as he often acknowledged, largely fulfilled Hirsch's vision during the first three decades of the twentieth century.

A week later, in early February 1899, just when his departure to New York appeared imminent, Hirsch preached a sermon called "Organization and Division of Labor." Again, he did not mince words, warning Jews would be the first victims of an imminent social revolution. "Make, make, make money is the one appeal from morning to night. If two or three can combine to make slaves of ten thousand there is no law, and, alas, no conscience to stay their wicked hands." He openly called on Jewish entrepreneurs to reorganize their businesses in a more humanely fashion—to serve as good models to American society. Nelson Morris and perhaps other members must have felt Hirsch was publicly censuring them. This at least was how the *Tribune* reporter interpreted the sermon: the "Congregation gave no indication of what impression the address made. Dr. Hirsch later said he always spoke his mind freely . . . and his congregation had become used to it." A few years earlier, Hirsch told the reporter, several members had resigned after he had criticized the business practices of big corporations; and afterwards he refrained from "attacking individuals."[32]

On February 27, 173 persons came to Sinai's synagogue for the most important meeting since the founding of the congregation. Fishell, Mandel, and Loeb presented the position of the board. New York, they admitted, offered Hirsch more opportunities. But Chicago, "this growing Empire City of the West is similarly situated." More, much more was a stake than the future of Judaism in Chicago:

> Not only have we in our midst thousands of our own people who require the guidance of a great leader . . . but there are many thousands of our citizens, non-Jews, toilers in the workshops, in the stores and in counting rooms, who look to our Rabbi as the champion of their rights and justice, and whose going away would leave them without one of their strongest friends. . . . [Hirsch has been] aiding in the purification and the elevation of public office and public trust. From every platform his strong and warning voice goes out against corruption, and for civic pride and civic honesty, for justice and for humanity.

In Hirsch, Chicago would lose a powerful civic guardian and advocate. And at Sinai, "we would find ourselves an army without a general, soldiers anxious to do duty, but with none to lead."

These were powerful and great words, especially if set against Hirsch's egocentric address to the (closed) February 10 meeting. The members present overwhelmingly supported the board. Eli B. Felsenthal stressed the utmost importance of keeping Hirsch. President Harper of the University of Chicago had told him Chicago simply could not afford to let Hirsch go, one of the five spiritual leaders in the city. Sinai's board had to keep the interest of Chicago in mind— and it did, as the opening statement clearly indicates. Harper had promised Felsenthal he would personally plead with Hirsch to remain in Chicago. Only Julius Rosenthal raised his personal objections, as he so often did. But this time he failed to grasp the magnitude of this occasion; he bored the other members with legalistic details about the risks of a life contract. Yet even he conceded in the end that he had nothing against Hirsch. The meeting voted almost unanimously for a life contract. A small delegation was dispatched to Hirsch's residence immediately to bring Hirsch to an impromptu celebration. But the rabbi refused to receive the ambassadors; supposedly he was unwell. It was widely reported by papers on February 28 that Hirsch would stay. But it appears he did not make up his mind for about a week. For several days, rumors and speculation were rife. The *American Israelite* even announced the name of Hirsch's successor in its March 9 edition—none other than Max Landsberg from Rochester, who had attended the Sunday service celebration in January. But Landsberg could not confirm the story. Sinai's Sunday service on March 5 drew a record crowd. Everybody wanted to know whether Hirsch would stay—or go. Only a few days after the service, Hirsch informed Temple Emanu-El he would remain in Chicago. On March 15, the president of Emanu-El confirmed this decision in a letter to Sinai. On March 17, Hirsch wrote the board that he had been greatly moved by the February 27 resolution and decided to remain at Sinai.

At the annual meeting on April 3, 1899, the congregation resolved to raise Hirsch's salary to $15,000. Two members actually proposed a much higher figure. Board member Conrad Witkowsky suggested $25,000 and was supported by Morris Selz, but the reaction spoke for itself: "Cries of 'Sit Down. We can get it! . . . We have not got it.'" Several members reacted angrily to Selz. Loewenthal, like Selz a charter member and former president, reminded the members present that Selz had not "taken an active interest in this congregation" for many years. Leo Fox accused Selz of obstructing the board. As a multimillionaire, he could easily afford higher dues, but many members could not. The members then compromised on $15,000.[33] Hirsch's contract was extended to fifteen years, after which it would automatically revert to a life contract. Why he was not given a life contract on the spot and why Hirsch accepted this deal remain unclear. The two men who had been openly critical of Hirsch, Fishell and Binswanger, resigned from the board but retained their Sinai membership. The affable and experienced Adolph Loeb was elected as the new president. A few weeks later, one of the most prominent members of the congregation tendered his resignation. On June 6, 1899, the meatpacking mogul Nelson Morris, the target of repeated attacks by Hirsch, informed the board he would leave "at once." According to Fishell, Hirsch commented, "The doors of Sinai swing out and swing in. Those that wish to go out can do so and those that wish to come in are welcome to come." Morris never returned.[34]

Why did Hirsch not accept Temple Emanu-El's call? He knew such an opportunity would in all likelihood not present itself again. The challenge, even for a rabbi of Hirsch's stature, however, should not be underestimated. Temple Emanu-El's board was composed of even more influential personalities than Sinai's—Hirsch would have to tread cautiously. To win over a less radically minded congregation, major theological concessions were unavoidable. And its pulpit was not as free as that of Sinai. Indeed, even if Temple Emanu-El can hardly be described as "Orthodox," Hirsch would have to publicly defend religious reforms he had ridiculed in previous years. Even under ideal circumstances, access to the city's elite circles would have been difficult. On his occasional visits to New York, Hirsch had attracted large crowds. But he could not take large audiences for granted on a regular basis. Other talented speakers, not least Felix Adler, were popular with a similar crowd Hirsch hoped to attract. Maybe—although that is hard to imagine—Sinai's rabbi recognized his shortcomings as he made the decision to stay in Chicago. He also had to consider his increasingly fragile health. The sincere and almost desperate support by the congregation and prominent Chicagoans made a strong impression on him. And the deal Sinai offered him was attractive, even though by accepting the new contract Hirsch too committed himself permanently to Sinai and would not be able to leave easily. But he had gained more than a better contract. As one of very few rabbis in America, Hirsch had emancipated himself almost completely from the board of his congregation. He had won exactly the freedoms he had outlined in his sarcastic address at the Sunday service celebration in January 1899. No longer would Hirsch politely make a suggestion, or ask the board for a short leave of absence. The congregation would try to fulfill his every wish. And in April 1899, the leading members of Sinai knew what Hirsch wanted: a new temple.

CHAPTER EIGHT

9.

IN 1892, THE organizing committee of the World's Columbian Exhibition in Chicago decided to put up a large statue of Queen Isabella of Spain in a prominent location on the exposition grounds. The Spanish queen was the sponsor of Columbus's expedition in 1492. But, in the same year, Isabella ordered the expulsion of Jews from Spain, and she was a major driving force behind the Inquisition. From a Jewish viewpoint, a person who was responsible for burning thousands of her Jewish subjects at the stake and brutally forced out many more was hardly an appropriate symbol for an event that promoted an inclusive and universal vision of America to the world. Emil G. Hirsch suggested erecting a statue of the German writer Gotthold Ephraim Lessing instead—the antithesis of Isabella. In his most famous work, *Nathan the Wise*, the enlightenment playwright and close friend of Moses Mendelssohn made a powerful case for toleration of the other and for the likeness of Judaism, Islam, and Christianity. For Lessing, no religion possessed the absolute truth. When somebody proposed a statue of Jesus instead of Isabella (or Lessing), Hirsch commented, "Those who carry his name upon their lips the oftenest, are not always true to his spirit.... they would not have admitted the carpenter's son had he applied to their fashionable schools because forsooth he was a Jew." Hirsch and other Jewish critics did not impress the organizing committee. Hirsch's references to Lessing and to the Jewishness of Jesus, however, hint at a deeper agenda that transcended the debate about the Spanish queen. The Isabella statue was soon forgotten, but Lessing's ideals guided the architects of a Jewish-Christian dialogue in America. Hirsch, several like-minded Jews and Christians, and Sinai played a decisive role in the early phase of this dialogue.[1]

The Isabella statue episode appeared to highlight the marginality of Jews. The 1890s witnessed increasing social discrimination against established Jews and anti-Semitic agitation against new immigrants. The dialogue with Christians was one attempt to work against exclusion, but it was hardly the only one. Exclusion affected not only Jews as a group in American society, or new Jewish immigrants who were often not even welcome in the circles of the established Jews but also Jewish women. At the World's Columbian Exposition, Jewish women made a successful and impressive attempt to overcome their marginalization—publicly as well as in an internal Jewish context. Several prominent Jewish women had been invited to join the organizing committee of a Jewish Congress. This event was to take place under the roof of the exhibition together with hundreds of other workshops and meetings. When it dawned on the women that the Jewish male organizers wanted to assign them a purely ceremonial role, they walked out. Two Sinai women, Hannah Solomon and Sadie American, took the lead and organized a separate Jewish Women's Congress. The congress exceeded the expectations of the organizers and led to the founding of the first national Jewish women's organization in America.[2]

In the 1890s, Jews, admittedly a tiny minority, were at once making a widely recognized claim to join the American mainstream and yet were reminded of their outsider status. The insider-outsider paradigm also applied internally, as the second example illustrates. Just as the inclusion of Jews on an official level coexisted with exclusion in certain social circles, the male Jewish establishment (with a few exceptions) refused to treat recent Jewish immigrants and Jewish women as equals. The agenda for increased Jewish participation and acceptance in American society and culture and the fight against discrimination and exclusion reflected the vision of Sinai as an explicitly modern American *and* Jewish congregation. Indeed, it was hardly a coincidence that some of the most prominent advocates of the emerging American Jewish women's movement and the early pioneers of a Jewish-Christian dialogue belonged to Sinai.

SINAI'S WOMEN MAKE THEIR CLAIM

Like other communal organizations, such as burial societies, most Jewish (and Protestant) women's associations in the United States did not affiliate with congregations before the 1880s. In contrast to Jewish (and Protestant) *Gemeinden* in Europe or the pre-1800 comprehensive congregation in America, mid-nineteenth-century congregations concentrated almost exclusively on the weekly service and the religious school. At Sinai, women had no formal status, similar to most Jewish and Christian congregations. They joined as dependants of a male. In some cases, a widow could take up the membership of her deceased husband, but she could not serve on the board. Before 1880, only a few lay leaders and rabbis took up the issue of women's roles within congregations. One, perhaps not quite surprisingly, was Isaac Mayer Wise. He recognized early on the importance of women to keep congregations viable, especially as professional lives drew men away from services and board meetings. But these voices remained isolated. Women, however, did not remain passive. Kohler's concern about the opposition of Sinai's "Ladies" to Sunday services in 1873 is a telling example.

In her detailed study about Jewish women and the formation of American Judaism, Karla Goldman emphasizes the "shift" that occurred around 1890. Mass immigration, rapid urbanization, industrialization, growing poverty in inner-city neighborhoods, and the rise of the Progressive movement created new possibilities for younger women to escape the confines of the home. Most of these women were native born and belonged to socially established families. Some were married, others still lived with their parents, a few were single and inventing new careers as social workers or as professional (and salaried) activists. During the 1880s, more Jewish women began to volunteer for Jewish philanthropic organizations and congregations as aid workers and teachers—at schools for the children of congregants and of immigrants. And women launched ambitious projects on their own. In 1882, Sinai's women set up the forerunner of the Jewish Training School.[3]

In the late 1880s, several Reform congregations encouraged women to form organizations under the umbrella of their respective synagogues. New York was an early center. The pioneering sisterhood at Temple Emanu-El in 1888 was inspired by a successful Protestant organization. This and other early sisterhoods worked mostly outside of their actual congregations, especially on behalf of Jewish immigrants. The Emanu-El women provided advice and support, organizing an employment bureau and various activities for immigrant children. Other Jewish congregations in New York soon followed suit. In Kansas City and Philadelphia, rabbis Henry Berkowitz and Joseph Krauskopf inspired similar women's associations.[4] At first glance, Sinai congregation lagged far behind. Yet Sinai's women had been organizing informally by 1882 (if not earlier), as the founding of the Industrial School indicates.

Around 1890, the first women began to move into leadership positions in Jewish communities. Sinai's women were prominently represented on the local and national level. The most visible figures in the early phase were Hannah Solomon and Sadie American. Solomon was the daughter of Michael and the niece of Henry Greenebaum. Thirty-two years old in 1890 and the mother of three children, she was well educated and deeply influenced by Hirsch's teachings. Solomon embodied the "club woman volunteer." Sadie American, who turned thirty in 1890 and was single, represented another constituency of women activists: the settlement worker. American too had grown up with Sinai congregation. She taught at Sinai's school during the 1890s, was a resident at the Maxwell Street Settlement, and was affiliated with several Progressive causes in Chicago. Three other influential members of the first generation of female community leaders in Chicago also belonged to Sinai. Julia Felsenthal, a daughter of Sinai's first rabbi, was also single and spent some time at the Maxwell Street Settlement and taught at Sinai's school. Babette Mandel and Lizzie T. Barbe were closer to Solomon. They belonged to wealthy families and were married to established businessmen. Two other women became the first female officers of Jewish community institutions in Chicago. Blanche Stolz, the wife of rabbi Joseph Stolz, was elected to the board of the United Hebrew Charities in 1891. In the following year, Johanne Loeb (another Sinai woman) replaced her, remaining on the board for almost ten years. Throughout the 1890s, Hirsch encouraged women to organize in congregations and the wider community. In an 1892 article, he deplored the social "restrictions" women faced. Qualified women should become lawyers, physicians, and even rabbis. But in his opinion, only a few "exceptional" individuals (like him) could aspire to such careers. Neither he nor most women rejected traditional gender roles. In an ideal world, he emphasized, women would not have to work but could devote their full attention to their families: "Her place is at home."[5]

The World's Columbian Exposition provided Jewish women with a unique opportunity. The tacit opposition by the male organizers of the Jewish Denominational Congress to including women was the trigger. Solomon and American decided to take the initiative. Although they had only a few months' time to organize the Jewish Women's Congress, they received support from Jewish women across the country.[6] The Jewish Women's Congress led to the founding the National Council of Jewish Women, the first national Jewish women's organization. Julia Felsenthal coined the name, Solomon was elected as first president, and American became the lead manager. After the congress, Solomon and American began to drum up support. In 1894, one thousand four hundred members were recruited; by 1896, four thousand women had joined. The council regarded itself as a religious and charitable organization. While not feminist, it provided Jewish women with a distinctive voice that could not be ignored. Solomon's main goal resembled that of other Jewish leaders at the World Parliament of Religions: to work for the acceptance of modern American Judaism as part of the religious mainstream. Jewish women, as she stressed at the 1893 congress, should help to spread modern Judaism:

> Women and men of all creeds are realizing that the ties that bind us are stronger than the differences that separate, that when the world is giving to Israel the liberty, long withheld, of taking its place among all religions, to teach the truths it holds, for the benefit of man and the glory of the creator, the place of the Jewish woman should not be vacant. . . . And we in this land of liberty and prosperity, in this Columbian era, should not forget the deeper tones struck in days of adversity. . . . Belonging to radical congregations, . . . we are loyal to our faith.[7]

At first glance, Solomon's speech expresses the universal sentiment of the World's Columbian Exposition. And as could be expected, she echoed the broad and inclusive vision of Sinai's founders and their appreciation of the universal American ideals. But not only did she emphasize that women had a role to play in the mission of (radical) Reform Judaism, she reminded her mostly Jewish audience of the long history of enforced Jewish marginalization. Like other Reform Jews who participated in the World Parliament of Religions, Solomon made it clear that Jews would not sacrifice Judaism. In 1895, Solomon described the role of the council with a sentence that was clearly inspired by Hirsch: "Not the individual, but the organization, is the unit of our society."[8] In 1897, on the occasion of a regular Sunday service, she became the first woman to address the congregation from the pulpit as the main speaker. In her lecture, she presented the agenda of the council, outlining the importance of religion and scientific charity for the work of the organization.[9]

A few days after her lecture, the *Advocate* opened its pages to several of the foremost Jewish women speakers from across the country. Hirsch had drawn up a catalog of questions to redefine the role of Jewish women in the synagogue. The survey aimed precisely at the point that Hirsch himself, Solomon, and other women had been making since the early 1890s. The engagement of Jewish women would revive congregations. But how would the most active women be able to fulfill their traditional duties as mothers and wives? The women participating in the survey belonged to the leading figures of the new movement. They all supported a more prominent role of women in congregations, for instance, as Sabbath schoolteachers. Yet the most symbolic question—"Should she occupy the pulpit?"—divided the respondents. Women rabbis did not match with the volunteer ideal promoted by the council. Professional training and the demands of spiritual leadership of a congregation could not be combined with the traditional duties of a Jewish woman. The division of opinion among the survey participants followed partly that between club women and settlement workers. Solomon "strongly oppose[d] the ministry for women," as did several other respondents. Mary M. Cohen of Philadelphia was openly in favor of female rabbis: "There is no sex in spirituality." Julia Felsenthal argued, along the lines of Hirsch, that highly talented women might eventually be fit for the rabbinate.[10] The responses demonstrate the potential and limitations of the new Jewish women's movement. The councilwomen were not revolutionaries but cautious reformers who remained strongly committed to bourgeois ideals of family, motherhood, and the home. Only a few were ready to move further, and they can hardly be described as radical feminists.

The first major conflict within the National Council of Jewish Women was not fought over different visions of womanhood in modern society but over an issue that was much more divisive: religion. As leaders of an organization with a religious platform, Solomon's and American's open identification with Sinai's cause—in particular Sunday services—soon triggered criticism. A prominent opponent of Solomon was Rebekah Kohut, whose late husband had been an early leader of Conservative Judaism. At the 1896 council meeting, Solomon faced her first serious challenge, because she supported the Sunday Sabbath. She managed to deflect the attack by officially keeping debates over religious issues off the agenda—if she or other women were speaking on behalf of the council. This move can be interpreted as a tacit admission that the council was not primarily a religious organization. Yet Solomon was now a public figure. Her every move and word soon found its way to more than a few publications sitting atop Jewish coffee tables across America. In 1895, a new Jewish weekly joined the aging *Deborah*. The *American Jewess* targeted a younger generation of established Jewish women. Rosa Sonneschein, the former wife of Reform rabbi Solomon Sonneschein, edited the paper from Chicago and supported the council—but not uncritically. Other papers, not least the *Reform Advocate*, covered Solomon's speeches and activities. Solomon simply could not separate her role as a prominent Sinai member from that as the official leader of the council. Eventually in

1905, she declined to run for another term. In the post-Solomon era, the council quickly moved away from its religious platform and concentrated almost completely on philanthropic work, especially on social projects with Jewish immigrant women.[11] The council's national secretary, Sadie American, oversaw this reorientation. She had been as vocal as Solomon in her support of Sunday services. But in 1900, she moved to New York. Here, as a salaried employee of the council, she concentrated successfully on managing the national organization. In addition she took on the leadership of the New York council chapter, whose members were overwhelmingly not radical Reformers. American's organizational skills, her enthusiasm, and her background as a settlement worker explain why she managed to keep her position.[12]

In hindsight, the strong reaction by Conservative and moderate Reform women was not surprising. Even the women who were active in the council tended to be more in tune with the religious tradition than their husbands, brothers, and even fathers. The radical Sinai women represented a vocal but relatively small minority. The marginalization of Sinai's women in an organization they had helped to create proved once more that overarching Jewish organizations in America were not viable on a religious platform.

The early history of the council raises a few questions: why did Solomon and other women organize under the auspices of the World's Columbian Exposition's Department of Religion, and why did they commit the Council to a religious mission—when they knew that other Jewish women did not share their radical views? A closer look at the early stages of a Jewish-Christian dialogue shows that Solomon's strong commitment to radical Reform Judaism had a more complex background.

OPENING A DIALOGUE

In November 1890, several Jewish and Christian ministers from Chicago met for a public workshop at the First Methodist Church with "the object of giving information and of promoting a spirit of inquiry therefore on the basis of mutual kindness." The main organizer was William Blackstone, a Protestant businessman. None of the participating rabbis and ministers knew much, if anything, about him. During the two-day interfaith workshop, Blackstone remained in the background. The speakers outlined their theologies and described their views of the other religion, primarily to learn and reexamine their own positions. In their talks, the rabbis and ministers explored basic questions, as the titles of their lectures indicate: "Why Israelites Do Not Accept Jesus as Their Messiah" (Bernhard Felsenthal); "The Attitude of Nations and of Christian People Toward the Jews" (Reverend E. P. Goodwin), "The Religious Conditions of Jews To-day and Their Attitude Towards Christianity" (Emil G. Hirsch).[13]

The beginning interfaith dialogue in this period hints at a major shift in American religious discourse. Already after the Civil War, some Christian leaders and the wider public treated Sinai and major Reform congregations in other cities with respect, but serious theological discussions between Jews and Christians remained rare. There were certainly exceptions. In Cincinnati, for instance, Reform rabbi Max Lilienthal exchanged pulpits with Christian colleagues as early as the 1870s. According to his biographer (and successor at Bene Israel), David Philipson, Lilienthal did "much" to build cordial relations between Jews and Christians in Cincinnati. In Chicago, a much bigger city, Jewish and Christian congregations supported each other after the 1871 fire. Yet apart from a few exchanges with liberal Protestant ministers like Robert Collyer, David Swing, and Hiram W. Thomas, Sinai, as an explicitly modern congregation, remained isolated. This changed during the 1880s. Admittedly, at the 1890 workshop, only two relatively small groups within Judaism and Christianity in America were represented—liberal Protestants and radical Reform Jews—or so it seemed. The climate for a dialogue had become much more convivial than in previous decades. Sinai was hardly typical, but comparable Reform congregations in other cities also opened up to their neighbors and stepped up their visibility, an indication of increasing acceptance and confidence. Moreover, as theology emerged as academic discipline in America, many Protestants recognized that German-trained Reform rabbis were serious theological scholars. In the last three decades of the nineteenth century, German models influenced divinity schools, new religion programs at research universities, and even religious seminaries.[14]

A scholar examining the American interfaith dialogue around the turn of the twentieth century on a purely theological level could easily overlook the absentees. By 1890, it was apparent that the mass immigration from eastern and southern Europe would have a major impact on American religious life. The overwhelming majority of the immigrants were Catholics, traditional (or secular) Jews, and Orthodox Christians. Hardly any recently arrived immigrant rabbis and scholars took part in interfaith discussions before 1914. Established "German" Jews and mostly Irish Catholics were well aware that immigration broadened the religious spectrum within their faiths considerably—and rapidly. The rise of Conservative Judaism in the 1880s was in part a response to the changing dynamic of American Jewish life in the early period of mass immigration. The dynamic of immigration also explains why rabbis like Hirsch and Kohler began to take an increasing interest in seminaries. In 1892, Hirsch wrote an enthusiastic report of his visit to Hebrew Union College, even commending Wise. Hirsch, a longtime critic of Cincinnati, began to recognize the importance of the college for the future of the Reform movement. In 1903, three years after Wise died, Kohler became the new president of HUC. He overhauled the curriculum and concentrated on the academic and professional training of future rabbis. Since Conservative Jews had established their own Jewish Theological Seminary in New York in 1886, Kohler decided to commit HUC more explicitly to the tenets of the Reform movement than Wise, who had kept the door open to more traditionally minded Jews.[15] Postgraduate institutions for training clergy required substantial funding and a long-term planning, but these institutions also provided the establishment with control over their respective movement. Around 1890, it was still too early to tell how many descendants of the new Jewish immigrants the Reform movement would be able to attract. One development, however, was apparent: many Jewish and Protestant immigrants did not affiliate with a congregation.

According to a statistic based on the 1890 census, in Chicago, about ten thousand Jews, a hundred thousand Protestants, and more than two hundred sixty thousand Catholics were affiliated. A little less than two-thirds of the one million Chicagoans was unaffiliated. In other American cities, the proportions differed. However, Catholics easily constituted the largest group in every big city. The high number of Catholics was only partly the result of the post-1880 mass immigration. Irish and German-speaking Catholics made up a considerable part of America's urban population in the 1860s and 1870s.[16]

The high rate of Catholic affiliation betrays the remarkable clout of the parish system. While American Protestants and Jews adapted the pluralist model in the first half of the nineteenth century, Catholics transplanted the European parish to America. Parish systems covered a clearly defined settlement area, usually dominated by one or two ethnic groups. In his study *Parish Boundaries*, John T. McGreevy shows why Jews and white Protestants displayed a much higher residential mobility than Catholics. The former groups left inner city immigrant neighborhoods as they moved up socially. Jewish and Protestant congregations followed their members. Therefore, a congregation like Sinai regularly had to spend considerable amounts on real estate and new buildings. Many Catholics remained tied to specific neighborhoods, built around "their" parish church. The tight organization of Catholic immigrant neighborhoods corresponded with a high degree of social control by the Catholic clergy. Many Catholic immigrants had little choice but to affiliate. For Catholics, however, sociability transcended "church" in a narrow sense; the parish system served as a social umbrella comprising dozens of associations and clubs. The success of this model was not lost upon Protestants and Jews.[17]

Admittedly, Jews were a small group, compared to Catholics. But even in colonial America, they had represented the largest non-Christian religion, and after 1880 their numbers increased. Jewish support for interfaith dialogue was driven by three interrelated concerns. The looming threat of anti-Semitism in the 1880s and 1890s made it almost compulsory for Jewish religious leaders to educate the public about Judaism. In an overwhelmingly Christian society, reaching out to Christian ministers was particularly important, because Americans had traditionally been exposed to anti-Jewish stereotypes from the Christian pulpit.[18] Even in a period of massive urbanization and social change, Christian ministers retained much moral authority beyond their respective congregations. The rise of anti-Semitism in Europe and to a growing extent in America, as well as the Jewish mass migration from eastern Europe, complicated efforts to involve Christian leaders in a dialogue and added urgency to this project.

A second motive followed from the Pittsburgh Platform and the rise of the second American-born generation. Leading Reformers felt they had fully arrived as Jews in America. In order to gain wider acceptance as part of the American mainstream, they could not stand apart but had to build lasting ties to like-minded Christians. Sinai congregation and Emil G. Hirsch were leaders in this project. The large number of Christians who attended Hirsch's Sunday services spoke for itself. Just as Jews were making their claim for official acceptance, the Catholic hierarchy in America pursued a similar goal. Catholics experienced enforced marginalization, discrimination, and hostility even more than Jews. The mass immigration from Europe strengthened anti-Jewish and anti-Catholic forces in America. But immigration also threatened to undermine the position of the Jewish and Catholic establishment. Yet in the short term, the steadily increasing number of Catholics and Jews gave their religious leaders more clout.

A third, more specific factor behind interfaith collaboration was the sincere interest shared by liberal Jewish and Christian theologians to define a permanent platform for an exchange of ideas. Jewish Reformers were unsettled by the rising strength of traditional Judaism in America. Regardless of real religious differences, liberal Jews and Protestants shared more among each other than with traditionally minded members of their own faiths. In Chicago, Hirsch quickly emerged as the leading Jewish advocate of a dialogue. From his first days in Sinai's pulpit, he built ties to leading Christian thinkers and theologians in the city.

The Jewish-Christian dialogue, as Susannah Heschel emphasizes in her study on Abraham Geiger, has long revolved around different interpretations of Jesus.

And Jesus was indeed a crucial figure for Hirsch's ethical and social justice theology. In his appreciation of Jesus, however, Hirsch was hardly uncritical. An 1892 lecture on the Crucifixion given to an audience of Reform Jews and liberal Protestants in Chicago illustrates his theological agenda. The lecture was published (with footnotes) and later reprinted, an indication of the importance Hirsch and Sinai attached to its content. At the outset Hirsch stated, "He [the Jew] need not deny, and he will not deny, the providential mission of Christianity, nor the rich blessings which it conferred upon the races of man." This disclaimer gave way to an exhaustive analysis that betrayed Hirsch's proficiency in Semitic languages and his commitment to biblical criticism. In the best tradition of Abraham Geiger, his teacher at the Berlin Hochschule in the early 1870s, Hirsch subjected the available sources to a detailed textual analysis and convincingly refuted Jewish responsibility for the Crucifixion. Of course, Hirsch was not the first American rabbi who confronted this issue. Isaac Mayer Wise published a detailed study of the Gospels already in 1874 to disprove widely held beliefs in Jewish responsibility in the Crucifixion. Hirsch, however, presented a much more scholarly analysis of the Gospels, their origins, and limitations than Wise did. Sinai's rabbi clearly aimed at a more educated readership, notably, Christian theologians and ministers. Like Geiger, Hirsch stressed the Jewish background of Jesus, describing him as one of the Pharisees.[19]

At first glance, the importance Hirsch and other Jewish Reform theologians attached to biblical criticism might appear to be an ill-judged move to open a serious dialogue with Christians in America. Only liberal Protestants shared a platform with Jews on this subject relatively early. But around 1890, biblical criticism was gradually making inroads with leading theologians, not quite surprising, as American universities established graduate schools and seminaries overhauled their curricula. One of the most influential proponents of biblical criticism in America was the first president of the University of Chicago, William Rainey Harper. Here, then, lies another reason why Harper was eager to recruit Hirsch for the University of Chicago in 1892, at the time of this lecture, and retain him if possible.[20] Hirsch's programmatic Crucifixion lecture, however, was no job-talk. His underlying motive was more fundamental: Sinai's rabbi consciously raised the core issue that at once separated and united Jews and Christians. Emphasizing the Jewishness of Christianity's founding figure seemed to constitute an even bigger affront than biblical criticism to many potential Christian partners for a dialogue. For Hirsch, as for his teacher Geiger, Jesus was not just born a Jew—he lived, preached, and died as a Jew—a thesis they based on biblical criticism. The view of Jesus as a Jew, however compelling, was anathema for Catholics and conservative Protestants. In Germany, liberal Protestant theologians who themselves were advocates of biblical criticism could not dispute the Jewishness of Jesus. Yet instead of acknowledging the pioneering work of Jewish theologians like Geiger, prominent Protestant scholars tried to disconnect Jesus from other Jews and Judaism. And they refused to enter into a dialogue with Jewish theologians such as Rabbi Leo Baeck around 1900.[21]

In the United States, the conditions for a Jewish-Protestant dialogue differed considerably, not just because of the clear-cut division of state and religion and the dynamic religious landscape. Around 1890, closer cooperation was an obvious choice for Reform Jews and liberal Protestants. Both faced the possible specter of marginalization within their own camp. Evangelical Protestantism was on the rise, and the arrival of traditional Jews and Catholics, the rise of Socialism, as well as the increasing strength of Conservative Judaism were developments liberal Jews and Protestants could not ignore.[22]

With his lecture on the crucifixion, Hirsch clarified the position of Reform Jews on the eve of the World's Columbian Exposition and the World Parliament of Religions in Chicago. Hirsch's unambiguous refutation of a Jewish responsibility for the Crucifixion (of a Jew) provides the chance to examine the possibilities and limitations of a Jewish-Protestant dialogue in America. In Chicago, Hirsch and his congregation faced two influential religious figures who represented opposing ends of the American Protestant spectrum: Jenkin Lloyd Jones and Dwight L. Moody.

JENKIN LLOYD JONES

The Welsh-born Jones was one of the most undogmatic Unitarians of his generation. In 1877, by then a rising figure in the Western Unitarian Conference and minister of a congregation in Janesville, Wisconsin, he expressed open support for biblical criticism. He reminded his fellow Christians that Jesus could not be divorced from his Jewish background: "He who declares that the living water from the great soul of Jesus has in it no foreign ingredients, no deposit belonging to the age, race, climate, and surroundings to which it belonged, refuses to apply the methods of analysis and distillation well known and well established by students to-day." In 1880, Jones relocated to Chicago to work permanently for the Western Unitarian Conference and focus on the editorship of his weekly journal, *Unity*. In 1882, *Unity* began printing some of Hirsch's sermons; in 1889, Hirsch joined *Unity*'s editorial board.[23]

In 1888, Sinai, All Souls, other liberal Protestants, and the Ethical Culture Society launched their first joint venture, the Chicago Institute for Instruction in Letters, Morals, and Religion. Its president, Franklin Head, was a well-known Chicago banker; Sinai member Julius Rosenthal served as vice president. The purpose of the institute was twofold. It offered a program of instructive evening lectures by educated speakers on various topics in the arts, sciences, and religion. The founders cited the Lowell and the Peabody Institutes in Boston and Baltimore, respectively, as models. But on a higher plane, the institute also served as common platform for members of different religious backgrounds. It was the obvious venue for Hirsch's 1892 Crucifixion lecture. In 1888, Sinai's rabbi volunteered to teach the first nine-week course: once-weekly evening classes on the Old Testament. For three dollars (or fifty cents per lecture) interested Chicagoans could attend the classes at the downtown Architectural Sketch Club in a room that offered seating for fifty people. According to Jones, the purpose of the institute was to overcome "the ignorance of intelligent men and women." He described the target group for Hirsch's course as "Sunday-school teachers, superintendents and students of religious thought and history." Hirsch's first class attracted more than fifty people and was well received. According to an observer, Hirsch did not present a formal talk, but came equipped with chalk and images to instruct the listeners. As on other occasions, he emphasized that he would not dismiss or ridicule the Bible but would not approach it uncritically, either.[24]

Not all liberal Protestants were ready for a dialogue with Jews. In an 1888 sermon, Jones recalled the worthy attempt by several "liberal ministers" in Chicago to reach beyond denominational lines and work together in a "fellowship." But while initially sympathetic to the idea, Jones withdrew when a majority decided to limit membership to Christians. Jones continued—in a sermon about Jesus—"I regretfully decided to stay outside with the saints and sinners who are proscribed by that phraseology. I will stay in the fellowship of Moses Montefiore and the truth-seeking and man-serving Jews everywhere. I will stay outside with Chunder Sen, Mozoomdar, and the white souls of India, with Emerson, Marcus Aurelius, Socrates, and Jesus."[25]

In 1884, Jones resigned from the Western Unitarian Conference to revive the Fourth Unitarian Church on the South Side of Chicago. Jones, a popular preacher, renamed it All Souls Church and turned it into a flourishing social congregation. In an 1894 portrait, a Chicago reporter characterized All Souls as a "home church." The "audience hall, libraries, and club-room" gave it a "charm that was "irresistible." All Souls was in some ways similar to Sinai, open to every person, regardless of her or his faith. Like Hirsch, Jones attracted large numbers of people from various backgrounds to his Sunday sermons.[26] Sinai and All Souls differed in regard to their membership: before 1900, Sinai's members constituted a small, tight-knit group of wealthy families. As a Christian congregation, All Souls admittedly had access to a larger pool of potential members, attracting a more-diverse and less-distinguished crowd. Many were upwardly mobile young men and women who were entering the middle class. This was exactly the group that aspiring social congregations like Sinai had to pull into their orbit in order to grow beyond a small group of closely connected businessmen. The private papers of some Sinai members reveal that for some, the border between radical Reform and Jones's nondogmatic Unitarianism was fluid. Sinai member Sophie Rosenwald, a younger sister of Julius and the wife of Sears and Roebuck executive Max Adler, sent her children not to Sinai's Sunday school but to All Soul's. Edward Morris, the son and successor of packinghouse owner and Sinai founder Nelson Morris, apparently did not belong to All Souls, nor did he convert. But Jones preached his funeral sermon in 1914.[27]

In 1885, Jones described Hirsch in a friendly pun as "our 'Fifth Unitarian' minister." Even more intriguing, from the perspective of Sinai congregation, was Jones's fierce opposition to dogma. His resignation from the Western Unitarian Conference and concentration on All Souls was related to a conflict within the Unitarian movement over the definition of the denomination as Christian. The conflict was resolved in 1892, but Jones opposed the compromise and distanced himself from organized Unitarianism. This background explains the growing unease Jones (and Hirsch) felt in discussions with some liberal Protestants who were not willing to seriously accept other religions as equals. In 1898, All Souls severed all ties with the Unitarian denomination. This made it easier for Sinai members and other Jews to affiliate with All Souls without formally joining the congregation. For many Jews in New York and Chicago, attending Felix Adler's lectures did not contradict their membership in a Reform congregation. Jones's view of Jesus is a perfect illustration of this transition. Similar to Hirsch, he portrayed him as a man of his time, an ethical teacher, and a role model whose message resonated beyond Judaism and Christianity. Sometime between 1884 and 1904, Jones stressed that any act of Christian appropriation diminished the importance of the actual Jesus for all people regardless of their religion, "Jesus wrote no creed, appointed no bishop, organized no church and taught no trinity. He framed no scheme of commercial atonement or sanguinary salvation to compromise the dignity, to impeach the justice, or to deny the love of the great God of the universe. Yet all these things are part and parcel of historic Christianity—so much a part of it that, taking these away, you have instead of Christianity only a blessed humanity left."[28] Nobody would have disagreed with this view more strongly than Jones's contemporary, Dwight L. Moody. As an

CHAPTER NINE

evangelical Christian, he regarded biblical criticism as blasphemy, and his view of the Jews explains why Hirsch spoke about Crucifixion in 1892, and perhaps more surprisingly, shows Hirsch's opposition to Zionism in a different light.

DWIGHT L. MOODY AND WILLIAM BLACKSTONE

Among the guests of the World's Columbian Exposition in September 1893 was a certain Adolf Stoecker, who until 1890 had been the chaplain at the court in Berlin—and a notorious anti-Semite. None other than Dwight L. Moody had invited this controversial figure to Chicago. In 1893, Moody was one of the most illustrious American Protestants. He is today regarded as a founding father of modern evangelical Protestantism in America. This legacy is even more remarkable, given Moody's lack of any formal education. His main accomplishment was to bring evangelical Protestantism to American cities during the second half of the nineteenth century. Moody was drawn to Stoecker, because he was a conservative social reformer and fierce opponent of Socialism who had long worked with the urban working class. As founder of the Berlin *Stadtmission* (city mission) Stoecker successfully combined social work with religious instruction. As Moody put it, "He is trying to do in Germany just what I am trying to do here—to reach the non-church-going masses with the gospel of Christ for their salvation." After 1880, Moody had gradually moved from his famous revivals to more extended campaigns targeting not evangelicals but working-class city migrants who were drifting away from the church. Like Stoecker, Moody opposed liberal reformers and socialists. Yet the Lutheran Stoecker was no evangelical, and his ambition was primarily political. In the late 1870s, he failed to rally workers around his socially conservative agenda. But when he began to add anti-Semitism to his political platform he attracted broad support from lower-middle-class voters—and became an attractive figure for Bismarck and the powerful Conservative Party. In 1892, Stoecker inserted an openly anti-Semitic clause into the Conservative Party program. Moody did not openly promote anti-Semitism, nor did he aim for political influence. But like other evangelicals, he believed in Jewish responsibility and guilt for the Crucifixion, and he supported attempts to convert Jews.[29]

Stoecker's visit became a public affair when the German-language publication *Staatszeitung* broke its initial silence. Its editors explained they had decided to cover the visit after securing Stoecker's promise not to speak about anti-Semitism. And indeed, Stoecker kept his promise: "I came not to attack the Jews, I came to preach the Word of God to my German brethren." After Stoecker's brief lecture, Moody turned to him and said, "We give you a warm welcome!

God bless you! We don't believe the newspapers! We believe the Bible! We have confidence in you! We love you!" In the *Reform Advocate*, Hirsch expressed nothing but scorn for the *Staatszeitung* for alienating its Jewish (and other) readers. In Hirsch's view, Stoecker was hardly a welcome guest, but at least he pronounced his anti-Semitism openly. Much more dangerous were "secret anti-Semites." This was a thinly disguised reference to Moody and his followers, especially to the above-mentioned William Blackstone, the organizer of the 1890 interfaith meeting.[30]

Upon Blackstone's suggestion, the ministers and rabbis had passed a resolution condemning the Russian government for supporting anti-Jewish violence. They also called on the American government to protest against the persecutions. While certainly sensible this seemingly innocent resolution was part of a "plan" Blackstone did not reveal to the participants. Blackstone was not a liberal Protestant, nor was he interested in opening a serious dialogue with Jews. In 1890, neither Bernhard Felsenthal nor Hirsch knew of Blackstone's true agenda. In 1887, he set up the Chicago Hebrew Mission, an institution openly supported by Moody. The "success" of this institution among immigrants remained negligible; according to its own publications, only a small handful of Jews were baptized in the 1890s.[31]

But Blackstone differed from other missionaries in Jewish immigrant neighborhoods. For him the mission was only one element of a larger endeavor that explains his "sympathy" with the persecuted Jews in Russia. Like Moody, Blackstone was an advocate of dispensationalist premillennialism. According to this deterministic belief, based on the apocalypse in the Gospel of John, at an unknown time in the future, all Jews will return to Palestine. They will rebuild the temple and establish a state. Their ruler will be a figure claiming to be the Jewish messiah—in reality, the Antichrist. The authentic Jesus Christ will return to Earth, destroy the Antichrist at Armageddon, and end his rule of terror. The few surviving Jews will recognize Jesus Christ as their true savior, immediately convert, and help to establish his earthly kingdom. This belief in the Second Coming explains why some evangelicals called for the Jewish return to Palestine, years before the first Zionist Congress met in Basel in 1897. The purpose of the Jewish missions was to "save" some Jews from their ultimate doom.[32]

Today, Blackstone is considered to be one of the pioneering Protestant "Zionists" in America. Soon after the interfaith meeting 1890, he began to call for an asylum for persecuted Jews from eastern Europe in Palestine. The call met with wide approval. The liberally minded public opinion was in favor, because he condemned the abuse and discrimination of Jews in Russia. Americans who opposed immigration and even anti-Semites probably sympathized with Blackstone's call, because Russian Jews would move to Palestine rather than America. Many Jews also reacted warmly to Blackstone's call, not least proto-Zionists. Some established Jews embraced Blackstone's Palestine plan, because it would reduce Jewish immigration. Emil G. Hirsch was not in principle opposed to Jewish life in Palestine, but he stated his position quite clearly: "We [Reform Jews] say, 'The country wherein we live is our Palestine, and the city wherein we dwell is our Jerusalem.' We will not go back . . . to form again a nationality of our own." In early 1891, Blackstone published the "Blackstone Memorial." This resolution called on President Benjamin Harrison to support the resettlement of Russian Jews in Palestine. Blackstone managed to assemble an impressive list of signatures: most Chicago ministers and rabbis signed. Among the signatories were Bernhard Felsenthal, Henry Greenebaum, Julius Rosenthal, and other members of Sinai, as well as prominent American businessmen, notably John D. Rockefeller and J. P. Morgan. Kaufmann Kohler also signed. One name, however, was missing. Emil G. Hirsch gave Blackstone credit for protesting against the intolerable conditions for Jews in the Russian Empire, but he recognized Blackstone's true intentions. He refused to sign. Other Jewish voices, such as the *American Israelite*, were also critical, but primarily because they opposed national Jewish aspirations as such. Nevertheless, many signatories did not express support with Blackstone but rather with persecuted Jews in Russia. Hirsch's primary reason for refusing to sign may well have been his fierce opposition to proto-Zionism and the concept of a Jewish race. Apart from rallying proto-Zionists in Chicago, the "Blackstone Memorial" had no immediate impact, but it stands out as an early attempt by evangelical Protestants to gain political influence.[33]

THE WORLD PARLIAMENT OF RELIGIONS AND THE AMERICAN CONGRESS OF LIBERAL RELIGIOUS SOCIETIES

Neither Jones's broad and inclusive vision nor Moody's proto-fundamentalism were representative of mainstream Protestantism in America, nor should the opposition between different positions be exaggerated. For instance, even during the 1890s, William Rainey Harper, a Baptist, entertained a close personal friendship with Moody, although their theological views had drifted apart. In 1891, Jane Addams briefly joined the executive committee of Blackstone's Chicago Hebrew Mission, even turning Hull House into the mission's headquarters. This peculiar (and short-lived) relationship is testament to Addams's openness and curiosity more than to any serious religious conviction.[34] Indeed, the divisions between American Protestants were still fluid and not yet as pronounced as they would be later in the twentieth century. Nevertheless, the acceptance of Catholics, Jews, and of other non-Christian religions as equals constitutes a litmus test in regard to the ultimate vision of American Protestants. The World's Columbian Exposition allows for a closer examination of the Jewish-Christian dialogue. The exposition symbolically represented a universal and optimistic vision of an American future and, at the same time, demonstrated the limited receptivity of Protestant and old-stock America to the cultural backgrounds of "other" Americans, whether they were Jewish, Catholic, or indeed, African American, Asian American, or American Indian.

The exposition presented an optimistic American vision of the dawning global age. The Greco-Roman architecture of the White City can be read in different ways. On a basic level, the symbolism expressed the close relationship between the universal and inclusive American creed and globalization, as the architects of the exposition imagined it. And yet a closer look reveals a more ambiguous, even exclusive and racist vision. Many visitors perceived the sharp contrast between the pristine, orderly, uniform, and utopian White City and the seemingly frenzied, diverse, and unclean real city—Chicago, marked by massive industrialization, social inequality, and mass immigration. The real grievances of America's mostly immigrant working class largely remained outside of the exposition's purview. African Americans were not given any role in the organizing committees. In fact, the ethnic and cultural transformation of America as it was literally unfolding outside of the exposition grounds conflicted with the uniform Columbian vision. The layout of the exposition grounds symbolically reflected America's view of the world. Closest to the White City were the developed European nations, further away and at the very bottom of a pseudoscientific hierarchy, Americans Indians and African tribes were exhibited as "primitives" and "savages."[35]

The exhibition's Department of Religion alone oversaw more than two hundred conventions, workshops, and smaller meetings, among them the Jewish Denominational Congress in late August, the Jewish Women's Congress in early September, and the World Parliament of Religions that same month. Leading representatives of the three branches of American Judaism attended the Jewish Denominational Congress. Reform rabbis dominated the proceedings, no recent immigrant or foreign Jew spoke, and Jewish women of course had organized their own meeting. Sinai, now the largest Jewish congregation in Chicago, and its famous rabbi stood very much at the center of these events. Hirsch spoke at the two congresses and to the parliament.[36]

The World Parliament of Religions was one of the best-attended and most talked-about conventions of the exposition. The meeting of representatives of

forty-five religions and denominations merits closer attention because leading American Protestants interacted with and listened to people who otherwise were depicted in stereotypical fashion. Jenkin Lloyd Jones was one of the
main planners. Hirsch was appointed as the sole Jewish representative to the
Parliament's organizing committee, together with the Catholic Archbishop of
Chicago—and fourteen local Protestant ministers. This proportion does not
reflect the reality on the ground. In 1893, affiliated Catholics outnumbered Protestants in Chicago. Even more revealing is the list of groups and religious figures
either not invited or relegated to the margins. Mormons were absent, as were
American Indians and the so-called primitive religions. African Americans and
non-Protestant women remained largely on the sidelines. The Jewish delegation comprised four leading Reformers: Hirsch, Kohler, Wise, and Berkowitz,
as well as rabbis Henry Pereira Mendes and Alexander Kohut, as representatives
of Orthodox and Conservative Judaism, respectively. No Jewish (or Catholic)
delegates from the rapidly growing immigrant communities were invited. The
Jewish and the Catholic delegations consisted entirely of Americans, in contrast
to the large Protestant cohort.

Richard Hughes Seager, the author of an insightful study about the parliament, describes the meeting as a failure. The agendas and expectations of the participating delegations were too far apart to be resolved. The Jewish and Catholic
delegations were primarily interested in gaining acceptance by leading Protestants, rather than opening a dialogue with other world religions. Most Protestants were not ready to recognize Hinduism and Buddhism (and Islam) as serious partners. Ironically, as Seager points out, instead of achieving greater unity,
the parliament was a "harbinger" of greater "plurality" in America. The parliament laid the foundation for the recognition of Jews and Catholics as part of
the American mainstream. The notion of America as a "Judeo-Christian" (rather
than Protestant) nation can be traced to the parliament. The acceptance of Catholics and Jews was in part an acknowledgement by the mainstream that the mass
immigration could not be reversed. Not coincidentally, during the 1880s and
1890s, the anti-immigrant movement gained strength and influence, especially
among American Protestants.[37]

Why did leading Protestants at the parliament give modern Judaism and even
Catholicism the stamp of approval? Accepting Catholicism and even recognizing Judaism as part of the Christian tradition were relatively easy steps for Protestants to take. Entering a serious dialogue with non-Christian religions other
than Judaism (a non-proselytizing religion), on the other hand, would have
undermined the all-embracing aspirations of many Protestants. Typical of the

welcoming sentiment towards Jews is the opening speech of Swedenborgian layman Charles Bonney, one of the main organizers of the exposition, to the Jewish Denominational Congress—the choice of the present tense is noteworthy: "Through all the Sacred Scriptures of the Old Testament, we walk side by side, . . . and if we part at the threshold of the gospels, it shall not be with anger, but with love." Non-Protestants too embraced Jews openly as Jews. In his address to the Jewish Women's Congress, the Catholic Archbishop of St. Paul, Minnesota, John Ireland, described the "preservation of the Hebrew people" as "one of history's greatest miracles." He then condemned anti-Jewish persecutions, past and present. At the parliament, the Greek Orthodox Archbishop of Zante deplored and forcefully rejected accusations of blood libel against Jews. This list could be continued. In fact, in his 1924 community history, Hyman Meites, a Zionist, commented, "the praise of Jews and Judaism heard at various religious congresses was so lavish that some [Jews] felt it was overdone."[38]

The Jewish establishment, of course, worked hard to achieve this outcome. Especially the Reform rabbis stressed the Jewish affinity to the universal agenda and the symbolic language of the exposition (except the Isabella statue). The Jewish pledge for inclusion was driven in no small part by the Jewish mass migration. The Americanization schemes for the new immigrants closely echoed the universal theme of the exhibition. Gabriel Bamberger, the director of the Jewish Training School, was recruited as a speaker at the Jewish Denominational Congress. For Hirsch, the importance of gaining recognition for modern Judaism was decisive—this explains why, in his own speech to the parliament, he did not touch on the need to overcome social inequality. Instead he tried to explain why modern Judaism could serve as a model for most other religions, in achieving greater unity. Buddhism, Christianity, and Islam had "emancipated themselves from the bondage of racial tests and national divisions" and adapted many "elements of the universal faith." But (modern) Judaism too was "no longer ethnic." As in earlier sermons and lectures, Hirsch explicitly rejected race: "Race is accidental, not essential, in manhood. Color is indeed only skin deep." The postracial and postethnic vision that defined Hirsch's concept of modern Judaism explains the frustration and open resentment he expressed towards the new Jewish immigrants in this period. The fear of traditional ghetto Judaism and the rise of proto-Zionism were undermining his vision of universal Judaism just as it was gaining increasing currency among non-Jews. As discussed previously, Hirsch's concept of modern Judaism was progressive and evolutionary. The traditional Judaism of the immigrants was, in his perception, inextricably tied to the past and un-American. Interestingly, the other Jewish delegates at the parliament, with the exception of Henry Berkowitz, talked about historic Judaism. Like most other delegates, their primary goal was to explain the main elements of their respective religion. Kohler, in typical fashion, gave an academic lecture, relating the ideal of "human brotherhood" to various biblical sources. Berkowitz focused on Judaism's relevance in present society, as indicated by the title of his lecture, "The Voice of the Mother of Religions on the Social Question." Yet only Hirsch presented an assessment of the present and a vision of the future, as if only he fully grasped the significance of this moment and the need to capture his audience.[39]

Some liberal Protestants and radical Reform Jews were eager to continue the exchange beyond 1893 and build a permanent liberal platform. In an 1894 article, Hirsch claimed liberals could not ignore the rise of the evangelical movement. They had to overcome their "isolation" and the "division of forces." The growing strength of traditional Judaism and Catholicism also required liberal cooperation across religious lines to avoid marginalization. The inclusive liberals saw themselves as the true standard bearers of the American creed as it had been proclaimed at the World's Columbian Exposition. However, not all liberal Protestants were ready to accept Jews. In 1893, a few months before the parliament, Hirsch apologized to Jones for not attending a meeting of the "Liberal Ministers Ass'n." Hirsch explained, "I stayed away because I distrust the 'liberalism' of some of the ministers. You and I, I fear, have but little sympathy in that body."[40]

The success of the parliament encouraged Hirsch, Jones, and another liberal Protestant minister from Chicago, Hiram W. Thomas to organize a permanent discussion forum, the American Congress of Liberal Religious Societies. This congress was made up of liberal Protestants, Universalists, Freethinkers, members of the ethical culture movement, and radical Reform Jews—overwhelmingly from Chicago. Most participating congregations were not affiliated with a denomination. Hirsch called on Sinai congregation to host the first congress, because "the Jew, so often charged with bigotry and clannish exclusiveness, is in very reality, the historically designated ensign bearer of *inclusive though* NOT *uniformed* humanity." It was the mission of Jews to spread the universal truths, but this did not mean Jews would exchange Judaism for "uniformity," a humanistic religion or liberal Protantism. Rather, the opposite would occur, for Hirsch the universal and ethical religion of the future was of course—Judaism.[41]

In May 1894, Thomas opened the first Congress of Liberal Religious Societies, thanking "noble Sinai Congregation" for its hospitality. A Jewish house of worship, Thomas declared, was a fitting location for the first Congress because "Judaism is our common mother, and Reform Judaism ceasing to be national, emphasizing the great truths of the one living God of righteousness, of brotherhood and love—that religion has become universal." Hirsch struck a somewhat different note by reminding the audience of the continuing persecution and discrimination of Jews, especially in Europe. He then outlined his vision of Judaism as the true "religion of practice" and as universal religion: "The basis of our fellowship is not belief. We ask no questions. Read the constitution of our society [Sinai congregation]. The word Jew does not even appear. Those of moral character wishing to fellowship with us are welcome in our house. We are Jews because history has assigned us a certain place." Echoing Thomas, Hirsch rejected Jewish "national" aspirations. After the congress, Hirsch reiterated his call for further dialogue and shared values. But he drew a clear line; the congress was not and could not be the "birthday party of a new religion." This was an explicit rejection of some Protestants, who expected Jews to join a new nondenominational universal but Christian religion.[42]

DIVERSITY VERSUS UNIFORMITY

In 1770, Moses Mendelssohn received a letter from a respected Protestant theologian from Switzerland, Johann Caspar Lavater. The Zurich deacon, who had visited Mendelssohn in Berlin a few years earlier, firmly believed the mass conversion of Jews and, consequently, the Second Coming of Christ, were imminent. Lavater urged Mendelssohn to immediately convert to Christianity. His conversion would inspire many Jews to follow him. Should he not want to convert, he should explain why Judaism was superior to Christianity. Mendelssohn did not take up Lavater's offer. In his brief reply letter he stressed that he would not convert: "I declare myself a Jew. I shall always remain a Jew." Lavater may have misunderstood Mendelssohn's expression of respect for Jesus. For Mendelssohn, Jesus was a Jewish rabbi who had neither renounced Judaism nor described himself as a divine figure. Almost a decade after Lavater's attempted conversion, Mendelssohn's friend Gotthold Ephraim Lessing published his play *Nathan the Wise*. The main character was modeled after the great Jewish philosopher. The play, a key text of the Western Enlightenment, stands for a competing vision to the all-embracing aspiration of Christianity Lavater represented. Lessing's Nathan challenged the traditional stereotype of the greedy and treacherous Jew as the "eternal" outsider and rootless stranger. The wise and tolerant Nathan was, as Amos Elon has observed, the exact opposite of the powerful Shylock image. More important, the play renounced the idea that a certain religion was superior to another. Lessing questioned absolutist dogma and made a powerful case for the acceptance of the other within, rather than without. For Lessing, religion was not a matter of one's faith but of ethical conduct, a message that defined Hirsch's social justice theology. *Nathan the Wise* presented a vision of Jewish inclusion in society that was based on mutual respect and did not require concessions or tests, let alone conversion.[43]

Although Chicago in the 1890s seemed to be a world apart from Berlin in the 1770s, the early phase of a Jewish-Protestant dialogue shows a striking resemblance to the earlier debate, not just because Jews and Protestants wrestled with some of the same issues. Hirsch's agenda, as we have seen, closely echoed that of Lessing and Mendelssohn. Repeatedly Hirsch had to defend Judaism. Protestants who could not accept the agenda of modern Judaism called on Jews to convert, blamed "them" for the Crucifixion of Jesus, or even perceived Jews through the deterministic prism of the Second Coming. Hirsch responded by describing the modern Jew as the harbinger of a universal ethical religion. The inclusive and universal ideal that Lessing expressed in *Nathan the Wise* defined Hirsch's agenda at the Columbian Exposition. Hirsch's concept of universal religion was postethnic, nondogmatic, humanistic, ethical, and rooted in modern Judaism. He and other Jewish speakers, not least Hannah Solomon, emphasized more than once that the eventual coming together under the roof of a universal religion would not entail a Jewish conversion to Christianity and would remain a vision, as long as Jews were discriminated and persecuted as Jews. On the other hand, as we have seen, Solomon and the other Sinai women faced strong opposition in the council because of their radical views. For more traditionally minded Jews Sunday services in particular represented a symbolic step towards Christianity. This hints at another irony. Hirsch and other radical Reform Jews were the driving forces behind winning acceptance for Jews among the American religious mainstream, but within the Jewish sphere they stood at the margins.

10.

"INSTITUTIONAL SYNAGOGUE"

APART FROM THE weekly service and special occasions, such as weddings or funerals, Sinai offered its members few venues for active participation. In this, Sinai resembled many Protestant and Jewish congregations in American cities at the time. Social status associated with the membership in an elite congregation like Sinai often outweighed a specific theological agenda. The spiritual and social crisis partly explains the appeal of innovative religious leaders like Felix Adler, Hiram W. Thomas, and, on the other end of the theological spectrum, Dwight L. Moody in the last third of the nineteenth century. They could present answers to the social question and attracted large audiences, including younger men and women. Tellingly, these ministers and their followers stood outside (or as Hirsch and Jones, on the fringe) of established denominations.

Rabbi Henry Pereira Mendes of the Orthodox Shearith Israel congregation in New York identified the core problem in 1885 when he emphasized the need to turn members from "listeners to participants."[1] As earlier in American religious history, an innovative solution came from the grass roots. The beginnings of the institutional Jewish congregation can be traced to the early and mid-1880s, not coincidentally, when American Jewish life entered a phase of transformation. To revive congregations, several younger rabbis realized, the role of all members, whether young or old, male or female, had to be redefined. They explicitly borrowed ideas from Catholic and Protestant congregations, an illustration of the permeability of denominational boundaries in the dynamic American setting.[2] Sinai's lay leaders, however, rejected this approach, primarily because the fortunes of the congregation had reversed spectacularly in the early 1880s. The rising fame of the charismatic rabbi, however, overshadowed and even exacerbated some of the persisting internal problems.

After Hirsch decided to stay in Chicago for good in 1899, he began to reassess the potential of the congregation. Sinai could be an outward oriented and "open" congregation with an ethical message, accessible to all Chicagoans regardless of their faith, and, at the same time, would be an "institutional synagogue" with a committed *Jewish* membership and wide-ranging social activities under its roof.[3] After the turn of the twentieth century, Sinai abandoned its splendid isolation and emerged as one of the largest social center synagogues in America. This chapter will examine why Sinai moved away from nondenominationalism and began to promote Jewish *Gemeinschaft* after 1900.

THE ROOTS OF TRANSFORMATION

The early beginnings of Sinai's reorientation reach back well into the 1890s. The leadership of Sinai's women in the National Council of Jewish Women and the forging of closer relations with liberal Protestants exposed rabbi, board, and members to new ideas. Hirsch repeatedly spoke and wrote about the social features of congregational life during the 1890s. He certainly noticed the rising anonymity at Sinai and other congregations he visited, and he knew about the positive impact of the changes Henry Berkowitz and Joseph Krauskopf and other younger rabbis like Moses Gries were introducing at their congregations. Krauskopf, who had succeeded Hirsch's father at Philadelphia's Keneseth Israel, and Gries, rabbi at Cleveland's Temple both especially openly sympathized with Sinai's radical Reform agenda and Sunday services. An even more obvious model was All Souls Church in Sinai's neighborhood. Jenkin Lloyd Jones may well have inspired an 1892 article by Hirsch about rethinking the concept of the congregation.

"A congregation" Hirsch wrote, "should represent, as it were, one family. . . . Congregations should . . . be the very center through which the social life of their members may pass." Members should come together regularly under the roof of the temple but in a sphere apart from the services and the formal business of the congregation for "spending a grateful hour of recreation." And, "the number of men and women is not large who feel that they are personally of some use for the larger organization of a congregation." Some congregations had already filled the social void; others "should lose no time to follow the example." This can be read as a clear hint for Sinai's board to draw some inspiration from All Souls. Jones promoted his congregation as a "home" and "family" for its members. In 1893, shortly after the World's Columbian Exposition, Hirsch lamented the shortcomings of congregations that were essentially "lecture associations." Jewish women should play a more proactive role in Reform congregations and receive formal recognition. Yet social activities, in his opinion, had to be refined and in accordance with the higher ethical mission and *Bildung*. "Some eastern] congregations," according to Hirsch, had "grown into veritable department stores." Fortunately, Chicago had resisted such "Barnumism."[4] In the early 1890s, Hirsch's thoughts on this issue still were shaped by the close exchange between Jews and liberal Protestants. Indeed, he might have still entertained the idea that non-Jews could belong to Sinai in some fashion.

The bitter power struggle between Hirsch and Sinai's board during the second half of the 1890s delayed the social congregation project. In one area, however, the board made a far-reaching decision that helped to ease the transition to a social congregation after 1900: the long-overdue reform of the membership system. Until the late 1880s, full membership in Sinai was beyond the reach of many urban professionals; members overwhelmingly were well-to-do businessmen. Some aspiring members perhaps could have afforded the membership dues of $100 per year, but full members were also obliged to acquire a pew and pay an annual pew tax ($30 in 1895). They were also expected to make special contributions, usually to balance shortfalls in the annual budget or to fund potentially costly projects, such as the renovation and extension of the temple. Since relatively few businessmen could afford such expenditures, Sinai membership conferred social status in the Jewish community. Ironically, Sinai was indeed a "family" before the mid-1890s, but hardly as Hirsch or Jones implied. The relatively few Sinai members were closely related through intermarriage. To expand the congregation, the dues system had to be overhauled. The board felt compelled to act only when the sons of several members could not afford to apply for membership. In 1888, Sinai amended its membership laws. Sons and sons-in-law of full members could now join as special members for $40 per year, without having to buy a pew (or make other special payments). However, young men *not* related to a Sinai member could only apply for full membership. It took another seven years before the congregation redefined its membership system more thoroughly, opening its doors to a broader stratum of the established Jewish community.

The revised 1895 constitution distinguished between four different membership categories. The conditions for "regular members" remained unchanged; the same applied to "special members," who enjoyed the same rights as regular members, with one exception: should the father or father-in-law of a special member leave Sinai (or pass away), the special membership would expire twelve months later. Newly introduced were the categories "associate member Class A" and "associate member Class B." These were designed for males who were not related to full Sinai members. Associates in Class A were married men unable to afford a pew. For $40 annually they were assigned two seats. Class B members were unmarried men who could not acquire a pew; for $16 annually they were allocated one seat. Associate members had limited voting rights within the congregation; they could not vote on real estate matters, nor could they hold elected office. The reform yielded tangible results. From 1895 to 1896, the membership grew by more than 10 percent, from 303 to 335. Half of the new members joined as special or associate members.[5]

Shortly after the membership reform, the board made another bold decision. The minutes for the April 1896 annual meeting mention the status of women for the first time: "One of the special features . . . was the admission of women to full membership in the Congregation, betokening once more that we are ever ready to move in line with the progressive spirit and tendencies of the age." Unfortunately the discussions leading to this change and the exact dates were not recorded. Yet the reform was clearly tied to the broader reorganization of the membership system in July 1895. Providing women with full membership rights appeared sensible, given the prominence of the congregation's women on the national stage, and the declared interest of women to become more involved in their congregations. Sinai was one of the first Jewish congregations in the country to take this step, but not the first in Chicago. A neighbor of Sinai, the radical Reform congregation Temple Isaiah, began admitting women as full members when it was founded in the previous year 1895. This congregation, led by Rabbi Joseph Stolz and its founder Henry Greenebaum, was a South Side offshoot of Sinai's daughter congregation, Zion. Most other Reform congregations offered full membership for women only after 1920.[6]

Gradually, the membership reform made an impact. However, Hirsch's rising profile also helped to pull in new members. Between the early 1860s and the early 1880s, the membership had hovered around 100; in 1875, Sinai had 80 members, in 1881, it had 86. Five years later, in 1886, after Hirsch had established himself, the number had risen to slightly over 150. And the congregation continued to grow: from 230 in 1890 to 335 in 1896, just after the membership reform, and up to 463 in 1900. These numbers may not appear spectacular but apart from the unmarried associate members most members had families with several children.

Therefore, the actual number of people affiliated formally with Sinai was much higher than the statistics indicate. In 1902, president Loeb remarked that 500 members translated into 2,000 "souls." By 1904, Sinai was the second largest Reform congregation in America with 512 members, and it continued to expand. Keneseth Israel in Philadelphia (506 members) had almost as many members in 1904; only Temple Emanu-El in New York (771) surpassed the two congregations. In Chicago, the second and third largest Reform congregations—KAM (170) and Temple Isaiah (100)—were much smaller than Sinai.[7] Nevertheless, even after the reform of its membership system, most Jews in Chicago could not aspire to join Sinai. For a working-class family with several children living on the West Side, far from Sinai's temple, $40 was a fortune. Nevertheless, by 1900, Sinai was almost twice as big as it had been in 1890 and was ready for further expansion.

A NEW VISION

In his report to the congregation on the occasion of the thirty-ninth annual meeting in April 1900, Sinai president Adolph Loeb briefly looked back at the severe "crisis" that had rocked the congregation in the previous year. The decision to retain the charismatic rabbi "under any and all circumstances," had given Sinai new strength and confidence. As was the president's duty, Loeb then revisited various events and activities of the previous twelve months. Near the end of his list he noted the death of a man who had never set foot into Sinai's temple, yet whose shadow hung over the congregation since its earliest days. Loeb described him as "the so-called Nestor of American Rabbis." He continued, "Whilst leaving it to others to extol praises of the many virtues and great accomplishments of the great Rabbi during his long and eventful life, I merely desire to record the fact that in the absence of Dr. Hirsch I deemed it proper to send an official telegram on part of our Congregation in this, their hour of grief." "So-called Nestor" was, of course, a reference to Isaac Mayer Wise, and the telegram was dispatched to his Cincinnati congregation Bene Yeshurun. Wise's opposition to Sinai's founding in 1861 and to its distinctive theology—not least to Sunday services—had become firmly entrenched in the congregation's institutional memory. Wise was also a synonym for the "union." As one of very few Reform congregations Sinai remained committed to nondenominationalism. Even in 1900, as soon transpired, many older members regarded Wise and the union with much suspicion.[8]

As Loeb sat down, Hirsch addressed the members present, not losing a single word about Wise. In his address, he described Sinai as the "pioneer congregation in the movement." Indeed, he wondered, "why should Sinai not have [a] thousand members?" The distribution of power within the congregation had changed in remarkable ways. The rabbi—not the president—presented the case for an ambitious new project. After 1880, Sinai's temple had become one of the best-attended houses of worship in the city of Chicago. But Hirsch and a few likeminded members felt the neo-Romanesque edifice with its beautiful ornaments was not in tune with the new age and Sinai's universal message. For Sinai's "new home," he aimed for a state-of-the-art modern building, in the Greek classical style, echoing Burnham's White City. "The church buildings of the future will differ radically from those so far erected. The new Sinai Temple about which I have to begin to dream as a near certainty, should be a home for all communal activities . . . it will serve purposes of worship, instruction, propaganda, philanthropy and sociability. Pioneer in so many departures I would have my beloved Congregation again become the pathfinder in this reform of Church architecture." In fact, the new building would not only serve "communal needs," it would also be a "a revenue producer." Concerts or big lecture events would help to cover the operating costs. The board voted to print Hirsch's message and distribute it to all members.[9]

Hirsch's address did not come as a big surprise. The board and members knew he wanted a new state-of-the-art temple, commensurate with his standing as one of Chicago's most respected preachers. But Hirsch had an even more ambitious goal. The key word in his short speech was "home"—exactly the concept that defined All Souls Church. It was hardly a coincidence that Jenkin Lloyd Jones and his congregation were in the final stages of planning a major extension to All Souls in 1900. The social center Jones envisioned clearly influenced Hirsch. During the 1890s, Jones had even suggested adding a bowling alley to his center to appeal to a bigger crowd and generate additional income.[10]

While All Souls pushed ahead with its project, Sinai postponed the building of the new temple for several years. Apart from Hirsch's illness-related absences, Sinai did not have a committed leadership team in place after President Gatzert stepped down in the mid-1890s after serving almost a decade. Gatzert and his predecessors, notably Berthold Loewenthal, were founders of the congregation and strongly identified with their temple. Presidents Fishell, Loeb, and Hart did not possess the necessary authority to steer the congregation into a new direction. This only changed in 1906 when a new administration came into office.

Before 1906, the board took one crucial decision when it pushed for membership in the organized Reform movement. The passing of Wise in 1900 removed the last symbolic obstacle. Although the case for joining the union was now overwhelming, several older members fiercely resisted this move. For more than forty years, Sinai had defined itself against Cincinnati. Indeed, Sinai's denomination was the nondenominational Congress of Liberal Religious Societies, a loose federation that cut across religious boundaries and included Jewish Reform congregations, the Chicago Ethical Culture Society, and liberal Protestants, such as All Souls Church.[11]

One year after the death of Wise, President Loeb proposed for the first time Sinai should join the union, especially since Sunday services were now an "accomplished fact." By 1900, several larger Reform congregations had adopted Sunday services, and the UAHC had repeatedly stressed it would not interfere. Hirsch supported Loeb, and the board was in favor. But in 1902, Loeb explained the board had decided to postpone a decision because several older members "vehemently opposed" it. This hints at the influence of the surviving founders, especially lawyer Julius Rosenthal. A powerful argument against union membership was the question of Wise's succession. But early in 1903, none other than Kaufmann Kohler accepted the presidency of Hebrew Union College, and thus the theological leadership of the UAHC. After leaving Chicago, Kohler had distanced himself from the radical positions he himself had espoused at Sinai. But Kohler and Sinai's leaders successfully repaired their fraught relationship. Kohler's move to Cincinnati provided the union supporters with the decisive momentum. In early April 1903, President Hart reiterated the call, pointing to Hirsch's "assurance" that with Kohler as the new head of the college, Sinai should join. Hirsch emphasized his brother-in-law would be a firm guardian against "false emotionalism" and "romanticism." Kohler was, after all, "a Chicago man." Sinai should give up its "dignified aloofness" to gain greater influence within the Reform movement. And so, almost thirty years after the founding of the UAHC, Sinai finally joined in 1903. This step seemed to mark the end of a long era of isolation within the Reform camp.[12]

SINAI'S NEW LEADERS

The eventual decision to join the UAHC and open the congregation to a broader social spectrum illustrates the growing influence of the second generation. Sinai's new lay leaders were American-born, exclusively male, and had been shaped by Hirsch's social theology. All were among the movers and shakers of the United Jewish Charities (after 1900, the Associated Jewish Charities). Several belonged to the families of the congregation's founders, an indication for the long reach of the Palatinate migration network. Harry Hart, the cofounder of the flourishing clothing firm Hart Schaffner & Marx, was the last president who was born in Europe. He had come to Chicago from Eppelsheim in 1858 as an eight-year-old. His successor, Moses Ernst Greenebaum, was the first man from the second generation to sit in the president's chair. His father, Elias, had just been elected as president of KAM when Moses was born in 1858. In 1877, he joined his father's bank and became its president in 1911. The younger Greenebaum was an important figure in Chicago mortgage banking and real estate. For years he played a prominent role in the Jewish community.[13] After Greenebaum assumed the presidency in 1906, he expressed his interest to serve for longer than a few years, providing Sinai with a degree of stability. As a member of one of the most respected Jewish families in Chicago, he possessed sufficient social capital; he enjoyed strong support and knew how to handle the eccentric rabbi. Instead of distancing himself from the congregation, Hirsch was more willing to yield to the board than some of his critics had expected after the bitter clashes of the late 1890s. Unlike the founders' generation, the new board members were younger than the rabbi and looked up to him.

The board's actual influence was somewhat reduced, because soon after his election Greenebaum and Hirsch fostered a small circle of committed members who steered the congregation successfully through the 1910s and 1920s. The five key figures were born between 1852 and 1866; they advised and intimately trusted each other in philanthropic and congregational matters. Their careers and actions betray the specific vision of Sinai as it entered the twentieth century: a strong commitment to the Jewish community, civic causes, social reform, and education.

Sinai treasurer Abraham G. Becker (born in 1857) was one of the most trusted and successful bankers in Chicago after 1900. The Beckers were closely related to the Schaffners. Both families belonged to the Palatinate network and had settled in Chicago around 1860; Abraham was born during a stopover in Warsaw, Ohio. Both families were members of Zion congregation, and as a teenager Abraham was active in the Zion Literary Association. The intertwined careers of Henry Greenebaum, Abraham Becker, and his later brother-in-law Herman Schaffner demonstrate the long reach of the Palatinate network and the boom-and-bust circles that were so characteristic for Chicago's economy. Henry Greenebaum's German National Bank provided the young Becker and Herman Schaffner with their first jobs in the early 1870s. Schaffner, also a member of Zion congregation, quickly rose to chief treasurer. After the bank's spectacular failure in 1877, Schaffner launched his own bank. Becker, a mere twenty years old, became his junior partner. In the early phase of the 1893 recession, Schaffner's bank faced bankruptcy. Instead of negotiating with his creditors, a desperate Schaffner took a boat and rowed out onto Lake Michigan. Several days later his body was discovered on the North Side lakeshore. Thus it fell to Becker to reorganize the bank under challenging circumstances. Becker was briefly arrested and faced several lawsuits by angry investors, but he managed to settle all claims. By 1900, A. G. Becker & Co. was a flourishing bank dealing in commercial paper. Becker spent much time and money for the United Hebrew Charities; he served as president of the Associated Hebrew Charities from 1903 to 1905 and again in 1914. Becker was also a major benefactor of the Chicago Art Institute.[14]

The best-known member of the small circle was Sears and Roebuck chief executive Julius Rosenwald (born in 1862). His election as vice president in 1910—a largely symbolic office—illustrates his status as Sinai's most committed member. Suffice it to say, Rosenwald, a prominent philanthropist, generously supported the congregation. He became a member of Sinai soon after moving to Chicago from New York in 1885 as a modestly wealthy businessman. Like many of his Jewish peers, he became a partner in a textile business. Rosenwald had grown up downstate, in Springfield, where his parents had settled after moving from northern Germany via Baltimore through several small towns in the South and Midwest. During the 1890s, Rosenwald joined Sears and Roebuck and reinvented the company's mail-order business. The secret behind Rosenwald's success was his competence as a manager and his keen sense for innovation. By 1900, he was wealthy enough to devote time and serious money to philanthropy. He evenly divided his donations between Jewish and civic causes. Rosenwald served for several years between 1909 and 1913 and again from 1915 to 1917 as president of Associated Jewish Charities. His engagement reflected Sinai's strong commitment to Chicago Jewish philanthropy, as he experienced it during the 1880s and 1890s as a young man. Sinai cofounder Isaac Greensfelder, a successful businessman and the longtime head of the United Hebrew Charities and its predecessor institutions, served as a role model for Rosenwald.[15]

Hirsch influenced more than Rosenwald's philanthropic mission as a spiritual teacher. The rabbi introduced Rosenwald to (in his view) deserving recipients, sometimes after the latter had contacted him rather than Rosenwald. For instance, a letter University of Chicago president Harper wrote Hirsch in 1904 about his first meeting with Rosenwald hints at the rabbi's role as a facilitator. Harper found Rosenwald to be a "most agreeable man," who would very likely support the university library. He continued, "His expressions of esteem for you were unbounded, and if the Library comes, it will be simple and solely because of his interest and affection for you." Rosenwald gave large sums to the university. On the occasion of his fiftieth birthday in 1912, for instance, he donated almost

$700,000 to several worthy causes. This spectacular gift was publicly announced: $250,000 each went to the university for the new geography building (Rosenwald Hall) and to the Associated Jewish Charities of Chicago. In May 1912, three months before he made his birthday gift public, Rosenwald became a trustee of the University of Chicago. After founding trustee (and fellow congregant) Eli B. Felsenthal, Rosenwald was the second Jew on the university board at a time when the Protestant elite began to shun even the most civically committed Jews. Later, Rosenwald made even more generous gifts to the university: in 1916, he pledged $500,000 for the medical school; he put $1,000,000 at the disposal of his fellow trustees in 1926; and he donated $2,000,000 for the construction of new residence halls in 1928.[16]

Rosenwald gave to many worthy causes, but not without carefully evaluating each case and seeking the advice of trusted figures in his immediate circle, such as Hirsch, Becker, and Julian Mack. In 1917, soon after being elected to the board of the Rockefeller Foundation, he established the Julius Rosenwald Fund as a foundation, reflecting a rethinking of his philanthropy. The philosophy of Rosenwald's philanthropy diverged from traditional giving by promoting a sustained approach, similar to the policy of other large foundations. The more than five thousand public schools he, together with Booker T. Washington, helped to set up across the American South for African American children were not entirely funded by the Rosenwald Fund. After 1917, a county or school district had to match the Rosenwald grant. Frequently the local African American population of a county raised a substantial part of the necessary funds. According to Sealander, the "scientific philanthropy" that Rosenwald, John D. Rockefeller, and Andrew Carnegie, along with their respective foundations, espoused sprang from two sources: the management philosophy of successful and innovative entrepreneurs with access to professional knowledge and, in a broad sense, social gospel.[17] Rosenwald primarily selected institutions and endeavors that advanced education and the arts. Admittedly, the same applied to Rockefeller, Carnegie, and many other American and European philanthropists at the time. Yet Rosenwald's upbringing as the child of upwardly mobile Jewish immigrants from central Europe, his membership in Sinai congregation, and his serious commitment to Reform theology point to a deeper source for two quite distinctive but closely related foci of his philanthropy for *not* specifically Jewish causes, the support of education and of African Americans.

As described in previous chapters, education and schools had a special meaning for Sinai's founders. Rosenwald had just joined Sinai when the congregation launched the state-of-the-art Jewish Training School. The older members of Sinai, as well as his own parents, belonged to the first generation of a marginalized group that had enjoyed a solid primary school education in the German states and had a high respect for *Bildung*. Rosenwald named his first son after the German Enlightenment writer Lessing, a figure revered by Hirsch and Jenkin Lloyd Jones. Rosenwald was not the first Sinai member who took up the cause of African Americans. Sinai's founders, notably Bernhard Felsenthal, Michael Greenebaum, and Julius Rosenthal, were declared abolitionists. Yet after the Civil War, the fate of African Americans receded in the background. The African American population of Chicago remained relatively small before World War I. Nevertheless, Hirsch repeatedly spoke up against racial injustice; on a few occasions he addressed African American audiences.

At a 1911 luncheon at the Republican Club in New York, where he shared a panel with W. E. B. DuBois, Hirsch questioned whether race had any scientific basis. If all people were "descended from one ape," nobody could make a serious case for the supposed superiority of one race over another. Race was not biologically determined; race prejudice had sociological causes. Hirsch singled out slavery as a major culprit. This institution had corrupted societies, because individuals were treated and gradually began to behave as "members of a class." The notion of a "chosen class with privileges that can't be taken away" was in Hirsch's view "essentially un-American." And he continued, "the American who harbors race prejudice is committing a crime against his Americanism."[18] In November 1912, Hirsch, who according to the African American daily *Chicago Defender* was the "greatest living American Hebrew" (an assessment he certainly agreed with), addressed 1,200 congregants at Chicago's African Methodist Episcopalian Bethel Church. Bethel, one of the most vibrant institutional churches in Chicago was, as Hirsch freely admitted, an inspiration for Sinai as an "institutional synagogue." Bethel's spiritual founder Reverdy C. Ransom, an African American minister and social gospel advocate, was like Hirsch an early member of the Hull House circle.[19]

But while impressive, such public statements were relatively rare. Nobody at Sinai openly opposed Rosenwald's commitment to African Americans, but none of his fellow congregants openly joined hands with him, with the exception of Hirsch and Julian Mack. The rabbi accompanied him on his first trip to Booker T. Washington's Tuskegee Institute in 1911. Judge Mack and his wife were his guests on the second trip in 1912. In early 1911 Mack and Rosenwald went to a personal meeting with President William Howard Taft to discuss establishing a YMCA for African Americans in Washington, D.C.[20]

Nevertheless, in his attempt to overcome racial divisions and discrimination, Rosenwald remained largely an isolated figure. His support was guided by serious concern, personal interest, and genuine curiosity. A key influence was Booker T. Washington, whom he first met in 1911 and who became his friend. Yet Washington, a regular visitor to Chicago, seems not to have made a deep impact on Sinai's members, with the exception of the rabbi. When Washington died in 1915, Hirsch contributed a personal tribute to the founder of Tuskegee to the *Chicago Defender*.[21] On one occasion, however, Sinai took a clear stand against race discrimination. This occurred before Rosenwald began to commit his philanthropy to African Americans in 1910–1911 and may have influenced him. After a brutal race riot in Springfield in 1908 on the eve of the Lincoln centennial, Hirsch joined the signers of a declaration calling for ending racial inequality and discrimination. Jane Addams, W. E. B. DuBois, Rabbi Stephen S. Wise, and the preacher of the Chicago Ethical Culture Society, William Salter also signed the declaration. This call led to the founding of the National Association for the Advancement of Colored People. Although Hirsch is regarded as a cofounder of the NAACP, he did not play a serious role in its organization. Naturally, the Springfield native Rosenwald extended his support to the NAACP, albeit on a relatively modest scale. In early 1912, Rosenwald and Jane Addams encouraged the leaders of the NAACP to hold their fourth annual meeting in Chicago. Sinai's imposing new temple was chosen as the opening venue under the banner "Our Common Humanity." On the podium were Jane Addams, Hirsch, the early civil rights leader and journalist Oswald Garrison Villard, the Yale graduate and linguist William Pickens (the only black person among this group), and the head of the Baha'i Faith, Abdul Baha, who was in town to lay the cornerstone of the Baha'i House of Worship in Wilmette. In the "mixed assemblage," as the *Tribune* noted, were Ida Wells and DuBois, who spoke on race discrimination on the following day."[22]

Julian William Mack (born in 1866) was the fourth and youngest member of Sinai's informal leadership circle. He did not occupy a formal office within the congregation, he had a relatively modest income, and he had no family connections to Sinai. But he accumulated much cultural and social capital before and after he came to Chicago from Cincinnati. Like a growing number of Jews born after the Civil War, he had not gone into business but had attended university. As a student, he helped to found the *Harvard Law Review* and later won a prestigious fellowship that took him from Harvard to the universities of Berlin and Leipzig. During the 1890s, Mack found his first job as a lawyer in the office of Sinai cofounder Julius Rosenthal. Mack also served as the chief manager of the United Hebrew Charities (on a voluntary basis). He worked closely with Jane Addams at Hull House and became a Progressive. According to an early Rosenwald biographer, it was Mack who introduced the philanthropist to Addams. Mack's commitment to the United and Associated Jewish Charities and his German education earned him the respect of Hirsch, who often criticized congregants who, unlike Mack, were wealthy but did not live up to their social responsibilities. Not surprisingly, Hirsch considered Mack, who was an articulate speaker, as a suitable candidate to replace him in the pulpit during his absences.[23]

In 1903, Chicago mayor Carter Harrison Jr. selected Mack as a candidate for the Cook County Circuit Court. This was a clever move. Unusually for a member of the Jewish establishment, Mack was a Democrat—like the mayor who owed his position to successfully mobilizing new immigrants. Against the background of sprawling vice in the city Harrison faced much criticism by city's Republicans, not least members of Sinai who were active in the civic reform movement, such as lawyer Lessing Rosenthal (the son of Sinai cofounder Julius Rosenthal). By picking a highly respected member of the Jewish establishment with social reform credentials, Harrison managed to co-opt his Jewish critics. Mack was well known among the Democrat Jewish electorate on the city's West Side and easily won the election. He was one of the first Jewish judges in America, a matter of great honor for Sinai—even for the committed Republican Hirsch. As a county court judge, Mack, true to his Progressive convictions, volunteered to serve on Chicago's juvenile court. Mack strongly pushed the case for reforming youths rather than sending them to jail. His reform court soon attracted attention across the nation.

In 1906, Mack helped cofound an effective Jewish lobby organization, the American Jewish Committee (AJC). Mack and the other founders, led by New York investment banker and philanthropist Jacob Schiff, ignored objections of the ineffectual B'nai B'rith. Hirsch, too, was initially critical, because he felt not laymen but rabbis (especially he himself) should represent American Jews. But a more forceful and professional lobby was needed: anti-Semitism was on the rise, immigration restrictions against Jews were widely discussed, and the precarious situation of Jews in the Russian Empire and Romania demanded a strong and unified Jewish response. Hirsch quickly overcame his skepticism and served on the AJC board in its first two years; Rosenwald joined the AJC executive committee in 1909.

By the end of the decade, Mack belonged to the national American Jewish leadership, and he became a regular guest in Washington. In 1909, he spoke as head of the Immigrants' Protective League and vice president of the AJC on behalf of Jewish immigrants in front of a congressional committee investigating the state of immigration; earlier that same year, outgoing president Theodore Roosevelt invited Mack to a conference on dependent children. Hirsch was also appointed as a member of the President's Commission for the Dependent Child. In 1910, the new president (and fellow Cincinnatian), William Howard Taft, appointed Mack to the new U.S. Commerce Court in Washington, ignoring protests by Illinois Republicans over the nomination of a Democrat. The new position allowed Mack to visit Chicago on a regular basis. Only in 1913, when he was appointed to the Circuit Court of Appeals in New York, did he give up his residence on the South Side. But he continued to visit Chicago frequently.[24]

The close relationship to Greenebaum, Becker, Rosenwald, and Mack, prominent figures who all deeply respected their rabbi, put Hirsch (born in 1852), the oldest member of the small circle, more at ease and prevented conflicts. The board gradually relieved Hirsch of his workload. In 1906, Sinai gave him an extended winter vacation. In the following years, Hirsch took longer leaves of absence, largely to recuperate from repeated bouts of illness. In 1906, the board set aside $2,000 for an assistant rabbi, though no one was hired. A few years later Hirsch began to groom his son-in-law, Gerson B. Levi, to be his successor. Levi was a graduate of the Conservative Jewish Theological Seminary in New York. After coming to Chicago in 1906 as the new rabbi of B'nai Sholom Temple Israel, he married Hirsch's daughter, Elsa. Levi's new congregation was quite small and straddled the borderline between Conservative and Reform Judaism. Levi joined the congregation shortly after it merged with Temple Israel. His duties left him sufficient time to preach regularly at Sinai.[25]

A large constituency within the congregation lacked formal or informal representation. Women were conspicuously absent, notably Hannah Solomon, who after her resignation as leader of the national council certainly would have been an obvious candidate for the board. Most urban Reform congregations admitted women to their boards only after 1920. As business leaders the board members hardly ever encountered women as equals. The policy on women resembles Sinai's lackluster position towards race relations. Sinai's women, however, did not remain passive.[26]

Women were continuously represented on the board of the United and Associated Jewish Charities of Chicago after the early 1890s. This is noteworthy, because Sinai continued to dominate this institution and the congregation board overlapped with that of the charities. None other than Solomon was elected to the board in 1900 when the Associated Jewish Charities was formally established at Sinai's temple. The long engagement of women's organizations on behalf of the Jewish community provided women with a better case for participation on the leadership level. Women quickly realized that the most promising path to gain official recognition within religious congregations was through organization and participation. The silent opposition of Sinai's male leaders to giving women more formal influence with the congregation beyond the right to full membership explains why several Sinai women created their own association during the 1890s that was a partner to—rather than a part of—Sinai congregation. The Chicago chapter of the National Council of Jewish Women was Sinai's sisterhood in all but name. In March 1896, the Chicago council chapter asked Sinai's board whether it would extend its support to a "religious school" on the West Side.

The council "religious school" opened its doors in January 1896. It aimed to reduce the influence of traditional Judaism by exposing specifically girls to the teachings of Reform Judaism and offsetting the impact of the much-dreaded cheder on Jewish boys. Of course, the girls could only attend the school after securing the consent of the parents. By 1898, the West Side Sabbath School was on a solid footing, thanks largely to Sinai's support. In later years, the school became known as the Sinai Mission School. Its curriculum and teaching staff overlapped with that of Sinai's own religious school. Superintendent Julia Felsenthal was officially in charge of the women teachers. In 1899–1900, the school enrolled about three hundred girls, and it was part of Sinai congregation in all but name. This transition also demonstrates the gradual retreat of the council from explicitly religious ventures. Sinai also opened its temple to women's associations. In 1908, for instance, Chicago council chapter, Johanna lodge, the Deborah Verein, and the Sarah Greenebaum lodge held their meetings at Sinai's temple.[27]

THE PATH TOWARD A NEW SYNAGOGUE

The successful transition to a younger leadership and lack of space partly explain why the building of the new temple finally went ahead in the fall of 1908. Another factor was the "inconvenient location" of the current temple, as president Greenebaum put it in his 1907 report for the members. During the 1890s, as the first African Americans settled on the Near South Side, members moved increasingly further south into more prestigious neighborhoods, particularly Hyde Park, Kenwood, and Grand Boulevard. Even for a large and wealthy congregation, the project required repeated fundraising drives. In 1909, Sinai bought a large parcel for a new temple and an adjacent social center in the heart of the Grand Boulevard neighborhood.[28]

In 1910, a year before Sinai's fiftieth anniversary, in the early stages of the construction, Hirsch reiterated his case for a new temple in an editorial for the *Reform Advocate*. A closer look at the article reveals a remarkable change of opinion. For Hirsch, the project of a new temple and a social congregation possessed renewed urgency. A more convenient location and larger sanctuary were essential, but his main concern was not to extend Sinai's reach among non-Jews but rather to redefine Sinai as a *Jewish* social congregation. After praising Sinai's legacy as an uncompromising radical Reform congregation and Sunday services, Hirsch emphasized Sinai was "intensely Jewish." He pointed to Orthodox Judaism as an inspiration for reorganizing Sinai. The formal and uncritical adherence to ancient rituals was certainly problematic in his eyes, yet Reform Judaism had become part-time Judaism, reduced for many to attending the weekly service, and it was eroding further. Orthodox Judaism should serve as model to revive Reform Judaism, because it "embraced the totality of life." Sinai's new "synagogue," Hirsch demanded, should reconnect with the Jewish tradition by throwing open its doors every day. It should be a "Beth-ha-Kenesseth and a Beth-ha-Midrash" (a house where members would assemble and a house of study) and a true *Gemeindehaus* (house of community).

What explains this change of mind? Hirsch himself gave the answer: Sinai "energized Jewish self-respect. Its members will not cringe or crawl to obtain social recognition. They have learned and that largely through the sermon preached to them that they can well afford to ignore the snobbish affections of the social anti-Semites."[29] After 1900, Sinai's members clearly felt the sting of anti-Semitic discrimination in the social sphere. Many of the once-influential Christian business leaders and politicians who had defended their Jewish colleagues, partners, and friends against anti-Semitism had passed away. Much of the discrimination established Jews encountered was informal. A short glance through the annual reports of various civic institutions reveals a conspicuous absence of Jews on the boards of the Chicago Symphony Orchestra, the Art Institute, and comparable institutions. Only two prominent Jews, Julius Rosenwald and Abraham G. Becker, became trustees of the Art Institute in the first three decades after 1900, although many wealthy Jewish families were among the members and supporters of the museum. And only Rosenwald's name is mentioned as a member of the extended board of the Chicago Symphony Orchestra.[30] The election of these two men, even of Rosenwald, who supported almost every cultural institution in Chicago, was exceptional. Established Jews retained their position as leaders only at civic institutions they had backed since their inception, especially at the Chicago Public Library and the University of Chicago.

Thus the project of an institutional congregation that offered Jews a "home" appeared more appealing. Hirsch's remarks must be seen in this changing context. His renewed appreciation of the Jewish tradition also found expression in the design of the new temple by architect Alfred S. Alschuler. On a first glance, the grand neoclassical structure did not betray any Jewish symbols, not on the exterior, not even inside the sanctuary—save for one exception. During a board meeting in November 1911, when the new building had been almost completed and the board discussed the dedication service, Hirsch alleged the late Dankmar Adler had forgotten to include the Sepher Torah during the 1891 renovation of the old temple—as if nobody had noticed it then or during the twenty years since. This symbol, Hirsch demanded, should be brought back, because, as the board minutes relate, "it was the distinctive sign of a Jewish Temple and its presence was not in any sense a symbol of orthodoxy; and he recommended strongly that it be restored in the new Temple." Of course, Adler was not at fault. Hirsch himself had asked the architect, who had been a committed member of KAM until his death in 1900, to remove the Sepher Torah. The board had donated the Torah scroll to the University of Chicago. Now, at the last minute, the Sepher Torah was brought back.[31] This decision betrays a turning away from the strong antiritual discourse of the 1880s and 1890s. The restoration of the Sepher Torah was a tacit admission that certain Jewish symbols and rituals mattered, even at a congregation widely known as one of the most radical exponents of the Reform movement.

The final price tag for the new temple was slightly over $500,000, indeed a princely sum in 1912. When the move to the new temple was imminent in 1911, Julius Rosenwald forwarded Sinai $50,000 for sale of the old temple and property on 21st Street and Indiana Avenue. This generous act helped Sinai to organize the move to the new premises in early 1912 without having to wait for the sale of the old premises. The sale of the pews yielded most of the needed funds. Rosenwald alone spent $5,000 for his own family pew and an additional $20,000 for pews the congregation would assign to members who could not afford to acquire their own pew. The dedication ceremonies attracted more than the two thousand people the sanctuary could accommodate. Among the guests of honor who spoke during the three-day dedication and celebration were Jane Addams, the rabbis Kaufmann Kohler and Joseph Krauskopf, and a few local notables such as Professor George Burman Foster, who taught at the University of Chicago Divinity School. Rabbis Stephen S. Wise and Samuel Sale could not attend because of illness. More noteworthy were the absentees. Addams and Foster were the only well-known guests who were not Jewish; the absence of the mayor, civic leaders, and Protestant ministers was yet another indication for increasing Jewish isolation.[32]

CHAPTER TEN

In his own sermon Hirsch looked back on more than thirty years in Sinai's pulpit. In retrospect, especially his comments about the attitude of liberal Christians toward Reform Judaism are noteworthy. By 1912, the liberal congress had lost much of its original enthusiasm, and Hirsch could not resist a sharp attack on liberal Protestants. During the 1880s and 1890s, Hirsch had often referred to Jesus as an ethical teacher, in part to open a dialogue with Christians. Now his comments about Jesus were more skeptical. Judaism, he argued, stood on firm ground. But was Christianity not largely based on one figure who was a Jew? "If this Jesus never lived, what about the originality of the religion ascribed unto him?" Hirsch implicitly rejected Christian calls for Jews to convert and pointed to the persecution of Jews in the Russian Empire—by Christians. Indeed, anti-Jewish hatred and discrimination only highlighted that the "covenant of Judaism" had lost nothing of its relevance in the present age. The sermon betrays

FIGURE 10. Temple of Chicago Sinai congregation at Grand Boulevard and 46th Street, Chicago, circa 1925. Courtesy of the Chicago Sinai Congregation.

Hirsch's disappointment over the silence of liberal Protestant theologians as anti-Semitism was spreading in Europe and America.[33]

Two days were devoted to the opening of the new Sinai Social Center, an indication of the importance the congregation attached to this new institution. Women dominated the first day. This was not just a symbolic recognition of the work women's organizations performed for Sinai and the Jewish community at large; the center was in part conceived as a permanent home for several women's organizations.[34] It was more than a "home" for Sinai's members. It was designed as a gateway for the Chicago Jewish community, but on Sinai's terms. The center owed its existence not simply to the idea of the social congregation. Four local "centers"—all closely related—provided inspiration: Hull House, Reverdy Ransom's Bethel Church (AME), the Chicago Hebrew Institute, and the Abraham Lincoln Center of All Souls Church. Several of Sinai's leaders had been associated with the Hull House circle from its earliest days, notably Hirsch, Mack, and Rosenwald. Hull House provided the space for several religious leaders and social reformers to discuss and experience the idea of the social center with a continuous program.[35] One was an African American minister who came to Chicago from Cleveland in the mid-1890s.

Reverdy Cassius Ransom joined Bethel Church (AME) in 1896 as a young preacher. Influenced by Progressivism and the Hull House circle, he turned his congregation into an "institutional church." Bethel organized a kindergarten, an employment bureau, a printing shop, and athletic facilities. Ransom enhanced the involvement of the congregation's members through a men's club and a women's conference. Bethel's targets were not just members of the congregation but poorer African Americans from the surrounding neighborhood. Ransom's institutional church combined the social congregation with aspects of the settlement idea. He left Chicago in 1904, but Bethel remained committed to the institutional model. Hirsch told the members of Bethel Church in late 1912 that Sinai as an "institutional synagogue . . . owes its inspiration[al] to the Institutional A.M.E. church."[36]

Another inspiration was the Abraham Lincoln Center of All Souls Church, situated only about a mile from Sinai's new temple, in Kenwood. Jenkin Lloyd Jones had long called for combining the social congregation with a social center that functioned as a "home" for his congregation but also as a neighborhood center. Abraham Lincoln Center opened its doors in 1905. Its origins reached back to the 1890s. In 1892, Jones envisaged a large settlement center with athletic facilities, a library, regular cultural programs, a kindergarten, a training school, and other social activities—even a bowling alley. Unlike Hull House, his center was sectarian, but not exclusive. Jones chose Lincoln as a name patron, because he transcended all divisions and symbolized inclusion. One inspiration was the Jewish Training School. Jones envisioned a similarly modern, multipurpose building, only larger. His nephew, Frank Lloyd Wright, who had worked for Dankmar Adler and Louis Sullivan when they designed the Jewish Training School in 1890, became the lead architect of the Lincoln Center. The building bears a strong resemblance to the school. Shortly before completion, Wright walked away because he and his uncle could not agree over the exterior design.[37]

Bethel Church, the Abraham Lincoln Center, and Sinai Social Center were closely related, not least because their spiritual leaders belonged to the Hull House circle. It is also striking that they appealed to rather different audiences. Bethel Church targeted the poor in its vicinity, in part because no other institution cared for destitute African Americans who had a very limited choice over where they could settle and worship. The church was based in the segregated Black Belt, and it could not hope to attract more than a few committed white members into its ranks. Jones, on the other hand, aimed at a potentially much larger constituency of Protestants and Jews, and he explicitly welcomed African Americans. This also explains the dimension of the Abraham Lincoln Center, a prominent multistory building.

During the dedication of the social center in 1912, Sinai's leaders stated they did not want to target the poor, although they were certainly welcome. The Jewish community already provided a wide range of options for poor Jews, ranging from employment bureaus, social services, child care, and the Jewish Training School. Apart from offering a better home for Jewish women's organizations Sinai aimed at the many unaffiliated Jews and especially their children. The center was not uncontroversial. There were concerns that religion would be sidelined by sports and entertainments. But it offered a competing vision to the Hebrew Institute.[38]

The Hebrew Institute was a settlement in all but name. But one crucial difference separated it from Hull House and other settlements. It was one of the first larger settlements in the United States founded and governed exclusively by the people it targeted. Several immigrants established the institute in 1903, to promote "education, civic training, moral and physical culture, the amelioration of the condition and social advancement of the Jewish residents of the city of Chicago." But in its first two years the institute existed only on paper. This changed when cofounder Nathan D. Kaplan approached the Chicago Council of Jewish Women chapter and became acquainted with Sinai member Johanne Loeb. She promoted the institute among her social circle at Sinai. The institute targeted Jewish immigrants, not least the younger generation. It promoted integration, albeit not on the terms of the established Jews. Most founders and leaders of the Hebrew Institute were well-known Zionists. But they refrained from giving the institute an openly Zionist or religious outlook, in order to include as many Jews as possible. In 1907, Hirsch openly embraced the institute, not coincidentally when he became concerned about anti-Semitism and social isolation. A lecture series he organized on behalf of the institute convinced leading Jewish philanthropists to open their purses. Julius Rosenwald and other established Jews funded the construction of a new building in the heart of the ghetto area on the West Side. The Hebrew Institute offered English classes, job training for men and women, social activities for children, and a wide array of physical activities, and it had a swimming pool.[39]

The growing success of the Hebrew Institute raises the question why its main benefactors created a competing center. Sinai's center and the new temple were inclusive: "Our gates are open to all that will enter, be they women or be they men, be they white or be they of other color, be they Jews, or be they non-Jews. Here shall be at home all who search for knowledge." This statement echoes once more the aspirations of the universal *Bildung* ideal. And the design of the center as a facility of educating and training of mind and body owed as much to enlightenment ideals as to the settlement model. Yet several speakers hinted quite openly at a narrower target audience. According to Hirsch the Center was "in no sense sectarian. . . . Yet probably it will attract (and it were wrong if it did not) in the main Jewish young men and Jewish young women." For Sinai, the Center offered a competing *Jewish* vision to the Hebrew Institute. Hirsch singled out the Hebrew Institute as "the very center of Zionist agitation."[40] This statement hints at a deeper conflict over the implications of defining Jewishness in America in the period of mass immigration. In the eyes of Sinai's leaders the Hebrew Institute instrumentalized its social and cultural program to turn especially younger immigrants into ethnic Jews, sidelining Americanization—and religion. Sinai Social Center belonged to a religious congregation. Like the Hebrew Institute, it emphasized Jewish *Gemeinschaft*, yet explicitly on religious and on inclusive American terms. The location of the Sinai Social Center—miles from the West Side immigrant neighborhood—limited its appeal among the large immigrant community. Yet the athletic facilities, particularly the basketball court and the swimming pool, pulled in hundreds of Jewish and Christian youths from across the South Side. Some were certainly children of members, quite a few belonged to other congregations, or their parents were unaffiliated. The center comprised several sports teams. Teenagers of both sexes competed in various disciplines with their Jewish and Christian peers across the city. Particularly successful were the Sinai Tankers, the male swimming team. They won several urban and regional competitions between 1918 and 1921, defeating YMCA sides, nonsectarian teams organized around natatoriums, and the Hebrew Institute. One of the most successful swimmers was Ethel Bilson, known as the "Medal-Some Mermaid" who won a number of competitions in the early 1920s. During a 1918 competition, the Tankers' victory depended on two Irish kids. This was testament to the ideal of inclusiveness and openness, at least in the period before growing numbers of African Americans moved to the Grand Boulevard neighborhood in the early 1920s.[41]

After the membership reform of 1895–1896, the decision to join the UAHC in 1903, the opening of the Sinai Social Center constituted the third decisive

FIGURE 11. The chess club at the Sinai Social Center, circa 1920. Courtesy of the Chicago Sinai Congregation.

step that transformed the congregation. In the early 1890s, Sinai attracted large audiences to its Sunday services, but the congregation was still controlled by the relatively small "family" of elderly immigrant founders. As members of the second generation joined the board, the congregation opened its ranks to a much broader group of established Jews. Soon after 1900, the optimistic vision to reach out beyond the Jewish community gradually eroded, and even Hirsch recognized the need to foster more Jewish *Gemeinschaft* among the established Jews in Chicago, many of whom were not affiliated with a synagogue—and among the new immigrants.

11.

AFTER 1900, Sinai began to draw its members from a broader stratum of the Jewish establishment. Only few immigrants attended Sunday services before 1920. If established Jews and immigrants encountered each other, frequently it was on unequal terms, as employers and employees or as providers and recipients of philanthropic aid. This chapter examines how the relationship between Sinai and the immigrants began to transform after the turn of the twentieth century, when members of the congregation interacted more frequently with individual immigrants. The decision by several Sinai members to support the Hebrew Institute in the first decade of the twentieth century hints at a changing approach and a departure from the paternalistic philanthropy of the last two decades of the nineteenth century. Instead of designing projects, regardless of recipients' specific needs, immigrants were treated as partners who could be trusted to shape and manage philanthropic institutions on their own. It is hardly surprising that many established Jews had ambivalent feelings about this transition. Hirsch was no exception. A leading advocate of the Hebrew Institute, he went out of his way to promote the new institution and encouraged members of Sinai to donate generously. Yet in 1912, during the opening of the Sinai Social Center, he accused the institute's leaders of "Zionist agitation."[1] In hindsight, Zionism rather than religion appears to be the leading symbolic issue dividing immigrants and established Jews.

But the reality was more complex. Hirsch, the highly paid rabbi of a prestigious urban Reform congregation and a fierce critic of Zionism, enjoyed much respect among leading Zionists in and beyond Chicago and many Jewish immigrants in Chicago. His frequent attacks against the exploitation of working-class Chicagoans certainly added to his reputation among many immigrants. Sinai's support of workers' rights faced an important test in late 1910, when thousands of Jewish and other immigrant garment workers joined one of the biggest strikes in Chicago history. Several of the key employers in the garment sector were members of Sinai congregation.

ZIONISM

In 1906, Russian Zionist Shmarya Levin visited Chicago. As a delegate of the first Duma, he gained prominence when he sharply protested against anti-Jewish violence and persecution. After the czar dissolved the Duma in July 1906, Levin moved to Berlin, where he had attended the Hochschule für die Wissenschaft des Judentums in the early 1880s. From there, he embarked on several lecture tours to the United States to rally support for Zionism and raise funds for the Jewish community in Palestine. During his Chicago visit, Levin first spoke to Zionists on the West Side. More surprisingly, he also gave a German address at the Standard Club to a select group of established Jews that included Hirsch, also a graduate of the Berlin Hochschule. According to several witnesses, Levin, a charismatic speaker, impressed the audience. He was the guest of honor at a banquet organized by local Zionists at a simple restaurant on the West Side. Among the invitees were Julius Rosenwald, Abraham G. Becker, and other Jews from the South Side. Levin was not the only Zionist who spoke to members of Sinai and other established Jews in Chicago in this period. Stephen S. Wise, a rising figure in the Reform movement who sympathized with Hirsch's social theology but was also an early advocate of Zionism, repeatedly preached at Sinai. In November 1914, after the beginning of the war in Europe, Sinai opened its temple to Louis Brandeis, who had just assumed the leadership of the American Zionists. None other than Shmarya Levin accompanied Brandeis.[2] Why did Sinai invite and listen to these figures?

Soon after 1900, established American Jews began to rethink their position toward the recent Jewish immigrants—not just in Chicago. At the beginning of the new century, even the most optimistic Americanizers among established Jews had to concede that their efforts had only a limited impact. Around 1900, the first American-born generation replaced the elderly founders on the boards of congregations and community institutions. The new leaders took a more open-minded approach to mass immigration. The numbers spoke for themselves: established Jews were increasingly marginalized. In 1904, the annual Jewish immigration crossed the threshold of a hundred thousand people for the first time, and in the following years the numbers remained high. In most years between 1900 and 1914, Jews made up about 10 percent of the annual immigration to the United States. In a period of mass immigration, these were remarkable statistics for a relatively small group. Chicago's Jewish population increased from about ten thousand in 1880 to a staggering three hundred thousand by 1920. Apart from New York, which had a Jewish population of well over a million in 1920, only Philadelphia and Warsaw matched the size of Chicago's Jewish community.

Most contemporaries linked the Jewish mass immigration to the United States with widespread anti-Jewish riots in the Russian Empire that followed in the wake of the notorious 1903 Kishinev pogrom. American Jewish leaders, who initially had seen the immigration as a threat to their own status, were seriously concerned about the safety of the large Jewish population in the Russian Empire. The founding of the American Jewish Committee in 1906 was driven by concerns over growing anti-Semitism at home; it also reflected the growing responsibility American Jews felt for distressed Jews abroad. The new body coordinated relations with Jews in western Europe and lobbied against immigration restrictions. On the local level, established Jews and immigrant leaders began to build closer ties. AJC cofounder Julian Mack engineered the election of Bernard Horwich, a Zionist, to the board of the Associated Jewish Charities in 1902, little more than ten years after the first woman had been elected to the board. The Chicago Hebrew Institute and the much more ambitious Kehillah project in New York depended on the cooperation between established Jews and immigrants.[3]

At first glance, Zionism might appear to be a minor matter, if set against other issues that divided newcomers from the longer settled Jews: class, religion, and strikingly different visions of communal Jewish life in America. Few American Jews joined Zionist organizations before 1914. Yet even though most Jews seemed indifferent to Zionism before 1914, the respective position on this issue emerged as pivotal litmus test as established and immigrant Jews debated different visions of Jewish life in America. For many established Jews, Zionism sharply contradicted a religiously defined American Jewish identity, while for most of its adherents Zionism reinforced an ethnic Jewish identity in a pluralist American setting. However, opponents and supporters of Zionism both shared a serious concern for the growing plight of Jews in eastern Europe.

Early on, Zionism in the United States evolved within a broad spectrum. Sharply different opinions on Zionism did not by default preclude cooperation, especially in times of crisis. Moreover, Zionism was not a fixed set of ideas; rather, it was a continuous debate. Most American Zionists were recently arrived immigrants. But several key figures in the early Zionist movement in the United States were "German" Reform Jews, especially rabbis.[4]

Chicago was one of the early centers of organized Zionism in America. The first proto-Zionist association in Chicago can be traced back to 1883, when several immigrants founded the Dorshei Sifrut Ha-Ibrith, an association that promoted the use of Hebrew. One of the founders was Bernhard Felsenthal, who then was still the rabbi of Zion congregation. After he retired from Zion's pulpit in 1887, he continued to participate at various public events and contributed articles to the Jewish press. Felsenthal was not close to Hirsch, but the two men respected each other as leading radical Reform theologians, even after Felsenthal began to promote Zionism openly in the late 1890s. Felsenthal's support of Zionism had deep roots. Already in 1869, he described Jews as a religion and "nation," based on "common descent." In an 1879 article, he depicted Jews "primarily as *Stammesgenossenschaft* [tribal community] and only on a secondary level as *Glaubensgenossenschaft* [religious community]."[5]

In the last third of the nineteenth century, many American Reform rabbis were quite comfortable expressing Jewish difference in racial terms, as Eric Goldstein has recently shown.[6] But to understand Hirsch's strong opposition to race and Felsenthal's support of the idea, events in central and eastern Europe around 1880 have to be taken into account. One development, anxiously followed by Jews in the United States, was the rise of modern anti-Semitism in Germany, France, and other European countries during the last two decades of the nineteenth century. This period witnessed not only the organization of a radical anti-Semitic movement but a paradigmatic shift to a secular and explicitly racist definition of Jews. At least as unsettling was the political impact anti-Semitism was making on the highest echelons of the German and French state. Several German anti-Semites, most famously the historian Heinrich Treitschke, were respected scholars who taught at leading universities. Educated Jews in Germany and beyond were deeply unsettled that leading representatives of *Bildung* gave the stamp of approval to an ideology that contradicted the inclusive and universalistic ideals of the Enlightenment. German anti-Semites were divided over many issues, but most agreed on one central goal: to revoke Jewish emancipation; some even demanded the expulsion of Jews. In an 1883 sermon, Hirsch compared anti-Semitism to an infectious disease for which the Atlantic was no obstacle. American Jews had to be on guard and fight such stereotypes. "Modern" Jews should pursue integration, Hirsch demanded, rather than withdrawing into a social ghetto.[7]

Two other seemingly related events coincided with the rise of modern anti-Semitism in Germany: a wave of pogroms across the Russian Empire in 1881 and a sudden increase in Jewish emigration from Russia in the same year. The pamphlet *Auto-Emancipation* by the Odessa physician Leon Pinsker was an early Jewish response to the 1881 pogrom wave. Like many educated Jews in eastern Europe, Pinsker had initially embraced Enlightenment ideals. But the pogroms convinced him that irrational forces constituted a serious threat and that only a sovereign Jewish state could protect Jews from such persecution. Pinsker suggested a suitable territory should be acquired at an unspecified location, primarily to serve as a safe haven for Jews from eastern Europe.[8]

If Felsenthal did not obtain a copy of Pinsker's pamphlet, he certainly knew about its central positions from discussions in the Jewish press in Europe. In 1883, German rabbi Isaak Rülf praised Pinsker's agenda and went a step further, describing Palestine as the national homeland for the Jewish people. Felsenthal's essay, "Some Thoughts on the Jewish Problem," published simultaneously with Rülf's essay, clearly echoes the debate in the German-Jewish public and betrays proto-Zionist influences. In Felsenthal's view, anti-Semitism constituted a grave threat for Jews as a people rather than as a religious community. Especially in the Russian Empire, the situation was precarious, but transplanting most Jews from eastern Europe to the United States at a time when the overwhelming majority of established Jews strongly opposed the mass immigration seemed impossible—. Thus Palestine was the obvious "asylum." Felsenthal called on American Jews to support a "Jewish commonwealth on the shores of the Jordan river" and the peaceful coexistence of Jewish settlers with the Muslim and Christian population of Palestine under Ottoman rule. In such views, however, Sinai's first rabbi differed sharply from Hirsch. In 1885, Hirsch urged American Jews to completely reject a national and specifically a "racial" identity, because promoting Jewish separateness would play into the hands of anti-Semites: "Antisemitism [*sic*] is legitimate, when the Jew is 'race-proud.'" Felsenthal, in sharp contrast, called on Jews to acknowledge their common ethnic background, *because* anti-Semites discriminated and persecuted Jews as a "race."[9]

When the first Zionist Congress convened in Basel in 1897, supporters of the idea in Chicago had organized. It is not exactly clear when the first Zionist association was formed, but several accounts by contemporaries point to 1896 as the founding date of the Chicago Zionist Organization, No.1. The Knights of Zion followed in 1897. Leon Zolotkoff, the founding editor of the influential Chicago Yiddish daily *Der Taeglicher Idisher Kuryer* (Daily Jewish Courier), represented Chicago's Zionists at the first Basel congress. Other figures on the local scene, apart from Felsenthal, were also immigrants from eastern Europe: Bernard Horwich, his brother Harris, Hyman Meites, the author of the 1924 community history, and several others.[10]

Felsenthal was the widely respected honorary leader of organized Zionist movement in Chicago. In Hirsch's eyes, however, Felsenthal's activities were irrational and driven by emotionalism. In a private letter to his predecessor, he described organized Zionism in 1898 as a "hoax." But Felsenthal was not the only Reform rabbi who supported Zionism. Rabbi Gustav Gottheil of Temple Emanu-El in New York also attended the 1897 Basel congress as an American delegate. He and his son, Richard Gottheil, who taught Semitic studies at Columbia; the young Stephen S. Wise; and the leading Conservative rabbi Marcus Mordecai Jastrow, an important influence on the young Hirsch, founded the Federation of American Zionists in 1898, together with leading representatives of the new immigrants, such as Zolotkoff. Another supporter was Rabbi Joseph Krauskopf at Philadelphia's Keneseth Israel Congregation. Felsenthal, whose health increasingly confined him to his home by the late 1890s, corresponded regularly with the older Gottheil, Jastrow, the young Wise, and another young Reform rabbi and Zionist, Judah L. Magnes. Since Hirsch left no papers, it ultimately remains unclear how he judged the decisions of men like Krauskopf or Wise who stood relatively close to him and whose motives for supporting Zionism could not be reduced to naïve emotionalism.[11]

It is noteworthy that Gottheil, the rabbi of America's most prestigious Reform congregation during the 1880s and 1890s, yielded to pressures of leading members and did not touch on Zionism on the pulpit. But support of Zionism was apparently not an obstacle for the Emanu-El board members when they selected Gottheil's successor. In 1906, they offered the position to Wise, who rejected the offer because he felt the board would restrict a free pulpit. Emanu-El then approached Magnes. He accepted in 1907 but left in 1910 for another New York congregation. The cause, however, was not related to his Zionist activities but to his growing alienation from Reform Judaism.[12]

Emil G. Hirsch is often portrayed as one of the most vociferous Jewish critics of Zionism in America.[13] In May 1897, on the eve of the first Basel congress, he described the "the new Zionist craze" as the "most dangerous symptom" that modern Jews faced. Fifteen years later, in 1912, Hirsch declared in a sermon to his congregation, "As long as I am in this pulpit Sinai Congregation will be

As a token of love and sincere esteem to my nephew Henry B. Kiefer from B. Felsenthal.

Jan'y 2. 1902.

FIGURE 12. Bernhard Felsenthal, 1902 (with a handwritten dedication to his nephew). Courtesy of the Chicago Sinai Congregation.

unalterably opposed to Zionism." Hirsch promoted the idea of a spiritual mission of Israel. Supporting the return even of the hard-pressed eastern European Jewish masses to Palestine would increase the isolation of Jews in the Diaspora, threatening the project of emancipation. "For me Israel's destiny foreshadowed in its very martyrdom and heroism is to be of greater service and meaning than what it can be if our rerise [*sic*] as a small political nation in a corner of anterior Asia is the ultimate goal of our checkered, tearwet, and blooded career." The list of Hirsch's acerbic comments about Zionism is long. Yet a closer examination reveals that his position on Zionism defies easy categorization. One seemingly obvious reason for his critical stance was his oft-repeated position that Jews were not a race. However, in 1895, Hirsch briefly reversed his position, describing Jews as a race. But even during these few months, Hirsch's concept of race was inclusive. In his view, children of mixed marriages were Jewish, if they identified with Judaism. Indeed, non-Jews should join: "If they decide to join us freely, let us accept them!" A "merely racial" Judaism was "doomed to fossilization." In a 1908 sermon at Sinai, Hirsch explicitly "urged [Jews] to wed Gentiles," as the *Chicago Tribune* put it. According to the paper, Hirsch presented intermarriage as "the solution to the Jewish problem." The alternatives were "emigration and segregation." Throughout history, Jews had intermarried; the "modern Jew" was no "Semite," and "there was no such thing as a Hebrew race."[14] Sinai's rabbi frequently made provocative—even insulting—statements. It would indeed be a mistake to draw general conclusions from a specific remark or editorial. In contrast to other scholar-rabbis like Kohler, Hirsch did not write academic tomes but was a public intellectual who reached out to a wide audience—often polemically, and not always consistently—commenting on issues of the day through sermons, speeches, and editorials.

The rise of proto-Zionism during the 1880s and Zionism toward the end of the 1890s and the engagement of critics like Hirsch were closely related to the situation of Jews in the Russian Empire and Romania. Hirsch's speeches, sermons, and statements during the first decade of the twentieth century reveal a conflicting picture. Orthodox rabbi Zvi Hirsch Masliansky, who visited Chicago in 1898, observed that Hirsch frequently changed his position on Zionism. Hirsch promoted radical Reform Judaism as an inclusive, postethnic, universalistic religion, as the very opposite of the Judaism of the ghetto. Yet his condemnation of the anti-Jewish persecution in eastern Europe, in a period of rising anti-Semitism at home, also betrays an appreciation of Jewishness and the Jewish Diaspora.[15]

A good example for the first view is an address Hirsch gave on the occasion of the celebration of the 250th anniversary of the first settlement of Jews in North

America on Thanksgiving Day 1905. Shortly before the long-planned celebration a series of brutal pogroms in the Russian Empire shocked the Jewish public in the West. The atrocities committed in late October in Odessa against Jewish women and children were particularly violent and troubling. In response, American Jewish leaders scaled down the central celebration in New York and used the speeches to rally support among the wider American public for Russian Jews. Hirsch, who spoke at a local celebration in Chicago, promoted America as the very opposite of Russia—a country where Jews were the quintessential insiders rather than members of an unwanted and marginalized minority. Judaism and Americanism, he argued, were not separates but indistinguishable composites. Modern Judaism and the American project both had strong roots in the Enlightenment, sharing a similar universal outlook: "*E pluribus unum* formulates a truth, radiantly visible in the vision of this day. By rejoicing as Jews we are accentuating our Americanism. And in similar manner the pride of our Americanism . . . is not a protest against, it is a proclamation of our fidelity to our Judaism." Hirsch rejected the traditional Judaism of the ghetto, the Judaism of "regretful retrospect." The religious idea of *Galut* (exile) and Zionism contradicted Jewish identification with America. "We cannot honestly declare that we are here in exile. We cannot honestly petition that we be led back to Palestine as our country. We have a country which is ours by the right of our being identified with its destinies, our being devoted to its welfare, our sharing its trials, our rejoicing in its triumphs." Modern Judaism—"our Reform Judaism"—based on a reinterpretation of the core principles of Judaism, was perfectly in tune with America. Indeed, according to Hirsch, Jewish principles, partly in Christian clothing, formed the basis of the American republic, because the Puritans acted in the spirit of ancient Jews: "Is not America's political creed the practical execution and activization [*sic*] of these fundamental conceptions of Judaism?"[16]

Hirsch's relationship with Chicago Zionist leader Leon Zolotkoff was strained. According to Masliansky, the editor of *Der Taeglicher Idisher Kuryer* repeatedly criticized Hirsch, highlighting the contradictions in his statements about Zionism. At the same time, Hirsch reached out to Zionists. A year before the 1897 Basel congress, he opened the *Reform Advocate* to Zionist critics of his positions.[17] After 1900, he fostered close personal ties with several new immigrants. Two Chicago Zionists, Philip Bregstone and Bernard Horwich, expressed admiration for Hirsch in their memoirs and described a number of amicable meetings between Sinai's rabbi and leading West Side personalities. On at least one occasion, Hirsch joined Horwich to collect small donations for the Hebrew Institute in the ghetto. After the notorious 1903 Kishinev pogrom, prominent members of both Jewish communities in Chicago met at the Standard Club to coordinate their response. As Bregstone recalls, Hirsch turned to the immigrant leaders and said: "We will join you! . . . We are all brothers in sorrow! As for me, use me wherever you see fit: if needs be I'll put on my phylacteries and prayer shawl; send me where you will." In a 1904 publication about the situation of Jews in Russia, Hirsch expressed sympathy for Zionism in Russia, because the movement and idea were mobilizing Russian Jews. But he also pointed out that Zionism would do "harm" in the United States. Several other Reform rabbis re-examined their anti-Zionist position in light of the Russian atrocities against Jews. The anti-Jewish riots of November 1905 in Russia triggered another collab-orative effort in Chicago. A few months before he was elected president of Sinai, Moses E. Greenebaum led a fundraising campaign for the victims among all Jews in the city. Bregstone singled out Hirsch as the figure who "bridged the gap of the Chicago river that divided the two classes of Jews: the South Side and the West Side." Several Sinai members spent much time and energy for overcoming the deep divide, notably Julian Mack, Babette Mandel, and Johanne Loeb.[18]

Hirsch's reaction to the death of Felsenthal in 1908 also illustrates concern for Jews in Russia and an appreciation of his predecessor's motives for supporting Zionism: "Like Felsenthal Sinai sympathizes with the sufferings, both physical and spiritual, of the Jews persecuted in darkest Russia and treacherous Rouma-nia. Like him we protest against a dogmatic and ecclesiastic limitation of the Jewish fellowship. Like him Sinai deplores the rise of anti-Semitism. But what in his declining years seemed to him to point out Israel's peril and to foretell Israel's perdition unless it withdrew into a political national Ghetto of its own making, is for us an all the more urgent appeal to continue the good fight for our rights and for the right." Hirsch did not deny that he was "respectfully dissenting" with the late Felsenthal's Zionist views.[19]

Early on, Hirsch recognized the great appeal of Zionism, especially for the op-pressed Jewish masses in eastern Europe, and their sympathizers abroad. Some of his closest fellow travelers, such as Reform rabbis like Joseph Krauskopf and even his congregant Julian Mack, turned to Zionism. Hirsch shared the deep con-cern of Zionists for the fate of Jews in Russia and Romania. But promoting the difference of Jews, not in religious but in racial terms, he reasoned, played into the hands of anti-Semites and threatened the status of Jews even in the United States. Hirsch's ideal of American Judaism as an exclusively religious fellowship held little attraction for many immigrants who defined Jewishness in secular terms. Hirsch was no Zionist. But his early and critical engagement with Zion-ism and Zionists and with leaders of the new immigrants can only be read as an attempt to influence the debate about Zionism and an American Jewish ethnicity. In hindsight, Sinai's rabbi appears as an influential, albeit rather reluctant, harbinger of American Zionism in its formative phase.

EMPLOYERS VERSUS WORKERS

Zionism was not the only issue dividing and yet simultaneously connecting established Jews and newcomers in Chicago and other American cities. Class divisions were much more acutely felt. Along with Polish, Lithuanian, and Italian immigrants, many Jewish men and women found work in Chicago's expanding textile industry. While the workers were much more ethnically diverse than in New York, where most garment workers and employers were Jews from eastern Europe, some of the most successful textile firms in Chicago around 1900 were owned by Jewish immigrants from central Europe. In 1875, more than a third of Sinai's eighty members managed manufacturing and retail businesses for clothes and shoes. Sinai members Bernhard Kuppenheimer, Isaac Greensfelder, Simon Florsheim, Joseph Schaffner, and Harry Hart founded major American textile firms, employing thousands of young immigrant workers who worked under challenging conditions in sweatshops near the city center.

Sinai's rabbi had long denounced the deplorable situation of the working class. After the 1894 Pullman Strike, Hirsch stepped up his criticism of unrestrained capitalism. In one of his most influential discourses, "The Inalienable Duties of Man," he outlined his social justice platform: "The individual is by society—Society is not by the individual. Society is the mother, the individual is the child." Hirsch demanded more rights for male and female workers and a redistribution of wealth and presented a far-reaching social reform program. This included a number of concrete proposals: a progressive income tax, a tax on luxury products, legislation on workers' rights, health and safety procedures in the work place, a state-administered social and health insurance scheme similar to the one Bismarck had introduced in Imperial Germany during the 1880s, a six-day working week, a ban of child labor, and the protection of female workers.[20]

Only a few members openly disagreed with Hirsch's demands for workers' rights. In 1899, meatpacker Nelson Morris, a founder of the congregation, resigned following repeated and thinly veiled attacks against him from the pulpit. His response remained the exception. In fact, during the conflict over Hirsch's imminent move to New York, Sinai's board proudly pointed to the "thousands of our citizens, non-Jews, toilers in the workshops, in the stores and in counting rooms [in Chicago], who look to our Rabbi as the champion of their rights and justice." Progressive causes and the strong commitment to the organized Jewish community were a hallmark of the congregation. Sinai's sympathy for workers' rights is noteworthy for another reason. Most established Protestant congregations, not to mention the Catholic Church, opposed organized labor. Chicago's Fourth Presbyterian Church, for instance, helped poor Chicagoans, but its leaders did not speak up on behalf of the working class. Only a few liberal congregations, like Sinai's close ally Unity Church, called for social justice and voiced support for the working class. The outcome of the 1910–1911 Chicago garment workers' strike illustrates that Hirsch's sermons and the board's statement had not fallen on deaf ears.[21]

On September 22, 1910, Hannah Shapiro, a young Jewish immigrant, along with more than a dozen other unorganized women, walked out, triggering one of the biggest strikes in Chicago history. Their sweatshop was part of Hart Schaffner & Marx, the largest textile firm in Chicago—and one of the largest producers of men's clothing in the world. Hart Schaffner & Marx was formed in 1887 when Joseph Schaffner formed a partnership with the brothers Harry and Max Hart and Marcus Marx. Like many firms founded by Jewish immigrants from central Europe in mid-nineteenth-century America, Hart Schaffner & Marx was a family firm. Schaffner, the Hart brothers, and Marx were relatives and belonged to the Palatinate migration network associated with Sinai (and Zion) congregation. Hart Schaffner & Marx quickly expanded; in 1910 the business employed a vast workforce. More than eight thousand men and women toiled in its forty-eight sweatshops. The success of the firm was in part built on a pioneering national advertising campaign. Schaffner and Harry Hart both had a keen sense of changing tastes marketing their suits successfully as a stylish brand. The working conditions were among the best in the sector. Years before Shapiro walked out, the management had made an effort to improve employee relations and raise hygiene standards in its workshops. Hart Schaffner & Marx did not contract work to small independently run sweatshops but employed its workers "inside." This practice prevented some of the worst abuses common in an industry that relied on unregulated contractors. Yet the company was not immune from competition and uneven business cycles. Repeatedly the management reduced wages and laid off staff. And the conditions at their workshops, as Schaffner conceded after the strike, were not acceptable. Indeed, in his testimony to the U.S. Commission on Industrial Relations in 1914, he wondered why the strike had not "occurred much sooner."[22]

The immediate cause for the walkout was a pay cut from 4¢ to 3.75¢ for a pair of pants. Variable pay was common practice in the industry. Even working ninety to one hundred hours, Hannah Shapiro still made less than ten dollars a week. In early October, organized male workers joined the protest, and by the middle of the month, most workers had walked out. Thousands of workers at other companies in Chicago also stopped working, and eventually more than forty thousand were participating. The unorganized women asked Jane Addams for assistance, and Hull House emerged as meeting point for the strikers. As chair of Chicago's Citizens Committee, Hirsch acted as mediator, along with Addams, Julian Mack, and others. They urged Schaffner to accept the unionization of the workers and convinced him that the working conditions in his shops were deplorable. At this point the struggle about pay and the actual working conditions moved to the sidelines, and the formal recognition of unions as legitimate representatives by employers emerged as the real pivot of the strike.

The Chicago strike began immediately after two major strikes in the New York garment industry. In November 1909, twenty thousand shirtwaist (blouse) makers had gone on strike in New York. Most were young girls not much older than twenty, and almost 70 percent were Jewish immigrants. The strike dragged on until February 1910, when a settlement was reached. The employers, themselves overwhelmingly Jewish immigrants from eastern Europe, agreed to better working conditions, but they refused to formally recognize the unions. This was less than the workers had fought for. But in hindsight, the strike strengthened organized labor because thousands of workers joined unions. The growing confidence of many workers led to an even bigger strike a few months later. In July 1910, the mostly male cloakmakers went on strike. This "Great Revolt" involved more than seventy thousand workers. In this sector, too, most workers and their employers were Jewish immigrants. Leading figures in the established Jewish community, including investment banker Jacob Schiff, respected lawyer Louis Marshall, and Boston attorney Louis D. Brandeis, mediated. They produced the Protocol of Peace that gave the workers a fifty-hour week, increased pay, and the "preferential union shop." The protocol served as a model for other industries. The preferential union shop represented a de facto recognition of the unions by the employers. The end of the strike in early September 1910 and its successful outcome provide the background for the events in Chicago a little more than two weeks later.[23]

Before 1914, organized labor in Chicago, one of the biggest industrial centers in the world, remained on the defensive. Continuous mass immigration and a rapidly diversifying industrial sector, however, do not sufficiently explain the limited leverage of unions over employers. Repeatedly, the latter defeated attempts to organize workers brutally and with support of federal troops, such as after the 1886 Haymarket protests, the 1894 Pullman strike, and another massive strike in 1904. The clothing sector had witnessed several largely unsuccessful attempts to unionize, reflecting the relative weakness of organized labor. The United Garment Workers (UGW), the Chicago Federation of Labor, and the Women's Trade Union League represented only a fraction of the workers. UGW's members were mostly native born, and the union leadership resented immigrants (because they drove down wages), singling out in particular Jews for criticism. The large firms, organized in the Chicago Wholesale Clothiers' Association ignored the unions.[24] Therefore, it was no great surprise when initially, in late October 1910, Hart Schaffner & Marx management claimed it paid the highest wages in the city and it would not deal with "agitators" claiming to represent its employees. Ironically, there was some truth to this statement. The rapidly spreading strike caught UGW by surprise, and the union was not able to secure a mandate from the workers. Following a call by Jenkin Lloyd Jones for arbitration, the Chicago City Council passed a motion in late November asking the mayor to mediate in the strike. But the Chicago Wholesale Clothiers' Association steadfastly refused to talk with union leaders who claimed to represent the striking masses. In early December, violent clashes with the police claimed the first casualty. Hart Schaffner & Marx, although by far the biggest firm, did not belong to the Wholesale Clothiers' Association. It crossed the line by talking with union representatives before early December, albeit without making progress. On December 4, the day after the death was reported, the *Chicago Tribune* announced a deal was in the making, and more important: Hart Schaffner & Marx would be ready to "recognize the Union." In the next few weeks, two men with very different backgrounds helped to bring about a peaceful resolution of the strike, Joseph Schaffner and a young employee, Sidney Hillman.[25]

Unlike Harry Hart, Schaffner kept a low profile in the congregation. At Hart Schaffner & Marx, their roles were reversed. Schaffner rather than Hart spoke for the firm, and he took charge during the strike. Schaffner and Hart were no cold-blooded capitalists. Both men had shown a disposition for charitable causes, similar to many other members of Sinai and of comparable Jewish congregations in other American cities. Hart served as vice president of the Associated Jewish Charities when he was elected president of Sinai. As a young man, Schaffner was active in the YMHA and was a prominent supporter of the second Jewish hospital in Chicago. Around the turn of the twentieth century, Schaffner was affiliated with the B'nai B'rith Cleveland Orphan Asylum. But his philanthropy was not limited to the Jewish sphere. According to the *New York Times* Schaffner's name "was on the list of membership of every national charitable organization in Chicago."[26] In short, Schaffner and Hart were the prototype of the socially responsible and civically committed businessmen. But they employed thousands of immigrant workers who barely made ends meet and faced extremely challenging working conditions. The death of the picketer in early December 1910 deeply unsettled them.

Schaffner's willingness, as leader of Chicago's largest clothing firm, to recognize a union as a legitimate partner constituted a bold step and was a blow to employers' interests in Chicago, well beyond the clothing sector. The UGW leaders quickly realized the significance of Schaffner's offer. But the strikers resented the union. Instead of providing the UGW leaders with a mandate, the workers staged several large demonstrations. By the end of December a group of articulate, unorganized Hart Schaffner & Marx workers, led by Sidney Hillman, Samuel Levin, Bessie Abramovitz, and Italian immigrant Anzuino Mariempietri, emerged as spokesmen. After the fatal shooting of another worker by the police in mid-December, this time in front of a Hart Schaffner & Marx workshop, and a more generous offer, the strikers agreed to talks. Schaffner conducted the negotiations with Hillman and other workers; the UGW remained excluded. Apart from some limited improvements for the workers the settlement established unions as legitimate representatives of workers—but only at Hart Schaffner & Marx. The settlement took effect on January 14, 1911. The workers at the other firms, the overwhelming majority, ended their strike a short time later, after failing to win concessions from the Chicago Wholesale Clothiers' Association.

Apart from the (apparently) limited success at one firm, the garment workers' strike failed. Many ringleaders were fired, wages remained low, and in some cases employers imposed even harsher conditions. But in hindsight, Schaffner's recognition of organized labor as a legitimate representative and partner constituted a turning point in the history of organized labor in Chicago, because it established a sphere where employers and workers could settle conflicts amicably. The other employers were reluctant to bow to the principles of the January 1911 agreement. Several ostracized Schaffner socially. In 1911 and 1912, Hillman tirelessly organized workers in Chicago, overcoming much distrust between different ethnic groups, gradually providing the labor movement with growing leverage. During his 1914 testimony, Schaffner stressed that the "fundamental cause of the strike" was the absence of a "channel" through which the workers could discuss "grievances" with the management. The January 1911 agreement created this channel. Schaffner's openness to change, his acknowledgement of intolerable conditions, and the communication skills of Hillman were indispensable to put the agreement on a firm footing, prevent further strikes, and reach mutually acceptable agreements. After Hart Schaffner & Marx agreed to a minimum wage for its female workers in 1916, Hillman commended the management for being "absolutely fair to organized labor." Only "few concerns in this country," he claimed, offered their workers similarly beneficial "conditions of labor."[27]

The Amalgamated Clothing Workers of America, formed in 1914 with Hillman as its first president, traced its roots to the January 1911 agreement. By 1919, after reaching several agreements with Hart Schaffner & Marx, the union counted more than forty thousand members in Chicago alone. Jews only represented less than a third of the workers in the industry but most union leaders were Jewish. Unlike in other industries they successfully overcame ethnic and even racial divisions, strengthening the bargaining power of the union.[28] Hillman emerged as one of the key players in the American union movement during the first half of the twentieth century. In 1937, looking back on a long period of peaceful relations that owed much to the initial agreement, Hillman stressed, "For fully 25 years . . . the Amalgamated Clothing Workers of America and Hart Schaffner & Marx cooperated in a labor-management relationship that was not only steady, unbroken and progressive, but also mutually beneficial. . . . Let us remember that these 25 years abounded in major disturbances, depressions, war and prosperity.'" Hillman attended Schaffner's funeral in 1918. At the funeral service, Hirsch praised Schaffner as a "business man whose prosperity had not dulled or dwarfed his sense of justice and his devotion to public welfare."[29]

The public condemnation of abuses common in the industry by a principal employer and the acceptance of organized labor opened a path for improving working conditions and labor relations in and beyond Chicago. Schaffner's critical reflection of his own role was remarkable, so was his sincere attempt to reach a good understanding with his workers, in a city known for ruthless oppression of organized labor.

HIRSCH'S DOWNFALL

By 1912, many members of huge and expanding Jewish immigrant community regarded Hirsch as their informal leader. His public empathy with the distressed Jews in eastern Europe, his support for the Hebrew Institute, his uncompromising stand against anti-Semitism, and his engagement for workers' rights earned him much respect among immigrants. He was a well-connected power broker and a nationally known social reformer. Neither traditional leaders like rabbis or businessmen, nor new leaders, who rose through local politics or unions, could claim to represent more than a segment of the large, heterogeneous, and constantly growing Jewish immigrant population. The dynamic of immigration undermined the power base of traditional leaders and provided Hirsch with an informal mandate. He stood above the various partly overlapping religious, ideological, *landsmanshaftlich* milieus in the ghetto. He was an articulate and professional leader—no opportunist—and widely respected throughout the city. And he was, after all, a rabbi.

Sinai was proud to have retained its illustrious rabbi. After 1900, Hirsch developed a more amicable relationship with the board and the congregation. In recognition of Hirsch's accomplishments, the board announced in 1918 that the annual meeting would be held on Hirsch's sixty-seventh birthday, May 22. But strangely, on that day, Hirsch was absent. Only one sentence in the president's annual report hints at a possible reason: "We wish to record our full recognition of his patriotism and loyalty and to make the full measure of true Americanism which we all share alike with him and which no one has a right to question."[30] It remains unclear who had questioned Hirsch's "Americanism." What is certain, however, is that Hirsch kept a low profile for almost a year. After returning to the pulpit, he never regained his former stature. During the First World War, he did not preach regularly due to repeated bouts of illness. But that probably was not the reason why he did not attend the annual meeting on his birthday. Several local scholars touch on the affair, but no account is fully accurate.[31] Unfortunately, it is not possible to reconstruct the internal debates in the boardroom of the congregation. It remains doubtful whether these were even recorded (or kept), given the precariousness of the situation. Nevertheless, the available sources, the 1914 speech, a published sermon, and the press coverage allow for a closer look.

World War I and its immediate aftermath put Jews across eastern Europe in great danger. Millions were displaced; tens of thousands were massacred in 1918–1919 alone. In 1914, American Jews put their differences aside to organize a support network. The newly elected American Zionist leader, Louis Brandeis, and Shmarya Levin spoke at Sinai in November 1914 to plead for the small Jewish community in Palestine that was cut off from European support. Hirsch, Becker, Bernard Horwich, and others organized a mass meeting in mid-December to raise funds for Jews in eastern Europe. When the United States entered the war in 1917, thousands of Jews volunteered across the United States, among them members of Sinai congregation. Military service was a visible testament of immigrant patriotism. Meites's extensive treatment of Jewish contributions to the American war effort in his 1924 history of the Chicago Jewish community clearly highlights the strong sense of American pride especially recent immigrants felt. Indirectly, however, Meites responded to widespread anti-Semitism during the mid-1920s when the volume was published.[32]

For understandable reasons, Meites passed over the communal hatred and real fear that rocked Chicago between 1914 and the early 1920s. For most Chicagoans, the European war was not a distant event. Like millions of Americans, they were torn between sorrow for close kin and enthusiasm for a specific cause. With its huge European immigrant population, Chicago became a microcosm of the European conflict. Within weeks after the beginning of the war in August 1914, invisible lines crisscrossed the city. Conspiracy theories were rife, and violent clashes erupted repeatedly. In contrast to their German, Polish, Czech, Irish, and African American neighbors, Jews largely remained on the sidelines. Jewish community leaders immediately recognized the potential dangers and kept a low profile. Many Jews tacitly sympathized with Germany and the Austro-Hungarian Empire, primarily because the two powers fought against the dreaded czar. Some Irish leaders also supported the German cause because they longed for a British defeat—and Irish independence. The impact of the war on Chicago and other northern cities reached even further. The drafting of many young males across Europe, internal restrictions on mobility, the British sea blockade against Germany, and German submarine warfare reduced the transatlantic migration, almost interrupting it by 1916. The demand for cheap and low-skilled labor pulled in rising numbers of African Americans from the South. The expansion of the so-called Black Belt on Chicago's South Side, an acute housing shortage, deep-seated racism, and the heated atmosphere sparked communal violence, directed not least against African Americans. Most Americans had little sympathy for the victims of these riots. They watched the ethnic demonstrations and violent clashes in the cities with great unease. The social fabric of American society seemed threatened.[33]

Since his arrival in 1880, Hirsch had occasionally lent his voice to the German community in Chicago. For instance, in 1912, he was the keynote speaker during a big fundraiser with the Chicago Symphony Orchestra for a Goethe monument in Lincoln Park. Among the attendees were many prominent members of Sinai and the German ambassador.[34] For German American leaders in Chicago and other American cities, the war offered the chance to revive the seemingly moribund community project following the decline of the German-speaking immigration after 1890. At the same time, the German government calculated to mobilize the support of millions of German Americans for its war effort, to weaken pro-British sentiments and keep the United States on the sidelines. In 1914–1915, Bernhard Dernburg, a former German colonial secretary, toured the United States to promote the German cause among immigrant communities—until the Wilson administration expelled him in June 1915. On December 10, 1914, Dernburg spoke in Chicago in front of a "cheering" audience of five thousand sympathizers of the German war effort. Hirsch had accepted an invitation to give a short address at this event. The wide support across ethnic lines for Germany in Chicago, the frenzied atmosphere at Medinah Temple, a large convention hall on the Near North Side, and Hirsch's tendency to make provocative statements set the scene for a notorious speech. Hirsch stressed the loyalty of German Americans to their adopted country, but he defended Germany and its army, notably the aggression against Belgium. Not surprisingly, Hirsch reserved his sharpest rebukes for Russia. "The Russians," and not the Germans, were the true "barbarians," having committed countless atrocities against their Jewish subjects before the war. Indeed, according to the *Chicago Tribune*, he stated, "the Jews all over the world ... are with Germany in this war." Hirsch also lashed out against England for supposedly denying Germany the right of self-determination. The speech culminated in an infamous passage (not mentioned by the *Tribune*): "Germany wants to be free. It learned freedom from Kant. . . . The German army is the categorical Imperative of duty."[35] The categorical imperative, the cornerstone of Immanuel Kant's moral philosophy, defines the essence of ethical practice. This principle stood at the center of Hirsch's social justice theology. Using the categorical imperative to justify war exceeded Hirsch's usual penchant for provocation. Only a few weeks later, as criticism of Dernburg mounted, the rabbi backtracked. In early February 1915, he stated in a speech on Abraham Lincoln to the National Garment Manufacturers Association, "He is an American who consecrates himself with the ideas of America without equivocation."[36]

After the American entry into the war in 1917, a notorious witch-hunt against "Germans" was unleashed across the nation. Chicago, a city with one of the largest German-speaking populations outside of Germany, was no exception. Within weeks, dozens of street names were anglicized, and private and public institutions ranging from hospitals to hotels changed their names. The Goethe monument in Lincoln Park, dedicated shortly before the war, was taken down to prevent its destruction. Several German activists were arrested. Unlike most German leaders, Hirsch remained a highly respected figure in the city. But after several months the campaign caught up with him. In April 1918, the *Chicago Tribune* reported anonymous members of Sinai congregation had accused Hirsch of being "not loyal" and harboring "pacifist tendencies." According to rumors, Sinai was about to split over the question whether to retain the rabbi. On April 12, 1918, the *Tribune* covered Hirsch's rebuttal on its first page, next to patriotic war cartoons and a story exposing that "German concerts and other entertainments of a strictly Teutonic character" were still continuing in Chicago. Sinai's president confirmed that one member had sent him an anonymous letter calling for "radical action" against Hirsch. Greenebaum rejected the criticism as unfounded. But he called for an immediate "vote of confidence." The *Tribune* reporter interviewed Hirsch at his home. The rabbi expressed doubt whether he would be "ousted" by Sinai. He did not deny his pro-German sentiments. And yes, he was a pacifist, having "been engaged in peace work for thirty years." He suspected "certain young men of good character . . . who seldom come to the services" behind the accusations. The anonymous letter was (in his opinion) based on a misunderstanding. During a recent sermon he had singled out the State Council for Defense for its problematic language but not for its basic policy. The council had praised the United States for entering the war "for the continuance of Christian civilization." Doubts regarding his loyalty were ludicrous, and he announced a nuanced response from his pulpit on the following Sunday.[37]

On April 13, a Saturday, the *Tribune* reported an interview with Greenebaum, who had discussed the "report against Dr. Hirsch" with several board members. In his opinion, "these stories about pro-Germanism are absolutely unwarranted. We shall not emphasize the matter by paying any further attention to it."[38] But the pressure was mounting. Would the illustrious and proud rabbi, one of the most prominent Chicagoans, become a victim of the anti-German crusade? And was there any substance to rumors that Sinai might split? Hours before the service on Sunday, April 14, people flocked to the temple. The 2,500 seats were quickly filled, more than 500 people were sitting and standing in the aisles. And at least 1,000 had to be turned away. The board had decorated the interior of the temple with national flags for the occasion.

Hirsch did not disappoint. The *Tribune* titled its article "Patriotic Fervor Marks Rabbi's Answer to Doubters." And indeed, Hirsch made a strong statement in favor of the war, "he affirmed his undivided, single-hearted allegiance to the nation's cause." Defending his pacifist position, he also condemned the "doctrine of hatred." The "Jewish doctrine" was "not to promote hate and resentment." This can be interpreted as cautious criticism of the agitation against supposed traitors. Yet a closer reading of the actual sermon betrays another side. The congregation expected Hirsch to distance himself unambiguously from his pacifist and pro-German positions in order to deflect further criticism. Suffice to say, several members, the sons of several members, and two of Sinai's Sunday school teachers had joined the U.S. Army and had been deployed. Yet Hirsch decided not to fully retract his earlier positions. American entry into the war, he boldly admitted, was not what he had "hoped" for: "When Congress had spoken for us, an American, I had no right to dissent. I had to obey the Law and I did obey it. Our enemy's government had invaded our sovereign rights. I had hoped that this might not come about." He also took issue with anti-German agitators. Demands that "every German shall have disappeared from the face of earth and German shall be a dead language," were preposterous. The "loyalty" of German Americans was "above suspicion." Obliterating German might only be the first step to ban every non-English language, and eventually even non-Christians. Hirsch reminded the congregation and the Chicago public that diversity was a core American principle that should not be sacrificed.

The *Tribune* reporter did not cover the unpatriotic part of Hirsch's sermon. Indeed, the *Tribune* clearly shielded Hirsch, a staunch Republican, against the worst accusations. Rather, the reporter described an impressive show of solidarity by his congregation. Immediately after the sermon, an "impromptu reception" unfolded on the pulpit, "hundreds of the congregation filing past the rabbi congratulating him upon his eloquence and announcing that they would stand by him." On the same evening, the Sinai Sisterhood gave a big patriotic reception to a hundred midshipmen from the Great Lakes Naval Station; Hirsch gave a short address. The congregation decided to print and publish the sermon "My Religion and the War"—and indication for the importance it attached to Hirsch's response.[39]

Hirsch managed to hang on to his job, but he lost his informal role as unofficial head of the Jewish community and influential moral voice in Chicago. There can be little doubt that the patriotic sermon he was forced to preach, his dependence on the congregation's support, and the realization how much symbolic capital he had wasted were devastating experiences for Hirsch. According to the report, the board prepared for the annual meeting in May 1919, Hirsch had not been preaching for a whole year. Even though many congregations canceled their services during the second half of 1918 following the outbreak of the influenza across the nation, Sinai offered regular services. Several illustrious speakers replaced Hirsch during his absence in 1918–1919, ranging from local rabbis like Joseph Stolz to Julian Mack and Stephen S. Wise. His son-in-law, Gerson B. Levi, preached on a regular basis and became Sinai's de facto rabbi. After his return in mid-1919, Hirsch was a diminished figure. Occasionally he spoke up against injustice, for instance, on the occasion of the notorious riot against African Americans in August 1919. In the *Reform Advocate* he compared the violence to the pogroms in Russia. But only few Chicagoans outside of the established Jewish community listened to him. One of these few friends, Gotthard Deutsch, who occupied the chair of history at Hebrew Union College in Cincinnati, also became the victim of the anti-German hysteria gripping the country. Deutsch, a pacifist who had repeatedly criticized one-sided pro-Allied reports in the Cincinnati press, almost lost his position after the United States entered the war.[40]

In 1921, on the occasion of his seventieth birthday, the *Reform Advocate* devoted a special issue to its founder and longtime editor. The issue contains dozens of addresses by friends and colleagues. Even though some of Hirsch's closest collaborators, such as William Rainey Harper and Jenkin Lloyd Jones, had died, the absence of non-Jews is striking. Only Jane Addams, the Illinois governor, one of the two U.S. senators for the state of Illinois, the Unitarian minister John Haynes Holmes, and a few professors of the University of Chicago congratulated him. Chicago's mayor was absent, as were urban reformers; national, state, and local political leaders; Protestant liberals; and the head of the Chicago Public Library and other institutions Hirsch had supported during his tenure at Sinai.[41]

Hirsch died on January 7, 1923, shortly after he had seemingly recovered from another bout of illness. With Hirsch, one of the last great American rabbis who was deeply steeped in nineteenth-century German culture left the scene. His predecessor and brother-in-law, Kaufmann Kohler, died three years later in 1926 in New York, after having retired in 1921 from Hebrew Union College. With the single exception of Sinai's former president Joseph L. Gatzert, the Sinai founders had all passed away a few years before Hirsch. Almost sixty-two years after its founding, an era in the history of Sinai congregation came to an end. Much hinged on the question of Hirsch's succession. The board members knew they had to act quickly.[42]

Part III.

DECLINE AND RENAISSANCE

12.

THE LOSS OF Emil G. Hirsch, even though it was not unexpected, was a severe blow. During the past forty-three years, Sinai and Hirsch had become inseparable. Sinai's rabbi had been more than a religious and spiritual leader. As son of Samuel Hirsch, son-in-law of David Einhorn, and as major theologian himself, he embodied radical Reform. Yet after more than four decades, the congregation was ready for a new and different kind of leadership. For all his intellectual brilliance and fame, Hirsch had been a remote and eccentric figure. He was frequently absent and did not foster personal relationships. When he died, Hirsch was one of the last German-trained Reform rabbis still serving a major American Jewish congregation.

Sinai's new rabbi came to Chicago in 1923 at a critical juncture, just as his predecessor had done forty-three years earlier. Following in the footsteps of an illustrious and powerful rabbi, however, was one of his lesser concerns. Just as in the 1880s, during the early stages of the Jewish mass migration and in the midst of Chicago's dramatic expansion, the new rabbi and Sinai's lay leaders had to redefine the congregation in a rapidly changing setting. The successful growth of Sinai after 1900 and the opening of the social center overshadowed a looming crisis. Sinai's constituency represented a tiny and decreasing part of the huge Jewish population in Chicago. In a period of increasing racial conflict and economic crisis the lofty universal aspirations of Classical Reform held little promise. One option to avoid a steady decline of the membership and further marginalization was to open the congregation to the Jewish immigrant community. Sinai Social Center was designed as a gateway for teenagers and young adults from this constituency. But convincing them (and their parents) to join a "German" temple as full-fledged members was a different matter. This crucial question was sidelined by the need to relocate to a different part of the city, as the area surrounding Sinai's temple and social center became part of the Black Belt. This final chapter will discuss how Sinai Congregation coped with these and other formidable challenges before and after World War II, when Chicago struggled to retain its position as a leading manufacturing center and commercial hub.

BETWEEN SEGREGATION AND ANTI-SEMITISM

The 1920s marked a transitional phase in American and American Jewish history. In the three decades before World War I, mass immigration boosted the population of America's big cities. Chicago's rapid and dramatic transformation after 1880 largely depended on European immigrants who were not Protestants. Small-town America, on the other hand, remained a world apart. A majority of "old stock" rural Protestants associated the cities with social disorder and moral decay. They favored isolationism, despised immigrants, opposed suffrage for women, and supported Prohibition, and in many parts of the country, the Ku Klux Klan. The broader shift toward exclusion and isolation after 1918 reflected this cultural divide and constituted a big challenge for urban America, especially in the wake of the Great Depression. During the 1920s and 1930s, race emerged as new and powerful source of tension over the ownership of urban space—in addition to labor conflicts, interethnic turf wars, and the rise of machine politics.[1] Sinai could not avoid being drawn into some of these conflicts, in part because it was locked into a quickly changing neighborhood. This was a new experience for a hitherto relatively privileged and sheltered congregation.

Declining immigration from Europe during World War I and postwar immigration restrictions created new opportunities for internal migrants, especially African Americans. At least fifty thousand moved to Chicago from the South between 1910 and 1920, most during the second half of the decade. The migration continued even through the Depression and increased again during World War II. Within a few years the sharply segregated Black Belt, a densely settled slum, grew into America's second largest center of African American life, after Harlem in New York. The first African American migrants, who for lack

of a better choice were forced to look for housing in neighborhoods border-
ing on the Black Belt, encountered severe and often violent resistance. To make
matters worse, employers exploited racial divisions, using African Americans as
strikebreakers.[2]

In 1918–1919, African Americans began moving into Grand Boulevard, home
to many Sinai members and its large temple and social center. Rather abruptly,
the congregation found itself on the front lines of a conflict over the shifting
boundary of the Black Belt. In April 1919, the *Chicago Tribune* reported that
Sinai would relocate. According to an unnamed source, Bethel Church (AME)
was close to acquiring Sinai's temple and social center. Bethel was a pioneering
institutional church serving upwardly mobile members of the African American
community. When contacted by the paper, representatives of both congregations would not confirm the story. However, according to the executive director
of the Sinai Social Center, Samuel D. Schwartz, "the influx of Negro residents"
drove many members further south into Kenwood and Hyde Park. One was
none other than Sinai's ailing rabbi who had moved to an apartment building
in Hyde Park.[3]

In November 1919, Hirsch had to defend himself against accusations of having
sold his residence to an African American family. In an interview with the *Tribune*, Hirsch stressed that not he but his son had sold the house—to a member
of Sinai who was white. This man, who was named by Hirsch's son and identified
in the article, apparently had resold the house hours after buying it. As in earlier
instances, Hirsch explicitly condemned race discrimination, but his explanation
for the sale appears evasive. For Hirsch, class rather than race determined his
choice of neighborhood; he preferred a "good black neighbor" to a "poor white
one." But instead of firmly rejecting the widespread practice of restrictive covenants, the unwritten stipulation not to sell real estate to African Americans,
Hirsch denied any responsibility. He had been recuperating in California, and
his son had completed the sale. Moreover, his wife could not find a white do-
mestic servant, because the home had been among the last in his area still occupied by a white family: "The block is full of colored persons, anyway." Hirsch,
already under the cloud of suspicion for lacking patriotism, had every reason to
be worried about his personal safety—and perhaps the safety of his son and the
Sinai member who had bought his house, not to mention the new occupants.
A residence on Grand Boulevard in close proximity to Sinai's temple had been
firebombed several months earlier because it was rented to "Negros." In a different part of the city, the home of the white landlord who openly admitted that
he rented to African Americans was also set on fire.[4] As the congregation's lead-

ers debated how to respond to the rapid transformation of their neighborhood, they also had to confront increasingly open anti-Semitic discrimination.[5]

Established Jews in Chicago formed a relatively small and dispersed group in neighborhoods that were dominated by Protestants. They were more vulnerable to discrimination in their professional and private lives than working-class and lower-middle-class Jews who lived in Jewish neighborhoods and frequently worked alongside and for other Jews. But the social and racial profiles of ethnic neighborhoods were fluid. As Jewish immigrants and their descendants moved into higher-skilled, blue- and white-collar occupations during the 1910s, they began moving from the garment district on the Near West Side to areas on the Northwest Side, the South Shore, and especially to North Lawndale on the West Side. Poles, Lithuanians, and Italians were also heading west and south. Yet not everybody was moving. The parish system tied Catholics to specific districts. A majority of German Catholics had relocated to new "American" parishes even before the 1920s, but some Irish and eastern European Catholics stayed put. Chicago's complex ethno-religious topography was one reason African American arrivals faced violent resistance as they tried to find housing in the vicinity of the old Black Belt in 1919.[6]

The decision of Sinai's leaders not to follow their members to Hyde Park and Kenwood when the congregation still had the option to do so was certainly understandable. Its temple and the state-of-the-art social center were just a few years old, and Kenwood and Hyde Park were within walking distance from the temple. Serving thousands of congregants and their families in rented quarters seemed impossible; completing a new building would have taken many years. And Sinai had long opposed race discrimination. Following the notorious August 1919 race riot, white homeowners formed the Kenwood and Hyde Park Property Owners Association (HPPOA). In the fall of 1919, the association pressured local real estate agents to join "our fight against the Negro." In November 1920, the HPPOA called on Sinai to become a corporate member. After a long discussion, the board refused because "it would be improper for Sinai Congregation to join such an organization." Thus Sinai did not relocate, even when almost all Jews in Chicago—including its own members—were on the move.[7]

By the mid-1920s, the number of Jews remaining in the ghetto on the Near West Side had dropped sharply, and the decaying area became part of the expanding Black Belt, like Grand Boulevard several miles to the south. At the same time, North Lawndale on the Far West Side emerged as one of the largest Jewish neighborhoods outside of New York, home to dozens of synagogues, Jewish schools, and a wide range of religious and secular institutions, including the Jewish People's Institute (the former Hebrew Institute).[8] Since the 1880s, recently immigrated Jews in Chicago had been divided into many subsections, defined by a combination of *Landsmanshaft*, family, religion, and class. The continuous expansion of the Jewish population before 1914 and the arrival of large numbers of new immigrants from different parts of eastern Europe undermined efforts to build an overarching community. In 1912, Orthodox leaders adapted the model of the established community and successfully organized the first major umbrella philanthropic organization, the Federated Orthodox Jewish Charities (FOJC). Secular Jews and other groups did not support the FOJC and formed their own networks. Ironically, the interruption of the immigration during World War I and postwar restrictions made it easier to overcome this fragmentation.

Some authors argue that the rise of anti-Semitism helped to bring established Jews and the many different groups among the immigrants closer together in the early 1920s.[9] But pragmatic considerations and financial constraints should not be discounted. Julius Rosenwald deserves most of the credit for engineering the merger of the two main philanthropic organizations into the Jewish Charities of Chicago on January 1, 1923. His sincere and generous backing of various immigrant and establishment institutions equipped him with the necessary authority to win over skeptics on both sides. Of course, nobody wanted to lose the support of the great philanthropist. From Rosenwald's perspective, the merger of Associated Jewish Charities and the FOJC was a logical step. As Marc J. Swatez has pointed out, the major incentive was to cut costs. Since the 1870s, Associated Jewish Charities mostly supported immigrants, and the work of both organizations and their affiliates overlapped. Bringing them under a single roof reduced the administrative overhead and freed funds for people in need.[10]

THE NEW RABBI

As in earlier moments in Sinai's history, much hinged on the search for a new rabbi. The ideal candidate was an energetic and well-educated young man with job experience who stood fully behind the radical Reform agenda. In the early 1920s, it was no easy task to find such a man. The fate of Sunday services in and beyond Chicago illustrates the declining appeal of radical Reform. During the 1890s, more than a dozen major congregations introduced Sunday services. Twenty years later, only one other large Reform congregation still attracted large crowds on Sundays, Cleveland's Temple. Their success owed much to their charismatic rabbi, Abba Hillel Silver. No wonder that just days after Hirsch's death, Sinai's board was considering him as a candidate. Silver was just thirty years old in 1923; he was an immigrant from eastern Europe and an outspoken Zionist.

But that was not a stumbling block. In June 1918, none other than Julian Mack became the president of the Zionist Organization of America. Several months after his election, in November 1918, Sinai invited Mack to be the main speaker for a Sunday service. Even staunch anti-Zionists recognized that Silver possessed the persona to fill Hirsch's shoes, appeal to the immigrant masses, and take Sinai in a new direction. But Silver was not inclined to leave Cleveland, as Julian Morgenstern, the president of Hebrew Union College, informed a member of Sinai involved in the search.[11] Beyond Sinai's reach was the man who continued Hirsch's mission more than any other figure. Stephen S. Wise was, of course, a Zionist, but he was a radical Reformer who did not regard ritual as central and who had a strained relationship with the organized Reform movement. Like Hirsch, whom he held in high respect, he was a charismatic speaker and considered himself as a trailblazer. At his Free Synagogue, he openly welcomed Christians and promoted social justice. In 1922 Wise challenged HUC and the UAHC by establishing his own rabbinical seminary, the Jewish Institute of Religion.[12]

A surprising omission on the board's shortlist was Gerson B. Levi. It was no secret that Hirsch wanted his son-in-law to succeed him. Levi had preached regularly at Sinai for almost two decades. During Hirsch's prolonged absences since mid-1918, he had become Sinai's rabbi in all but name. Levi also took over the editorship of the *Reform Advocate*. But now, after Hirsch's death, several influential members, the so-called Committee of Fifty, openly voiced their opposition to Levi in a letter to president Greenebaum. Although they provided no reason, it is likely that these members objected to Levi's Conservative training and his stronger commitment to the Jewish tradition. The board quickly settled on another candidate. At thirty-three years of age, Sinai's new rabbi, Louis L. Mann, was young but not inexperienced. Mann was born in Louisville in 1890 into a German family. After graduating from the University of Cincinnati and Hebrew Union College, he joined the small Reform congregation Mishkan Israel in Hamden, Connecticut, as rabbi in 1913. Although he completed a doctoral dissertation in psychology at nearby Yale where he also taught comparative ethics for a couple of years, Mann was not a scholar-rabbi in the tradition of his German-trained predecessors. At Mishkan Israel, Mann had become an advocate of the social congregation. He was no Zionist, but remained largely silent on the issue, recognizing its potential divisiveness. Mann could not match Hirsch's great talent as a speaker, but he was not shy and quickly settled into the new job.[13]

To have a young man at the helm who did not carry Hirsch's baggage certainly was a liberating experience. Mann's inaugural sermon, preached on Rosh

Hashanah 1923, betrays pragmatism and modesty. Mann made a strong case for continuity, expressing his strong belief in the social congregation and in social justice, the hallmark of Hirsch's theology. "Whenever and wherever ideals are shattered, whenever man is overlooked for mammon and morals for money," he assured the members, Sinai and "this pulpit" would not "remain silent." This was no empty promise. Like his predecessor, Mann did not hesitate to sharply criticize the exploitation of the poor, corruption in local politics, and the rise of organized crime. Mann warned the congregation not to isolate itself from society or other Jews. But he did not raise the question whether Sinai should recruit new members among the immigrant community, nor did he touch on the issue of race.[14]

Serving a congregation of thousands of people certainly constituted a big change for the new rabbi. For average members, who were not involved in the congregation beyond attending services and the occasional event, Mann remained a distant figure throughout his tenure, in part because he had to negotiate a busy schedule. Mann could draw on an experienced board that had steered the congregation successfully through the difficult last years under Hirsch. He could also lean on Samuel Disraeli—"S.D."—Schwartz, the executive director of the Sinai Social Center. This office, created in 1918, was indispensable to manage the expansion of the activities and the growing demand. According to one estimate, up to ten thousand persons passed through the Sinai Social Center or temple during some weeks in the 1920s. Schwartz had grown up in Chicago in an Orthodox home. His father, Moritz Schwartz, was one of officers of the Hungarian immigrant congregation Agudath Achim. Schwartz graduated from the University of Chicago and taught English classes at the Hebrew Institute before moving to the Sinai Social Center in 1914. Schwartz was much more intimately involved with the daily business of the congregation than Mann. In addition to managing the center and recruiting speakers for the Sinai Forum, the lecture series, he emerged as intermediary between the members and the officers, and eventually even as unofficial associate rabbi who by the 1940s officiated at funerals when Mann was not available.[15]

REJECTING RECONSTRUCTIONISM

Sinai remained an influential player in Chicago Jewish life during the 1920s and 1930s but moved to the sidelines. In part, this was only natural. In a huge and diverse community even a large congregation carried much less weight than in the tight-knit established community. Yet Sinai's declining influence had deeper roots. The congregation isolated itself within a transforming Jewish community, locally and nationally, stubbornly sticking to its radical—or as it was now described, Classical Reform—legacy.

The perhaps most influential figure in American Judaism after 1920, together with Stephen S. Wise, was Mordecai Kaplan, the father of Reconstructionist Judaism. Because he came to America at a relatively young age, he moved at ease in the American setting but was intimately connected with Jewish learning. Kaplan grew up in a rabbinical family and attended a secular university and a rabbinical seminary. After graduating with a master's in sociology from Columbia, he obtained his rabbinical degree from the Jewish Theological Seminary, where he assumed a teaching position in 1909. Like most immigrants, Kaplan came to Conservative Judaism not from the traditional wing of Reform but from Orthodox Judaism.

Reconstructionism evolved as Kaplan began to distance himself from his Orthodox origins and shows some similarity to the agenda of the early Reform movement: Kaplan, a Zionist, rejected Jewish chosenness and questioned the applicability of rigid religious laws in modern society. Judaism had to respond to the transformation of modern society or would become obsolete. Of course, Reconstructionism differed from early Reform in its emphasis on Jewish peoplehood. As Jonathan D. Sarna emphasizes, the impact of Reconstructionism as a movement was limited, but Kaplan's message resonated far beyond his immediate circle, especially the all-embracing concept of Judaism as a "religious civilization" rather than a religion defined by a system of laws. Kaplan encouraged Jews to embrace Jewish culture in all its expressions. The foundation was the synagogue center. Kaplan envisaged the synagogue (center) as "the Jew's second home . . . his club, his theatre, and his forum." Existing centers of Reform congregations pursued a similar agenda. But even though they were successful, their founders had not managed to combine religion and sociability sufficiently. Zionism and Jewish culture helped to bridge the divide between "shul and pool." Because he positioned himself at the center of American Jewish life, Kaplan, rather than his Reform forerunners, popularized the synagogue center. Reconstrucionist synagogue centers appealed to the many immigrant Jews and especially their children who were at home in America who questioned the rigid demands of Orthodoxy but valued the Jewish tradition and defined themselves increasingly in ethnic terms.[16]

The rise of Reconstructionism in the 1920s occurred in a period of growing religious indifference among Jews and Christians, and especially among the younger generation. According to an estimate by the American Jewish Committee in 1919, only about 20 percent of American Jews were affiliated in some form with a congregation. And at many congregations, attendance was lagging. In response, many Reform congregations began to reexamine their theological position and looked toward the immigrants and their descendants as members. Kaplan's call for reconnecting with a Jewish way of life cannot be disconnected from developments outside of the synagogue. In a period of increasing anti-Semitism, established and immigrant Jews gradually conceived of themselves as members of a single and not insignificant group in America's larger cities. They watched the precarious situation of the Jewish masses in eastern Europe, where many American Jews had family ties, and a further tightening of already-restrictive immigration protocols by President Hoover in 1930. The anti-Semitic terror of the Nazi regime in a country with a seemingly well-integrated Jewish community was deeply unsettling. Thus the anti-Zionist position of many Reformers eroded. The 1937 Columbus Platform illustrates the shift. After heated discussions the participating Reform rabbis defined Judaism in religious and ethnic terms. The platform contained a passage in support of Zionism, tellingly without mentioning the actual "Z" word.[17]

Initially, Sinai seemed isolated from these changes. More than two hundred families joined Sinai in the months after the arrival of Louis L. Mann, pushing the membership for the first time over one thousand people. Sunday services were so well attended that loudspeakers had to be installed in the adjacent social center, because the two thousand seats in the temple were filled. In 1925, Sinai (with a membership of 1,101) had almost as many members as Temple Emanu-El in New York (1,132). Three other Reform congregations were even larger: the two Philadelphia Reform congregations Keneseth Israel (1,456) and Rodeph Shalom (1,389) and Silver's Temple congregation in Cleveland (1,200). Several other congregations had about one thousand members: Cleveland's Anshe Chesed (1,000), Beth El in Detroit (1,080), Rodeph Shalom in Pittsburgh (1,194), and the Baltimore Hebrew congregation (932). The size of the two Cleveland and the two Philadelphia congregations was partly the result of a lack of competition. Both cities had only two Reform congregations respectively, and Detroit and Pittsburgh had just one. While impressive at first glance, these numbers actually confirm the decline of Reform in the urban context. Only in Chicago and New York did the movement manage to put down firm roots.

Two Reform congregations were located in the immediate vicinity of Sinai. Temple Isaiah grew strongly, from about 100 members in 1904 to 434 in 1925. KAM had a respectable 380 members in 1925. Several smaller Reform congregations served different parts of the city. In 1928–1929, eleven congregations in Chicago belonged to the UAHC. Even if family members are added to the approximate 2,500 members, an estimated 10,000 affiliated Reform Jews represented little more than 3 percent of Chicago's Jewish population of around 300,000. But this small minority still was overwhelmingly composed of self-employed businessmen and entrepreneurs, professionals, and white-collar employees. The organized Jewish community could not ignore this relatively established group.[18]

The new rabbi provided a new sense of stability and optimism. At the 1924 annual meeting, President Greenebaum praised Rabbi Mann for spearheading a "revival" of the congregation. He stressed the absence of controversies and factionalism, a clear hint that the last years under Hirsch had been difficult.[19] The Sinai Sisterhood, which had been founded in 1914–1915 to develop "the long neglected family life of the Congregation," was the most active element in the congregation. The Sinai Sisterhood symbolizes the transition to congregational sisterhoods after 1910. Its more than six hundred members (in 1924) organized various social events, raised funds for projects within the congregation, and cooperated with other Jewish and non-Jewish women's associations. Only after Hirsch's death did the sisterhood demand formal representation. In 1924, Babette Mandel became the first female member on Sinai's board. In the following year, the sisterhood gained a second seat.[20] In 1926, Jennie Franklin Purvin took over the presidency from Lizzie T. Barbe. Purvin was one of the most energetic women in the congregation. A past president of the Chicago chapter of the National Council of Jewish Women, she seemed a safe candidate for the board in the late 1920s, but she was passed over. Deeply frustrated, she and her husband resigned from the congregation in 1931. Purvin turned her energies elsewhere. In 1933, she became a board member of the Chicago Public Library, and she played a leading role in the redevelopment of Chicago's lakefront. This success perhaps explains why she overcame her disappointment and returned Sinai in 1939, remaining active in the sisterhood well into the 1950s.[21]

In 1926, Purvin, in her role as president of the sisterhood, directed a survey of Sinai's 1,153 members. More than 50 members had moved to the northern suburbs. In the early stages of this small migration, Sinai had even established a branch in Winnetka. In 1920, President Greenebaum joined the 40 or so families, mostly current or former Sinai members, for the dedication ceremony. Emil G. Hirsch agreed to conduct services on a regular basis. But the experiment was short-lived. The distance proved too far, and illness prevented Hirsch from preaching. A few months after Hirsch's death, the branch members set up the independent North Shore Congregation in Glencoe. Sinai's lack of interest was understandable. In 1926, more than half of the members (60 percent) lived within a two-mile radius of the temple on the South Side, and 80 percent lived within a 2 1/2-mile radius—primarily outside of the Black Belt, in nearby Hyde Park. According to census data, in 1920, African Americans made up about 30 percent of the Grand Boulevard neighborhood where Sinai's temple was located. Ten years later, in 1930, the number had risen to 95 percent.[22]

RELOCATION AND DEPRESSION

In January 1926, Mann urged the board to relocate. But it took more than a year before any decisions were taken. In his report to a February 1927 meeting of the congregation, the rabbi did not mince his words: Sinai was now "in the very heart of the colored district." The service attendance, though still strong, was lagging because people had the "most unpleasant experiences" in the vicinity of the temple. A rather intriguing proposition was to move to the Loop, Chicago's central business district, and combine the new temple and center with an office building. Apart from earning a steady rental income, a "metropolitan synagog[ue]" would attract Jews from all over the city, as well as visiting businessmen. Yet apart from the huge costs involved, one member admitted honestly, "the mere sight of the loop on the day of rest would take away from the restfulness of the day." And the business district seemed hardly an appropriate site for the congregation's school and social center.[23]

At the annual meeting two months later, it was resolved to sell the temple and the center and to move to Hyde Park. Now, the situation had apparently become intolerable. "The intrusion of undesirable elements into our neighborhood," as S. D. Schwartz put it, had forced the center to cancel many of its programs. Mann's comments from the February meeting were printed as part of the annual report. But the text was carefully edited: the word "colored" was replaced by the word "new." The board did not want to publicize the fact that race was the real driving factor behind the decision to relocate. Sinai entered into negotiations with Bethel Church (AME) about the sale of the temple. The board bought a plot in Hyde Park. Members contributed the lion share, but $315,000 had to be borrowed. Architect Alfred S. Alschuler began to work on a design for a temple with 2,400 seats with an adjacent building for the center. But the talks with Bethel dragged on without result. By 1928, the board members were getting cold feet. Was it wise to spend millions of dollars for a new temple and center if Hyde Park, too, would soon become part of the Black Belt? The board decided to sell the empty plot, and the idea to move to the Loop was again discussed. The congregation still had not found a solution by October 1929.[24]

Within months after the Wall Street crash, all plans were put on hold. Many members stopped paying their dues. The congregation owed over $300,000 to a bank and an even higher sum to its members—for a piece of land it officially owned but would not use. As the economic outlook for the American economy worsened by the day, the traditionally wealthy congregation, for the first time in its history, faced the real possibility of dissolution. Mann and Schwartz voluntarily offered to reduce their salaries. At the 1931 meeting, the board admitted, "The situation is desperate." That year, the Sinai Social Center was effectively closed; only some of the facilities like the basketball courts remained in use. Across the country, countless congregations downsized or closed. Temple Emanu-El in New York lost almost half of its members. Like other congregations, Sinai retained nonpaying members on its rolls because it did not want to push people barely making ends meet into even deeper trouble. A severe consolidation program kept the congregation solvent and brought the debt down. In 1933, the membership stood at 987, but Sinai still owed $170,000—and that did not include the much larger sum members had provided out of pocket.

During the early 1930s, the rabbi, executive director, and board pulled together to keep the congregation afloat, strenuously avoiding a discussion over the responsibility for the disastrous real estate deal or lamenting the unattractive location of the temple. In 1932, at the height of the crisis, President Greenebaum resigned. His mortgage bank, like the businesses of many members, was struggling. The main cause for the resignation, however, was his deteriorating health. Eventually, Sinai's wealthiest member single-handedly saved Sinai. Julius Rosenwald made sure that the administrators of his estate, led by his son, Lessing, would protect "his" congregation. In 1935, the Rosenwald estate covered the lion's share of the amount Sinai had paid for the plot and borrowed from members, under stipulation that the board would settle the mortgage debt of $170,000. The eventual sale of the land yielded the remainder. The deal was sealed in early 1936. In the end, Sinai had spent almost $1,000,000 for nothing but sorrows. The temple was still in the same location as in 1926, and a move was not an option for the foreseeable future.[25]

DEFENDING SINAI'S BRAND

At Sinai's seventy-fifth anniversary celebration in 1936, keynote speaker Abba Hillel Silver, a regular guest and friend, described Sinai as a "national institution." He commended especially its pulpit, a strong "'voice' in American Israel" for seventy-five years.[26] This was no hollow praise. Mann built himself a national reputation by adapting Hirsch's model of a socially engaged pulpit. Throughout the 1920s and 1930s, Mann joined Silver, Mordecai Kaplan, and several other rabbis who preached against intolerance, reminding a largely unreceptive American audience of the benefits of religious and cultural diversity. Early on, Mann earned the wrath of the pro-Republican *Chicago Tribune* for his attacks on the corrupt administration of Republican Chicago mayor William Hale Thompson. After he had openly criticized a retired admiral for promoting a jingoistic concept of American nationhood at the 1927 American Citizenship Foundation Banquet, the paper denounced him as "clerical demagogue."[27]

Mann recognized the importance of continuing the dialogue with liberal Protestants against considerable odds. He developed ties to Protestant ministers and congregations in Chicago, especially through the Fellowship of Faith program and regular pulpit exchanges. Mann was also among the founders of the National Conference of Christians and Jews in 1927. Solomon B. Freehof, his colleague at KAM, was a close collaborator. In 1933, the two rabbis, leading Christian ministers, and social reformers launched Re-Thinking Chicago, a series of informal but influential conferences on urban reform.[28]

In 1936, Mann joined other rabbis across the country in denouncing a series of anti-Jewish editorials in the *Christian Century*. The Chicago-based weekly, the main forum of liberal Protestantism after 1920, was popular with many Jewish readers who embraced its rejection of Hitler and anti-Semitism. In 1936, however, editor and publisher Charles Clayton Morrison attacked American Jews as a group, depicting Judaism as an "alien element in American democracy." In his eyes, Judaism was not universal and inclusive, but exclusive, hereditary, and thus, "racial." Morrison's editorials were especially discouraging for Sinai and its rabbi. The silence of other Protestants proved more disappointing than Morrison's editorials. Only Reinhold Niebuhr, one of the editors and a regular speaker at Sinai, openly condemned Morrison. In his own response, Mann took issue with Morrison's idea that Jews could to be blamed for anti-Semitism by supposedly isolating themselves from the rest of society. Several other rabbis responded to Morrison in the pages of the *Christian Century*, reiterating their appreciation of religious pluralism. Mordecai Kaplan identified the main motive behind Morrison's attack—the narrow-minded conviction that only (Protestant) Christianity possessed the absolute truth, combined with the expectation that Jews should become Christians. This was no basis for a serious dialogue. For Mann, the Jews were "primarily a *religious* people." This was a thinly veiled rejection of Zionism but also a critique of the race concept. Mann went on, accusing Morrison of promoting an American utopia that came rather close to the Nazi ideal of racial (and racist) homogeneity. Here, Mann echoed Hirsch's opposition to the race concept (and consequently to Zionism). Morrison, rather feebly, defended himself by stating that his criticism had been directed exclusively against Zionists, even though his original article explicitly took issue with Judaism and religious diversity in America. Neither Morrison nor his Jewish critics touched upon the deplorable situation of African Americans.[29]

The highlight of his career, in retrospect, was Mann's speech at the 1941 meeting of the Union of American Hebrew Congregations in Detroit. The meeting occurred at a challenging moment, in the second year of World War II, when isolationism was strong and American Jews could do little to protect their European coreligionists from Nazi terror. The Depression and the war overshadowed the growing crisis of the organized Reform movement. His reputation as a straight talker earned Mann the dubious honor of assessing the state of the Union at the Detroit convention. Sinai's rabbi openly spoke about what few dared to say publicly: the union had lost its voice and vision—and its mission. Candidly, Mann accused the UAHC of neglecting Reform Judaism, particularly in the big cities. Referring to the widely known inauguration sermon of his predecessor at Sinai, "Crossing the Jordan," Mann urged the union leaders to take Hirsch's notion of "building" Reform to heart. The union should create a professional public relations operation and devise a sustained fundraising strategy. The speech, still known by its powerful refrain, "while the Union slept" (inspired by Winston Churchill), had the desired effect, triggering an overhaul of the organization.[30]

From Sinai's perspective, two points in this speech are noteworthy. Classical Reform, Mann argued, had "overemphasized the intellectual aspect of the movement to the neglect of the mystical elements." And in his eyes a renewed effort was needed to pull the large number of unaffiliated Jews in urban America into existing and new congregations. Yet within the walls of his own congregation, the otherwise-engaged and provocative reformer Mann displayed a surprisingly conservative and cautious side. He did not put his weight behind major changes in the liturgy or theology and did not favor experiments. Sinai continued to stand apart from mainstream Judaism and follow its own trajectory. This policy had served the congregation well in the past and seemed to be a promising path, even in the challenging years of the Depression. The weekly attendance at Sinai's Sunday services remained remarkably strong throughout the 1930s and 1940s, and the members became more involved rather than less. Like other American congregations, Sinai served as a safe haven during the difficult years of the Depression. But over time, the tacit rejection of the Reconstructionist message isolated Sinai from the larger Jewish community.[31]

In March 1935, the Chicago Rabbinical Association (CRA) blamed Sinai for violating the Sabbath. The congregation had scheduled theater performances (of a not specifically religious nature) at the temple on Friday nights and had sold tickets (a supposedly commercial activity). Surprisingly, the Jewish Charities (the forerunner of the Jewish Federation) backed the CRA. This was a particularly worrying development. But the congregation was not easily intimidated. In a formal letter, President Robert Sonnenschein warned the Jewish Charities in no uncertain terms not to interfere with the autonomy of a congregation, vigorously defending Sinai's interpretation of the Sabbath: "Sinai believes in the Talmudic dictum that 'the Sabbath was made for man and not man for the Sabbath.'" A week later, Sonnenschein sent conciliatory letters to the CRA and Jewish Charities. He stressed Sinai did not want to provoke further conflict and would avoid scheduling Friday night entertainments in the future. Instead of drawing a line under the whole affair, the CRA fanned the flames by asking all rabbis in Chicago to read a prepared statement censuring Sinai from the pulpit. Mann speculated the real motive behind the CRA attack was to bully Sinai into abolishing Sunday services. The board decided to wait, because the Jewish Charities could not afford to alienate a major congregation (and contributor). And indeed, a few months later, as rumors were spreading that Sinai would sever its ties with the organized Jewish community, the Jewish Charities hastened to reassure Sinai of its continued "cooperation": "The recent unpleasant incident" should be "looked upon as a closed affair."[32] In hindsight, the public attack by the CRA and the Jewish Charities only corroborated Sinai's commitment to its radical Reform legacy—and Sunday services. But the incident also highlighted the growing marginalization of Sinai.

In the mid-1930s, growing numbers of Jewish emigrants from Nazi Germany began to arrive in Chicago. Earlier than other Jewish congregations and associations in America, Sinai opened its doors to the "newcomers." From 1936, different emigrant rabbis conducted German services on every fourth Friday night at Sinai's temple. Initially, most members of the congregation were sympathetic. Sinai expected to recruit new members from a constituency considered susceptible to their brand of Reform. German mainstream Liberal Judaism had emerged during the second half of the nineteenth century as a result of the compromise between Reformers and traditional Jews within the state-regulated *Einheitsgemeinde*. Few Sinai members realized that German-style Liberal Judaism differed considerably from the radical Reform legacy. Soon, criticism mounted. During a meeting in April 1938, a board member stated that for "an ultra-reform Congregation . . . an orthodox Religious Service, even though done by and for Newcomers, was out of place." Hannah Solomon, who now (finally) sat on the board, disagreed and defended the services. Reform was a broad camp without a "uniform procedure of worship." The "newcomers ought to be allowed to determine their own mode of worship."

Ironically, a major cause for the growing unease was the unexpected success of the services. Regular attendance hovered between three hundred and five hundred; six hundred emigrants came to the 1937 Rosh Hashanah service. Only a few could afford to join, yet patience was wearing thin fast. A leading critic was the rabbi. In May 1938, Mann stated that "he did not under any circumstances want a Newcomers' Congregation carrying on activities within the doors of Sinai in the German language." Nurturing a traditionally Jewish constituency within its own walls, Mann feared, would undermine Sinai's radical Reform platform, just when external pressure from the CRA was mounting. And of course, Sinai might be accused (again) of lacking in patriotism and harboring pro-German sentiments from a public that had limited sympathy for suspicious foreigners—even if they were refugees from Nazi terror.[33]

The skepticism, however, remained largely confined to the boardroom. Sinai's actions betray remarkable virtue. In the late 1930s, S. D. Schwartz helped a number German Jews come to Chicago by signing affidavits, a key requirement for obtaining a visa to the United States—but also a great financial risk for him as sponsor. Among the refugees who received affidavits from Schwartz were Ida Lazarus, the daughter of Sinai's second rabbi, Isaak L. Chronik, and Hans Eugen Simmel, the son of the famous sociologist Georg Simmel. In the fall of 1938, the congregation began a search for a rabbi who would preach regularly to the newcomers. When the board tried to contact the preferred candidate, Fritz Bamberger, in January 1939, it transpired he had been arrested after the notorious *Kristallnacht* pogrom on November 9–10, 1938. With support from Illinois governor (and Sinai member) Henry Horner and the State Department, the board brought Bamberger to Chicago. Bamberger had a doctoral degree in philosophy and had taught at the Berlin Hochschule für die Wissenschaft des Judentums, but he was not a rabbi. It remains unclear why Sinai selected Bamberger. In Chicago, Bamberger assumed a teaching position at the small College of Jewish Studies. This position, in fact, allowed him to enter the United States outside of the immigration quota. For a small honorarium, he conducted German services at Sinai. He soon emerged as an articulate speaker for the refugees and became the Chicago head of the Council of Refugee Organizations. Yet the perceived pressure on Sinai to not tolerate un-American activities grew. During a June 1940 meeting, a board member (with a rather German-sounding name) "believed it urgently necessary to have the Newcomers learn American ways and traditions as quickly as possible." The services continued.[34]

At a lengthy May 1942 gathering devoted to the newcomer services, a committee that included Bamberger and Mann argued for continuing German services for another year. The report stressed the commitment to "*Americanize* them [the newcomers] as quickly as feasible." The men and women attending the services were sympathetic to Sinai's brand of Reform. Emigrants who favored traditional services had many alternatives in Chicago, yet Sinai was their preferred option. Sinai had managed to pull one thousand of the approximately six thousand refugees on Chicago's South Side into its orbit. It was crucial not to "lose" them. Several members prepared a report in favor of discontinuing the services. They pointed out that the emigrants faced much resentment from other Jews in Hyde Park, unintentionally supporting the case for continuing the services. The overriding concern of these members was Americanization at any cost. Sinai could and should not tolerate "a foreign group as a foreign entity." A majority of the board voted for continuing the services for another year.[35]

SINAI FORUM

Mann supported German services at Sinai only halfheartedly, and he favored American isolationism. On Rosh Hashanah 1939, less than two weeks after the German attack on Poland and its large Jewish population, Mann told his congregation it was "the Rosh Hashanah obligation of America . . . to remain neutral." Mann was no coward. This statement and his critical line toward the newcomers reflect a socially conservative side that was at odds with the radical legacy of his predecessors in Sinai's pulpit. Rabbi Jacob I. Weinstein, the new rabbi at KAM, preached a different Rosh Hashanah message, openly voicing doubts about the merits of "nonintervention."[36]

The members respected Mann, but he was not loved, unlike S. D. Schwartz. After the closure of the social center in 1931, S. D. became the executive director of the congregation and Sinai's second rabbi in all but name. In the mid-1930s, in a period of great financial pressure, the board discussed raising Schwartz's much-reduced salary, proof of his growing stature and importance. One board member emphasized that Schwartz was easily the "most popular man in the Congregation." Although he kept a low profile, Schwartz was Sinai's main recruiter and fundraiser. And he was the man behind the greatest success in the post-Hirsch era: the Sinai Forum.[37]

> Jews, Catholics, Protestants, and agnostics, fundamentalists, and modern-
> ists, pacifists, . . . conservatives, and communists, Darrow the doubter and
> James M. Gray the Moodyite, Beard the historian, and Dreiser, the novel-
> ist, all are welcomed to its teaching forum.[38]

This characterization, taken from a 1930 *Tribune* article about the congregation, conveys the buzz the Sinai Forum exerted across the city. For Schwartz, as
he explained in the same article, the lecture series provided "education through
sharp stimulation." Listeners would only reexamine and possibly redefine their
own position if they were exposed to strong dissent, a provocative thesis, or a
controversial speaker. With this agenda, the forum successfully translated the
Enlightenment ideas of continuous education and debate into the intellectual
climate of the 1920s and 1930s. After a slow start, the forum took off in the
1920s and continued through the Depression. In some years it generated urgently needed income. Audiences ranged from 1,800 to 3,500. Often crowds had
to listen to lectures through loudspeakers in adjacent rooms. Many attendees
were not members of Sinai, nor were they Jewish. Among the regular (and less
controversial) speakers between the 1920s to the 1950s were Abba Hillel Silver
and Reinhold Niebuhr. Schwartz even lured such illustrious figures as Eleanor
Roosevelt to the Sinai Forum. During the 1940s, at the beginning of his career,
Leonard Bernstein came repeatedly to Sinai to discuss modern American music.
The program ranged in topic from politics to theology to academics—even occasional entertainments and concerts. A young Yehudi Menuhin performed at
a forum event in early 1945. One of the highlights came in November 1941, four
weeks before the Japanese attack on Pearl Harbor, when the German writer and
Nobel Prize laureate Thomas Mann spoke at Sinai. He (rather than the reluctant
rabbi) made a powerful case against isolationism and for the defeat of Nazism.
"Anything—without any conceivable exception, anything—is better than Hitler." Only a complete destruction of the Nazi regime offered the possibility to
reconnect with Germany's "better traditions."[39]

In October 1944, thirty-two years after the dedication, Sinai finally left its
temple on Grand Boulevard, selling the compound with the center to the Catholic Archdiocese of Chicago. The papers of the congregation do not contain evidence for an unusual level of threats or harassment, let alone conflicts between

Chicago Sinai Cong. Archives

FIGURE 13. The Sinai Forum: S. D. Schwartz (left), Reinhold Niebuhr (center), and Louis Mann (right), at Hyde Park High School, January 21, 1946. Courtesy of the Chicago Sinai Congregation.

Sinai members and African American residents. Apart from the occasional interfaith meeting, Sinai had not used its location to build deeper ties to its African American neighbors. While Sinai officially opposed racism, the Sinai Social Center informally excluded African American youths and adults from the neighborhood throughout the 1920s, in contrast to the nearby Abraham Lincoln Center. Jenkin Lloyd Jones had encouraged African Americans to use the center when it opened in 1905, But by the early 1920s, as more African Americans settled in the area and flocked to the Lincoln Center, the number of white patrons dropped. All Souls Church left Kenwood in 1922. Race was the overarching factor behind

Sinai's move in 1944. After renting quarters for the school, services, and other activities at different locations in Hyde Park, the board pushed ahead with the building project. It was Sinai's misfortune that the federal government selected the lot Sinai had bought for a veterans' hospital. In a relatively benign real estate market, the relocation was uncomplicated but added two years to the period of homelessness. On March 5, 1950, on the eve of Sinai's eighty-ninth anniversary, the new temple building, designed by Friedman, Alschuler & Sincere, was dedicated on the corner of 54th Street and South Shore Drive. The massive building accommodated over 1,800 people in a central sanctuary. A small chapel was designed for family events. The temple had classrooms, but the social center, though included in the original design, was never built.[40]

FALLING BEHIND

The 1950s witnessed a remarkable renaissance of the Reform movement in the United States. In 1937–1938, the UAHC counted 290 congregations with about 50,000 family members. By 1956, the number had risen to 520 congregations with over 250,000 members. In 1956, the Chicago metropolitan area was home to 16 Reform congregations. Sinai had an impressive 1,603 members, but Temple Sholom, a mainstream Reform congregation on the North Side, had overtaken Sinai with 1,870 members. Sinai's Hyde Park neighbors KAM (750) and Isaiah Israel (615) also increased their membership. The main growth areas of the Reform movement, however, were the suburbs and the "golden cities" in California and Florida. A disproportionate share of the Jewish Sun Belt migrants, especially in West Los Angeles, hailed from Chicago. In 1956, several Reform congregations were located in Chicago's northern suburbs, and their numbers and membership were increasing. It was uncertain whether Hyde Park, situated several miles south of the Loop and surrounded by the Black Belt, would retain its status as a middle-class neighborhood.[41]

On a first glance, Sinai's well-attended annual meeting in June 1954 did not betray a crisis. Even though the cost of the new temple was considerable, the economic troubles of the 1930s and 1940s belonged to the past. To relieve especially Mann of his duties, the congregation employed an assistant rabbi in the late 1940s. After the move to the new temple in 1950, the membership jumped from about 1,000 to 1,600 in a few months. Seven hundred children were enrolled in the congregation's school, and various associations, from the Men's Club (founded in 1929) to the Sisterhood, were flourishing. In his report, incoming president Harvey Kaplan accentuated Sinai's distinctiveness in no uncertain terms:

Sinai is one of the great congregations not only of America but of the world. Sinai has been unique from the day of its birth. . . . Our Congregation . . . is the most liberal not only in Chicago and the United States but in the world. . . . Sinai is unique in that it has not been guilty of slipping backward from classic Reform Judaism as have so many Reform Congregations in our country. We have a mission and deeply feel that time will vindicate our ultra-liberal interpretation of Judaism.[42]

Throughout its history, Sinai had a complicated relationship to the Reform mainstream. But from the 1870s to the 1920s, the congregation had been a controversial but widely respected trendsetter. The introduction of Sunday services, the abolition of Saturday services, the close cooperation with liberal Protestants, the push for social reform and education in Chicago, and the successful Sinai Social Center had provoked much debate (and criticism) but influenced Reform congregations across America. In 1954, however, President Kaplan could not hide the fact that his congregation had been theologically marginalized. Throughout the nineteenth century, Sinai had forged ahead in the name of innovation and progress. After 1920, the congregation failed to respond to social change and the expectations of a changing constituency.

Many illustrious Jewish and Christian theologians were invited to Sinai between 1920 and 1960—but Mordecai Kaplan was not among them. When he celebrated his seventieth birthday in 1951, twelve rabbis on Chicago's South Side devoted their sermons to Kaplan, among them several Reformers like Jacob Weinstein at KAM and Morton Berman at Temple Isaiah Israel. Sinai's senior rabbi, however, did not; instead, Sinai's assistant rabbi, Richard Hertz, congratulated Kaplan.[43] Sinai's theological marginalization was symbolically intertwined with the isolated location of the congregation on Chicago's South Side. The same members who were strongly committed to "ultra-liberal" Reform also preferred a neighborhood that held little promise for a congregation of Sinai's size.

The congregation's leaders were quite aware of the looming challenges. In the early phase of the prolonged homelessness, when the congregation still had the possibility to move to an alternative location, some members voiced opposition to Hyde Park, as President Emil Kitzinger put it in a letter to the rabbi in 1945, "because of the negro situation." Hyde Park was the home of the majority of Sinai's members, but in order to sustain itself, Sinai had to look for members in other parts of the city. Therefore, Sinai redefined itself as a "metropolitan" congregation, as a synagogue with a large share of members who commuted from different parts of metropolitan Chicago, including the suburbs. In his message to the 1949 annual meeting, on the eve of the move to the new temple, Kitzinger's successor, Joseph Rosenberg, claimed Sinai, unlike its smaller neighbors KAM and Temple Isaiah Israel, was *not* "a neighborhood, local congregation." In a similar vein, Richard Hertz depicted Sinai in 1951 as a "citywide temple" and as "metropolitan Temple: a cathedral congregation for all Chicagoland." He continued, pointing to other permanent Hyde Park monuments: "Here we shall remain, along with the University of Chicago, the Museum of Science and Industry, the Illinois Central Railroad, and the Outer Drive. A temple cannot chase real estate booms."[44]

Its home in Hyde Park forced Sinai to take a position in neighborhood's complex racial politics. By tacitly supporting neighborhood associations and through restrictive covenants, the University of Chicago had prevented African

Chicago Sinai Archives

FIGURE 14. Temple of Chicago Sinai congregation in Hyde Park, 1990. Courtesy of the Chicago Sinai Congregation.

CHAPTER TWELVE

Americans from settling in Hyde Park until the late 1940s. As the Black Belt began to expand into Kenwood and the western section of Hyde Park, the university adopted a more sophisticated strategy, rallying the residents and the city behind a campaign against crime and slum expansion. Most residents, represented by the Hyde Park Kenwood Community Conference (HPKCC), opposed racism but felt cornered by rising crime and a weak police presence. Following a widely reported kidnapping of a white woman by a "Negro burglar" in May 1952, the university organized a mass meeting. Two thousand five hundred Hyde Parkers attended. Rabbi Mann was elected to a committee to organize a body that became known as the South East Chicago Commission (SECC). In June, Mann became one of the SECC district chairmen. The *Tribune* article covering the founding meeting left little doubt that only the university possessed the financial and political clout and the determination to contain the expansion of the Black Belt. With the backing of the Democratic machine in city hall, headed since 1956 by Mayor Richard S. Daley, the energetic SECC executive director, Julian Hirsch Levi, and university chancellor, Lawrence A. Kimpton, pushed through an ambitious and ruthless urban renewal scheme. The run-down residential areas were largely cleared and taken over by the university. Aggressive policing of building code violations was used to condemn buildings, most of which were occupied by African Americans. "Urban renewal" saved the university and became a model for other inner-city universities that bordered segregated and crisis-ridden neighborhoods. As Arnold Hirsch has shown in his study *The Making of the Second Ghetto*, this policy did little to address the worsening racial segregation, let alone its causes.

Urban renewal proved to be a mixed blessing, especially for a large Jewish congregation like Sinai with a relatively limited constituency compared to Christian congregations. By raising economic and social profiles and reducing the number of residential units, the influx of less-affluent, and by default mostly nonwhite Chicagoans was "successfully" reversed. But relatively high rents, limited choice of housing, and, above all, public schools that could not match their suburban counterparts, were hardly incentives for younger white couples with children to settle in Hyde Park. Even before 1950, homeownership in Hyde Park had only been an option for a few wealthy families occupying homes too large for small families with limited income. Most Hyde Park residents rented apartments. These could not compete with the space and amenities of suburban homes. Moreover, the renewal of Hyde Park lasted into the 1960s, and crime remained a constant concern, especially as the conditions in adjacent areas of the Black Belt deteriorated further during the 1960s and 1970s.[45]

Sinai considered itself a Hyde Park institution, and it valued its longstanding relationship to the university. Mann was affiliated with the Department for Oriental Languages and Literatures. Julian H. Levi, the SECC director and the driving force behind the Hyde Park renewal program, was the grandson of Emil G. Hirsch, the son of Gerson B. Levi, and a member of Sinai. In 1962, the university appointed Levi to a professorship in urban studies. His brother, Edward Hirsch Levi, also a member of Sinai, had served as dean of the law school since 1950 and later as the university's first provost. In 1968, he assumed the presidency of the university, and in 1975, President Gerald Ford appointed him attorney general of the United States. While Sinai attracted fewer faculty members than KAM, its members continued the long tradition of philanthropy towards the university. In 1965, the Joseph and Helen Regenstein Foundation gave $10,000,000 to the university for the new library building. The Regenstein Library joined other buildings named after Sinai members.[46]

More noteworthy than Sinai's role in the ambiguous neighborhood politics of Hyde Park was its passivity in the struggle for civil rights in the 1950s and 1960s.[47] Particularly striking is the silence of Rabbi Mann, whose predecessor was, after all, one of the founders of the NAACP. Instead, Rabbi Weinstein of KAM, Sinai's neighbor in Hyde Park, emerged as an outspoken critic of the hidden agenda behind the renewal policy. He criticized residential segregation soon after his arrival at KAM in the late 1930s, arguing that Jews could not deplore anti-Semitic discrimination if they did not fight racism. Throughout the 1950s, Weinstein made no secret of his fierce opposition to segregation. He supported the fight against crime and slumlords, a serious issue for KAM and its members. However, Weinstein accused the city and Mayor Daley of promoting segregation rather than integration, betraying the legacy of Lincoln: "People who live differently come to think differently and a city, like a house, divided into rich and poor, black and white, cannot stand." In the 1960s, Weinstein gained national recognition for his support of civil rights, and he emerged as an early critic of the Vietnam War.[48] Thus Weinstein continued the tradition of social action and dissent in the name of universal ideals that once had been the hallmark of Sinai.

Between the 1920s and 1950s, Sinai lost its role as a national leader, a process that can be traced back to the early 1920s. The unsatisfactory location contributed to the theological and intellectual marginalization, but so did the unwillingness to reach out proactively to the large constituency of nonestablishment Jews—and to its African American neighbors. Rabbi Mann did not live up to the model of his predecessor, who for all his personal weaknesses had promoted social action and forged many relationships. From the 1950s to the 1980s, the

CHAPTER TWELVE

board was torn between the determination of its aging members to stay put and the gradual realization that especially married couples with small children preferred the comfort of the suburbs to a racially mixed urban neighborhood with an uncertain future. By the late 1950s, Sinai began to lose members, and it failed to attract younger families with children. The confirmation photographs taken since the 1940s are perhaps the most powerful illustration of the growing crisis. In the 1950s, Mann and his associate rabbi still confirmed dozens of children every year. But even before Mann retired in 1962, classes were visibly shrinking. By the 1970s, only a few children were left.[49]

EPILOGUE

ʕ̤ʔ

IN 1961, A FEW months after the inauguration of John F. Kennedy, Sinai celebrated its centennial. There was little sign of a dawning new era. In a small brochure, Louis L. Mann outlined Sinai's distinctive theological platform. Sinai was a "liberal" congregation and committed to change. "Strangely enough," he wondered, "the tendency at this time is backward, not forward." Mann, now in his thirty-eighth year in Sinai's pulpit, glossed over Zionism and civil rights. He did not touch on Sinai's long record of promoting social justice at a time when Hyde Park was in the midst of the controversial urban renewal program. Radical Reform had become a sacred tradition that was detached from the social reality, in contradiction to its progressive spirit and social justice legacy. Zionism and civil rights mobilized especially younger men and women involved in Jewish congregational life during the 1950s and 1960s. Sinai, already located in a neighborhood not very promising for younger couples with children, did not pull these Jews into its orbit. Thus the congregation situated itself, literally and symbolically, on the margins. Admittedly, since its founding, Sinai had kept some distance to the Reform mainstream and the organized movement. Yet in the decades before 1920, Sinai was a controversial but influential trendsetter. By the time it celebrated its centennial, the congregation still enjoyed some respect, but in theological terms it was marginal player with limited appeal.

Mann retired in 1962. His successor, Samuel E. Karff, faced a difficult task. Karff was Sinai's first rabbi who did not hail from a "German" family and who openly embraced Zionism. He pushed for a stronger participation of the congregation in the social life and politics of Hyde Park and tried to draw especially the remaining younger members closer to the congregation, with some success. At a 1963 meeting, board member Jeannette Segal supported the case for involvement in Hyde Park, candidly admitting, "We have been proud isolationists for too many years." Karff cautiously brought Sinai closer to the Reform mainstream. Under his auspices, some elements of the traditional liturgy were reintroduced. In 1956, Sinai had revived Friday evening services, now Saturday (morning) services made a comeback. But Sunday services remained.[1]

The late 1960s witnessed a growing migration of Sinai members to the Near North Side, and to a smaller extent to the suburbs, against a background of an accelerating movement of white Chicagoans out of the city. In 1973, the number of members remaining in Hyde Park dropped below 50 percent. The share of younger members with children fell dramatically. Karff now openly called for a move, reminding the board of its "responsibility . . . to safeguard the future of Sinai." The Hi-Rise Fellowship program of the early 1970s was a response to the declining service attendance, especially on Sundays. Karff and an assistant rabbi regularly conducted short services in several condominium buildings on the Near North Side. Later in the decade, the congregation rented facilities for regular services in the same area. The Genesis Project fostered closer relationships between members living in different parts of the city. Informal Bible study circles met regularly in the homes of members. Although various scenarios were discussed, ranging from mergers with other Hyde Park or suburban congregations to establishing branches, no obvious location in the city, not even on the Near North Side, was considered promising enough.[2]

It would be too simplistic to blame Sinai's leaders for misjudging the complex dynamic of Chicago's changing social and economic topography. The inability of Sinai to find its appropriate place *in* the city also betrays a larger crisis. Deindustrialization, racial segregation, and machine politics exacerbated social and economic divisions in post-1950 Chicago and other northern cities. According to one urban sociologist, postwar Chicago represents "a classic case of white flight."[3] Urban Jewish congregations were particularly vulnerable, because they catered to a small and clearly defined subset of the constituency, which was least likely to remain in the cities. Relatively well-educated and skilled men and women found better job opportunities and more comfort in the suburbs. Even members (and potential members) who continued to work in the city—for law firms, in the financial sector, or at universities—headed for the suburbs, especially if they had children. In addition to rising crime and racial tensions, Chicago's public schools could not compete with their better-funded suburban counterparts. After 1950, many larger urban Jewish congregations in the Midwest and on the East Coast followed their members to the suburbs (or locations on the urban fringe), sometimes by merging with suburban congregations. Some smaller and midsize congregations dissolved. At the same time, new congregations were established in the suburbs, and existing ones, such as Sinai's erstwhile branch, the Glencoe-based North Shore congregation, were expanding. Thus the virtual conflict between its gradually aging members living in Hyde Park and increasingly on the Near North Side, and potential younger members for whom the city held little promise threatened the existence of Sinai Congregation.[4]

The Hi-Rise Fellowship program and the Genesis Project illustrate the gradual decentralization of the congregation. Neither project though could stem the decline and fulfill the vision of a metropolitan congregation. Yet the board (and most members) opposed a move, in part because they could not agree on an alternative location. In 1974, Karff left Sinai for a large and expanding Reform congregation in Houston, a city that was booming in the 1970s. Sinai struggled for years to find a successor, an indication of the growing crisis. Only in the late 1980s did much persuading by Karff's successor, Howard Berman, and lobbying

Chicago Sinai Archives

FIGURE 15. "Services Sunday Morning," outside of Temple of Chicago Sinai congregation in Hyde Park, circa 1985. Courtesy of the Chicago Sinai Congregation.

by the first woman president, Miriam Letchinger, initiate a change of mind. The board reasoned, correctly as it would turn out, that Sinai would only be able to live up to its aspirations as a metropolitan congregation by locating in the center of Chicago. As required by the bylaws, the decision was put to a vote. The members overwhelmingly voted in favor of the move, and it occurred in 1998.[5]

Today, Sinai is a thriving metropolitan congregation. Even though most members live in the vicinity of the temple, some commute from different parts of the city and the suburbs. Sinai's new home on the Near North Side straddles Chicago's central shopping and entertainment districts and is within easy reach of residential areas like Lincoln Park and Lakeview that are pulling younger people, even couples with children, back into the city. In 2010, the congregation had almost a thousand members, including a growing share of families with children, and it has continued to attract new members.[6] Sinai has tried to rekindle the radical spirit of its pre-1920 years. Berman and his successor, Michael Sternfield, have performed interfaith marriages without requiring the conversion of the non-Jewish partner. The latter are encouraged to join the congregation as full members. Non-Jewish members, from a wide range of religions and faiths, enjoy the same rights as other members, including the right to serve as elected officers on the board. Suffice to say, Sunday services are still celebrated. Today, of course, Sinai is hardly the only Jewish congregation with a platform that provokes criticism from more traditionally minded Jews.[7] What is remarkable, however, is that the congregation has been committed to an explicitly radical interpretation of the Jewish tradition since 1861. Already in 1886, Sinai president Berthold Loewenthal proudly stressed Sinai's "distinction of being the best abused congregation on this continent."[8]

In his recently published survey of American Judaism, Jonathan D. Sarna makes a case for the forces of "renewal," questioning pessimistic scenarios of the disappearance of Jews as a group in the near future. The history of Sinai congregation supports this thesis.[9] However, in its history Sinai faced a number of severe challenges. Only three years after its founding, a large faction walked out and established a separate congregation, after a majority of the members refused to give rabbi Bernhard Felsenthal an extended contract. During the 1870s, radical and moderate members clashed repeatedly over the introduction of Sunday services. The conflict was only resolved after Kaufmann Kohler's departure in 1880. After America entered World War I, Emil G. Hirsch misjudged the frenzied atmosphere in Chicago. His criticism of the war and his pro-German stance put his congregation in great danger. The disastrous real estate deal in 1928 would have forced the board to dissolve the congregation, had Julius Rosenwald not

FIGURE 16. Temple of Chicago Sinai congregation at Delaware Place, Chicago, 2007. Photo by the author.

stepped in and provided the urgently needed funds. The move to downtown Chicago in the 1990s came almost too late. In hindsight, the risks associated with the relocation are easily overlooked.

Why did Sinai endure? Especially three aspects have to be considered: the theological platform, the role of the religious and lay leadership, and the social and economic context.

The theology of Sinai was strongly influenced by the universal *Bildung* ideal. *Bildung* informed the civic activism of the congregation's members in the first sixty years of the congregation. Emil G. Hirsch successfully translated *Bildung* into the social context of a rapidly industrializing and expanding metropolis, combining it with social action. Felix Adler and his Ethical Culture Society were an important influence. It was no coincidence that the main institutions and causes Sinai and its members supported outside of the synagogue were related to education. At least one member of Sinai sat on the board of the Chicago Public

Library from its founding in 1872 well into the twentieth century; in the 1890s, Hirsch served as head of that board. Several members of the congregation were appointed to Chicago's Board of Education during the second half of the nineteenth century. Sinai members donated large sums to the University of Chicago in its first decades. Julius Rosenwald's philanthropy was strongly influenced by the social justice theology of Hirsch—and very likely by the state-of-the-art Jewish Training School. Rosenwald committed much of his funds to education-related causes. *Bildung* and social action were also the foundation for the multiple relationships the congregation forged in Chicago during the four decades after 1880. Indeed, in those forty years, Sinai had a persuasive theological platform, a capable rabbi who realized the potential of the congregation and opened its doors to the wider community, and many like-minded partners who shared the congregation's vision. Sinai was committed to nondenominationalism and did not consider itself as part of the Reform mainstream, even after joining the Union of American Hebrew Congregations in 1903. Yet between the 1880s and the 1920s, Sinai and its rabbi occupied a central position in the social and civic life of Chicago.

The gradual decline during World War I and the increasing marginalization in the following decades had several causes. Hirsch's successor, Louis L. Mann, closely identified with Sinai's radical Reform platform but was unable and unwilling to adapt it to the changing circumstances. Although Sinai had capable and experienced lay leaders, Mann inherited a position that gave him much more influence than he could have hoped for. After the dramatic 1899 leadership struggle, the board had yielded much of its authority to its rabbi. In hindsight, the relatively powerful position of a socially conservative and cautious rabbi contributed to the loss of its erstwhile influence—especially during the Depression, when the board was preoccupied with keeping the congregation afloat.

The relationships Sinai forged before 1914 withered, and the congregation was increasingly isolated. In part, this was the conscious choice by the rabbi and the board, for instance, when African Americans were de facto excluded from the Sinai Social Center during the 1920s. Even the German Jewish "newcomers" were not received with open arms, as the internal board discussions reveal. Yet the impact of growing anti-Semitism, social and racial conflicts, and the Depression cannot be dismissed. Many of Sinai's Progressive Era collaborators had passed away, and the conditions for building relationships were not as convivial as they had been in the 1890s. The affair over the anti-Jewish editorials in the *Christian Century* highlights a growing distance by liberal Protestants to Jews. Nevertheless, especially in the years after World War II, Sinai could have chosen a different path but did not. Even after it located in Hyde Park, many opportunities were missed.

Just like Sinai's gradual decline since the 1920s is a prism of Chicago's struggle with economic crisis, deindustrialization, segregation, and suburbanization, its renaissance in recent years reflects the remarkable turnaround of a city that appeared doomed in the late 1960s. The adoption of Schiller Elementary School in 2008 has a special meaning in light of congregation's history. Reaching out to an overwhelmingly African American constituency from the former Cabrini Green housing project connects with the older legacy of the congregation in regard to social action in general and to African Americans in particular. Without a doubt, Sinai's founders, Emil G. Hirsch, Julian Mack, and Julius Rosenwald, would have happily embraced this project, devoted to a school named after a founding father of the *Bildung* ideal, the German poet Friedrich Schiller, and to the education of children who are deprived of resources and equal opportunities.[10]

ABBREVIATIONS

AJA	American Jewish Archives (Cincinnati)
AJC	American Jewish Committee
AJHQ	*American Jewish Historical Quarterly*
AJHS	American Jewish Historical Society
AJS	Associated Jewish Charities (of Chicago)
AZ	*Allgemeine Zeitung des Judenthums* (Leipzig)
CHM	Chicago History Museum
CJA	Chicago Jewish Archives
CSC	Chicago Sinai Congregation
FOCA	Federated Orthodox Charities of Chicago
HUC	Hebrew Union College
ISZ	*Illinois Staatszeitung*
KAM	Kehilath Anshe Ma'ariv
NAACP	National Association for the Advancement of Colored People
NCJW	National Council of Jewish Women
RA	*Reform Advocate* (Chicago)
UAHC	Union of American Hebrew Congregations
UHC	United Hebrew Charities (Chicago)
UHRA	United Hebrew Relief Association (Chicago)

NOTES

INTRODUCTION

1. See http://www.calvaryumc-philly.org/templates/System/details.asp?id=25808&PID= 234386 (accessed August 19, 2010).

2. Michael P. Conzen, "Jewish Congregations on the Move in Chicago, 1849–2002," *Encyclopedia of Chicago*, ed. James Grossman, Janice L. Reiff, and Ann Durkin Keating (Chicago: University of Chicago Press, 2004), 691.

3. "Operation Push Buys Temple for $200,000," *Jet Magazine*, July 13, 1972, 13.

4. Martin Luther King Jr., "Why Jesus Called A Man A Fool" (sermon, Mt. Pisgah Missionary Baptist Church, Chicago, Illinois, August 27, 1967), repr. in *A Knock at Midnight: Inspiration From the Great Sermons of Reverend Martin Luther King, Jr.*, ed. Clayborne Carson and Peter Holloran (New York: Warner Books, 2000), 141–64.

5. Thomas Philpott, *The Slum and the Ghetto: Neighborhood Deterioration and Middle-Class Reform, Chicago, 1880–1930* (Oxford: Oxford University Press, 1978), 337–40; Dominic A. Pacyga, *Chicago: A Biography* (Chicago: University of Chicago Press, 2010), 225–27; Adam Cohen and Elizabeth Taylor, *American Pharaoh: Mayor Richard J. Daley. His Battle for Chicago and the Nation* (Boston: Little, Brown, 2000), 184–90, 331–32.

6. Michael A. Meyer, *Response to Modernity: A History of the Reform Movement in Judaism* (New York: Oxford University Press, 1988), 304; *Chicago Tribune*, April 29, 1912.

7. Introduction to *Portraits of Twelve Religious Communities*, ed. James P. Wind and James W. Lewis, vol. 1 of *American Congregations* (Chicago: University of Chicago Press, 1994), 1–2; see also Martin E. Marty, "Public and Private: Congregation as a Meeting Place," in *New Perspectives in the Study of Congregations*, ed. James P. Wind and James W. Lewis, vol. 2 of *American Congregations* (Chicago: University of Chicago Press, 1994), 133–66; James P. Wind, *Places of Worship: Exploring their History* (Walnut Creek, CA: Altamira Press, 1997);

Martin E. Marty, *Modern American Religion: The Irony of It All 1893–1919* (Chicago: University of Chicago Press, 1986).

8. Chicago Sinai Congregation, Social Action Committees, http://www.chicagosinai .org/social_action/face_to_face.cfm (accessed May 10, 2010).

9. Naomi Cohen, *What the Rabbis Said: The Public Discourse of Nineteenth-Century American Rabbis* (New York: New York University Press, 2008); Jeffrey S. Gurock, *Orthodox Jews in America* (Bloomington: Indiana University Press, 2009).

10. Peter Eisenstadt, *Affirming the Covenant: A History of Temple B'rith Kodesh, Rochester, New York, 1848–1998* (Rochester, NY: Temple B'rith Kodesh, 1999); Fred Rosenbaum, *Visions of Reform: Congregation Emanu-El and the Jews of San Francisco 1849–1999* (San Francisco: Judah L. Magnes Museum, 2000); noncommissioned studies include Karla Goldman and Jonathan D. Sarna, "From Synagogue-Community to Citadel of Reform: The History of K. K. Bene Israel (Rockdale Temple) in Cincinnati, Ohio," in Wind and Lewis, *American Congregations*, 1:159–220; Melissa Fay Greene, *The Temple Bombing* (Reading, MA: Addison-Wesley, 1996); innovative general studies dealing with the history of Jewish congregations include *The American Synagogue: A Sanctuary Transformed*, ed. Jack Wertheimer (Cambridge: Cambridge University Press, 1987); Alan Silverstein, *Alternatives to Assimilation: The Response of Reform Judaism to American Culture 1840–1930* (Hanover, NH: University Press of New England, 1994); Ewa Morawska, *Insecure Prosperity: Small-Town Jews in Industrial America, 1890–1940* (Princeton, NJ: Princeton University Press, 1996), esp. 135–75; Wind, *Places of Worship*, 78–81; David Kaufman, *Shul with a Pool: The "Synagogue-Center" in American Jewish History* (Hanover, NH: University Press of New England, 1999); Karla Goldman, *Beyond the Synagogue Gallery: Finding a Place for Women in American Judaism* (Cambridge, MA: Harvard University Press, 2000).

11. Meyer, *Response to Modernity*; see also Jonathan D. Sarna, *American Judaism: A History* (New Haven, CT: Yale University Press, 2004). For studies that take the European background into account, see Stefan Rohrbacher, "From Württemberg to America, A 19th Century German-Jewish Village on its Way to the New World," *AJA* 41 (1989): 142–71; Tobias Brinkmann, *Von der Gemeinde zur "Community": Jüdische Einwanderer in Chicago 1840–1900* (Osnabrück: Universitätsverlag Rasch, 2002); Tony Michels, *A Fire in Their Hearts: Yiddish Socialists in New York* (Cambridge, MA: Harvard University Press, 2005); Eli Lederhendler, *Jewish Immigrants and American Capitalism, 1880–1920: From Caste to Class* (Cambridge: Cambridge University Press, 2009); Rebecca Kobrin, *Jewish Bialystock and Its Diaspora* (Bloomington: Indiana University Press, 2010).

12. Perry R. Duis, *Challenging Chicago: Coping with Everyday Life, 1837–1920* (Urbana: University of Illinois Press, 1998); Dominic A. Pacyga, *Polish Immigrants and Industrial Chicago: Workers on the South Side, 1880–1922* (Columbus: Ohio State University Press, 1991); John T. McGreevy, *Parish Boundaries: The Catholic Encounter with Race in the Twentieth-Century Urban North* (Chicago: University of Chicago Press, 1996); Kathleen Neils Conzen, "Immigrant Religion and the Public Sphere: The German Catholic Milieu in America," in

German-American Immigration and Ethnicity in Comparative Perspective, ed. Wolfgang Helbich and Walter Kamphoefner (Madison, WI: Max Kade Institute, 2004), 69–116.

13. An early publication of (the mostly German-language) documents relating to Sinai's founding, including letters exchanged between the board and a committee charged with organizing the printing in 1897: Bernhard Felsenthal, *The Beginnings of the Chicago Sinai Congregation: A Contribution to the Inner History of American Judaism* (Chicago: Ettlinger, 1898).

CHAPTER 1

1. Hyman L. Meites, *History of the Jews of Chicago* (Chicago: Chicago Jewish Historical Society, 1924), 114–16; Walter Kamphoefner, *The Westfalians: From Germany to Missouri* (Princeton, NJ: Princeton University Press, 1987); John Bodnar, *The Transplanted: A History of Immigrants in Urban America* (Bloomington: Indiana University Press, 1985), 57–58; Charles Tilly, "Transplanted Networks," in *Immigration Reconsidered: History, Society and Politics*, ed. Virginia Yans-McLaughlin (New York: Oxford University Press, 1990), 78–95.

2. Reminiscences of Jacob Greenebaum Sr. (Biographical File, CJA); see also Hannah Solomon, *Fabric of My Life* (New York: Bloch, 1946).

3. From 1815 to 1880, a hundred thousand emigrated from the territory of Imperial Germany (Jacob Toury, *Soziale und politische Geschichte der Juden in Deutschland 1848–1871* [Düsseldorf: Droste, 1977], 43); from 1830 to 1914, the number was two hundred thousand from the same region (Avraham Barkai, *Branching Out: German-Jewish Immigration to the United States 1820–1914* [New York: Holmes & Meier, 1994], 9–10); and from 1820 to 1880, two hundred and fifty thousand emigrated from central and eastern Europe (Hasia R. Diner, *The Jews of the United States, 1654 to 2000* [Berkeley: University of California Press, 2004], 87).

4. Dirk Hoerder, *Cultures in Contact: World Migrations in the Second Millennium* (Durham, NC: Duke University Press, 2002), 331–32.

5. Monika Richarz, ed., introduction to *Jüdisches Leben in Deutschland: Selbstzeugnisse zur Sozialgeschichte 1780–1871* (Stuttgart: DVA, 1976), 27; David Sorkin, "The Impact of Emancipation on German Jewry: A Reconsideration," in *Assimilation and Community: The Jews in Nineteenth Century Europe*, ed. Jonathan Frankel and Steven Zipperstein (Cambridge: Cambridge University Press, 1991), 177–98 (esp. 180).

6. Toury, *Soziale und politische Geschichte*, 43; Barkai, *Branching Out*, 9–10; Diner, *The Jews of the United States*, 87; Arthur Ruppin, *Soziologie der Juden* (Berlin: Jüdischer Verlag, 1930), 1:126.

7. For an account of Jewish departure that emphasizes political factors, see Naomi Cohen, *Encounter with Emancipation: The German Jews in the United States 1830–1914* (Philadelphia: Jewish Publication Society, 1984), 4–17. Diner acknowledges economic factors but stresses the influence of anti-Jewish violence and oppressive state policies (*The Jews of the United States*, 85–88); Jonathan Sarna also emphasizes the differences between Jewish and

Christian migrants (*American Judaism: A History* [New Haven, CT: Yale University Press, 2004], 64).

8. Reinhard Rürup, *Emanzipation und Antisemitismus: Studien zur "Judenfrage" der bürgerlichen Gesellschaft* (Frankfurt: Fischer, 1987), 27–46.

9. Jacob Toury, "Jewish Manual Labour and Emigration: Records from some Bavarian Districts (1830–1857)," *Leo Baeck Institute Yearbook* 16 (1971): 45–62; Sigrid Faltin, *Die Auswanderung aus der Pfalz nach Nordamerika im 19. Jahrhundert* (Frankfurt: Peter Lang, 1989), 56; Ira Katznelson, "Between Separation and Disappearance. American Jews on the Margins of American Liberalism," in *Paths of Emancipation. Jews, States, and Citizenship*, ed. Ira Katznelson and Pierre Birnbaum (Princeton, NJ: Princeton University Press, 1995), 169.

10. Tobias Brinkmann, *Von der Gemeinde zur "Community": Jüdische Einwanderer in Chicago 1840–1900* (Osnabrück: Universitätsverlag Rasch, 2002), 39–59; Barkai, *Branching Out*, 9–10.

11. Diner, *The Jews of the United States*, 85–88; Cohen, *Encounter with Emancipation*, 4–17. Another study that emphasizes the impact of violence on Jewish life between 1815 and 1848 is Stefan Rohrbacher, *Gewalt im Biedermeier: Antijüdische Ausschreitungen in Vormärz und Revolution 1815–1848/49* (Frankfurt: Campus, 1993). An account emphasizing the economic transformation is Brinkmann, *Von der Gemeinde*, 59–65. On Bohemia, see reprinted and translated sources in Guido Kisch, "The Revolution of 1848 and the Jewish 'On to America' Movement," *AJHQ* 38 (1948–49): 185–231.

12. Herman Eliassof and Emil G. Hirsch, "The Jews of Illinois: Their Religious and Civic Life, their Charity and Industry, their Patriotism and Loyalty to American Institutions, from their earliest settlement in the State unto present time," *RA*, May 4, 1901, 318.

13. Ibid., 50, 70, 79, 81, 112, 286 (Leopold Maier's reminiscences), 287, 317; "Letters from Grandma Mandel's Attic": David Liebmann (Oberndorf) to Frank and family, April 1854; father Mendel Ries (Aufhausen) to the dear children, January 3, 1848, Biographical File, CJA; *New York Times*, July 16, 1865 (see passenger list of the ship *America*); for sources on individual biographies see: Brinkmann, *Von der Gemeinde*, 67–79.

14. See the index in *Chicago: Its History and its Builders* (Chicago: privately printed, ca. 1914); Eliassof and Hirsch, "Jews of Illinois," 318; Meites, *History of the Jews of Chicago*, 435.

15. Bernhard Friedberg, "Samuel Adler," *Jewish Encyclopedia*, ed. Isidore Singer (New York: Funk and Wagnalls, 1901), 1:199; for obituaries, see the June 11, 1891, issue of the *New York Times*; *New Yorker Staatszeitung*, June 21, 1891.

16. Bernhard Felsenthal, Reisenotizen (June 4, 1854–1857, n.d.), Felsenthal Papers, MS-153, AJA.

17. *AZ*, May 17, 1853, 255.

18. On Felsenthal's attempts to introduce religious reforms in Madison, see Amy Hill Shevitz, *Jewish Communities on the Ohio River: A History* (Lexington: University of Kentucky Press, 2007), 71–74.

19. Herbert Heaton, "Economic Change and Growth," in *The New Cambridge Modern History: X. The Zenith of European Power*, ed. J. P. T. Bury (Cambridge: Cambridge University Press, 1964), 22–48 (esp. 36); on Leopold Mayer's journey, see Eliassof and Hirsch, "Jews of Illinois," 286.

20. For a migration network from Franconia that dominated the early Jewish community in Columbus, Ohio, see Marc Lee Raphael, *Jews and Judaism in a Midwestern Community: Columbus, Ohio 1840–1975* (Columbus: Ohio Historical Society, 1979), 35–58.

21. Stefan Rohrbacher, "From Württemberg to America, A 19th Century German-Jewish Village on its Way to the New World," *American Jewish Archives* 41 (1989): 142–71; Cornelia Östreich, *"Des rauhen Winters ungeachtet . . .": Die Auswanderung Posener Juden nach Amerika im 19. Jahrhundert* (Hamburg: Dölling und Galitz, 1997), 171–72; Tilly, "Transplanted Networks," 84–88.

22. Jacob Rader Marcus, ed., *Memoirs of American Jews 1775–1865* (Philadelphia: Jewish Publication Society, 1955–56), 2:107; Henry Feingold, *Zion in America: The Jewish Experience from Colonial Times to the Present* (New York: Twayne Publishers, 1974), 73; Hasia R. Diner, *A Time for Gathering: The Second Migration 1820–1880*, vol. 2 of *The Jewish People in America*, ed. Henry Feingold (Baltimore, MD: Johns Hopkins University Press, 1992), 66–68; Joshua Trachtenberg, *Consider the Years: The Story of the Jewish Community of Easton, 1752–1942* (Easton, PA: Temple Brith Sholom, 1944), 125.

23. William Toll, *The Making of an Ethnic Middle Class: Portland Jewry over Four Generations* (Albany: State University of New York Press, 1982), 10; Gerald Sorin, *A Time for Building: The Third Migration 1880–1920*, vol. 3 of *The Jewish People in America*, ed. Henry Feingold (Baltimore, MD: Johns Hopkins University Press, 1992), 3; Raphael, *Jews and Judaism in a Midwestern Community*, 35–36; Diner, *A Time for Gathering*, 65; Shevitz, *Jewish Communities on the Ohio River*, 47–64.

24. Abraham Kohn, diary, 1842–1843 (New York: Leo Baeck Institute, Memoir Collection, ME 951). A translation of parts of the diary from the original German into English can be found in Abram Vossen Goodman, "A Jewish Peddler's Diary 1842–1843," *American Jewish Archives* 4 (1951): 81–111; Leopold Furth, Biographical File, CJA.

25. For sources on individual migrants, see Brinkmann, *Von der Gemeinde*, 71–80; Gerhard Foreman, Biographical File, CJA; Ira Nelson Morris, *Heritage from My Father: An Autobiography* (New York: privately printed, 1947), 2–3; Louise Carroll Wade, *Chicago's Pride: The Stockyards, Packingtown, and the Environs in the Nineteenth Century* (Chicago: University of Illinois Press, 1987), 84–92, 203.

26. Jenny R. Gerstley, "My Childhood in Early Chicago," Gerstley, Biographical File, CJA; Eliassof and Hirsch, "Jews of Illinois," 376.

27. German Press Club of Chicago, ed., *Biographical and Industrial Prominent Citizens and Industries of Chicago* (Chicago: privately printed, 1901), 133; Brinkmann, *Von der Gemeinde*, 75; Eliassof and Hirsch, "Jews of Illinois," 395–96.

28. Brinkmann, *Von der Gemeinde*, 75–80; Stephen G. Mostov, "Dun and Bradstreet Reports as a Source of Jewish Economic History: Cincinnati, 1840–1875," *American Jewish History* 72 (1983): 333–53 (esp. 342); Stephen G. Mostov, "A 'Jerusalem' on the Ohio: The Social and Economic History of Cincinnati's Jewish Community, 1840–1875" (PhD diss., Brandeis University, 1981). On Jews in small towns, see Lee Shai Weissbach, *Jewish Life in Small-Town America* (New Haven, CT: Yale University Press, 2005); Shevitz, *Jewish Communities on the Ohio River*.

29. Diner, *Jews of the United States*, 87.

30. Barkai, *Branching Out*, 9, 15; Diner, *Jews of the United States*, 87; Jonathan D. Sarna, *American Judaism: A History* (New Haven, CT: Yale University Press, 2004), 64. On the diverse backgrounds of "German" immigrants, see Walter D. Kamphoefner, "German Emigration Research, North, South, and East: Findings, Methods, and Open Questions," in *People in Transit: German Migrations in Comparative Perspective 1820–1920*, ed. Dirk Hoerder and Jörg Nagler (Cambridge: Cambridge University Press, 1995), 19–33; Nancy Green, "The Comparative Method and Poststructural Structuralism: New Perspectives for Migration Studies," in *Migration, Migration History, History: Old Paradigms and New Perspectives*, ed. Jan and Leo Lucassen (Bern: Peter Lang, 1997), 70.

31. Reminiscences of Jacob Greenebaum Sr.; Jacob Toury, "Der Eintritt der Juden ins deutsche Bürgertum," in *Das Judentum in der Deutschen Umwelt 1800–1850*, ed. Hans Liebeschütz and Arnold Paucker (Tübingen: Siebeck Mohr, 1977), 142–46; Paula Hyman, "The Social Contexts of Assimilation: Village Jews and City Jews in Alsace," in *Assimilation and Community: The Jews in Nineteenth-Century Europe*, ed. Jonathan Frankel and Steven J. Zipperstein (Cambridge: Cambridge University Press, 1992), 111–14.

32. John Higham, *Send These To Me: Immigrants in Urban America* (Baltimore, MD: Johns Hopkins University Press, 1975), 123.

33. See the annual reports of the United Hebrew Relief Society in Chicago (established in 1859); these are kept at the Chicago Jewish Archives; for the background; see Brinkmann, *Von der Gemeinde*, 168–74, 249–78.

34. Richarz, introduction to *Jüdisches Leben in Deutschland*, 17–18; Toury, *Soziale und politische Geschichte*, 30.

35. Diner, *Jews of the United States*, 82–83.

36. Avraham Barkai, "German-Jewish Migrations in the Nineteenth Century," *Leo Baeck Institute Year Book* 30 (1985): 301–18 (esp. 311); Rohrbacher, "From Württemberg to America," 153; Toury, "Jewish Manual Labour and Emigration," 59; Maldwyn Allen Jones, *American Immigration* (Chicago: University of Chicago Press, 1960), 111; Mack Walker, *Germany and the Emigration 1816–1885* (Cambridge, MA: Harvard University Press, 1964), 75.

37. *Jüdische Geschichte in Berlin: Bilder und Dokumente* (exhibition catalog), ed. Reinhard Rürup (Berlin: Hentrich, 1995), 134, 142–47.

38. Simone Lässig, *Jüdische Wege ins Bürgertum: Kulturelles Kapital und sozialer Aufstieg im 19. Jahrhundert* (Göttingen: Vandenhoeck & Ruprecht, 2004), esp. 26–34.

39. Roger Daniels, *Coming to America: A History of Immigration and Ethnicity in American Life* (New York: Harper, 1990), 150.

40. See biographies in Eliassof and Hirsch, "Jews of Illinois."

CHAPTER 2

1. Kathleen D. McCarthy, *Noblesse Oblige: Charity & Cultural Philanthropy in Chicago 1849–1929* (Chicago: University of Chicago Press, 1982), 13; Thomas Philpott, *The Slum and the Ghetto: Neighborhood Deterioration and Middle-Class Reform, Chicago, 1880–1930* (Oxford: Oxford University Press, 1978), 7–8; Tobias Brinkmann, *Von der Gemeinde zur "Community": Jüdische Einwanderer in Chicago 1840–1900* (Osnabrück: Universitätsverlag Rasch, 2002), 83–97. For a general overview, see Richard Sennett, *Families against the City: Middle Class Homes of Industrial Chicago 1872–1890* (Cambridge MA: Harvard University Press, 1970), 23; William Cronon, *Nature's Metropolis: Chicago and the Great West* (New York: Norton, 1991); Witold Rybczynski, *City Life: Urban Expectations in a New World* (New York: Scribner, 1995), 110–15; Paul Boyer, *Urban Masses and Moral Order in America 1820–1920* (Cambridge, MA: Harvard University Press, 1978).

2. *Israelite* (Cincinnati), February 3, 1860.

3. Jonathan D. Sarna, *American Judaism: A History* (New Haven, CT: Yale University Press, 2004), 96–97.

4. *Israelite*, September 30, 1859.

5. Michael A. Meyer, *Response to Modernity: A History of the Reform Movement in Judaism* (New York: Oxford University Press, 1988), 238–44; *Die Deborah* (Cincinnati), August 24, 1855; Stanley Nadel, "Jewish Race and German Soul in Nineteenth-Century America," in *American Jewish History* 77 (1987): 6–26 (esp. 9–10).

6. Meyer, *Response to Modernity*, 243–44; on the conference, see *Sinai* (Baltimore), February 1856, 4–10.

7. On the term synagogue-community, see Sarna, *American Judaism*, 52–61; for one hundred thousand (1815–1880), see Jacob Toury, *Soziale und politische Geschichte der Juden in Deutschland, 1848–1871* (Düsseldorf: Droste, 1977), 43; for two hundred thousand (1830–1914), see Avraham Barkai, *Branching Out: German-Jewish Immigration to the United States 1820–1914* (New York: Holmes & Meier, 1994), 9–10.

8. Lee Shai Weissbach, "The Jewish Communities of the United States on the Eve of the Mass Migration," in *American Jewish History* 78 (1988): 79–108; Weissbach, *Jewish Life in Small-Town America* (New Haven, CT: Yale University Press, 2005).

9. *AZ*, July 27, 1846.

10. Robert S. Adler, *The Family of Max and Sophie R. Adler* (Chicago: privately printed, 1972), Biographical File, CJA; *History of Sangamon County, Illinois: Together with Sketches of Its Cities, Villages and Townships, Portraits of Prominent Persons, and Biographies of Representative Citizens. History of Illinois* (Chicago: Illinois Inter-State Publishing Company, 1881), 709.

11. Herman Eliassof and Emil G. Hirsch, "The Jews of Illinois: Their Religious and Civic Life, their Charity and Industry, their Patriotism and Loyalty to American Institutions, from their earliest settlement in the State unto present time," *RA*, May 4, 1901, 286.

12. *Israelite*, August 8 and 15, 1856. The description of Chicago is taken from Isaac Mayer Wise, *Reminiscences: Translated from the German and Edited with an Introduction by David Philipson* (Cincinnati, OH: Leo Wise, 1901), 298; in his reminiscences, Wise places his first visit in July 1855, very likely by mistake.

13. Bernhard Felsenthal and Hermann Eliassof, *History of Kehillath Anshe Maarab: Issued under the Auspices of the Congregation on the Occasion of Its Semi-Centennial Celebration, Nov. 4, 1897* (Chicago: KAM, 1897), 23; *Occident* (Philadelphia), January 1855, 526; Bernhard Felsenthal, "A Contribution to the History of the Israelites in Chicago," unpublished manuscript, 1863, see Col. Felsenthal, Bernhard, Box 130, CHM archive; Morris Gutstein, *A Priceless Heritage: The Epic Growth of Nineteenth Century Chicago Jewry* (New York: Bloch, 1953), 434; on the mistaken naming, see Emil G. Hirsch, "Deutsches Judenthum," in *Die Geschichte einer Wunderstadt*, ed. Eugen Seeger (Chicago: Max Stern, 1892), 397–401 (esp. 397); Mayer is quoted in Eliassof and Hirsch, "Jews of Illinois," 287; on "indifference" in Chicago, see *Occident* (Philadelphia), January 1857, 586.

14. *Die Deborah* (Cincinnati), August 8, 1855; *Israelite*, July 8, 1859.

15. *Israelite*, August 8 and 15, 1856.

16. Notes by Emil G. Hirsch for Sunday Service (?), November 22, 1922, [Chicago] Sinai Congregation Records, MS collection 56, AJA, quoted in Sinai Papers, AJA. The collection is chronologically organized, and the files can be traced by the respective date. With the exception of entries in the minute books, which are specifically referenced, all following references in this and the following chapters refer to the respective date. For a detailed inventory, see http://americanjewisharchives.org/aja/FindingAids/Sinai.htm (accessed May 10, 2010).

17. Ira Katznelson and Pierre Birnbaum, "Emancipation and the Liberal Offer," in *Paths of Emancipation: Jews, States, and Citizenship*, ed. Ira Katznelson and Pierre Birnbaum (Princeton, NJ: Princeton University Press, 1995), 20–22; the classic study with a German focus remains Jacob Katz, *Out of the Ghetto: The Social Background of Jewish Emancipation, 1770–1870* (Cambridge, MA: Harvard University Press, 1973); on the modern Jewish experience outside of Germany, see Miriam Bodian, *Hebrews of the Portuguese Nation: Conversos and Community in Early Modern Amsterdam* (Bloomington: Indiana University Press, 1997); Lois C. Dubin, *The Port Jews of Habsburg Trieste: Absolutist Politics and Enlightenment Culture* (Stanford, CA: Stanford University Press, 1999). For the term "response to modernity," see Meyer, *Response to Modernity*.

18. Michael A. Meyer, *The Origins of the Modern Jew: Jewish Identity and European Culture in Germany, 1749–1824* (Detroit: Wayne State Press, 1967), 144–82.

19. Meyer, *Response to Modernity*, 62–99 (quote, 89).

20. George L. Mosse, *German Jews beyond Judaism* (Bloomington: Indiana University

Press, 1985), 3; see also David Sorkin, *The Transformation of German Jewry, 1780–1840* (New York: Oxford University Press, 1987).

21. Simone Ladwig-Winters, *Freiheit und Bindung: Zur Geschichte der Jüdischen Reformgemeinde zu Berlin von den Anfängen bis zu ihrem Ende 1939* (Berlin: Hentrich & Hentrich, 2004), 55–102; David Philipson, *The Reform Movement in Judaism*, new and rev. ed. (New York: Macmillan, 1931), 253–57.

22. Letters from Kaufmann Kohler to Bernhard Felsenthal, April 6, 1869, and June 7, 1869, Felsenthal Papers, Box 1 (correspondence), AJHS. Kohler wrote on April 6, "Für ein großes, freies Judenthum will ich wirken u. dazu will mir das schlaff gewordene religiöse Leben in Deutschland durchaus keinen Wirkungskreis in Aussicht stellen."

23. Meyer, *Response to Modernity*, 62–99, 264–95; Maria T. Baader, "From 'the Priestess of the Home' to 'the Rabbi's Brilliant Daughter': Concepts of Jewish Womanhood and Progressive Germanness in *Die Deborah* and the American Israelite, 1854–1900," *Leo Baeck Institute Yearbook* 43 (1998): 47–72.

24. The most comprehensive biographical overview remains Kaufmann Kohler, "David Einhorn: The Uncompromising Champion of Reform. A Biographical Essay," *Yearbook of the Central Conference of American Rabbis* 19 (1909): 215–70.

25. Quoted in Meyer, *Response to Modernity*, 138, 246 (original emphasis).

26. On the term "priest people," see Exodus 19:6.

27. Quoted in Gershon Greenberg, "The Significance of America in David Einhorn's Conception of History," *AJHQ* 63 (1974): 160–84 (quote on 163).

28. Meyer, *Response to Modernity*, 245–47 (see p. 216 for the term "religious reality").

29. *Sinai*, February 1856, 4–10.

30. Todd Endelman, *The Jews of Britain 1656 to 2000* (Berkeley: University of California Press, 2002), 113.

31. Meyer, *Response to Modernity*, 245.

32. Emma Felsenthal, *Bernhard Felsenthal: Teacher in Israel* (New York: Oxford University Press, 1924), 1–10.

33. Ibid.

34. Letter from David Einhorn to Bernhard Felsenthal, March 10, 1857, Felsenthal Papers, Box 1 (correspondence), AJHS.

35. Felsenthal, *Teacher in Israel*, 24–25; Shevitz, *Jewish Communities on the Ohio River: A History* (Lexington: University of Kentucky Press, 2007), 70–71.

36. *Israelite*, October 16, 1857.

37. *Israelite*, February 26 and April 16, 1858. On a possible connection to the *Lichtfreunde* movement in New York and the German states, see Cornelia Wilhelm, "An Ambivalent Relationship: Isaac M. Wise and the Independent Order of B'nai B'rith," in *New Essays in American Jewish History*, ed. Pamela S. Nadell, Jonathan D. Sarna, and Lance J. Sussman (Jersey City: KTAV, 2010), 155–73 (esp. 158–60).

38. Bernhard Felsenthal, *The Beginnings of the Chicago Sinai Congregation: A Contribution to the Inner History of American Judaism* (Chicago: Ettlinger, 1898), 10; *Sinai*, March and April 1859. The founding of the *Reformverein* in 1858 is sometimes confused with the founding of the congregation. See, e.g., Sydney Ahlstrom, *A Religious History of the American People*, rev. ed. (New Haven, CT: Yale University Press, 2004), 578.

39. Letter from Gerhard Foreman and others to Samuel Adler, November 24, 1858; the original could not be located but the letter was reprinted in Bernhard Felsenthal, *Kol Kore Bamidbar: Ueber jüdische Reform—Ein Wort an die Freunde derselben* (Chicago: Chas. Heß, 1859), 33–35; see also *Sinai*, March 1859.

40. *Sinai*, June 1859, 153–55; Daniel Bluestone, *Constructing Chicago* (New Haven, CT: Yale University Press, 1991), 63–103.

41. *Israelite*, July 8, 1859 (repr. from the *Chicago Daily Democrat*). Einhorn recognized the true intentions of the Christian visitor and criticized Wise for reprinting the letter (*Sinai*, August 1859, 218).

42. Letter from David Einhorn to Bernhard Felsenthal, November 30, 1858, and January 20, 1859, Felsenthal Papers, Box 1 (Correspondence), AJHS; *Sinai*, March and April 1859.

43. Bernhard Felsenthal, *Jüdisches Schulwesen in Amerika: Ein Vortrag gehalten am 13. Dezember 1865 in der "Ramah-Loge" zu Chicago von Bernhard Felsenthal Prediger der Zionsgemeinde daselbst* (Chicago: Albert Heunisch, 1866), 36.

44. Felsenthal, *Kol Kore Bamidbar*, 25.

45. Ibid.

46. Ibid., 19–20; David Einhorn, "Felsenthal's *Kol Kore Bamidbar*," *Sinai*, May 1859, 115.

47. Felsenthal, *Kol Kore Bamidbar*, 22–23.

48. Letter from Samuel Adler to Gerhard Foreman and others, December 21, 1858, in Felsenthal, *Kol Kore Bamidbar*, 35–37; the original letter is located in Felsenthal Papers, Box 2 (miscellaneous correspondence), AJHS.

49. Felsenthal, *Kol Kore Bamidbar*, 32.

50. Meyer, *Response to Modernity*, 248.

51. Felsenthal, *Kol Kore Bamidbar*, 14–15.

52. For Wise as an Americanizer, see Sefton D. Temkin, *Isaac Mayer Wise: Shaping American Judaism* (Oxford: Littman, 1992); for Felsenthal and Einhorn as "Germanizers," see Hasia R. Diner, *A Time for Gathering: The Second Migration 1820–1880*, vol. 2 of *The Jewish People in America*, ed. Henry Feingold (Baltimore, MD: Johns Hopkins University Press, 1992), 221; on Wise's vision of a Jewish denomination, see Wilhelm, "An Ambivalent Relationship," 158.

53. Deborah Dash Moore, *B'nai B'rith and the Challenge of Ethnic Leadership* (Albany: State University of New York Press, 1981), 7; Cornelia Wilhelm, *The Independent Orders of B'nai B'rith and True Sisters: Pioneers of a New Jewish Identity, 1843–1914* (Detroit: Wayne State Press, 2011).

54. *Report of the Eighth Annual General Convention of the Independent Order B'nai B'rith* (Cincinnati, 1859), 33; Wilhelm, "An Ambivalent Relationship," 158–67.

55. *First Annual Report of the United Hebrew Relief Association of Chicago* (Chicago, 1860); Tobias Brinkmann, "'Praise upon You: The U.H.R.A.!': Jewish Philanthropy and the Origins of the First Jewish Community in Chicago 1859–1900," in *The Shaping of a Community: The Jewish Federation of Metropolitan Chicago*, ed. Rhoda Rosen (Chicago: Spertus Press, 1999), 24–39; for the term "secular kehillah," see Jonathan D. Sarna, "The Halakha According to B'nai B'rith," in *Rav Chesed: Essays in Honor of Rabbi Dr. Haskel Lookstein*, ed. R. Medoff (Jersey City: KTAV, 2009), 2:165–82.

56. For research on organized Jewish philanthropy and its impact on Jewish identity, see especially Rainer Liedtke, *Jewish Welfare in Hamburg and Manchester, c. 1850–1914* (Oxford: Oxford University Press, 1998); Derek J. Penslar, *Shylock's Children: Economics and Jewish Identity in Modern Europe* (Berkeley: University of California Press, 2001); Tobias Brinkmann, "Ethnic Difference and Civic Unity: A German-American Comparison of Jewish Communal Philanthropy in the Nineteenth Century City," in *Philanthropy, Patronage and Civil Society: Experiences from Germany, Great Britain and North America*, ed. Thomas Adam (Bloomington: Indiana University Press, 2004), 179–97; and Susan Ebert, "Community and Philanthropy," in *The Jews of Boston*, ed. Jonathan D. Sarna and Ellen Smith (Boston: Northeastern University Press, 1995), 211–37.

57. *AZ*, January 12, 1864 (emphasis added).

58. Ebert, "Community and Philanthropy," 212; Walter Ehrlich, *Zion in the Valley: The Jewish Community of St. Louis* (Columbia: University of Missouri Press, 1997), 1:220–24; Robert Rockaway, "Ethnic Conflict in an Urban Environment: the German and the Russian Jew in Detroit, 1881–1914," *AJHQ* 60 (1970/71): 133–50.

59. Brinkmann, *Von der Gemeinde*, 171.

60. Ibid., 90; *Israelite*, September 30, 1859, and June 10, 1870.

61. Cronon, *Nature's Metropolis*, 68–74; Wolfgang Schivelbusch, *The Railway Journey: The Industrialization of Time and Space* (Berkeley: University of California Press, 1987).

62. Letter from David Einhorn to Bernhard Felsenthal, June 2, 1859, Felsenthal Papers, Box 1 (correspondence), AJHS; *Israelite*, September 30, 1859; January 13, 1860 .

63. *Israelite*, January 13, 1860.

64. *Sinai*, November 1859.

65. Felsenthal, *The Beginnings of the Chicago Sinai Congregation*, 30–35.

66. *Israelite*, November 30, 1860; memorandum signed by Henry Greenebaum and Lazarus Silverman, May 1909, Sinai Papers, AJA.

67. Herman Eliassof, "Sinai's Progress: Interesting Facts from the History of the Chicago Sinai Congregation," special edition, "Jews of Illinois Number. Especially Devoted to the Dedication of the new Sinai Temple and Social Center," *RA*, March 16, 1912, 141–45; Felsenthal, *The Beginnings of the Chicago Sinai Congregation*, 30–35. On the name, see also Emil G. Hirsch, "Sinai's Half Century, A Discourse Preached April 23, 1911," *RA*, May 6, 1911.

1. E. Brooks Holifield, "Toward a History of American Congregations," in *New Perspectives in the Study of Congregations*, ed. James P. Wind and James W. Lewis, vol. 2 of *American Congregations* (Chicago: University of Chicago Press, 1994), 33–40.

2. Mary Ryan, *Civic Wars: Democracy and Public Life in the American City during the Nineteenth Century* (Berkeley: University of California Press, 1997).

3. Bertram Korn, *American Jewry and the Civil War* (Philadelphia: Jewish Publication Society, 1951), 117–19; Simon Wolf, *The American Jew as Patriot, Soldier and Citizen* (Philadelphia: Levytype, 1895), 425–47.

4. Bernhard Felsenthal, "Die Juden und die Sclaverei," *ISZ* (Chicago), June 6, 1862 (repr. in *Sinai*, July 1862, 158–63 [under its original title]); *AZ*, August 5, 1862 (without title under the rubric "Nordamerika"); Bernhard Felsenthal, "Negerrecht und Judenrecht," *ISZ*, July 9, 1862.

5. Theodore J. Karamanski, *Rally 'Round the Flag: Chicago and the Civil War* (Chicago: Nelson-Hall, 1993), 107.

6. *Chicago Times-Herald*, June 9, 1895 (on Leopold Mayer); Eugen Seeger, ed., *Die Geschichte einer Wunderstadt* (Chicago: Max Stern, 1892), 106–7, 410; Madison C. Peters, "How the Jews Won Fame as Brave Fighters During the Civil War," *Chicago Tribune*, December 27, 1908.

7. Wolf, *The American Jew as Patriot, Soldier and Citizen*, 425–26; Max J. Kohler, "Jews and the American Anti-Slavery Movement," *The Menorah* 20 (March 1896): 143–59 (esp. 158); Seeger, *Die Geschichte einer Wunderstadt*, 124; Bessie Louise Pierce, *A History of Chicago: From Town to City 1848–1871* (Chicago: University of Chicago Press, 1940), 210.

8. *Sinai*, August 1862, 200–1; *AZ*, September 2, 1862; Emma Felsenthal, *Bernhard Felsenthal: Teacher in Israel* (New York: Oxford University Press, 1924), 33–34.

9. Letter from War Department, Washington City, to B. Felsenthal, Minister of Sinai Congregation, January 10, 1863, Felsenthal Papers, Box 2 (miscellaneous correspondence), AJHS; see also Joakim Isaacs, "Ulysses Grant and the Jews," *American Jewish Archives* 17 (1965): 3–16.

10. Felsenthal, *Teacher in Israel*, 33.

11. *ISZ*, August 15, 1862.

12. Korn, *American Jewry and the Civil War*, 117.

13. *ISZ*, August 15, 1862; *Sinai*, September 1862, 232. On the number of Jews in Chicago, see Bernhard Felsenthal, "A Contribution to the History of the Israelites in Chicago," manuscript 1863, Collection Felsenthal, Bernhard, Box 130, CHM.

14. *ISZ*, August 20, 1862; repr. in *Sinai*, September 1862, 231 (the original is probably lost).

15. Michael A. Meyer, *Response to Modernity: A History of the Reform Movement in Judaism* (New York: Oxford University Press, 1988), 250; Isaac M. Fein, "Baltimore Rabbis during the Civil War," *AJHQ* 51 (1961): 67–86; Sefton D. Temkin, "Isaac Mayer Wise and the

Civil War," *American Jewish Archives* 15 (1963): 120–63; Jacob R. Marcus, *The Americaniza-tion of Isaac Mayer Wise* (Cincinnati, OH: privately printed, 1931), 10.

16. *Third Annual Report of the UHRA* (Chicago, 1862). The determined action made in-deed big news "throughout the land"—and even beyond (*Cincinnati Volksfreund*, August 16, 1862; *AZ*, October 7, 1862).

17. Hyman L. Meites, *History of the Jews of Chicago* (Chicago: Chicago Jewish Histori-cal Society, 1924), 88–89; Wolf, *The American Jew as Patriot, Soldier and Citizen*, 164; Ed-mond S. Meany, *Governors of Washington, Territorial and State* (Seattle: University of Wash-ington Press, 1915), 43–44 (Salomon served as governor of the Washington Territory from 1870–1872).

18. Quoted in Meites, *History of the Jews of Chicago*, 97.

19. See handwritten reminiscences, Henry Greenebaum Papers, 1852–1914 (CHM); Meites, *History of the Jews of Chicago*, 84; Isaac Markens, "Lincoln and the Jews," *Publications of the American Jewish Historical Society* 17 (1909), repr. in Abraham Karp, ed., *The Jewish Experience in America: Selected Studies from the Publications of the American Jewish Historical Society* (Waltham, MA: American Jewish Historical Society, 1969), 3:220–76.

20. Edward H. Mazur, *Minyans for a Prairie City: The Politics of Chicago Jewry, 1850–1940* (PhD diss., University of Chicago, 1974), 80–81; Herman Eliassof and Emil G. Hirsch, "The Jews of Illinois: Their Religious and Civic Life, their Charity and Industry, their Patriotism and Loyalty to American Institutions, from their earliest settlement in the State unto pres-ent time," *RA*, May 4, 1901, 317; Alfred Theodore Andreas, *History of Chicago: From Earliest Period to the Present Time* (Chicago: A. T. Andreas, 1884–1886), 1:573; David Ward Wood, *History of the Republican Party and Biographies of its Supporters: Illinois Volume* (Chicago: Lincoln Engraving Co., 1895), 174.

21. Walter Ehrlich, *Zion in the Valley: The Jewish Community of St. Louis* (Columbia: Uni-versity of Missouri Press, 1997), 1:56; Robert Rockaway, *The Jews of Detroit* (Detroit: Wayne State University Press, 1986), 23–24; on Cincinnati, see Jonathan D. Sarna, "'A Sort of Para-dise for the Hebrews': The Lofty Vision of Cincinnati Jews," in *Ethnic Diversity and Civic Identity: Patterns of Conflict and Cohesion in Cincinnati since 1820*, ed. Jonathan D. Sarna and Henry Shapiro (Urbana: University of Illinois Press, 1992), 148.

22. Seeger, *Die Geschichte einer Wunderstadt*, 129, 415; on Salomon as "German candi-date," see *ISZ*, November 12, 1865; *Israelite*, January 14, 1870.

23. Jonathan D. Sarna, "The 'Mythical Jew' and the 'Jew Next Door' in Nineteenth-Century America," in *Anti-Semitism in American History*, ed. David Gerber (Urbana: Uni-versity of Illinois Press, 1986), 57–70; *Chicago Tribune*, April 12, 1867.

24. Letter from David Einhorn to Bernhard Felsenthal, June 21, 1861, Felsenthal Papers, Box 1 (correspondence), AJHS.

25. On Collyer's engagement for a public library and support for the poor, see Andreas, *History of Chicago*, 2:439–40.

26. *Zeichen der Zeit* (Chicago), April 15, 1869, 60.

27. *Occident* (Philadelphia) July 1863, 188.

28. Felsenthal, *The Beginnings of the Chicago Sinai Congregation*, 35; for the map, see E. Whitefield (Creator), *Map of the Business Portion of Chicago* (Chicago: Rufus Blanchard, 1862), ICHi-27737, CHM; Felsenthal provides June 21 as the date, but this day was a Friday; the actual service was conducted on June 22, 1861. This date was also mentioned in an internal board memo in 1875 (Sinai board to members, June 20, 1875, Sinai Papers, AJA).

29. *Constitution and By-Laws of the Sinai Congregation of Chicago* (Chicago, 1861); *Hymnen gesammelt und herausgegeben auf Kosten der Sinai Gemeinde in Chicago* (Chicago, 1861); Meites, *History of the Jews of Chicago*, 97; Felsenthal, *The Beginnings of the Chicago Sinai Congregation*.

30. Jonathan D. Sarna, "Seating in the American Synagogue," in *The American Synagogue: A Sanctuary Transformed*, ed. Jack Wertheimer (Cambridge: Cambridge University Press, 1987), 363–94 (esp. 366–72).

31. *Constitution and By-Laws of the Sinai Congregation*; deed for sale of "First English Ev. Lutheran Church," on Monroe between Wells and Clark, for $1,200, April 15, 1861, Sinai Papers, AJA; Meites, *History of the Jews of Chicago*, 97.

32. Notes for a talk, handwritten by Emil G. Hirsch, probably on the occasion of Sinai's twenty-fifth anniversary celebration, May 16, 1886, Sinai Papers, AJA. Hirsch wrote, "[Sinai was] Founded under the impulse given to Reform-Judaism in America by Dr. Einhorn's 'Sinai' and called after that invaluable periodical."

33. *ISZ*, May 22, 1861 (also *AZ*, June 25, 1861); on Geiger, see Susannah Heschel, *Abraham Geiger and the Jewish Jesus* (Chicago: University of Chicago Press, 1998).

34. *Sinai*, June 1861, 135–42.

35. Letter from David Einhorn to Bernhard Felsenthal, May 31, 1861, Einhorn Papers, Box 1, Folder 2, AJA.

36. Letter from David Einhorn to Bernhard Felsenthal, June 2, 1861, and December 20, 1861, Einhorn Papers, Box 1, Folder 2, AJA.

37. Letter from David Einhorn to Bernhard Felsenthal, June 28, 1861, Einhorn Papers, Box 1, Folder 2, AJA; *Sinai*, August 1861, 228; *Sinai*, June 1861, 159, 162.

38. Felsenthal, *Teacher in Israel*, 29.

39. Letter from David Einhorn to Bernhard Felsenthal, April 24, 1864, Felsenthal Papers, Box 1 (correspondence), AJHS.

40. Rima Lunin Schultz, *The Businessman's Role in Western Settlement: the Entrepreneurial Frontier, Chicago 1833–1872* (PhD diss., Boston University, 1985), 77; Alan Silverstein, *Alternatives to Assimilation: The Response of Reform Judaism to American Culture 1840–1930* (Hanover, NH: University Press of New England, 1994), 28.

41. Felsenthal, *The Beginnings of the Chicago Sinai Congregation*, 37; Felsenthal, *Teacher in Israel*, 31–32.

42. Henry Greenebaum, A. Rubel, H. S. Rosenthal, and Bernhard Felsenthal, untitled

statement arguing for a new congregation on Chicago's West Side, July 18, 1864, Felsenthal Papers, MS-153, AJA.

43. Bernhard Felsenthal to Henry Greenebaum and others, July 21, 1864; employment contract, August 16, 1864, Felsenthal Papers, MS-153, AJA; *Inter Ocean* (Chicago), February 12, 1876; Eliassof and Hirsch, "Jews of Illinois," 340.

44. Felsenthal, *The Beginnings of the Chicago Sinai Congregation.*

45. Bernhard Felsenthal, *Jüdisches Schulwesen Amerika. Ein Vortrag, gehalten am 13. Dezember 1865 in der 'Ramah-Loge' zu Chicago von Bernhard Felsenthal, Prediger der Zionsgemeinde daselbst* (Chicago: Albert Heunisch, 1866); report of History Committee, Meeting of Executive Board, 13 April 1901, Sinai Papers, AJA. No source confirms the meeting between Schönemann and Geiger in 1865, but in 1866 Geiger asked Felsenthal in a letter how Chronik (whom he had recommended for the post) was doing (letter from Abraham Geiger to Bernhard Felsenthal, September 26, 1866, repr. in *Die Deborah, Neue Folge* 1 (1901), 213; the original is located in Felsenthal Papers, Box 2 (miscellaneous correspondence), AJHS.

46. Felsenthal, *Jüdisches Schulwesen in Amerika: Ein Vortrag gehalten am 13. Dezember 1865 in der "Ramah-Loge" zu Chicago von Bernhard Felsenthal Prediger der Zionsgemeinde daselbst (Chicago: Albert Heunisch, 1866)*, 31.

47. *New York Times*, July 16, 1865.

48. Report of History Committee, Meeting of Executive Board, April 13, 1901, Sinai Papers, AJA; David Philipson, *The Reform Movement in Judaism*, new and rev. ed. (New York: Macmillan, 1931)250–57.

49. Israel Joseph Benjamin, *Drei Jahre in Amerika 1859–1862* (Hannover: Riemschneider, 1862), 112. In 1874, Kaufmann Kohler stressed the late Geiger's "alienation towards Reform in America" (see *Gedächtniß Feier für Dr. Abraham Geiger. Chicago, den 17. November 1874* [Chicago, 1874]; see also Michael A. Meyer, "German-Jewish Identity in Nineteenth-Century America," in *Toward Modernity: The European Jewish Model*, ed. Jacob Katz [New Brunswick, NJ: Transaction, 1987], 247–67, [esp. 259]).

50. Bessie Louis Pierce, *A History of Chicago*, volume 3, *The Rise of a Modern City 1871–1893* (Chicago: University of Chicago Press, 1957), 20–24.

51. *Sinai*, June 1860, 260; *AZ*, August 21, 1860, October 30, 1860. The best biographical profile of Chronik remains the excellently researched piece by Esther Eugenie Rawidowicz, "I. L. Chronik and his *Zeichen der Zeit*," in *The Chicago Pinkas: On the Anniversary of the College of Jewish Studies*, ed. Simon Rawidowicz (Chicago: College of Jewish Studies, 1952), 137–76; see also Michael Brocke and Julius Carlebach, eds., *Biographisches Handbuch der Rabbiner, Die Rabbiner der Emanzipationszeit in den deutschen, böhmischen und großpolnischen Ländern 1781–1871*, vol. 1, part 1, comp. Carsten Wilke (Munich: Saur 2004), 231–32.

52. *Zeichen der Zeit*, August 15, 1869, 116–17; October 15, 1869, 152; the only remaining original copy of *Zeichen der Zeit* survives at the University of Maryland library at College Park.

53. *Zeichen der Zeit*, June 6, 1869, 105.

54. *ISZ*, June 16, 1867 (quote); August 4, 1867.

55. *ISZ*, December 9, 1867.

56. Andreas, *History of Chicago*, vol. 3, 830.

57. Contract between Sinai Congregation and Rosehill Cemetery, July 15, 1867, Sinai Papers, AJA; Eliassof and Hirsch, "Jews of Illinois," 323.

58. *Protokolle der Rabbiner-Conferenz abgehalten zu Philadelphia, vom 3. bis zum 6. November 1869* (New York: S. Hecht, 1870), 10, 13; for an English translation of the proceedings, see Sefton D. Temkin, *The New World of Reform* (London: Leo Baeck College, 1971); *Zeichen der Zeit*, November 15, 1869, 162; Eliassof and Hirsch, "Jews of Illinois," 323; letter from David Einhorn to Bernhard Felsenthal, February 21, 1870, Felsenthal Papers, , Box 1 (correspondence), AJHS; Meyer, *Response to Modernity*, 256–58.

59. Meites, *History of the Jews of Chicago*, 110.

60. For the broader context, see Cornelia Wilhelm, "An Ambivalent Relationship: Isaac M. Wise and the Independent Order of B'nai B'rith," in *New Essays in American Jewish History*, ed. Pamela S. Nadell, Jonathan D. Sarna, and Lance J. Sussman (Jersey City: KTAV, 2010), 155–173; Cornelia Wilhelm, *The Independent Orders of B'nai B'rith and True Sisters: Pioneers of a New Jewish Identity, 1843–1914* (Detroit: Wayne State Press, 2011); Jonathan D. Sarna, "The Halakha According to B'nai B'rith," in *Rav Chesed: Essays in Honor of Rabbi Dr. Haskel Lookstein*, ed. R. Medoff (Jersey City: KTAV, 2009), 2:165–82.

61. *Report of the Annual Meeting of the District Grand Lodge No. 2 IOBB, Held in Chicago* (Cincinnati, 1862), 11–12.

62. Ibid., 13.

63. Gary Edward Polster, *Inside Looking Out: The Cleveland Jewish Orphan Asylum 1868–1924* (Kent, OH: Kent State University Press, 1990), 6, 10–24.

64. *Proceedings of the Annual Meeting of the District Grand Lodge No. 2, Held in Milwaukee* (Cincinnati, 1867), 7–8.

65. *ISZ*, November 13, 1867; Wilhelm, "An Ambivalent Relationship," 169.

66. *Report of the Proceedings of the Constitutional Grand Lodge of the IOOB* (New York, 1865–1872).

67. *Report of the Executive Committee of the Constitutional Grand Lodge 1872/1873* (New York, 1873), 191.

68. *First Annual Report of the District Grand Lodge No. 6 IOBB and Constitution and By-Laws and Rules* (Chicago, 1869), 8–10; *AZ*, September 22, 1868 (repr. in *ISZ*).

69. For a detailed discussion of this key question, see Sarna, "The Halakha According to B'nai B'rith," 165–82; Wilhelm, *The Independent Orders of B'nai B'rith and True Sisters*.

70. Tobias Brinkmann, "Charity on Parade—Chicago's Jews and the Construction of Ethnic and Civic 'Gemeinschaft' in the 1860s," in *Celebrating Ethnicity and Nation: American Festive Culture from the Revolution to the Early Twentieth Century*, ed. Jürgen Heideking and Geneviève Fabre, (New York: Berghahn, 2001), 157–74.

71. *ISZ*, September 4, 1867; *AZ*, October 15, 1867; *Israelite*, September 13, 1867.

CHAPTER 4

1. Carl Smith, *Urban Disorder and the Shape of Belief: The Great Chicago Fire, the Haymarket Bomb and the Model Town of Pullman* (Chicago: University of Chicago Press, 1995), 22–25.

2. *Israelite*, October 20; October 27, 1871.

3. *Jewish Times* (New York), November 3, 1871; *Israelite*, October 20, 1871; Walter Ehrlich, *Zion in the Valley: The Jewish Community of St. Louis (Columbia: University of Missouri Press, 1997)*, 1:220–24; J. Jenny R. Gerstley, "My Childhood in Early Chicago," Gerstley, Biographical File, CJA.

4. Eugen Seeger and Eduard Schlaeger, *Chicago: Entwickelung, Zerstörung und Wiederaufbau der Wunderstadt* (Chicago: Max Stern, 1872), 59, 82, 92; Karen Sawislak, *Smoldering City: Chicagoans and the Great Fire, 1871–1874* (Chicago: University of Chicago Press, 1995).

5. "For Mayor, Henry Greenebaum," *Chicago Tribune*, October 21, 1871 (I am grateful to Miriam Joyce for drawing my attention to this article); *Jewish Times*, October 27, 1871; business correspondence, H. Greenebaum Papers, CHM.

6. Seeger and Schlaeger, *Chicago*, 136–37; Bernhard Felsenthal and Hermann Eliassof, *History of Kehillath Anshe Maarab: Issued under the Auspices of the Congregation on the Occasion of Its Semi-Centennial Celebration, Nov. 4, 1897* (Chicago: KAM, 1897), 49; report of board of directors of the Chicago Sinai Congregation to the members, November 19, 1871; report of board of directors of the Chicago Sinai Congregation to the members, April 21, 1872, Sinai Papers, AJA; Herman Eliassof and Emil G. Hirsch, "The Jews of Illinois: Their Religious and Civic Life, their Charity and Industry, their Patriotism and Loyalty to American Institutions, from their earliest settlement in the State unto present time," *RA*, May 4, 1901, 343.

7. Report of the board of directors of the Chicago Sinai Congregation to the members, November 19, 1871, Sinai Papers, AJA; *Chicago Tribune*, June 17, 1879.

8. Michael A. Meyer, *Response to Modernity: A History of the Reform Movement in Judaism* (New York: Oxford University Press, 1988), 270–71.

9. Sawislak, *Smoldering City*, 117–18; Smith, *Urban Disorder and the Shape of Belief*, 70–77; Kathleen D. McCarthy, *Noblesse Oblige: Charity & Cultural Philanthropy in Chicago 1849–1929* (Chicago: University of Chicago Press, 1982), 66.

10. *Jewish Times*, November 3, 1871; *Israelite*, November 24, 1871; *ISZ*, December 25, 1871; Sawislak, *Smoldering City*, 117–18.

11. Sawislak, *Smoldering City*, 225–27, 258; Smith, *Urban Disorder and the Shape of Belief*, 103–4.

12. Letter from Raphael Guthmann to Sinai, November 27, 1871; letter from Benedict Schlossman to Sinai, September 27, 1872, Sinai Papers, AJA.

13. The Home for Aged Jews of Chicago, Drexel Av. and 62nd Street, *Sixth Annual Report, May 1896–May 1897* (Chicago, 1897); record book of admissions, Home for Aged Jews Papers, CJA.

14. *Historic City: The Settlement of Chicago* (Chicago: Dept. of Development and Planning, 1976), 42–43; Janet L. Abu-Lughod, *New York, Chicago, Los Angeles: America's Global Cities* (Minneapolis: University of Minnesota Press, 1999), 51–54.

15. Ira Nelson Morris, *Heritage from My Father* (New York: privately printed, 1948), 4; Louis Wirth, *The Ghetto* (Chicago: University of Chicago Press, 1928), 173–74; Hyman L. Meites, *History of the Jews of Chicago* (Chicago: Chicago Jewish Historical Society, 1924), 133–34; Witold Rybczynski, *City Life: Urban Expectations in a New World* (New York: Scribner, 1995), 115; William Bross, *History of Chicago: What I Remember of Early Chicago* (Chicago: Jansen, McClurg & Co., 1876), 120.

16. Richard Sennett, *Families against the City: Middle Class Homes of Industrial Chicago 1872–1890* (Cambridge MA: Harvard University Press, 1970), 25–31; Ross Miller, *Here Is the Deal—The Buying and Selling of a Great American City* (New York: Knopf, 1996), 209.

17. William Cronon, *Nature's Metropolis: Chicago and the Great West* (New York: Norton, 1991), 345–46; Smith, *Urban Disorder and the Shape of Belief*; Ross Miller, *American Apocalypse: The Great Fire and the Myth of Chicago* (Chicago: University of Chicago Press, 1990); Sawislak, *Smoldering City*; Miller, *Here Is the Deal*, 209; Rybczynski, *City Life*, 115.

18. Cronon, *Nature's Metropolis*, 65–93, 280–312.

19. Bernhard Felsenthal, "The Jews of Chicago," in *Discovery and Conquest of the Northwest*, ed. Rufus Blanchard (Wheaton, IL: Blanchard and Co., 1880), 5:628–34 (quote on 631).

20. "Our Germans," *Chicago Tribune*, December 2, 1872; John Higham, *Send These To Me: Immigrants in Urban America* (Baltimore, MD: Johns Hopkins University Press, 1975), 123. On Morris, see Morris, *Heritage from My Father*, 3; Bessie Louise Pierce, *A History of Chicago*, vol. 3, *The Rise of a Modern City 1871–1893* (Chicago: University of Chicago Press, 1957), 111; U.S. Bureau of the Census, 1870, Illinois, Cook Co., Chicago, 4th Ward (Washington, DC: Bureau of the Census, 1870; *Chicago Tribune*, April 13, 1890.

21. Tobias Brinkmann, *Von der Gemeinde zur "Community": Jüdische Einwanderer in Chicago 1840–1900* (Osnabrück: Universitätsverlag Rasch, 2002), 289–90.

22. *American Israelite*, October 29, 1875.

23. Brinkmann, *Von der Gemeinde*, 287.

24. Benjamin Willem de Vries, *From Pedlars to Textile-Barons: The Economic Development of a Jewish Minority Group in the Netherlands* (Amsterdam: North-Holland, 1989); Hannelore Oberpenning, *Migration und Fernhandel im "Tödden-System": Wanderhändler aus dem nördlichen Münsterland im mittleren und nördlichen Europa* (Osnabrück: Rasch, 1996); Steven Fraser, "Combined and Uneven Development in the Men's Clothing Industry," *The Business History Review* 57 (1983), 522–47.

25. Marsha Rozenblit, "Choosing a Synagogue: The Social Composition of Two German Congregations in Nineteenth-Century Baltimore," in *The American Synagogue: A Sanctuary Transformed*, ed. Jack Wertheimer (Cambridge: Cambridge University Press, 1987), 327–62.

26. Alan Silverstein, *Alternatives to Assimilation: The Response of Reform Judaism to American Culture 1840–1930* (Hanover, NH: University Press of New England, 1994), 28.

27. Standard Club, *Articles of Incorporation, Club Annals, Officers and Directors, By-Laws, House Rules, Roster of Members* (Chicago: Standard Club, 1912).

28. "Our Germans," *Chicago Tribune*, December 2, 1872.

29. Kaufmann Kohler to the president of Sinai, November 3, 1873, Sinai Papers, AJA.

30. Simone Ladwig-Winters, *Freiheit und Bindung: Zur Geschichte der Jüdischen Reformgemeinde zu Berlin von den Anfängen bis zu ihrem Ende 1939* (Berlin: Hentrich & Hentrich, 2004), 65; David Philipson, *The Reform Movement in Judaism* (New York: Macmillan, 1931), 253–54, 374.

31. *Inter Ocean* (Chicago), August 22, 1873.

32. Eliassof and Hirsch, "Jews of Illinois," 324; letters from David Einhorn to Kaufmann Kohler, January 21, 1872, February 25, 1872, August 28, 1873, and January 23, 1874, Einhorn Papers, Box 1, Folder 3, AJA.

33. Letter from Kaufmann Kohler to the president of Sinai, December 1, 1873, Sinai Papers, AJA (original emphasis).

34. Signature list, December 3, 1873, Sinai Papers, AJA.

35. Signature list, December 18, 1873, Sinai Papers, AJA.

36. Esther Eugenie Rawidowicz, "I. L. Chronik and his *Zeichen der Zeit*," in *The Chicago Pinkas: On the Anniversary of the College of Jewish Studies*, ed. Simon Rawidowicz (Chicago: College of Jewish Studies, 1952) 146–47; see also the obituary (with "Sinai" misspelled and wrong dates) in *AZ*, January 29, 1884; Silverstein, *Alternatives to Assimilation*, 28.

37. Karla Goldman, *Beyond the Synagogue Gallery: Finding a Place for Women in American Judaism* (Cambridge, MA: Harvard University Press, 2000), 121–29; Brinkmann, *Von der Gemeinde*, 432–34; Daniel Bluestone, *Constructing Chicago* (New Haven, CT: Yale University Press, 1991), 79.

38. Most scholars provide a different date: January 15, 1874. The reason for this mistake is the celebration of the twenty-fifth anniversary of the introduction of Sunday services on January 15, 1899. January 15, 1874, actually fell on a Thursday.

39. Report, President Loewenthal, March 29, 1874, Sinai Papers, AJA; Goldman, *Beyond the Synagogue Gallery*, 163.

40. *Inter Ocean* (Chicago), April 26, 1874 (repr. from the *American Israelite*).

41. *Jewish Times*, April 17, 1874; Kerry Marc Olitzky, "The Sunday-Sabbath Controversy" (rabbinical Thesis Hebrew Union College, Cincinnati, 1981), 29; *American Israelite*, April 3, May 1, 1874; Meyer, *Response to Modernity*, 255.

42. Meyer, *Response to Modernity*, 291.

43. Felsenthal and Eliassof, *History of Kehillath Anshe Maarab*, 49.

44. *Annual Report of M. M. Gerstley, President of Kehilath Anshe Mayriv, to the Congregation, Chicago, August 16th, 1874* (Chicago: Max Stern, 1874).

45. Sinai board to members, November 19, 1874, Sinai Papers, AJA; Eliassof and Hirsch, "Jews of Illinois," 325.

46. *Gedächtniß—Feier für Dr. Abraham Geiger. Chicago, den 17. November 1874* (Chicago, 1874).

47. Quoted in Silverstein, *Alternatives to Assimilation*, 44–45; Meyer, *Response to Modernity*, 260–61; Annual report of the board to the members, September 11, 1873, Sinai Papers, AJA; Morton M. Berman, *Our First Century 1852–1952: Temple Isaiah Israel* (Chicago: Temple Isaiah Israel, 1952), 16–18; Eliassof and Hirsch, "Jews of Illinois," 294.

48. Letter from R. Rubel and Albert Felsenthal to the Board of Representatives of the Jewish Congregations in Cincinnati, June 29, 1873, Sinai Papers, AJA.

49. Letter from Moritz Loth to Berthold Loewenthal, August 2, 1874, Sinai Papers, AJA.

50. Report by Sinai board to members, June 20, 1875, Sinai Papers, AJA.

51. Written address from Sinai president [Loewenthal] to members, April 18, 1875, Sinai Papers, AJA.

CHAPTER 5

1. *Annual Report of M. M. Gerstley, President of Kehilath Anshe Mayriv, to the Congregation, Chicago, August 16th, 1874* (Chicago: Max Stern, 1874).

2. *Annual Report of M. M. Gerstley*; *Israelite*, March 15, 1872, and November 5, 1875; Bernhard Felsenthal and Hermann Eliassof, *History of Kehillath Anshe Maarab: Issued under the Auspices of the Congregation on the Occasion of Its Semi-Centennial Celebration, Nov. 4, 1897* (Chicago: KAM, 1897), 43.

3. Daniel Bluestone, *Constructing Chicago* (New Haven, CT: Yale University Press, 1991), 95.

4. Letter from Kaufmann Kohler to President Snydacker, October 21, 1877, Kohler Papers, MS-29, Box 1, Folder 4, AJA.

5. *AZ*, January 7, 1879.

6. David Kaufman, *Shul with a Pool: The "Synagogue-Center" in American Jewish History* (Hanover, NH: University Press of New England, 1999), 13–14; Leon A. Jick, "The Reform Synagogue," in *The American Synagogue: A Sanctuary Transformed*, ed. Jack Wertheimer (Cambridge: Cambridge University Press, 1987), 85–110 (esp. 92).

7. *Inter Ocean*, June 21, 1879.

8. Kaufmann Kohler, "Morality," *Chicago Tribune*, February 19, 1877.

9. "A Notable Wedding," *Inter Ocean*, June 21, 1877.

10. Benny Kraut, *From Reform Judaism to Ethical Culture: The Religious Evolution of Felix Adler* (Cincinnati, OH: Hebrew Union College Press, 1979), 154–65.

11. *American Israelite*, June 25, 1875; *Nineteenth Annual Report of the Executive Board of the United Hebrew Relief Association For the Year 1877–1878* (Chicago: Rubovits, 1878), 5–8 ("Jewish boys of tender age can be seen on our streets and in immoral quarters engaged in peddling matches . . . and in similar more vicious employments" [8]).

12. Kaufman, *Shul with a Pool*, 56–68.

13. *Israelite*, March 9, 1866.

14. *American Israelite*, November 16, December 21, and December 28, 1877, and March 1, 1878 (quote); semi-annual report, March 21, 1877, Sinai Papers, AJA.

15. Minutes of Sinai Literary Society 1877/78, CHM; *Occident* (Chicago), November 22, 1878; *ISZ*, March 23, 1878.

16. "Dr. Adler: The Sinai Literary Association," *Chicago Tribune*, March 21, 1878; Kaufmann Kohler, "Dr. Felix Adler," *Chicago Tribune*, March 22, 1878.

17. Kraut, *From Reform Judaism to Ethical Culture*.

18. Quoted in Kraut, *From Reform Judaism to Ethical Culture*, 109; Michael A. Meyer, *Response to Modernity: A History of the Reform Movement in Judaism* (New York: Oxford University Press, 1988), 265–66. On living conditions on the Lower East Side during the 1870s, see Dorothee Schneider, *Trade Unions and Community: the German Working Class in New York City 1870–1900* (Urbana: University of Illinois Press, 1994), 11–16.

19. Sydney Ahlstrom, *A Religious History of the American People*, rev. ed. (New Haven, CT: Yale University Press, 2004), 744–45, 779–85 ("the liberals led the Protestant churches into the world of modern science, scholarship, philosophy, and global knowledge" [783]); on Collyer's call to suppress workers' protests by force, see Carl Smith, *Urban Disorder and the Shape of Belief: The Great Chicago Fire, the Haymarket Bomb and the Model Town of Pullman* (Chicago: University of Chicago Press, 1995), 108–9.

20. Bluestone, *Constructing Chicago*, 101–3; *American Israelite*, November 5, 1875; Alfred Theodore Andreas, *History of Chicago: From Earliest Period to the Present Time* (Chicago: A. T. Andreas, 1884–1886), 3:827–28: Smith, *Urban Disorder and the Shape of Belief*, 349; Martin Marty, "Protestants," in *Encyclopedia of Chicago*, ed. James Grossman, Janice L. Reiff, and Ann Durkin Keating (Chicago: University of Chicago Press, 2004), 652–55.

21. Kraut, *From Reform Judaism to Ethical Culture*, 114–23; Meyer, *Response to Modernity*, 265–66; Kaufmann Kohler, "Dr. Felix Adler," *Chicago Tribune*, March 22, 1878.

22. Kohler, "Dr. Felix Adler."

23. *ISZ*, March 23, 1878.

24. For reprinted letters from the *Tribune* and *Staatszeitung*, see "A Newspaper Controversy," *American Israelite*, April 12, 1878. The page with the reprinted letters was recently digitized by the American Jewish Archives, see http://americanjewisharchives.org/wise/attachment/3988/TIS-1878-04-12-001.pdf (accessed August 22, 2011).

25. Julius Rosenthal, "Dr. Felix Adler," *Chicago Tribune*, March 23, 1878.

26. *American Israelite*, April 12, 1878 (repr. from *Chicago Tribune*).

27. "Dr. Kohler has had his revenge; he has abused me in the press and privately; he abused his pulpit on yesterday by heaping personal abuse and insults on me; he has abused our youth publicly . . . he has abused Dr. Felix Adler in a shameful manner" (Julius Rosenthal, "IV Document. Julius Rosenthal's Reply to the above," in "A Newspaper Controversy," *American Israelite*, April 12, 1878).

28. *ISZ*, March 28, 1878, see also for the original English version of the speech: "Dr. Felix Adler on the Advance of Liberalism in This Country," *Chicago Tribune*, March 27, 1878.

29. *Jewish Advance*, January 3, 1879.

30. Meyer, *Response to Modernity*, 267–68; Jonathan D. Sarna, "Converts to Zionism in the American Reform Movement," in *Zionism and Religion*, ed. Shmuel Almog, Jehuda Reinharz, and Anita Shapira (Hanover, NH: University Press of New England, 1998), 188–203 (esp. 193).

31. Bernhard Felsenthal, *Zur Proselytenfrage im Judenthum* (Chicago: Rubovits/Breslau; E. Franck, 1878), 29–34; Kaufmann Kohler, "Religion und Race," *ISZ*, September 10 and September 12, 1878; Felsenthal, "Jüdische Nationalität," *ISZ*, March 24, 1877; Felsenthal, "Religion und Race," *ISZ*, September 11, 1878.

32. Minutes of Sinai Literary Society 1877/78, April 22, 1878, CHM; *Jewish Advance*, February 21, 1879.

33. Letter from Kaufmann Kohler to the President of Sinai, June 9, 1879, Sinai Papers.

34. Report by president and board, 1879 [no precise date], Sinai Papers, AJA.

35. "Two Sundays," *Chicago Tribune*, June 17, 1879.

36. Gerson B. Levi, introduction to *My Religion* by Emil G. Hirsch (New York: Macmillan, 1925), 11, 23; David Einhorn Hirsch, *Rabbi Emil G. Hirsch, The Reform Advocate* (Chicago: Whitehall Company, 1968); *RA*, May 21, 1921 (special issue on the occasion of Emil Hirsch's seventieth birthday). See especially the addresses by Hirsch's fellow students at the Hochschule, Samuel Sale and Emanuel Schreiber, on pages 376 and 381, respectively. Frank H. Vizetelly, "Emil G. Hirsch," *Jewish Encyclopedia*, ed. Isidore Singer (New York: Funk and Wagnalls, 1901–1906), 6:410; Anja Becker and Tobias Brinkmann, "Transatlantische Bildungsmigration: Amerikanisch-jüdische Studenten an der Universität Leipzig 1872 bis 1914," *Leipziger Beiträge zur jüdischen Geschichte und Kultur* 4 (2006): 61–98.

37. Minutes from special meeting, February 19, 1880, Sinai Papers, AJA; Meyer, *Response to Modernity*, 262–63.

38. William Clark, *Academic Charisma and the Origins of the Research University* (Chicago: University of Chicago Press, 2006), 449–52, 462–66.

39. Becker and Brinkmann, "Transatlantische Bildungsmigration," 61–98; Kaufmann Kohler, "Obituary of Emil G. Hirsch," *Central Conference of American Rabbis Yearbook* 33 (1923): 145–55. Hirsch often praised the German university system: see *Occident* (Chicago), September 27, 1889.

40. Letter from Emil G. Hirsch to Godfrey Snydacker, July 6, 1880, Sinai Papers, AJA.

41. Minutes from special meeting, February 19, 1880, Sinai Papers, AJA.

42. *Occident* (Chicago), November 21, 1879.

43. Among the men who preached repeatedly at Sinai after Kohler's departure was Henry Gersoni, a reform-minded publicist from the Russian Empire who edited the *Jewish Advance*, a short-lived German- and English-language weekly in Chicago. See Jacob Kabakoff,

Halutzei ha-Sifrut ha-Ivrit ba-Amerikah (Tel Aviv and Cleveland, 1966), 82–84, 92–95 (in Hebrew); Tobias Brinkmann, *Von der Gemeinde zur "Community": Jüdische Einwanderer in Chicago 1840–1900* (Osnabrück: Universitätsverlag Rasch, 2002), 333–34.

CHAPTER 6

1. Arthur Ruppin, *Soziologie der Juden* (Berlin: Jüdischer Verlag, 1930), 1:126; Jonathan D. Sarna, ed., *The American Jewish Experience* (New York: Holmes & Meier, 1986), 296.

2. For a remarkable assessment by Hirsch see his speech on the occasion of the twenty-fifth anniversary of the founding of Zion congregation, see *Occident* (Chicago), September 27, 1889.

3. Michael A. Meyer, *Response to Modernity: A History of the Reform Movement in Judaism* (New York: Oxford University Press, 1988), 264–95.

4. Thomas Philpott, *The Slum and the Ghetto: Neighborhood Deterioration and Middle-Class Reform, Chicago, 1880–1930* (Oxford: Oxford University Press, 1978), 8; Witold Rybczynski, *City Life: Urban Expectations in a New World* (New York: Scribner, 1995), 110–15; Neil Harris, ed., *Grand Illusions: Chicago's World's Fair of 1893* (Chicago: Chicago Historical Society, 1993); Bessie Louise Pierce, *A History of Chicago: From Town to City 1848–1871* (Chicago: University of Chicago Press, 1940), 481–82; Bessie Louise Pierce, *A History of Chicago: The Rise of a Modern City 1871–1893* (Chicago: University of Chicago Press, 1957), 515–16.

5. Hyman L. Meites, *History of the Jews of Chicago* (Chicago: Chicago Jewish Historical Society, 1924), 141, 162–63; *The South Shore Temple Year Book 1926* (Chicago: South Shore Temple, 1926), 21.

6. *The Crossing of the Jordan: Inaugural Sermon before the Sinai Congregation by the Rev. Dr. E.G.,[sic] Hirsch, Chicago, September 5th, 1880* (Chicago, 1880).

7. Annual reports, April 4, 1881, March 20, 1882, April 1, 1885, and March 31, 1886; minutes of special meeting, August 24, 1880 (draft contract with the new rabbi discussed), Sinai Papers, AJA.

8. Alan Silverstein, *Alternatives to Assimilation: The Response of Reform Judaism to American Culture 1840–1930* (Hanover, NH: University Press of New England, 1994), 212. Gottheil had briefly served the Berlin Reform Temple in the late 1850s as an assistant to Holdheim before moving to a congregation in Manchester, England; in 1873, he accepted the position as successor of Samuel Adler at Temple Emanu-El (see Richard Gottheil, *The Life of Gustav Gottheil: Memoir of a Priest in Israel* [Williamsport, PA: Bayard Press, 1936], 6–39.

9. "American Hebrew Congregations," *New York Times*, July 13, 1881.

10. *Occident* (Chicago), January 27, 1882. On Herman Felsenthal, see *New York Times*, September 4, 1899 (obituary).

11. *Occident* (Chicago), January 27, 1882; Talmud, Berachot 61b.

12. *Occident* (Chicago), January 27, April 28, and October 6, 1882; *Chicago Times*, September 27, 1882.

13. Emil Hirsch, "Reformed Judaism, A Discourse Delivered in 1882, Before Sinai Congregation," *Occident* (Chicago), February 23 and March 2, 1883 (original emphasis); on the hospital, see diary of the superintendent of the Michael Reese Hospital, United Hebrew Relief Association Chicago; 1883–1887, CJA; Herman Eliassof and Emil G. Hirsch, "The Jews of Illinois: Their Religious and Civic Life, their Charity and Industry, their Patriotism and Loyalty to American Institutions, from their earliest settlement in the State unto present time," *RA*, May 4, 1901, 309.

14. Letters from Emil G. Hirsch to the board, March 2, 1883; March 27, 1883, Sinai Papers, AJA.

15. *Occident* (Chicago), June 1, 1883; see also the June 8, 1883 edition.

16. *Occident* (Chicago), August 3, September 14, and October 5, 1883; for an overview, see Bernhard Felsenthal and Hermann Eliassof, *History of Kehillath Anshe Maarab: Issued under the Auspices of the Congregation on the Occasion of Its Semi-Centennial Celebration, Nov. 4, 1897* (Chicago: KAM, 1897).

17. *Occident* (Chicago), April 14, 1882, and December 14, 1883 ("You must take me with all my faults"). See, for instance, letter from S. Rosenbaum to Joseph Gatzert, March 26, 1889 (resigned because of "ungentlemanly conduct of Rev. Dr. Hirsch"), Sinai Papers, AJA. David Philipson, *My Life as an American Jew: An Autobiography* (Cincinnati, OH: John G. Kidd & Son, 1941), 87–89.

18. *Occident* (Chicago), November 9 and November 16, 1883; Emil G. Hirsch, "Luther as a Man: His Strength and His Weakness," *Chicago Tribune*, November 12, 1883.

19. Emil G. Hirsch, "Deutsches Judenthum," in *Chicago: Die Geschichte einer Wunderstadt*, ed. Eugen Seeger (Chicago: privately printed, 1892), 397–401 (original emphasis) (esp. 400).

20. *Occident* (Chicago), October 26, 1883.

21. *RA*, May 29, 1897; Emil G. Hirsch, *Ethical Materialism: A Discussion Before the Sinai Congregation* (Chicago: Rubovits, 1888); Emil G. Hirsch, *Mediaeval Civilization: Synopsis of a Discourse delivered before the Chicago Sinai Congregation by Rev. Dr. E. G. Hirsch* (Chicago: Occident, 1883); Tobias Brinkmann, *Von der Gemeinde zur "Community": Jüdische Einwanderer in Chicago 1840–1900* (Osnabrück: Universitätsverlag Rasch, 2002), 412–13. Hirsch joined the board of the UHRA in 1886 (*28th Annual Report of the UHRA 1886/87* [Chicago, 1887]).

22. *Occident* (Chicago), June 8, 1883.

23. Benny Kraut, "A Unitarian Rabbi? The Case of Solomon H. Sonneschein," in *Jewish Apostasy in the Modern World*, ed. Todd Endelman (New York: Holmes & Meier, 1987), 272–308; *Inter Ocean*, November 16, 1887; Karla Goldman and Jonathan D. Sarna, "From Synagogue-Community to Citadel of Reform: The History of K. K. Bene Israel (Rockdale Temple) in Cincinnati, Ohio," in *Portraits of Twelve Religious Communities*, ed. James P. Wind and James W. Lewis, vol. 1 of *American Congregations* (Chicago: University of Chicago Press, 1994), 180–83.

24. Meyer, *Response to Modernity*, 267.

25. Ibid.; Emil G. Hirsch, *Reform Judaism—Discourse at the Celebration of Dr. Samuel Hirsch's 70th Anniversary Delivered by His Son, the Rabbi of Chicago Sinai Congregation* (Philadelphia, 1885), 6, 7, 10, 15 (original emphasis); *New York Times*, June 28 and July 12, 1885.

26. David Philipson, "The Pittsburg Platform," *Central Conference of American Rabbis Yearbook* 45 (1935): 3; see also *Occident* (Chicago), July 17, 1885, November 13, 1885, and February 11, 1887; Meyer, *Response to Modernity*, 235–244, 262, 290; David Kaufman, *Shul with a Pool: The "Synagogue-Center" in American Jewish History* (Hanover, NH: University Press of New England, 1999), 10–50; Eliassof and Hirsch, "Jews of Illinois," 294.

27. Emil G. Hirsch, "The Antithesis between Race and Religion," *Occident* (Chicago), November 6, 1885.

28. Eric Goldstein, *The Price of Whiteness: Jews, Race, and American Identity* (Princeton: Princeton University Press 2006), 26–31.

29. "Jew and Catholic United," *New York Times*, June 25, 1888; for a marriage between a formerly Presbyterian woman and a male member of Sinai, see *Chicago Tribune*, March 13, 1899.

30. Kaufman, *Shul with a Pool*, 16; *Occident* (Chicago), October 12, 1883, November 8, 1889, and June 13, 1890; Meyer, *Response to Modernity*, 269.

31. Emil G. Hirsch, *The Jew and the Greek—A Discourse before Sinai Congregation, December 2nd, 1888* (Chicago: Chicago Sinai Congregation, 1888).

32. Emil G. Hirsch, "Darwin und der Darwinismus," *Der Zeitgeist*, June 22, 1882; Hirsch, "Phrasen," *Der Zeitgeist*, November 23, 1882; Hirsch, "Evolution," in *Jewish Encyclopedia*, ed. Isidore Singer (New York: Funk and Wagnalls, 1901), 5:281–82; Meyer, *Response to Modernity*, 274. For background, see essays in Geoffrey Cantor and Marc Swetlitz, eds., *Jewish Tradition and the Challenge of Darwinism*, (Chicago: University of Chicago Press, 2006).

33. *Occident* (Chicago), December 15, 1882; Bernard Martin, "The Religious Philosophy of Emil G. Hirsch," *American Jewish Archives* 4 (1952): 66–82; Meyer, *Response to Modernity*, 275. In 1885, Hirsch declared, "the overgrown Man-God must go" (*Occident* [Chicago], September 4, 1885).

34. Quoted in Benny Kraut, *From Reform Judaism to Ethical Culture: The Religious Evolution of Felix Adler* (Cincinnati, OH: Hebrew Union College Press, 1979), 225.

35. *Occident* (Chicago), March 27, 1885; see also letter from Berthold Loewenthal to members, March 27, 1885, Sinai Papers, AJA (original emphasis).

36. Letter from Emil G. Hirsch to Berthold Loewenthal, April 6 and 7, 1885, and letter from Berthold Loewenthal to Emil G. Hirsch, April 8, 1885, Sinai Papers, AJA (original emphasis).

37. *Extract From Proceedings of Chicago Sinai Congregation at Annual Meeting, March 26th, 1885, and Special Meeting, April 9th, 1885* (Chicago: Max Stern, 1885); for a German Jewish report accusing Sinai of "almost abolishing Judaism," see *AZ*, July 28, 1885.

38. Minutes, April 9, 1885, Sinai Papers, AJA.

39. Letter from Emil G. Hirsch to board, March 25, 1886, Sinai Papers, AJA.

40. Emil G. Hirsch, "The Antithesis between Race and Religion," *Occident* (Chicago), November 6, 1885 (original emphasis).

41. *Occident* (Chicago), June 15, 1883 (Rosenthal becomes member), and December 18, 1885. See also Society of Ethical Culture of Chicago, Preamble and Constitution, Ethical Humanist Society of Chicago Papers; Box II-11; minutes of meetings, Board of Trustees, October 5, 1882–November 10, 1892, Box I-1, University of Illinois, Chicago, Library, Historical Collections; Stanton Coit, introduction to *Ethical Religion* by William Mackintire Salter (London: Watts, 1905), 8.

42. Kerry Marc Olitzky, "The Sunday-Sabbath Controversy" (rabbinical thesis, Hebrew Union College, 1981), 56–57; for an overview of Sunday services, see *Inter Ocean*, November 16, 1887; on Cleveland, see *Inter Ocean*, December 31, 1888; on San Francisco, see Fred Rosenbaum, *Visions of Reform: Congregation Emanu-El and the Jews of San Francisco 1849–1999* (San Francisco: Judah L. Magnes Museum, 2000), 84; on the Zion congregation, see *Occident* (Chicago), April 16, 1886; Goldman and Sarna, "From Synagogue-Community to Citadel of Reform," 180–83; Leon A. Jick, "The Reform Synagogue," in *The American Synagogue: A Sanctuary Transformed*, ed. Jack Wertheimer (Cambridge: Cambridge University Press, 1987), 91.

43. Meyer, *Response to Modernity*, 265–69 (quote on 265).

44. Quoted in Meyer, *Response to Modernity*, 388; Silverstein, *Alternatives to Assimilation*, 129.

45. *Proceedings of the Pittsburg Rabbinical Conference, November 16, 17, 18, 1885, Published by the Central Conference of American Rabbis in Honor of the Eightieth Anniversary of the Birth of Rabbi Kaufmann Kohler* (Richmond, VA, 1923), 23; for background, see Meyer, *Response to Modernity*, 265–70; Robert Southard, "The Theologian of the 1885 Pittsburgh Platform: Kaufmann Kohler's Vision of Progressive Judaism," in *Platforms and Prayer Books: Theological and Liturgical Perspectives on Reform Judaism*, ed. Dana Evan Kaplan and Ellen Umansky (New York: Rowman and Littlefield, 2002), 61–78.

46. *Occident* (Chicago), November 26, 1885 (repr. from *Inter Ocean*); Rosenthal said, "The basis of our present civilization is corrupted, for it is nothing else than selfishness and individualism, upon which the present state of social life is built."

47. Goldstein, *The Price of Whiteness*, 29; *Proceedings of the Pittsburg Rabbinical Conference*, 30, 34, 36, 38, 39.

48. *Occident* (Chicago), May 21, 1886. Loewenthal was not exaggerating; according to the German Jewish *AZ*, Sinai's reforms were widely condemned. In a satirical article one of its editors compared Sinai's rabbis with the most radical leaders of the French Revolution (*AZ*, June 29, 1886).

49. Carl Smith, *Urban Disorder and the Shape of Belief: The Great Chicago Fire, the Haymarket Bomb and the Model Town of Pullman* (Chicago: University of Chicago Press, 1995), 101–76; *Inter Ocean*, November 7, 1887; *New York Times*, November 6 and 14, 1887; Irving

Cutler, *The Jews of Chicago: From Shtetl to Suburb* (Urbana, IL: University of Illinois Press, 1996), 55; for background, see Paul Avrich, *The Haymarket Tragedy* (Princeton, NJ: Princeton University Press, 1984).

50. For further information see Schmidt's papers: Collection Ernst Schmidt, CHM; *RA*, September 8, 1900; see also Axel W.-O. Schmidt, *Der Rothe Doktor von Chicago: Ein Deutsch-Amerikanisches Auswandererschicksal: Biographie des Dr. Ernst Schmidt, 1830–1900, Arzt und Sozialrevolutionär* (Frankfurt am Main: Peter Lang, 2003).

CHAPTER 7

1. Hyman L. Meites, *History of the Jews of Chicago* (Chicago: Chicago Jewish Historical Society, 1924), 430 (list of Jewish trustees of the Chicago Public Library); *First Annual Report of the Board of Directors of the Chicago Public Library* (Chicago: Lakeside, 1873), 10; see also *Twenty-Sixth Annual Report of the Board of Directors of the Chicago Public Library* (Chicago: Chicago Public Library, 1898) for a list of all board members from 1872–1873 to 1898.

2. "Dr. Emil G. Hirsch Speaks," *Chicago Tribune*, October 10, 1897.

3. Board of the United Hebrew Charities, "Forty Years of the United Hebrew Relief Association of Chicago and the United Hebrew Charities of Chicago, October, 1859—October, 1899," *Eleventh Annual Report of the United Hebrew Charities of Chicago for the Year 1898/99* (Chicago: Ettlinger, 1899), appendix pp. 1–4; *Twenty-Ninth Annual Report of the United Hebrew Relief Association of Chicago 1887/88* (Chicago: Ettlinger, 1888), 5–17; Herman Eliassof and Emil G. Hirsch, "The Jews of Illinois: Their Religious and Civic Life, their Charity and Industry, their Patriotism and Loyalty to American Institutions, from their earliest settlement in the State unto present time," *RA*, May 4, 1901, 316; obituary of Isaac Greensfelder, *Chicago Tribune*, November 15, 1913.

4. Yaakov Ariel, "Miss Daisy's Planet: The Strange World of Reform Judaism in the United States 1870–1930," in *Platforms and Prayer Books: Theological and Liturgical Perspectives on Reform Judaism*, eds. Dana Evan Kaplan, Ellen Umansky (New York: Rowman and Littlefield, 2002), 49–60.

5. Standard Club, *Articles of Incorporation, Club Annals, Officers and Directors, By-Laws, House Rules, Roster of Members* (Chicago: Standard Club, 1912); obituary of Julius Rosenthal, *Chicago Legal News*, May 21, 1905.

6. *Inter Ocean*, June 21, 1877; *Occident* (Chicago), March 17, 1882.

7. Alan Silverstein, *Alternatives to Assimilation: The Response of Reform Judaism to American Culture 1840–1930* (Hanover, NH: University Press of New England, 1994), 102; on ethnic leadership, see Victor R. Greene, *American Immigrant Leaders 1800–1910: Marginality and Identity* (Baltimore, MD: Johns Hopkins University Press, 1987).

8. Paul Boyer, *Urban Masses and Moral Order in America 1820–1920* (Cambridge, MA: Harvard University Press, 1978), 143–55.

9. Kathleen D. McCarthy, *Noblesse Oblige: Charity & Cultural Philanthropy in Chicago 1849–1929* (Chicago: University of Chicago Press, 1982), 106–7.

10. *First Annual Report of the United Hebrew Charities of Chicago for the Year 1888–89* (Chicago: Ettlinger, 1889).

11. Letter from Julian Mack to Bella Freund, in minutes of the UHC, Vol. 1; June 6, 1894, CJA; Brinkmann, "'Praise upon you: The U.H.R.A.!'," 24–39.

12. McCarthy, *Noblesse Oblige*, 108–11; Rivka Lissak, *Pluralism & Progressives: Hull House and the New Immigrants, 1890–1919* (Chicago: University of Chicago Press, 1989), 1–24. Hirsch is mentioned in passing by Louise W. Knight, *Citizen: Jane Addams and the Struggle for Democracy* (Chicago: University of Chicago Press, 2005). Hirsch and other Jewish members of the circle are not mentioned by Jean Bethke Elshtain, *Jane Addams and the Dream of American Democracy: A Life* (New York: Basic Books, 2002).

13. Hirsch and Eliassof, "Jews of Illinois," 361; Charles Zeublin, "The Chicago Ghetto," in *Hull House Maps and Papers: A Presentation of Nationalities and Wages in a Congested District of Chicago*, ed. Residents of Hull House (New York: T. Y. Crowell, 1895), 91–111 (quote on 100); Philip P. Bregstone, *Chicago and Its Jews: A Cultural History* (Chicago: privately printed, 1933), 49; *Chicago Tribune*, November 15, 1916 (on Maxwell Street Settlement).

14. Thomas Wakefield Goodspeed, *A History of the University of Chicago—The First Quarter-Century* (Chicago: University of Chicago Press, 1916), vii–viii, 87; William M. Murphy and D. J. R. Bruckner, eds., *The Idea of the University of Chicago—Selections from the Papers of the First Eight Chief Executives of the University of Chicago from 1891 to 1975* (Chicago: University of Chicago Press, 1976), 7; Richard J. Storr, *Harper's University: The Beginnings. A History of the University of Chicago* (Chicago: University of Chicago Press, 1966), 39–42, 234; Steven J. Diner, *A City and Its Universities: Public Policy in Chicago, 1892–1919* (Chapel Hill: University of North Carolina Press, 1980), 15; obituary of Eli B. Felsenthal, *New York Times*, December 3, 1937; communication on acquisition of Semitic library, May 5, 1893, Sinai Papers, AJA; Peter M. Ascoli, *Julius Rosenwald: The Man Who Built Sears, Roebuck and Advanced the Cause of Black Education in the American South* (Bloomington: Indiana University Press, 2006), 55.

15. *RA*, May 4, 1901.

16. McCarthy, *Noblesse Oblige*, 129; Boyer, *Urban Masses*, 164; Diner, *A City and Its Universities*, 69; "To Feed the Hungry," *Chicago Tribune*, December 10, 1893 (founding of Civic Federation); "Cash to Crush Fraud," *Chicago Tribune*, November 13, 1894 (contains Hirsch's speech); "Nathan in Bakers' Seat," *Chicago Tribune*, April 23, 1897 (Nathan elected president); *New York Times*, January 27, 1927 (obituary of Lyman Gage).

17. Carl Smith, *Urban Disorder and the Shape of Belief: The Great Chicago Fire, the Haymarket Bomb and the Model Town of Pullman (Chicago: University of Chicago Press, 1995)*, 200–31.

18. Hannah Solomon, *Fabric of My Life* (New York: Bloch, 1946), 93; Papers of Rose Haas Altschuler, CJA.

19. *Twenty Fourth Annual Report of the United Hebrew Relief Association of Chicago*

1882/83 (Chicago: Ettlinger, 1884); Emil G. Hirsch, "Was nun?" [What now?], *Der Zeitgeist*, July 20, 1882.

20. Hirsch, "Back to the Soil," *RA*, October 3, 1903.

21. "Send them to Palestine," *Chicago Tribune*, February 16, 1891; "Our Russian Exiles," *Chicago Tribune*, July 19, 1891 ; "In Chicago's Ghetto," *Chicago Tribune*, February 2, 1896; *RA*, March 1, 1902.

22. Peter Pulzer, *The Rise of Political Anti-Semitism in Germany & Austria*, rev. ed. (Cambridge, MA: Harvard University Press, 1988), 27–70.

23. K. L., "The Jewish Problem in the World's Fair City," *RA*, April 8, 1893.

24. Hasia R. Diner, *A Time for Gathering: The Second Migration 1820–1880*, vol. 2 of *The Jewish People in America*, ed. Henry Feingold (Baltimore, MD: Johns Hopkins University Press, 1992), 191–93; Daniel J. Tichenor, *Dividing Lines. The Politics of Immigration Control in America* (Princeton, NJ: Princeton University Press, 2002), 114–49; Moses Rischin, *The Promised City: New York's Jews 1870–1914* (Cambridge, MA: Harvard University Press, 1962), 95–98.

25. *Ninth Annual Report of the UHC* 1896/97 (Chicago: Ettlinger, 1897), 7; Zeublin, "The Chicago Ghetto," 91–111 (quotes on 94, 96, 103, 105, 110); on background, see Kathryn Sklar Kish, "Hull House Maps and Papers: Social Science as Women's Work in the 1890s," in *The Social Survey in Historical Perspective 1880–1940*, ed. Martin Bulmer, Kevin Bales, and Kathryn Sklar Kish (Cambridge: Cambridge University Press, 1991), 111–47.

26. *RA*, April 14, 1894 (original emphasis).

27. Emil G. Hirsch, "A Great Danger," *RA*, April 13, 1895.

28. *RA*, August 30, 1902.

29. *Sixth Annual Report of the UHC 1893/94* (Chicago, 1894).

30. *RA*, October 7, 1899.

31. *First Annual Report of the Jewish Training School* (Chicago: Ettlinger, 1890), 8.

32. Smith, *Urban Disorder and the Shape of Belief*, 201.

33. Derek J. Penslar, *Shylock's Children: Economics and Jewish Identity in Modern Europe* (Berkeley: University of California Press, 2001), 117–18.

34. Tobias Brinkmann, "Between Vision and Reality: Reassessing Jewish Agricultural Colony Projects in 19th Century America," *Jewish History* 21 (2007): 305–24.

35. Meites, *History of the Jews of Chicago*, 586.

36. Minutes of the Jewish Industrial School, 1882–1890, November 18, 1882, AJA.

37. *Occident* (Chicago), October 1, 1886 (quote) and October 22, 1886; minutes of the Jewish Industrial School, April 29, 1887, AJA; Felix Adler, "A New Experiment in Education," *Princeton Review* 1 (1883), 143–57; Morris Gutstein, *A Priceless Heritage: The Epic Growth of Nineteenth Century Chicago Jewry* (New York: Bloch, 1953), 253; McCarthy, *Noblesse Oblige*, 89–93; Charles Alpheus Bennett, *History of Manual and Industrial Education, 1870 to 1917* (Peoria: Manual Arts Press, 1937), 347–60, 373–75.

38. *Second Annual Report of the Jewish Training School* (Chicago: Ettlinger, 1891), 10; minutes of the Jewish Industrial School, May 17, 1888, and May 7, 1890, AJA; Karl Knoop and Martin Schwab, *Einführung in die Geschichte der Pädagogik: Pädagogen-Porträts aus vier Jahrhunderten* (Heidelberg: UTB, 1981), 160–65; Bennett, *History of Manual and Industrial Education*, 416–19; *Handbook of the Jewish Training School of Chicago: A Summary of the Organization and Work of the School* (Chicago: privately printed, 1912), 8–13.

39. *Third Annual Report of the Jewish Training School* (Chicago: Ettlinger, 1892), 10–11, 52–53; *Second Annual Report of the Jewish Training School*; *RA*, September 24, 1894.

40. *Second Annual Report of the Jewish Training School*; *Third Annual Report of the Jewish Training School*, 7, 20; *Fifth Annual Report of the Jewish Training School* (Chicago: Rubovits, 1894), 8–9; *Seventh Annual Report of the Jewish Training School* (Chicago: Ettlinger, 1896); *Handbook of the Jewish Training School of Chicago*, 30; Gabriel Bamberger, "Training Schools," in *Judaism at the World's Parliament of Religions: Comprising the Papers on Judaism Read at the Parliament, at the Jewish Denominational Congress, and at the Jewish Presentation*, ed. Union of American Hebrew Congregations (Cincinnati, OH: R. Clarke, 1894), 334–38.

41. Brinkmann, "Between Vision and Reality."

42. Bamberger, "Training Schools," 334; Joseph Siry, "The Abraham Lincoln Center in Chicago," *Journal of the Society of Architectural Historians* 50 (1991): 235–65 (esp. 238–43); *RA*, September 24, 1894; *Handbook of the Jewish Training School*, 21–22; Gutstein, *Priceless Heritage*, 255.

43. *Handbook of the Jewish Training School of Chicago*, 45–54; Meites, *History of the Jews of Chicago*, 327, 429–30; Gutstein, *Priceless Heritage*, 256; Eliassof and Hirsch, "Jews of Illinois," 285; Louis Wirth, *The Ghetto* (Chicago: University of Chicago Press, 1928), 192, 278; Edward H. Mazur, *Minyans for a Prairie City: The Politics of Chicago Jewry, 1850–1940* (PhD diss., University of Chicago, 1974), 95–96; Siry, "The Abraham Lincoln Center in Chicago," 241; Theodore Andreas, *History of Chicago: From Earliest Period to the Present Time* (Chicago: A. T. Andreas, 1884–1886), 3:443; David Ward Wood, *History of the Republican Party and Biographies of its Supporters: Illinois Volume* (Chicago: Lincoln Engraving Co., 1895), 174; "Joseph Stolz, Dean of Reform Rabbis, is Dead," *Chicago Tribune*, February 8, 1941.

44. Ascoli, *Julius Rosenwald*, 135–53.

CHAPTER 8

1. Kaufmann Kohler, "A Tribute to the Memory of Emil G. Hirsch," *RA*, May 26, 1923.

2. Stephen S. Wise, a great admirer of Hirsch and, like him, a charismatic speaker, also dominated his Free Synagogue congregation during the first decades of the twentieth century (Michael A. Meyer, *Response to Modernity: A History of the Reform Movement in Judaism* [New York: Oxford University Press, 1988], 303).

3. Emil G. Hirsch, "Woman in the Pulpit," *RA*, November 11, 1893.

4. David Kaufman, *Shul with a Pool: The "Synagogue-Center" in American Jewish History* (Hanover, NH: University Press of New England, 1999), 17.

5. Letters from Emil G. Hirsch to board, March 22, 1889; annual reports, March 28, 1889, March 31, 1890, April 4, 1891; letter from S. Eisendrath to board, March 30, 1891, Sinai Papers, AJA; Herman Eliassof and Emil G. Hirsch, "The Jews of Illinois: Their Religious and Civic Life, their Charity and Industry, their Patriotism and Loyalty to American Institutions, from their earliest settlement in the State unto present time," *RA*, May 4, 1901, 328; "Big Prices for Pews Expected at the Sinai Congregation Sale Today," *Chicago Tribune*, September 6, 1892; see quotation from board minutes by Herman Eliassof, "Sinai's Golden Jubilee," *RA*, May 6, 1911, 460 (1894 board meeting on donation of Sepher Torah to the University of Chicago).

6. On the shifting of High Holiday services, see the remark by August Binswanger, meeting of executive board with rabbi, April 25, 1898, Sinai Papers, AJA.

7. Zvi Hirsch Masliansky, *Memoirs: An Account of my Life and Travels* (Jerusalem: Ariel, 2009), 262–64, 270–71, 276–77; Moses J. Gries, *The Jewish Community of Cleveland* (Cleveland, OH: privately printed, 1910), 5–6.

8. Report of the board, March 28, 1892, Sinai Papers, AJA.

9. Emil G. Hirsch, "Universal Religion and Judaism," *RA*, October 14, 1893.

10. Alan Silverstein, *Alternatives to Assimilation: The Response of Reform Judaism to American Culture 1840–1930* (Hanover, NH: University Press of New England, 1994), 85, 89–91, 98, 107, 154; Felicia Herman, "From Priestess to Hostess: Sisterhoods of Personal Service in New York City, 1887–1936," in *Women and American Judaism: Historical Perspectives*, ed. Pamela Nadell and Jonathan D. Sarna (Hanover, NH: University Press of New England, 2001), 148–81; Jonathan D. Sarna, *JPS: The Americanization of Jewish Culture, 1888–1988* (Philadelphia: Jewish Publication Society, 1989), 17; Kaufman, *Shul with a Pool*, 20–46. Another important rabbi was Solomon Schindler (Arthur Mann, "Solomon Schindler: Boston Radical," *New England Quarterly* 23 [1950]: 453–76).

11. Berkowitz, quoted in Kaufman, *Shul with a Pool*, 25; E. Brooks Holifield, "Toward a History of American Congregations," in *New Perspectives in the Study of Congregations*, ed. James P. Wind and James W. Lewis, vol. 2 of *American Congregations* (Chicago: University of Chicago Press, 1994), 38–42; Edward R. Kantowicz, "The Ethnic Church," in *Ethnic Chicago: A Multicultural Portrait*, ed. Peter d'A. Jones and Melvin G. Holli (Grand Rapids, MI: Eerdmans, 1995), 574–603; see also Kantowicz, "Polish Chicago: Survival through Solidarity," in Jones and Holli, *Ethnic Chicago*, 173–198.

12. "Urges Endowments by Jews: Dr. Hirsch Would Have Wealthy Hebrews Give Largely to Universities and Art," *Chicago Tribune*, January 30, 1899.

13. Silverstein, *Alternatives to Assimilation*, 26; Fred Rosenbaum, *Visions of Reform: Congregation Emanu-El and the Jews of San Francisco 1849–1999* (San Francisco: Judah L. Magnes Museum, 2000), 79.

14. Silverstein, *Alternatives to Assimilation*, 96.

15. Moses Rischin, *The Promised City: New York's Jews 1870–1914* (Cambridge, MA: Harvard University Press, 1962); Sven Beckert, *The Monied Metropolis: New York City and the Consolidation of the American Bourgeoisie, 1850–1896* (New York: Cambridge University Press, 2001), 323–34.

16. Annual report, April 6, 1896, Sinai Papers, AJA; "Hirsch May Quit Chicago," *Chicago Tribune*, January 21, 1899; "Dr. Gottheil's Successor," *New York Times*, February 1, 1899.

17. Special meeting of executive board, June 9, 1897, minute book, Sinai Papers, Box 10, Folder 1, AJA; "The Assembly in Honor of Dr. Hirsch," *RA*, June 26, 1897; Eliassof, "Sinai's Golden Jubilee," 460.

18. The biographical information was taken from the biographies in Eliassof and Hirsch, "Jews of Illinois," and Hyman L. Meites, *History of the Jews of Chicago* (Chicago: Chicago Jewish Historical Society, 1924); information on the age, birthplace, and occupation for two men, Bernard Cahn and a Julius Loeb, could not be verified.

19. For biographies, see Eliassof and Hirsch, "Jews of Illinois"; *Chicago Tribune*, April 23, 1897 (Nathan), December 17, 1892 (Moses Bensinger), October 15, 1904 (Moses Bensinger), November 5, 1911 (Mandel), and March 13, 1934 (Binswanger). On Binswanger's involvement in Sonneschein's departure from Shaare Emeth, see the dossier he prepared for Bernhard Felsenthal (who was asked for an opinion) on behalf of the board in 1886 (Shaare Emeth [board] to Felsenthal, June 24, 1886, Felsenthal Papers, Box 2 [miscellaneous correspondence], AJHS).

20. Letter from Emil G. Hirsch to Joseph Gatzert, June 4, 1891; Emil G. Hirsch to M. Spier (president of Jewish congregation in New Haven, Hirsch accepts invitation), March 1, 1897; Emil G. Hirsch to board, December 27, 1897 (speaks in Pittsburgh and later at Cornell University as "University Preacher"), Sinai Papers, AJA.

21. Meeting of executive board with rabbi, April 25, 1898, Sinai Papers, AJA.

22. Emil G. Hirsch to Albert Fishell, May 2, 1898, minute book, Sinai Papers, AJA.

23. Kaufmann Kohler to Emil G. Hirsch and board, December 5, 1898, minute book, Sinai Papers, Box 10, Folder 1, AJA.

24. Chicago Sinai Congregation, *Report of the Services in Commemoration of the Twenty-Fifth Anniversary of the Institution of Sunday Services, 1874–1899—Chicago January 15, 1899* (Chicago: Chicago Sinai Congregation, 1899), printed as special issue of *RA* (January 21, 1899), 15–22.

25. Ibid., 84–94.

26. Collection of undated press clippings on of Sunday services celebration in January 1899, Sinai Papers, AJA; *American Israelite*, January, 19 1899.

27. "Hirsch May Quit Chicago," *Chicago Tribune*, January 21, 1899; "Dr. Gottheil's Successor," *New York Times*, February 1, 1899; *Report of the Services in Commemoration of the Twenty-Fifth Anniversary of the Institution of Sunday Services*—special issue of *RA*, January 21, 1899. For a reprint of Gustav Gottheil's letter, see also Richard Gottheil, *The Life of Gustav Gottheil: Memoir of a Priest in Israel* (Williamsport, PA: Bayard Press, 1936), 186.

28. Eliassof, "Sinai's Golden Jubilee," 463.

29. Letter from Albert Fishell to Gerson B. Levi, April 26, 1921, Sinai Papers, AJA.

30. "Dr. E. G. Hirsch Whacks Trusts," *Chicago Tribune*, January 2, 1899.

31. "Urges Endowments by Jews," *Chicago Tribune*, January 30, 1899.

32. "Hirsch Sees Woe. Sounds a Warning that a Revolution Confronts Society," *Chicago Tribune*, February 6, 1899; on the background of the meat scandal, see *New York Times*, January 26, 1899; see also Sinai board minutes, April 25, 1898, Sinai Papers, AJA.

33. Annual meeting, April 3, 1899, minute book, Sinai Papers, Box 10, Folder 1, AJA; "Hirsch May Quit Chicago," *Chicago Tribune*, January 21, 1899; "Hirsch to Remain Here: Sinai Congregation to Retain its Rabbi for Life," *Chicago Tribune*, February 28, 1899; *Chicago Times-Herald*, February 28, 1899; "Dr. Gottheil's Successor," *New York Times*, February 1, 1899; *American Israelite*, February 16, 1899, and March 9, 1899.

34. Nelson Morris to board, June 6, 1899; Albert Fishell to Gerson B. Levi, April 26, 1921, Sinai Papers, AJA; *RA*, May 21, 1921 (recollections of Fishell on the occasion of Hirsch's seventieth birthday, see p. 421).

CHAPTER 9

1. Quoted in Hyman L. Meites, *History of the Jews of Chicago* (Chicago: Chicago Jewish Historical Society, 1924), 177; Amos Elon, *The Pity of it All: A Portrait of the German-Jewish Epoch 1743–1933* (New York: Picador, 2003), 62–63.

2. Pamela S. Nadell, *Women Who Would Be Rabbis: A History of Women's Ordination 1889–1985* (Boston: Beacon Press, 1999), 34; Faith Rogow, *Gone to Another Meeting: The National Council of Jewish Women 1893–1993* (Tuscaloosa: University of Alabama Press, 1993), 9–35; Hannah Solomon, *Fabric of My Life* (New York: Bloch, 1946), 82–83.

3. Tobias Brinkmann, *Von der Gemeinde zur "Community": Jüdische Einwanderer in Chicago 1840–1900* (Osnabrück: Universitätsverlag Rasch, 2002), 321–23, 433; Kaufmann Kohler to president of Sinai, December 1, 1873, Sinai Papers, AJA; Karla Goldman, *Beyond the Synagogue Gallery: Finding a Place for Women in American Judaism* (Cambridge, MA: Harvard University Press, 2000), 181.

4. Goldman, *Beyond the Synagogue Gallery*, 176–79, 182–83; Jenna Weisman Joselit, "The Special Sphere of the Middle-Class American Jewish Woman: The Synagogue Sisterhood, 1890–1940," in *The American Synagogue: A Sanctuary Transformed*, ed. Jack Wertheimer (Cambridge: Cambridge University Press, 1987), 206–25.

5. Rogow, *Gone to Another Meeting*, 9–10, 21; *Fourth Annual Report of the UHC for 1891/92* (Chicago, 1892); Meites, *History of the Jews of Chicago*, 132; Goldman, *Beyond the Synagogue Gallery*, 178–88; Emil G. Hirsch, "The Position of Woman," *RA*, March 5, 1892; see also Hirsch, "The Modern Jewess," *American Jewess* (Chicago), April 1, 1895, 10–11.

6. Rogow, *Gone to Another Meeting*, 9–35; Solomon, *Fabric of My Life*, 82–83.

7. Rogow, *Gone to Another Meeting*, 9–35; *Papers of the Jewish Women's Congress: Held at Chicago, September 4, 5, 6 and 7, 1893* (Philadelphia: Jewish Publication Society of America,

1894); Richard Hughes Seager, *The World's Parliament of Religions: The East/West Encounter, Chicago, 1893* (Bloomington: Indiana University Press, 1995), 45; address by Hannah Solomon, in *Papers of the Jewish Women's Congress*, 10–11. For an interpretation of the council as feminist, see Mary McCune, *The Whole Wide World, Without Limits: International Relief, Gender Politics, and American Jewish Women, 1893–1930* (Detroit: Wayne State University Press, 2005), 19–20.

8. Hannah Solomon, "The Practical Results of Women's Clubs" (speech at Illinois State Federation, Peoria, 1895), repr. in Solomon, *A Sheaf of Leaves* (Chicago: privately printed, 1911), 53–59. The quoted sentence was inspired by Hirsch: "The individual is by society— Society is not by the individual. Society is the mother, the individual is the child" (see Emil G. Hirsch, "The Inalienable Duties of Man I," *RA*, May 8, 1897, 189). Rogow, *Gone to Another Meeting*, 75–78, 91.

9. Hannah Solomon, "The Council of Jewish Women: Its Work and Possibilities," *RA*, February 27, 1897 (the service took place on February 14, 1897); invitation from the Sinai board to Hannah Solomon, February 10, 1897, Hannah Solomon Papers, AJA.

10. "Woman in the Synagogue," *RA*, February 20, 1897.

11. Rogow, *Gone to Another Meeting*, 97–101, 115, 118.

12. Sadie American, "Organization" (address), in *Papers of the Jewish Women's Congress*, 218–62. On American, see Elizabeth M. Holland, "Sadie American," in *Women Building Chicago 1790–1990: A Biographical Dictionary*, ed. Rima Lunin Schultz and Adele Hast (Bloomington: Indiana University Press, 2001), 35–38; Martha Katz-Hyman, "Sadie American," in *Jewish Women: A Comprehensive Historical Encyclopedia*, http://jwa.org/encyclopedia/article/american-sadie (accessed May 29, 2009).

13. *Inter Ocean*, November 23, 1890. Felsenthal stressed in 1894 that he previously had not known about Blackstone's involvement in Jewish Missions (*Unity*, July 26, 1894).

14. David Philipson, *Max Lilienthal, American Rabbi: Life and Writings* (New York: Bloch, 1915), 96; Alan Silverstein, *Alternatives to Assimilation: The Response of Reform Judaism to American Culture 1840–1930* (Hanover, NH: University Press of New England, 1994), 134–36.

15. *RA*, July 2, 1892; Silverstein, *Alternatives to Assimilation*, 137–38.

16. Bessie Louise Pierce, *A History of Chicago: The Rise of a Modern City 1871–1893* (Chicago: University of Chicago Press, 1957), 545.

17. John T. McGreevy, *Parish Boundaries: The Catholic Encounter with Race in the Twentieth-Century Urban North* (Chicago: University of Chicago Press, 1996), 7–28.

18. Frederic Cople Jaher, *Scapegoat in the New Wilderness: The Origins and the Rise of Anti-Semitism in America* (Cambridge, MA: Harvard University Press, 1994), 140–42, 154.

19. Susannah Heschel, *Abraham Geiger and the Jewish Jesus* (Chicago: University of Chicago Press, 1998), 11, 218; Emil G. Hirsch, *The Crucifixion—Viewed from a Jewish Standpoint—A Lecture delivered by invitation before the Chicago Institute for Morals, Religion and Letters* (Chicago: Rubovits, 1892), 4 (quote); Isaac Mayer Wise, *The Martyrdom of Jesus of*

Nazareth: A Historical-Critical Treatise on the Last Chapters of the Gospel (Cincinnati, OH: American Israelite, 1874); see also Harris Weinstock, *Jesus the Jew and Other Addresses* (New York: Funk and Wagnalls, 1902), 11–37.

20. Martin E. Marty, *Modern American Religion: The Irony of It All 1893–1919 (Chicago: University of Chicago Press, 1986)*, 38–41; James P. Wind, *The Bible and the University: The Messianic Vision of William Rainey Harper* (Atlanta: Scholars Press, 1987). In 1892, Hirsch was a speaker of honor at the fiftieth anniversary of the St. Paul's Universalist Church on Chicago's Near South Side (*Chicago Tribune*, December 20, 1892).

21. Elon, *The Pity of it All*, 47; Christian Wiese, *Challenging Colonial Discourse: Jewish Studies and Protestant Theology in Wilhelmine Germany* (Leiden: Brill, 2006), 159–216.

22. Marty, *Modern American Religion*, 193–250.

23. Jenkin Lloyd Jones, "Water, An Ante-Vacation Sermon" (1877), in *A Search for an Infidel: Bits of Wayside Gospel: Second Series* (New York: Macmillan, 1901), 136; *Unity*, March 1, 1882.

24. *Unity*, October 27, November 3, and November 17, 1888; on Franklin Head, see his obituary in *Chicago Historical Society, Annual Report for the Year Ending October 31, 1914* (Chicago: CHS, 1914), 57.

25. Jenkin L. Jones, "The Spiritual Leadership of Jesus—What Does It Consist In?" *Unity*, December 15, 1888; Keshab Chandra Sen and Protap Chunder Mozoomdar were famous Hindu theologians who both reflected about the relationship between Hinduism and Christianity during the second half of the nineteenth century.

26. "All Souls' Church," *Chicago Evening Post*, September 12, 1892.

27. *The Family of Max and Sophie R. Adler*, comp. Robert S. Adler (Chicago: privately printed, 1972), Papers of Max and Sophie Adler, CJA; obituary of Morris, *Chicago Historical Society, Annual Report for the Year Ending October 31, 1914* (Chicago: CHS, 1914), 59.

28. Thomas E. Graham, "Jones, Jenkin Lloyd," American National Biography Online, http://www.anb.org/articles/08/08-00774.html (accessed June 23, 2009); Jenkin Lloyd Jones, *Nuggets from a Welsh Mine* (Chicago: Unity, 1904), 44.

29. Marty, *Modern American Religion*, 209–12; James F. Findlay Jr., *Dwight L. Moody: American Evangelist: 1837–1899* (Chicago: University of Chicago Press, 1969); Leonard Dinnerstein, *Antisemitism in America* (New York: Oxford University Press, 1994), 38; Yaakov Ariel, *Evangelizing the Chosen People: Missions to the Jews in America, 1880–2000* (Chapel Hill: University of North Carolina Press, 2000), 45; D. A. Jeremy Telman, "Adolf Stoecker: Anti-Semite with a Christian Mission," *Jewish History* 9 (1995): 93–112.

30. Henry Burns Hartzler, *Moody in Chicago or the World's Fair Gospel Campaign* (Chicago: Fleming H. Revell, 1894), 96–124 (quotes on 97, 99); in 1883, the *Staatszeitung* had described itself as the "most unswerving opponent of the ghastly Stoeckerism" (*ISZ*, October 15, 1883); *RA*, September 9, 1893.

31. Ariel, *Evangelizing the Chosen People*, 27–28; Ariel, "An American Initiative for a Jewish State: William Blackstone and the Petition of 1891," *Studies in Zionism* 10 (1989): 125–37

(esp. 128–29); On reports about the mission work among Jewish immigrants in Chicago see: *The Jewish Era, A Christian Quarterly* 1 (January 1892), 3 (January 1894).

32. Ariel, *Evangelizing the Chosen People*, 10; Marty, *Modern American Religion*, 209–12, 223.

33. For an overview, see Ariel, "An American Initiative for a Jewish State," 131; for the signature list and the text of the Blackstone memorial, see Meites, *History of the Jews of Chicago*, 687–90.

34. Ariel, *Evangelizing the Chosen People*, 25–26.

35. Seager, *The World's Parliament of Religions*, 3–23.

36. Union of American Hebrew Congregations, *Judaism at the World's Parliament of Religions: Comprising the Papers on Judaism Read at the Parliament, at the Jewish Denominational Congress, and at the Jewish Presentation* (Cincinnati, OH: Robert Clarke, 1894).

37. Seager, *The World's Parliament of Religions*, 44–45, 172–75; Seager, general introduction to *Dawn of Religious Pluralism: Voices from the Parliament of Religions, 1893* (La Salle, IL: Open Court, 1993), 8–10.

38. Union of American Hebrew Congregations, *Judaism at the World's Parliament of Religions*, xxi, 410, 412–13; Meites, *History of the Jews of Chicago*, 181.

39. Union of American Hebrew Congregations, *Judaism at the World's Parliament of Religions*, 386–90.

40. Letter from Emil G. Hirsch to Jenkin L. Jones, March 24, 1893, Jenkin Lloyd Jones Collection, Box II, Folder 10, Special Collections Research Center, University of Chicago Library.

41. *Unity*, April 19, 1894 (repr. from *RA*; original emphasis); Seager, *The World's Parliament of Religions*, 129.

42. The First American Congress of Liberal Religious Societies, Proceedings (part 1), in *Unity*, May 31, 1894, 166, 168–69, 171; on Thomas, see Thomas Wakefield Goodspeed, *The University of Chicago Biographical Sketches* (Chicago: University of Chicago Press, 1922), 335–58.

43. Elon, *The Pity of It All*, 47–48 (Mendelssohn quoted on p. 48), 62–64.

CHAPTER 10

1. Quoted in Karla Goldman, *Beyond the Synagogue Gallery: Finding a Place for Women in American Judaism* (Cambridge, MA: Harvard University Press, 2000), 180.

2. David Kaufman, *Shul with a Pool: The "Synagogue-Center" in American Jewish History* (Hanover, NH: University Press of New England, 1999), 20–46.

3. "The Institutional Church," *Chicago Defender*, November 16, 1912 (quote attributed to Emil G. Hirsch).

4. Emil G. Hirsch, "The Social Features of Congregational Life," *RA*, February 27, 1892; Hirsch, "Woman in the Pulpit," *RA*, November 11, 1893; Hirsch, "A Communal Need," *RA*,

April 20, 1895. On All Souls, see the extensive portrait "All Souls' Church," *Chicago Evening Post*, September 12, 1892.

5. Special board meeting, April 16, 1888; annual meeting, April 2, 1900; annual report of the board, April 6, 1896, Sinai Papers, AJA; Chicago Sinai Congregation, *Constitution. Adopted July 1st 1895* (Chicago: Chicago Sinai Congregation, 1895).

6. Annual report, April 6, 1896, Sinai Papers, AJA; Faith Rogow, *Gone to Another Meeting: The National Council of Jewish Women 1893–1993* (Tuscaloosa: University of Alabama Press, 1993), 73; Goldman, *Beyond the Synagogue Gallery*, 192–96; Hyman L. Meites, *History of the Jews of Chicago* (Chicago: Chicago Jewish Historical Society, 1924), 518.

7. *Proceedings of UAHC, 1903–7, Volume 6* (Cincinnati, OH: May & Kreidler, 1907), 5072–76; Adolph Loeb, address, 41st annual meeting, April 15, 1902, Sinai Papers, AJA.

8. Minute book, 39th annual meeting, April 2, 1900, Sinai Papers, AJA.

9. Report from E. G. Hirsch to congregation, March 16, 1900, Sinai Papers, AJA.

10. Miss Ernestine Witkowsky, petition to the board (concert), minute book, February 28, 1881, Box 9, Folder 6; minute book, 39th annual meeting, April 2, 1900, Box 10, Folder 1, Sinai Papers, AJA. On Jones's vision, see Joseph Siry, "The Abraham Lincoln Center in Chicago," *Journal of the Society of Architectural Historians* 50 (1991): 235–65; for a planned bowling alley at a conservative institutional synagogue in New York, see Jonathan D. Sarna, *American Judaism: A History* (New Haven, CT: Yale University Press, 2004), 248.

11. *RA*, July 2, 1892; board meeting, September 27, 1902 (Hirsch participates), Sinai Papers, AJA.

12. Minute book, 40th annual meeting, April 1, 1901; board meeting, May 27, 1901; minute book, 41st annual meeting, April 15, 1902, Box 10, Folder 1, Sinai Papers, AJA; "42nd Annual Meeting, April 6, 1903," *RA*, April 4, 1903; "Thirtieth Annual Report [of the UAHC]," in *Proceedings of the Union of American Hebrew Congregations, 77th-80th Annual Reports, July 1, 1950-June 30, 1955* (Cincinnati, OH: UAHC, 1956), 4807 (Sinai paid dues for the first time in April 1903).

13. Meites, *History of the Jews of Chicago*, 511; *The Book of Chicagoans: A Biographical Dictionary of Leading Living Men of the City of Chicago*, ed. Albert Nelson Marquis (Chicago: Marquis, 1911), 281; "Large Additions to the Relief Fund," *Chicago Tribune*, November 19, 1905 (Greenebaum raising funds for Russian Jews).

14. "Herman Schaffner & Co. Fail," *New York Times*, June 4, 1893; "Is Found in the Lake, Body of Herman Schaffner, the Missing Banker" *Chicago Tribune*, June 15, 1893; Meites, *History of the Jews of Chicago*, 293; Marquis, *The Book of Chicagoans*, 49.

15. Edwin R. Embree and Julia Waxman, "Julius Rosenwald: Philanthropist," *Phylon* 9 (1948), 215–28; Marquis, *The Book of Chicagoans*, 581–82; Meites, *History of the Jews of Chicago*, 229.

16. Letter from William Rainey Harper to Emil G. Hirsch, December 1, 1904, William Rainey Harper Papers, Box VII, Folder 16, Special Collections Research Center, University

of Chicago Library; "New Men on College Board," *New York Times*, May 26, 1912; "Gives Away $687,000. Julius Rosenwald Makes Birthday Donations to Charity and Education," *New York Times*, August 12, 1912; Brandon L. Johnson with Daniel Meyer, John W. Boyer, and Alice Schreyer, *Building for a Long Future: The University of Chicago and its Donors: 1889–1930*, Department of Special Collections, University of Chicago Library, May 2, 2001–December 31, 2001, http://www.lib.uchicago.edu/e/spcl/excat/donorsint.html (accessed December 3, 2009).

17. Judith Sealander, "Curing Evils at their Source: The Arrival of Scientific Giving," in *Charity, Philanthropy, and Civility in American History*, ed. Lawrence Jacob Friedman, and Mark Douglas McGarvie (Cambridge: Cambridge University Press, 2003), 217–39 (esp. 233); Sealander, *Private Wealth & Public Life: Foundation Philanthropy and the Reshaping of American Social Policy from the Progressive Era to the New Deal* (Baltimore, MD: Johns Hopkins University Press, 1997), 69–73; Peter M. Ascoli, *Julius Rosenwald: The Man Who Built Sears, Roebuck and Advanced the Cause of Black Education in the American South* (Bloomington: Indiana University Press, 2006), 217; Mary S. Hoffschwelle, *The Rosenwald Schools of the American South* (Gainesville: University Press of Florida, 2006), 225–38.

18. "Danger to Nation in Race Prejudice," *New York Times*, March 5, 1911.

19. "The Institutional Church," *Chicago Defender*, November 16, 1912; Calvin S. Morris, *Reverdy C. Ransom: Black Advocate of the Social Gospel* (Lanham, MD: University Press of America, 1990), 105.

20. Ascoli, *Julius Rosenwald*, 83–92.

21. Ascoli, *Julius Rosenwald*, 83–92; "Appointed by Providence, Says Rabbi Hirsch," *Chicago Defender*, November 20, 1915; Hoffschwelle, *The Rosenwald Schools*, 28–35.

22. Ascoli, *Julius Rosenwald*, 160–61; "Rabbi Hirsch Offers the Use of His Mammoth Temple Free of Charge," *Chicago Defender*, January 20, 1912; "Final Plans for Fourth Meeting," *Chicago Defender*, April 27, 1912; "Speakers Encourage and Tell of Advance," *Chicago Defender*, May 4, 1912; "Negro's Advance Told by Villard," *Chicago Tribune*, April 29, 1912; *The Crisis*, March 1912, 203 (outlining Julius Rosenwald's role in bringing the conference to Chicago).

23. Anja Becker and Tobias Brinkmann, "Transatlantische Bildungsmigration: Amerikanisch-jüdische Studenten an der Universität Leipzig 1872 bis 1914," *Leipziger Beiträge zur jüdischen Geschichte und Kultur* 4 (2006): 61–98 (esp. 94–95); Morris Robert Werner, *Julius Rosenwald: The Life of a Practical Humanitarian* (New York: Harper & Brothers, 1939), 90–94; Harry Barnard, *The Forging of an American Jew: The Life and Times of Judge Julian W. Mack* (New York: Herzl Press, 1974), 51.

24. Barnard, *The Forging of an American Jew*, 56–58, 82–85, 117–19; 47th annual meeting, April 6, 1908; 48th annual meeting, April 6, 1909; 58th annual meeting, May 22, 1919, Sinai Papers, AJA; report of the American Jewish Committee, in *American Jewish Yearbook* 10 (1908–09), ed. Herbert Friedenwald (Philadelphia: Jewish Publication Society, 1909), 237.

25. Meites, *History of the Jews of Chicago*, 506; Emil G. Hirsch to the board (requesting

leave of absence), March 26, 1904; 50th annual meeting, April 3, 1911; 43rd annual meeting (report by president Harry Hart), April 4, 1904; 45th annual meeting, April 2, 1906; board meeting, October 31, 1910, Sinai Papers, AJA; Alan Silverstein, *Alternatives to Assimilation: The Response of Reform Judaism to American Culture 1840–1930* (Hanover, NH: University Press of New England, 1994), 100.

26. Goldman, *Beyond the Synagogue Gallery*, 191–96.

27. Meites, *History of the Jews of Chicago*, 581; 47th annual meeting, April 6, 1908; annual report, April 6, 1896; Rosalie Sulzberger, NCJW, Chicago Section, to board, March 17, 1896, March 16, 1898; Julia Felsenthal to board, May 30, 1900, Sinai Papers, AJA. Sinai closed the West Side school in 1926: Louis Mann to board, January 6, 1926, Sinai Papers, archive, CSC.

28. Report by Emil G. Hirsch for the annual meeting, March 23, 1908; Moses E. Greenebaum, annual report for 1906–1907, April 1, 1907; 48th annual meeting, April 6, 1909; 49th annual meeting, April 13, 1910; special meeting of the board, October 4, 1911, Sinai Papers, AJA; Thomas Philpott, *The Slum and the Ghetto: Neighborhood Deterioration and Middle-Class Reform, Chicago, 1880–1930* (Oxford: Oxford University Press, 1978), 337; Kaufman, *Shul with a Pool*, 46–48; Meites, *History of the Jews of Chicago*, 394.

29. Emil G. Hirsch, "The Proof of the Pudding," *RA*, April 16, 1910.

30. *Bulletin of the Art Institute of Chicago* (Chicago: The Art Institute, 1924), 68; Ascoli, *Julius Rosenwald*, 299; *The Chicago Symphony Orchestra: Thirteenth Session 1903–1904, Program Notes* (Chicago: Orchestral Association, 1903); *The Chicago Symphony Orchestra: Twenty-Sixth Session 1916–1917, Program Notes* (Chicago: Orchestral Association, 1916); *The Chicago Symphony Orchestra: Thirty First Session 1921–1922, Program Notes* (Chicago: Orchestral Association, 1921).

31. Board meeting, November 27, 1911, Sinai Papers, AJA; on influences on the design, see Samuel D. Gruber, "Arnold W. Brunner and the New Classical Synagogue in America," *Jewish History* 25 (2011): 69–102 (esp. 85).

32. 49th annual meeting, April 13, 1910; special meeting of the board, October 4, 1911, in minute book, Sinai Papers, AJA; report of the building fund, November 27, 1911; board meeting, April 29, 1912 (sale of old temple); 51st annual meeting, May 22, 1912, in board minutes, Sinai Papers, AJA; *Chicago Record Herald*, March 4, 1912; "The Dedication of the New Sinai Temple," special issue, *RA*, March 9, 1912; "Jews of Illinois Number," special issue, *RA*, March 16, 1912; Meites, *History of the Jews of Chicago*, 235.

33. Emil G. Hirsch, sermon, in "Jews of Illinois Number," 156–62.

34. Ibid., 166–70.

35. Ascoli, *Julius Rosenwald*, 55.

36. *Chicago Defender*, November 16, 1912; Annetta L. Gomez-Jefferson, *The Sage of Tawawa: Reverdy Cassius Ransom, 1861–1959* (Kent, OH: Kent State University Press, 2002), 53–74.

37. Siry, "The Abraham Lincoln Center in Chicago," 235–65.

38. Gotthard Deutsch, rabbi and professor at Hebrew Union College, recalled in 1921, referring to the Center's pool, "the 'Salvation by the Plunge,' as Dr. Hirsch once called it in

his inimitable sarcasm is surely making progress. A Gamaliel of our day might apply to the synagog [*sic*] what the Gamaliel of the second century said of the bath of Aphrodite: the temple has become an annex to the bath (Abodah Zarah, 44b)" (*RA*, May 21, 1921, 407–9).

39. Quoted in Meites, *History of the Jews of Chicago* (from the 1903 constitution of the Hebrew Institute), 218. For an overview, see *History of the Jews of Chicago*, 220–26; Kaufman, *Shul with a Pool*, 118–20.

40. "Jews of Illinois Number," 177–81; 51st annual meeting, May 22, 1912, Sinai Papers, AJA.

41. *Chicago Tribune*, August 25, 1918, December 7, 1919, and December 4, 1921; Philip P. Bregstone, *Chicago and Its Jews: A Cultural History* (Chicago: privately printed, 1933), 219; Linda J. Borish, "Jewish Women, Sports, and History," in *Sports in Chicago*, ed. Elliott J. Gorn (Urbana: University of Illinois Press, 2008), 62–77 (esp. 65); Philpott, *The Slum and the Ghetto*, 337.

CHAPTER 11

1. "Jews of Illinois Number," special issue, *RA*, March 16, 1912, 177–81.

2. Philip P. Bregstone, *Chicago and Its Jews: A Cultural History* (Chicago: privately printed, 1933), 78; Bernard Horwich, *My First Eighty Years* (Chicago: Argus, 1939), 189, 261–262; "Jews of Illinois Number," 162 (message by Stephen S. Wise); 49th annual meeting, April 13, 1910 (on Wise visit); board minutes, February 23, 1913 (Wise gave sermon at Sinai); 58th annual meeting, May 22, 1919, Sinai Papers, AJA; "Brandeis Seeks Aid for Jews," *Chicago Tribune*, November 8, 1914.

3. H. S. Linfield, "Statistics of the Jews," *American Jewish Year Book* 30 (1928/29): 258–59; Arthur Ruppin, *Soziologie der Juden* (Berlin: Jüdischer Verlag, 1930), 1:67–86; Horwich, *My First Eighty Years*, 254; Arthur Goren, *New York Jews and the Quest for Community: The Kehillah Experiment 1908–1922* (New York: Columbia University Press, 1970).

4. Hyman L. Meites, *History of the Jews of Chicago* (Chicago: Chicago Jewish Historical Society, 1924), 150–52; Anita Libman Lebeson, "Zionism Comes to Chicago," in *The Early History of Zionism in America*, ed. Isidore S. Meyer (New York: American Jewish Historical Society, 1958), 155–90 (esp. 162); see also "Zionist Organization of Chicago," undated booklet, in "Zionist Organization of Chicago," CJA (on Levin's visit in 1907, see p. 9); "Chicago," *Die Welt* (Vienna), January 21, 1898 (article on Zionist organizations in Chicago); Eli Lederhendler, *Jewish Immigrants and American Capitalism, 1880–1920: From Caste to Class* (Cambridge: Cambridge University Press, 2009), 104.

5. Meites, *History of the Jews of Chicago*, 150–51; Lebeson, "Zionism Comes to Chicago"; Bernhard Felsenthal, *Kritik des Christlichen Missionswesens insbesondere der "Judenmission"* (Chicago: Ed. Bühler's Buchhandlung, 1869), 13; *Jewish Advance* (Chicago), March 7, 1879.

6. Eric Goldstein, *The Price of Whiteness: Jews, Race, and American Identity* (Princeton: Princeton University Press 2006), 28–29.

7. Amos Elon, *The Pity of it All: A Portrait of the German-Jewish Epoch 1743–1933* (New York: Picador, 2003), 210–20; Peter Pulzer, *The Rise of Political Anti-Semitism in Germany & Austria*, rev. ed. (Cambridge, MA: Harvard University Press, 1988), 71–120; Emil G. Hirsch, "Antisemitism—A Discourse Delivered Before the Chicago Sinai Congregation," *Occident* (Chicago), January 19, 1883.

8. Walter Laqueur, *A History of Zionism* (New York: Holt, Rinehart and Winston, 1972), 70–73.

9. Isaak Rülf, *Aruchas Bas-Ammi. Israels Heilung. Ein ernstes Wort an Glaubens- und Nichtglaubensgenossen* (Frankfurt: Kauffmann, 1883); see also "Israel's Heilung" (review by an anonymous author), *AZ*, October 9, 1883, 662–66; Bernhard Felsenthal, "Some Thoughts on the Jewish Problem," *Occident* (Chicago), April 27, 1883; Emil G. Hirsch, "The Antithesis between Race and Religion," *Occident* (Chicago), November 6, 1885.

10. Meites, *History of the Jews of Chicago*, 196–203; Horwich, *My First Eighty Years*, 231; Lebeson, "Zionism Comes to Chicago," 173–74; "Chicago," *Die Welt*, January 14, 1898 (Zionism in Chicago).

11. Felsenthal, *Teacher in Israel*, 74–75, 79. letter from Emil G. Hirsch to Bernhard Felsenthal, October 11, 1898, Felsenthal Papers, MS-153, AJA: "I do not share your emotional engagement for Zion, yes, I am even going so far, with your exception, to suspect the movers and shakers of this movement in America of running a hoax" (original in German, my translation). Martin P. Beifield, "Joseph Krauskopf and Zionism: Partners in Change," *American Jewish History* 75 (1985): 48–60; Mark A. Raider, *The Emergence of American Zionism* (New York: New York University Press, 1998), 13–14.

12. Leon A. Jick, "The Reform Synagogue," in *The American Synagogue: A Sanctuary Transformed*, ed. Jack Wertheimer (Cambridge: Cambridge University Press, 1987), 94; Melvin I. Urofsky, *A Voice That Spoke for Justice: The Life and Times of Stephen S. Wise* (Albany: State University of New York Press, 1982); Stephen S. Wise, *Challenging Years: The Autobiography of Stephen Wise* (New York: Putnam, 1949); *New York Times*, January 9, 1923 (Wise described the deceased Hirsch as "the greatest preacher of his generation."); Norman Bentwich, *For Zion's Sake: A Biography of Judah L. Magnes* (Philadelphia: Jewish Publication Society, 1954).

13. Gerald Sorin, *Tradition Transformed: The Jewish Experience in America* (Baltimore, MD: Johns Hopkins University Press, 1997), 139.

14. *RA*, May 29, 1897; Meites, *History of the Jews of Chicago*, 292; Hirsch, quoted in Bernard Martin, "The Religious Philosophy of Emil G. Hirsch," *AJA* 4 (1952): 80; *Chicago Record Herald*, March 4, 1912; Emil Hirsch, "The Philosophy of the Reform Movement in American Judaism," in *Reform Judaism—A Historical Perspective—Essays from the Yearbook of the Central Conference of American Rabbis*, ed. Joseph L. Blau (New York: KTAV, 1973), 24–44 (quote, 42); the original appeared in *Yearbook of the Central Conference of American Rabbis* 5 (1895): 90–122; Goldstein, *The Price of Whiteness*, 30, 88; "Jews are Urged to

Wed Gentiles," *Chicago Tribune*, November 16, 1908; for controversies between Hirsch and Gustav Gottheil, see Richard Gottheil, *The Life of Gustav Gottheil: Memoir of a Priest in Israel* (Williamsport, PA: Bayard Press, 1936), 192–93.

15. Zvi Hirsch Masliansky, *Memoirs: An Account of my Life and Travels* (Jerusalem: Ariel, 2009), 265.

16. *The Two Hundred and Fiftieth Anniversary of the Settlement of the Jews in the United States* (New York: New York Co-operative Society, 1906), 148–63 (original emphasis); see also Arthur Goren, *The Politics and Public Culture of American Jews* (Bloomington: Indiana University Press, 1999), 30–47; on the 1905 Odessa pogrom, see Robert Weinberg, "Anti-Jewish Violence and Revolution in Late Imperial Russia: Odessa, 1905," in *Riots and Pogroms*, ed. Paul R. Brass (New York: New York University Press, 1996), 56–88.

17. Masliansky, *Memoirs*, 265; *RA*, September 12, 1896 (pro-Zionist article).

18. Horwich, *My First Eighty Years*, 275–86; Bregstone, *Chicago and Its Jews*, 97, 120, 137, 204–05; Emil G. Hirsch, "The Future of the Russian Jew in America," in *Russia at the Bar of the American People: A Memorial of Kishinef*, ed. Isidor Singer (New York: Funk and Wagnalls, 1904), xv–xxx (esp. xxvi); "Large Additions to the Relief Fund," *Chicago Tribune*, November 19, 1905; Jonathan D. Sarna, "Converts to Zionism in the American Reform Movement," in *Zionism and Religion*, ed. Shmuel Almog, Jehuda Reinharz, and Anita Shapira (Hanover, NH: University Press of New England, 1998), 193–203.

19. "Bernhard Felsenthal, Memorial Address Delivered by Dr. Joseph Stolz," *Yearbook of the Central Conference of American Rabbis* 18 (1908): 161–67; annual meeting, March 23, 1908, Sinai Papers, AJA.

20. Emil G. Hirsch, "The Inalienable Duties of Man I," *RA*, May 8, 1897; Hirsch, "The Inalienable Duties of Man II," *RA*, May 15, 1897; Hirsch, "Individual & Society," *RA*, May 29, 1891; Hirsch, "Modern Heretics," *RA*, June 13, 1896; Hirsch, "The Problem of Poverty," *RA*, February 20, 1897.

21. For a complaint by a congregant who felt he was unjustly attacked by Hirsch as an exploiter, see board minutes April 25, 1898, Sinai Papers, AJA; for the characterization of Morris by Sinai's president Albert Fishell, see *RA*, May 21, 1921, 421. Marilee Munger Scroogs, "Making a Difference: Fourth Presbyterian Church of Chicago," in *Portraits of Twelve Religious Communities*, ed. James P. Wind and James W. Lewis, vol. 1 of *American Congregations* (Chicago: University of Chicago Press, 1994), 464–519 (esp. 491).

22. Youngsoo Bae, *Labor in Retreat: Class and Community Among Men's Clothing Workers of Chicago, 1871–1929* (Albany: State University of New York Press, 2001), 85–115; Steven Fraser, *Labor will Rule: Sidney Hillman and the Rise of American Labor* (New York: Free Press, 1991), 40–76; Matthew Josephson, *Sidney Hillman: Statesman of American Labor* (Garden City, NJ: Doubleday, 1952), 47–58; Bregstone, *Chicago and Its Jews*, 208. Schaffner's 1914 testimony is quoted in Meites, *History of the Jews of Chicago*, 460; see also N. Sue Weiler, "Walkout: The Chicago Men's Garment Workers' Strike, 1910–1911," *Chicago History*

8 (1979): 238–49; Karen Pastorello, *A Power Among Them: Bessie Abramowitz Hillman and the Making of the Amalgamated Clothing Workers of America* (Urbana: University of Illinois Press, 2008), 24–28.

23. Irving Howe, *Immigrant Jews of New York, 1881 to Present* (New York: Schocken, 1976), 296–304.

24. Bae, *Labor in Retreat*, 47–90; Fraser, *Labor will Rule*, 43, 59.

25. *Chicago Tribune*, October 23, December 3, and December 4, 1910; Josephson, *Sidney Hillman*, 52; Bae, *Labor in Retreat*, 88.

26. Herman Eliassof and Emil G. Hirsch, "The Jews of Illinois: Their Religious and Civic Life, their Charity and Industry, their Patriotism and Loyalty to American Institutions, from their earliest settlement in the State unto present time," *RA*, May 4, 1901, 309, 355; *Menorah* (New York) 28 (1900), 40; *Survey* (New York), May 4, 1918 (obituary); *New York Times*, April 20, 1918 (obituary); Marcus Marx did not play an active role in the management (see *Chicago Tribune*, August 5, 1921 [obituary]).

27. Josephson, *Sidney Hillman*, 52–56; Bae, *Labor in Retreat*, 99–111; letter from Sidney Hillman to Hart Schaffner and Marx, April 26, 1916, repr. J. E. Williams, Sidney Hillman, and Earl Dean Howard, *The Hart Schaffner & Marx Labor Agreement: Being a Compilation and Codification of the Agreements of 1911, 1913, and 1916 and decisions rendered by the Board of Arbitration* (Chicago: privately printed, 1916), see appendix following p. 41. For an overview of the agreements, see also Earl Dean Howard, *The Hart Schaffner & Marx Labor Agreement: Industrial Law in the Clothing Industry* (Chicago: privately printed, 1920); Bregstone, *Chicago and Its Jews*, 210; Fraser, *Labor will Rule*, 68–76. Schaffner's 1914 testimony is quoted in Meites, *History of the Jews of Chicago*, 460.

28. Lizabeth Cohen, *Making a New Deal: Industrial Workers in Chicago 1919–1939* (Cambridge: Cambridge University Press, 2008), 47–48.

29. Hillman, quoted in *Time*, April 19, 1937; obituary of Joseph Schaffner, *Survey*, May 4, 1918.

30. 57th annual meeting, May 22, 1918, Sinai Papers, AJA; see also *RA*, May 25, 1918.

31. Melvin G. Holli, "The Great War Sinks Chicago's German *Kultur*," in *Ethnic Chicago*, ed. Melvin G. Holli and Peter d'A. Jones (Grand Rapids, MI: Eerdmans, 1981), 260–311; Dominic A. Pacyga, *Polish Immigrants and Industrial Chicago: Workers on the South Side, 1880–1922* (Columbus: Ohio State University Press, 1991), 193–94; Meites, *History of the Jews of Chicago*, 335; Horwich, *My First Eighty Years*, 313; on Hirsch's illness-related absences, see 54th annual meeting, April 5, 1915, Sinai Papers, AJA.

32. For a detailed account of these efforts with name lists, see Meites, *History of the Jews of Chicago*, 255–316.

33. Meites, *History of the Jews of Chicago*, 255–316; *Chicago Tribune*, November 8, 1914. More research on this important chapter in Chicago history is required. The best (but limited) overview remains Holli, "The Great War Sinks Chicago's German *Kultur*." On the

Great Migration to Chicago, see James Grossman, *Land of Hope: Chicago, Black Southerners, and the Great Migration* (Chicago: University of Chicago Press, 1991).

34. "Sing at Goethe Memorial," *Chicago Tribune*, March 17, 1912.

35. "Dernberg [*sic*] Lays Blame for War on the English," *Chicago Tribune*, December 11, 1914, "U.S. May Expel Dr. Dernburg," *Chicago Tribune*, May 12, 1915, "Wilson Expects Berlin to Yield," *Chicago Tribune*, June 13, 1915; for a reprint of Hirsch's speech, see *Jahrbuch der Deutschen in Chicago für das Jahr 1916: mit einer vollkommenen Geschichte des europäischen Krieges* (Chicago: Michael Singer, 1916), 30–32; for a relatively unbiased overview, see Frederick C. Luebke, *Bonds of Loyalty: German-Americans and World War I* (De Kalb: Northern Illinois University Press, 1974).

36. "New Meaning," *Chicago Defender*, February 20, 1915.

37. "Hirsch Replies to Charge That He is Not Loyal," *Chicago Tribune*, April 12, 1918.

38. "Congregation Satisfied With Hirsch's Views," *Chicago Tribune*, April 13, 1918.

39. 57th annual meeting, May 22, 1918, Sinai Papers, AJA; Emil Hirsch, *My Religion and the War, A Discourse by Emil G. Hirsch, April 14, 1918* (Chicago: Chicago Sinai Congregation, 1918), repr. *RA*, April 27, 1918; "Dr. Hirsch Voices Loyalty Before Crowd of 3,000," *Chicago Tribune*, April 15, 1918.

40. 58th annual meeting, May 22, 1919, Sinai Papers, AJA, Guido Dobbert, "The Ordeal of Gotthard Deutsch," *American Jewish Archives* 20 (1968): 129–55.

41. *RA*, May 21, 1921; on Hirsch's comparison, see Goldstein, *The Price of Whiteness*, 148.

42. For biographies and dates, consult the index of Meites, *History of the Jews of Chicago*; Hirsch's obituary was printed in the *Chicago Tribune* (January 8, 1923; the funeral was January 10, 1923) and Kaufmann Kohler wrote "Emil G. Hirsch," *Central Conference of American Rabbis Yearbook* 33 (1923): 145–55; "The Week: Rabbi Hirsch," *Chicago Defender*, January 13, 1923; see also the extensive memorial issue of the *RA* with recollections by close friends and colleagues (*RA*, May 26, 1923).

CHAPTER 12

1. John Higham, *Strangers in the Land: Patterns of American Nativism 1860–1925* (New York: Atheneum, 1977), 264–77.

2. James R. Grossman, *Land of Hope: Chicago, Black Southerners, and the Great Migration* (Chicago: University of Chicago Press, 1989), 123–60; Arnold Hirsch, *Making the Second Ghetto: Race and Housing in Chicago, 1940–1960* (Cambridge: Cambridge University Press, 1983), 16; Lizabeth Cohen, *Making a New Deal: Industrial Workers in Chicago 1919–1939* (Cambridge: Cambridge University Press, 2008), 34, 38–51. For a detailed treatment of African American migration to and settlement in Chicago, see Thomas Philpott, *The Slum and the Ghetto: Neighborhood Deterioration and Middle-Class Reform, Chicago, 1880–1930* (Oxford: Oxford University Press, 1978).

3. Dominic A. Pacyga, *Polish Immigrants and Industrial Chicago: Workers on the South*

Side, 1880–1922 (Columbus: Ohio State University Press, 1991), 224–28; "Bethel Church Moves to Buy New Property," *Chicago Tribune*, April 20, 1919.

4. "Rabbi Hirsch's Old Home Sold to Negro Tenant," *Chicago Tribune*, November 5, 1919, "Club Asked to Oust Man Who Rents to Negro," December 4, 1919.

5. Leonard Dinnerstein, *Antisemitism in America* (New York: Oxford University Press, 1994), 85–87.

6. James Grossman, *Land of Hope: Chicago, Black Southerners, and the Great Migration* (Chicago: University of Chicago Press, 1991), 127; John T. McGreevy, *Parish Boundaries: The Catholic Encounter with Race in the Twentieth-Century Urban North* (Chicago: University of Chicago Press, 1996), 9–38, Cohen, *Making a New Deal*, 31–33.

7. Eric Goldstein, *The Price of Whiteness: Jews, Race, and American Identity* (Princeton: Princeton University Press 2006), 68; "Hyde Parkers Swear to Hold on Color Line," *Chicago Tribune*, October 21, 1919; letter from Kenwood Property Association to Sinai congregation, November 29, 1920, Box 11, Folder 3, minute book, Sinai Papers, AJA.

8. Hirsch, *Making the Second Ghetto*, 4; Pacyga, *Polish Immigrants and Industrial Chicago*, 224–28; Irving Cutler, *The Jews of Chicago: From Shtetl to Suburb* (Urbana: University of Illinois Press, 1996), 122.

9. Jonathan D. Sarna, *American Judaism: A History* (New Haven, CT: Yale University Press, 2004), 220.

10. Cohen, *Making a New Deal*, 58–61, 94–97; Marc J. Swatez, "The Role of the Jewish Federation of Metropolitan Chicago," in *The Shaping of a Community: The Jewish Federation of Metropolitan Chicago*, ed. Rhoda Rosen (Chicago: Spertus Press, 1999), 53–63.

11. Kerry Marc Olitzky, "The Sunday-Sabbath Controversy" (rabbinical thesis, Hebrew Union College, 1981), 89–96; Julian Morgenstern to Julius H. Meyer, February 23, 1923, Sinai Papers, AJA; Marc Lee Raphael, *Abba Hillel Silver: A Profile in American Judaism* (New York: Holmes & Meier, 1989); Harry Barnard, *The Forging of an American Jew: The Life and Times of Judge Julian W. Mack* (New York: Herzl Press, 1974), 213; "Mack on Peace and Jews," *Chicago Tribune*, November 22, 1918.

12. Sarna, *American Judaism*, 195–96; Michael A. Meyer, *Response to Modernity: A History of the Reform Movement in Judaism* (New York: Oxford University Press, 1988), 302–3.

13. "The Committee of 50" (Atlantic City) to M. Greenebaum, January 15, 1923; 62nd annual meeting, April 22, 1923 (president's report), Sinai Papers, AJA; obituary for Louis Mann, *Chicago Tribune*, February 2, 1966; Kerry M. Olitzky, *The American Synagogue: A Historical Dictionary and Sourcebook* (Westport, CT: Greenwood, 1996), 79.

14. Louis Mann, inaugural sermon, September 10, 1923, Sinai Papers, AJA.

15. Philip P. Bregstone, *Chicago and Its Jews: A Cultural History* (Chicago: privately printed, 1933), 219–21; 57th annual meeting, May 22, 1918, Sinai Papers, AJA; letter from Emil Kitzinger to Edgar Greenebaum, board minutes, July 23, 1945 (Schwartz as de facto associate rabbi), Sinai Papers, AJA; Meyer, *Response to Modernity*, 304.

16. David Kaufman, *Shul with a Pool: The "Synagogue-Center" in American Jewish History* (Hanover, NH: University Press of New England, 1999), 228–41; Sarna, *American Judaism*, 245–49 (Kaplan quotes, 247).

17. Sarna, *American Judaism*, 224–27; Meyer, *Response to Modernity*, 319–23.

18. 60th annual meeting, May 22, 1921; 62nd annual meeting, April 22, 1923; 63rd annual meeting, April 20, 1924, Sinai Papers, AJA; *Proceedings of Union of American Hebrew Congregations* (Cincinnati, OH: May & Kreidler, 1903–07), 6:5072–76; *Fifty-First Annual Report of the Union of American Hebrew Congregations 1925* (Cincinnati, OH: May & Kreidler, 1925), 9857–64; Hyman L. Meites, *History of the Jews of Chicago* (Chicago: Chicago Jewish Historical Society, 1924), 521, 526.

19. Felicia Herman, "From Priestess to Hostess: Sisterhoods of Personal Service in New York City, 1887–1936," in *Women and American Judaism: Historical Perspectives*, ed. Pamela Nadell and Jonathan D. Sarna (Hanover, NH: University Press of New England, 2001), 148–81; board minutes, December 4, 1923 and September 16, 1924; 63rd annual meeting, April 20, 1924, Sinai Papers, AJA.

20. 54th annual meeting, April 5, 1915; board minutes, December 4, 1923 and September 16, 1924; 63rd annual meeting, April 20, 1924, Sinai Papers, AJA; *Chicago Sinai Temple Sisterhood Yearbook 1925/26*, Jennie Franklin Purvin Collection, MS-502, AJA.

21. Karla Goldman, "Jennie Franklin Purvin," in *Women Building Chicago: A Biographical Dictionary*, ed. Rima Lunin Schultz and Adele Hast (Bloomington: Indiana University Press, 2001), 727–29; *Chicago Sinai Temple Sisterhood Yearbook 1925/26*; letter from Jennie F. Purvin to S. D. Schwartz, October 2, 1931; letter from Jennie F. Purvin to M. E. Greenebaum, January 29, 1932; letter from Albert Ellbogen (Sinai president) to Jennie F. Purvin, August 24, 1939, Purvin Collection, MS-502, AJA; Linda J. Borish, "Jewish Women, Sports, and Chicago History," in *Sports in Chicago*, ed. Elliott J. Gorn (Urbana: University of Illinois Press, 2008), 70–72.

22. *Chicago Sinai Temple Sisterhood Yearbook 1926/27*; Cohen, *Making a New Deal*, 34; *Service Honoring Past Presidents of the Congregation, Sabbath Eve, March Twenty-Ninth 1957* (Glencoe, IL: North Shore Congregation, 1957); Pacyga, *Polish Immigrants and Industrial Chicago*, 225.

23. Report by Louis Mann, January 6, 1926; special meeting, February 22, 1927, Sinai Papers, CSC.

24. 66th annual meeting, April 10, 1927 (including papers over the acquisition of a plot in Hyde Park), Sinai Papers, CSC.

25. James O'Donnell Bennett, "Sinai Temple to Build Anew in Hyde Park," *Chicago Tribune*, January 5, 1930; obituary for Julius Rosenwald, *Chicago Tribune*, January 7, 1932; obituary for M. E. Greenebaum, *Chicago Tribune*, June 23, 1934; 70th annual meeting, June 4, 1931; 71st annual meeting, June 19, 1932; 72th annual meeting, October 15, 1933; board meetings, November 19, 1935, November 25, 1935, March 19, 1936, and April 16, 1936, Sinai Papers, CSC; Meyer, *Response to Modernity*, 307.

26. Printed copies (typewritten) of the speeches, Seventy-Five Anniversary-Celebration, Palmer House, October 25, 1936, Sinai Papers, CSC; "Sinai Members to Celebrate 75th Birthday," *Chicago Tribune*, October 4, 1936.

27. Kathleen McLaughlin, "Rabbi Rips into Admiral's Plea for U.S. Defense," *Chicago Tribune*, February 23, 1927; Louis Mann, "Echoes from the American Citizenship Foundation Dinner" (sermon, February 27, 1927), Sinai Papers, AJA.

28. Jacob H. Dorn, "Religion and Reform in the City: The Re-Thinking Chicago Movement of the 1930s," *Church History* 55 (1986): 323–37 (esp. 331–32); "Moslem Prayer Call Session," *Chicago Tribune*, May 10, 1929, "Dr. Mann Warns of Intolerance Among Varied Faiths," *Chicago Tribune*, April 14, 1931, John Evans, "Jew, Christian Find Common Ground is Big," *Chicago Tribune*, February 19, 1945; board meetings (interfaith), February 21, 1935, and May 2, 1960, Sinai Papers, CSC.

29. "The Jewish Problem" (editorial), *Christian Century*, April 29, 1936; Louis L. Mann, "Jewish Integrity and Tolerance," *Christian Century*, May 13, 1936 (original emphasis); "Jews, Christians and Democracy," *Christian Century*, May 13, 1936; see also Arnold M. Eisen, The Chosen People in America: A Study in Jewish Religious Ideology (Bloomington: Indiana University Press, 1983), 33–36.

30. Meyer, *Response to Modernity*, 308; Louis L. Mann, "The Failures of the Union and Where Do We Go from Here" (address delivered at the 37th Council of UAHC, Detroit April 28, 1941), in *Sixty-Seventh Annual Report of the UAHC* (Cincinnati, OH: UAHC, 1941), 188–202.

31. Mann, "The Failures of the Union and Where Do We Go from Here"; Martin Marty, *Modern American Religion*, vol. 2, *The Noise of Conflict, 1919–1941* (Chicago: University of Chicago Press, 1991), 251.

32. Letter from Abraham L. Lassen (Chicago Rabbinical Association) to Robert Sonnenschein (Sinai president), March 28, 1935; special board meeting, April 2, 1935; Sinai to Jewish Charities of Chicago, April 3, 1935; letter from Robert Sonnenschein to Mr. Rittman (Jewish Charities), April 11, 1935; letter from Robert Abraham L. Lassen, April 13, 1935; special board meetings, April 24, 1935, May 16, 1935, and September 12, 1935, Sinai Papers, CSC.

33. Board meetings, September 16, 1937, April 21, 1938, May 19, 1938, September 22, 1938, and October 22, 1938, Sinai Papers, CSC.

34. board meetings, January 3, 1939, March 7, 1939, June 18, 1940; 77th annual meeting, October 23, 1938; report on newcomers, May 8, 1941; letter from Albert Ellbogen (Sinai president) to U.S. Consul, Berlin, December 15, 1939 (copy); letter from American National Bank and Trust Co. of Chicago to U.S. Consul in Berlin (copy), December 12, 1939; Sworn affidavit for Ida Lazarus by S. D. Schwartz, March 10, 1941, Sinai Papers, CSC; "Central Europe Refugees Hold Rally Sunday," *Chicago Tribune*, November 26, 1942. For background, see Leon A. Jick, "The Reform Synagogue," in *The American Synagogue: A Sanctuary Transformed*, ed. Jack Wertheimer (Cambridge: Cambridge University Press, 1987), 100.

35. Board meeting, May 12, 1942; "Report of Special Committee To Evaluate Newcom-

ers Activity," May 12, 1942; untitled report (arguing for discontinuing newcomer services), May 12, 1942, Sinai Papers, CSC (original emphasis). Bamberger moved to New York, where he pursued a successful career in journalism as editor-in-chief of *Coronet* magazine and executive director of Esquire, Inc., in the 1950s and 1960s. He later taught at Hebrew Union College in New York (see obituary for Fritz Bamberger, *New York Times*, September 24, 1984).

36. John Evans, "Rabbis Exhort Flocks to Keep Nation Neutral," *Chicago Tribune*, September 14, 1939.

37. Board meeting, undated memo (on Schwartz), ca. 1936, Sinai Papers, CSC.

38. James O'Donnell Bennett, "Sinai Temple to Build Anew in Hyde Park," *Chicago Tribune*, January 5, 1930 (detailed portrait of the congregation and its activities).

39. S. D. Schwartz, "The Sinai Public Forum," *Character* 1 (February/March 1935); programs (small selection): Thomas Mann, November 3, 1941 (Thomas and Louis Mann were not related); Yehudi Menuhin, February 12, 1945; Reinhold Niebuhr, January 21, 1946; Leonard Bernstein, December 8, 1947; Abba H. Silver, January 16, 1950, Sinai Papers, CSC.

40. Farewell celebration, October 1, 1944; Leonard Bernstein, "What is American Music?"—Sinai Temple Forum, held at KAM temple, December 8, 1947; internal memo from Louis Mann, June 20, 1944, Sinai Papers, CSC; letter from Emil Kitzinger (Sinai president) to S.D. Schwartz, ca. July 1944, Sinai Papers, AJA; *Chicago Tribune*, July 16, 1944, March 28, 1948, March 5, 1950, and May 7, 1961; Philpott, *The Slum and the Ghetto*, 337–40; Hirsch, *Making the Second Ghetto*, 136.

41. *Proceedings of the Union of American Hebrew Congregations, 77th–80th Annual Reports, July 1, 1950–June 30, 1955* (Cincinnati, OH: UAHC, 1956); Jick, "The Reform Synagogue," 102; Sarna, *American Judaism*, 282–93; Deborah Dash Moore, *To the Golden Cities: Pursuing the American Jewish Dream in Miami and L.A.* (Cambridge, MA: Harvard University Press, 1996), 36.

42. "President's Message for the 88th Annual Meeting," November 20, 1949, Sinai Papers, AJA; 93rd annual meeting, June 27, 1954, Sinai Papers, CSC.

43. "Rabbis' Sermons to Pay Homage to Dr. Kaplan, 70," *Chicago Tribune*, May 10, 1951.

44. Emil Kitzinger (president) to Louis Mann, July 30, 1945, Sinai Papers, AJA; "President's Message for the 88th Annual Meeting"; Richard C. Hertz, "The Founding Fathers of Sinai" (sermon), *Chicago Sinai Bulletin*, December 13, 1951, Sinai Papers, CSC.

45. Hirsch, *Making the Second Ghetto*, 135–70; "Vote Hyde Park Council Aid in Fight on Crime," *Chicago Tribune*, March 28, 1952, "2,500 at Rally Draft Drive to Fight Crime in Hyde Park," *Chicago Tribune*, May 20, 1952, "District Chairmen Chosen for War on Crime on South Side," *Chicago Tribune*, June 20, 1952, "Decide High Rise Co-Op Soon," *Chicago Tribune*, February 6, 1964, "In Hyde Park Residents Fight Renewal Plan," *Chicago Tribune*, May 26, 1968; board meeting, May 6, 1968, Sinai Papers, CSC.

46. "Levi Heads U. of Chicago," *Chicago Tribune*, September 15, 1967, "Stick Around They Told Edward Levi," *Chicago Tribune*, November 10, 1968 (portrait of Edward Levi), John

McCarron, "Julian Levi's Parting Shot: Worried About Chicago," June 15, 1980 (portrait of Julian Levi); "The House of Books," *Chicago Tribune*, November 25, 1965.

47. "Rabbi Karff Urges School Race Control: Bar Some Negroes to Keep Integration," *Chicago Tribune*, February 1, 1965, "Rabbi Cautions Negro Leaders on Flare-Ups," *Chicago Tribune*, May 17, 1965.

48. Quoted in an address of Weinstein gave to the Committee on Planning and Housing of the City Council of Chicago on September 22, 1958, in Janice J. Feldstein, ed., *Rabbi Jacob J. Weinstein: Advocate of the People*, (New York: KTAV, 1980), 115. See also "Rabbi Decries Decay of Ellis Av. Residence," *Chicago Tribune*, February 19, 1953, and "Rabbi, Negro Will Discuss Racial Unity," *Chicago Tribune*, February 24, 1963; "Clerics Blast City on Slums," *Chicago Tribune*, December 10, 1959; obituary for Jacob Weinstein, *New York Times*, November 3, 1974.

49. 97th annual meeting, June 9, 1958, Sinai Papers, CSC; the confirmation photographs are preserved by the congregation; *The Herald* (Chicago), November 17, 1976 (about the attempt to revive the Forum after a twenty-year hiatus).

EPILOGUE

1. Chicago Sinai Congregation, *Centennial Anniversary 1861–1961* (Chicago: privately printed, 1961); 100th annual meeting, June 12, 1961; "Temple Marks 100th Birthday," *Chicago Tribune*, May 7, 1961, "Mann to Quit Post at Sinai," *Chicago Tribune*, April 23, 1962; obituary of Louis L. Mann, *Chicago Tribune*, February 2, 1966; "Pull-No-Punches Talks by Rabbi Draw Listeners," *Chicago Tribune*, May 28, 1967 (portrait of Samuel Karff); 95th annual meeting, June 13, 1956; board meeting, February 4, 1963; board meeting, November 1, 1971, Sinai Papers, CSC; Jonathan D. Sarna, *American Judaism: A History* (New Haven, CT: Yale University Press, 2004), 308–15.

2. Board meetings, January 11, 1971, February 1, 1971, June 11, 1973, and October 10, 1977, Sinai Papers, CSC; "Project Unites Temple," *Chicago Tribune*, April 19, 1973.

3. Janet L. Abu-Lughod, *New York, Chicago, Los Angeles: America's Global Cities* (Minneapolis: University of Minnesota Press, 1999), 230.

4. Sarna, *American Judaism*, 282–92.

5. Interview with Miriam and Marvin Letchinger, Chicago, June 15, 2009.

6. Board meeting, February 4, 1963, board meeting, October 5, 1964, letter from Alan Altheimer (president of the Chicago Federation of the UAHC) to Sinai Board, November 10, 1964, Sinai Papers, CSC.

7. Sarna, *American Judaism*, 368.

8. *Occident* (Chicago), May 21, 1886.

9. Sarna, *American Judaism*, esp. 272–374.

10. Pauline Dubkin Yearwood, "The inspiring story of how members of a Chicago synagogue on the Gold Coast are working with students at a Chicago public school near Cabrini-Green," *Chicago Jewish News*, October 10, 2008, http://www.chicagojewishnews .com/story.htm?sid=1&id=252364 (accessed May 10, 2010).

INDEX

𝄢

AJC (American Jewish Committee), 232, 245,
274. *See also* J. Mack, J. Schiff *Allgemeine
Zeitung des Judenthums* (Leipzig): Chicago
Jews, 50; on I. L. Chronik in Amsterdam, 70;
critical of Reform Judaism in Chicago, 103;
Felsenthal on abolition, 56; Jewish emigration,
17. *See also* L. Philippson
All Souls Church (Chicago), 169, 209, 210, 221,
225, 226, 238, 285. *See also* Abraham Lincoln
Center; J. Addams; E. G. Hirsch; J. L. Jones;
F. L. Wright
Alschuler, Alfred S., 4, 236, 277
Alschuler, Rose, 157
Alzey, 17
Amalgamated Clothing Workers of America,
258
American Congress of Liberal Religious Socie-
ties, 217, 218, 226, 237
American Hebrew (New York), 188
American Israelite. See *Israelite*
American Jewess (Chicago), 202
American Jewish Committee. *See* AJC (Ameri-
can Jewish Committee)
American, Sadie: co-organizer of Jewish
Women's Congress, 198; Maxwell Street
Settlement, 155; NCJW leader, 200, 203;
young Sinai member, 153. *See also* NCJW;
H. Solomon
Amsterdam, 70
Ansbach, 25
Anshe Chesed (New York), 91, 95
Anshe Chesed (Cleveland), 275
Anshe Emeth (Albany), 34, 63, 65
Anti-Jewish discrimination: AJC and, 232, 245;
in Chicago, 60, 61, 235, 259, 271, 279, 280;
Christian Century, 279, 280; emigration from
Europe, 15; in Germany, 159, 160, 211, 246,
247; Grant's order #11, 57; hampers dialogue
with Christian leaders, 206; impact of modern
anti-Semitism in the United States, 160, 211,
212, 238, 246, 247; and racism towards African
Americans, 290; Rothschilds as target, 78; in
Russia, 247, 251, 252, 261; social discrimination
towards established Jews, 198; A. Stoecker
visit to Chicago, 211, 212
Armour, Philip D., 148, 149
Art Institute of Chicago, 180, 228, 235

Associated Jewish Charities of Chicago. *See*
UHRA
Atlanta, GA, 35

Baha, Abdul, 231
Baha'i Faith, 231
Baltimore, MD, 31, 36, 38, 41, 43, 59, 65, 71, 90,
93, 99, 115, 119, 129, 134, 142, 183, 228, 275. *See
also* D. Einhorn; Har Sinai; E. G. Hirsch;
S. Sale; B. Szold
Baltimore Hebrew congregation, 275
Bamberger, Fritz, 282, 283
Bamberger, Gabriel: background and association
with F. Adler, 166; director of Jewish Train-
ing School, 166; at Jewish Denominational
Congress, 216; on mission of Jewish Training
School, 168, 169
Barbe, Lizzie T., 200, 276
Barbe, Martin, 183
Bavaria, Jewish emancipation, 14, 15
Basel, 212, 247, 248, 251
Beard, Charles A., 284
Becker, Abraham G., 227, 228, 233, 235, 244, 259
Bederkesa, 36
Beethoven, Ludwig van, 39
Bene Israel (Rockdale Temple) (Cincinnati), 6,
142, 204. *See also* M. Lilienthal, D. Philipson,
I. M. Wise
Bene Yeshurun (Cincinnati), 34, 96, 98, 179, 224.
See also I. M. Wise
Bensinger, Moses, 183
Berkowitz, Henry: influence on E. G. Hirsch,
221; institutional congregation, 175, 176;
sisterhood, 199; at World Parliament of
Religions, 215, 217
Berlin, 26, 28, 68, 39, 52, 63, 64, 68, 69, 93, 95,
107, 115–17, 130, 135, 141, 180, 207, 211, 218,
219, 231, 244, 282. *See also* M. Mendelssohn;
Reform Judaism
Berlin Reform Temple: founding, 39, 40; S.
Friedländer, 52, D. Holdheim, 64; separate
seating of men and women, 63; Sunday
services, 69
Berlin *Stadtmission*, 211
Berman, Howard, 296
Berman, Morton, 287
Bernstein, Leonard, 3, 284

conversion: to Judaism, 112; Jewish conversions to Christianity, 151, 212, 213; J. C. Lavater's attempt to convert M. Mendelssohn, 218, 219

Crucifixion, 207–11, 219

Daley, Richard S., 289, 290

Darrow, Clarence, 3, 284

Darwinism, 138

Dayton, OH, 18

Deborah Verein, 234

Dernburg, Bernhard, 260, 261

Detroit, MI, 20, 60, 72, 82, 83, 142, 275, 280

Deutsch, Gotthard, 263, 264

Dewey, John, 149

Die Deborah (Cincinnati), 34, 202. *See also*
I. M. Wise

Dirmstein, 16, 22

Dispensionalist premillennialism, 212, 218

Dreiser, Theodore, 3, 284

Du Bois, W. E. B., 230, 231

1848–1849 revolution, 13, 58

82nd Illinois Volunteer Regiment, 58, 59

Einhorn, David: abolition of slavery, 59; candidate for Sinai rabbi, 64–67; Civil War and escape from Baltimore, 64, 65; correspondence with B. Felsenthal, 45, 52, 66; correspondence with K. Kohler, 94, 95; conflict with I. M. Wise, 42–53; as Germanizer, 46–48; move to New York, 72; opposition of Sunday services, 94, 95; *Sinai* monthly, 42; theology, 41, 42. *See also* B. Felsenthal; A. Geiger; E. G. Hirsch; K. Kohler; I. M. Wise

Eliel, Gustav, 23, 91

Ellinger, Moritz: B'nai B'rith leader, 49; editor of *Jewish Times*, 97

Ely, Richard T., 163

Emanu-El (San Francisco), 142, 179

Enlightenment: and anti-Semitism, 246; and Jewish emancipation, 13; and Jewish Reformers, 19; Lessing's *Nathan the Wise*, 197, 218; and L. Pinsker, 247; relationship between roots of modern Judaism and the American republic, 251; and Sinai forum, 284. See also *Bildung*; G.E. Lessing

Eppelsheim, 11, 12, 16, 17, 19, 20, 24, 227

Eppelsheim migration network: business partnerships, 227, 254; founding of Sinai, 44; profile and emigration 15–20, 24; legacy in Chicago, 16, 183

Evansville, IN, 36

Federated Orthodox Jewish Charities. *See* FOJC (Federated Orthodox Jewish Charities

Fellheim, 22

Felsenthal, Bernhard: B'nai B'rith, 73–76; Civil War, 55–62; correspondence with D. Einhorn, 45, 52, 66; 1878 F. Adler visit, 111, 112; death, 252; as Germanizer, 46–48; as historian of Chicago Jewry, 67, 86; journey to America, 17–20; and E. G. Hirsch, 248, 252; move to Chicago, 43; photo, *249*; rabbi in Madison, IN, 43; resigns from Sinai, 66; signer of Blackstone Memorial, 213; Sinai Congregation rabbi, 65; slavery, 56, 57, 230; speaks at 1890 interfaith workshop, 203, 204; theology, 46–48; youth and training, 17; Zion congregation rabbi, 67; Zionist, 112, 246–48. *See also* D. Einhorn; Eppelsheim migration network; G. Foreman; H. Greenebaum; *Kol Kore Bamidbar*; I. M. Wise; Zion congregation; Zionism

Felsenthal, Eli: member of Sinai literary association and host of F. Adler in 1882, 127; son of Herman Felsenthal, 169; University of Chicago trustee, 156, 194, 229; supports E. G. Hirsch, 194

Felsenthal, Herman, 60, 169

Felsenthal, Julia, 200, 202, 234

Felsenthal, Marcus, 18

Fishell, Albert, 181, 182, 186, 187, 190, 191, 194, 195, 225

Florsheim Shoe Company, 150

Florsheim, Simon, 253

FOJC (Federated Orthodox Jewish Charities), 271

Frankel, Zacharias, 39

Freehof, Solomon B., 279

Free Kindergarten, 166

Friedländer, Salomon, 52

Friedman, Alschuler & Sincere, 286

Flomersheim, 16

Forchheim, 25

E. G. Hirsch; K. Kohler; *Kol Kore Bamidbar*; Pittsburgh Platform; Reform Judaism

Ramah lodge, 73–76. *See also* B'nai B'rith; B. Felsenthal; H. Greenebaum

Ransom, Reverdy C., 230, 238. *See also* Bethel Church; Hull House

Reconstructionism, 274. *See also* M. Kaplan

Reform Advocate (Chicago): as community paper, 152; editorship of G. Levi, 170; on H. Solomon, 202; special issue devoted to E. G. Hirsch, 264; on women in the synagogue, 201, 202; on Zionism, 251. *See also* E. G. Hirsch

Reform Judaism: and acceptance by Protestant establishment, 206; affiliation, 171, 172, 189, 224, 234, 241, 242, 275, 276, 280; America as outpost of Reform, 68; Amsterdam, 70; Berlin as early center, 68, 69; biblical criticism, 207, 208; *Bildung*, 39; in central Europe, 30, 38, 39, 68; Classical Reform Judaism, 280; Conservative Judaism, 134; ethical culture, 128; dialogue with Christians, 203–19; German-Jewish press, 38; historiography, 6; indifference and crisis during 1870s, 101, 103, 111, 112; institutional congregation, 175–79; 220–26, 238–42; mixed seating, 63; origins and rationale, 38, 39; Pittsburgh Platform, 142–44; "Protestantized" service, 103; race, 246; renaissance in the 1950s, 286; ritual, 139; social question, 104, 125; Unitarians, 62, 133; wealth, 90; women, 96, 97, 198–203; at World Parliament of Religions, 215; and Zionism, 246–53. *See also* D. Einhorn; B. Felsenthal; A. Geiger; E. G. Hirsch; S. Hirsch; K. Kohler; Pittsburgh Platform; Radical Reform Judaism; I. M. Wise; UAHC

Regenstein, Joseph and Helen, 290

Rochester, NY, 20

Rockdale Temple (Cincinnati). *See* Bene Israel

Rockefeller, John D., 155, 213, 229

Rodeph Shalom (Philadelphia), 275

Rodeph Shalom (Pittsburgh), 275

Roosevelt, Eleanor, 3, 284

Roosevelt, Theodore, 233

Rosehill Cemetery (Chicago), 72

Rosenberg, Joseph, 288

Rosenthal, Julius: as abolitionist, 230; calls for clemency for Haymarket anarchists, 146, 147; Chicago Fire and Chicago Relief & Aid Society, 83; Chicago Germans, 77; clash with K. Kohler over 1878 F. Adler visit, 110, 111; early supporter of Reform, 37; 1865 Europe trip, 68; founder of Chicago Republican party, 60; member of first Chicago Public Library board, 148; member of Union League Club, 151; objects to E. G. Hirsch life contract, 194; opposes UAHC membership, 226; on Pittsburgh Platform, 143; proponent of Sunday services, 114, 129; raises funds for Jewish Training School, 166; vice-president of Chicago Institute for Instruction in Letters, Morals, and Religion, 209. *See also* Chicago Public Library; E. G. Hirsch; M. Selz

Rosenthal, Lessing, 232

Rosenwald, Julius: African Americans, 5, 229–31, 299; and AJC, 232; businessman, 228; emigration of parents, 35, 36; engineers merger of FOJC and UHRA successor organization, 271; W. R. Harper, 228; Hull House, 154; influence of Jewish Training School, 169; inspiration by I. Greensfelder, 228; inspiration by E. G. Hirsch, 153, 193, 228–31; and Sinai Congregation, 5, 153, 169, 193, 228–33, 236, 278, 297–99; scientific philanthropy, 229; support for University of Chicago, 156, 228, 229; trustee of Art Institute, 235; at Tuskegee Institute, 230; and UHRA (and successor organizations), 228–31, 271; B. T. Washington, 229–31; and Zionism, 244. *See also* J. Addams; E. G. Hirsch; J. Mack; Sears and Roebuck

Rosenwald, Lessing, 230, 278

Rosenwald, Sophie, 210

Rosenwald schools, 169, 229

Rubel family, 16

Rülff, Isaak, 247

Sacramento, CA, 19

Sarah Greenebaum lodge, 234

St. Louis, MO, 20, 31, 35, 51, 60, 72, 75, 97, 133, 135, 142, 166, 183. *See also* A. Binswanger; S. Sale; Shaare Emeth; S. Sonneschein

St. Louis Manual Training School, 166

Sale, Samuel, 130, 135, 143, 144, 236

Salomon, Edward: Chicago alderman, 60; 1867 parade, 77; leads 82nd Illinois Volunteer Regiment at Gettysburg, 59; saves life of slave, 56

Salter, William Mackintire, 141, 231

San Francisco, CA, 35, 152, 153, 175, 179

Scammon, Jonathan Young, 61

Schaack, Michael, 145

Schaffner, Herman, 227

Schaffner, Joseph, 253–58

Schaffner, Nathan, 16

Schaumburg, IL, 164

Schiff, Jacob, 180, 232, 255

Schiller, Friedrich, 39, 152

Schlossman, Benedict, 84

Schmidt, Ernst, 62, 146, 147

Schönemann, Benjamin, 52, 68, 144

schools. See *Bildung*; Jewish Training School; Rosenwald schools

Schwartz, Moritz, 273

Schwartz, Samuel D., 269, 273, 277, 278, 282–85, *285*

Sears and Roebuck, 210, 228. *See also* J. Rosenwald

Second Coming. *See* dispensionalist premillennialism

Segal, Jeannette, 294

Selz, Morris, 22, 114, 195

Sepher Torah: reinstated at Sinai in 1911–12, 236; removal at Sinai in 1891–92, 172; removal at Tifereth Israel (Cleveland), 172, 173

Shaare Emeth (St. Louis), 97, 133, 135, 142, 183, 334n19

Shapiro, Hannah, 254

Silver, Abba Hillel, 3, 271, 272, 275, 278, 279, 284

Simmel, Georg, 282

Simmel, Hans Eugen, 282

Sinai Congregation: abolition of Saturday services, 139–41; African Americans, 5, 230, 231, 238, 268–70, 277, 285, 288–90, 298, 299; and American Congress of Liberal Religious Societies, 217, 218, 226; athletic facilities, 241; attendance of service, 101, 129, 171, 280; Bethel Church as inspiration for "institutional synagogue," 230, 238; branch congregation on North Shore, 276; budget, 90, 222; celebrates founding in 1886, 144; celebrates E. G. Hirsch, 181, 182; celebrates twenty-fifth anniversary of Sunday services, 186–88; cemetery, 72; centennial 1961, 293; Chicago Board of Education, 60, 169, 298; Chicago Jewish community, 149–52; Christians attend Sunday services, 97, 133, 171, 206; civic engage-

ment, 78; civil rights, 290; clash with Chicago Rabbinical Association, 281; construction of new temple in 1911, 236; controversy over F. Adler 1878 visit, 107–12; criticized by other Jews, 174; dues, 90, 222, 223; Civil War, 55–62; economic background of members, 86–91; expresses support for E. G. Hirsch, 194; founding, 42–53; Genesis Project, 294; Hebrew Institute, 240; Hi-Rise Fellowship program, 294; as Hyde Park institution, 288, 289; impact on B'nai B'rith, 49–51, 72–76; impact of Great Depression, 278; influenced by All Souls Church, 209, 210, 221, 225; institutional congregation, 178, 220–26, 230, 238–42; interfaith marriages, 296; introduction of Sunday services in 1874, 91–98; invites Jewish refugees from Nazi Germany, 281–83; Jewish Training School, 162–69; Kenwood and Hyde Park Property Owners Association, 270; language of service, 101, 129; liberal Protestants, 62; literary society, 106, 107, 112; liturgy, 63; marginalization in Chicago and nationally, 287, 290, 293, 296; Men's Club, 286; merger talks with KAM, 97, 98, 129; membership, 62, 87, 171, 222–24, 275, 278, 286, 291, 294, 296; membership as expression of social status, 222; as metropolitan congregation, 287, 288, 296; mixed seating, 63, name of the congregation, 64; 1926 survey of members, 276; nondenominationalism, 137; origin of members, 88; Pittsburgh Platform, 142–44; Progressives, 152–57; pursuit of D. Einhorn as rabbi, 65, 66; reform of the membership system, 222, 223; relationship between board and rabbi, 139–41, 178–96, 226–34; relationship with University of Chicago, 193; relocation from Black Belt, 277, 278, 285, 286; renovation of Sinai temple 1891–92, 172; ritual, 139, 236; J. Rosenwald, 5, 153, 169, 193, 228–33, 236, 278, 297–99; search for rabbi, 64–69, 72, 114, 115–17, 271, 272; Sepher Torah removal, 172, 236; Sinai Forum, 283, 284, *285*; Sinai Social Center, 238–42; sisterhood, 263, 276, 286; social and economic profile of members, 63, 86–91, 222, 253, 276; split and founding of Zion congregation, 67; synagogues, 62–64, 90, 91, 101, *102*, *173*, 234–38, *237*, 284, 286, *288*, 296, *297*; UAHC, 99, 225, 226; unaffiliated

Talladega, AL, 36

Temple Emanu-El (New York): accepts decision by E. G. Hirsch to remain in Chicago, 195; as described by E. G. Hirsch, 191; 1896 offer to E. G. Hirsch, 181; 1899 offer to E. G. Hirsch, 189; founding, 31; during Great Depression, 278; institutional congregation, 176; membership in 1904, 224; membership in 1925, 275; mixed seating, 63; profile, 195, 196; Rabbi Samuel Adler, 17, 38; sisterhood, 176, 199. *See also* G. Gottheil; J. Schiff

Temple Isaiah (Temple Isaiah Israel, KAM Isaiah Israel) (Chicago): founding, 223; membership in 1904, 224; membership in 1925, 275; membership in 1956, 286; rabbi congratulates M. Kaplan, 287; women as full members, 223. *See also* J. Stolz

Temple Sholom (Chicago). *See* North Side Hebrew Congregation

Temple, The. *See* Tifereth Israel

Thomas, Hiram W.: as ally of Sinai, 204; and American Congress of Liberal Religious Societies, 217, 218; appeal, 220; nondenominationalism, 137; Sunday lectures and founding of People's Church, 109. *See also* J. L. Jones; E. G. Hirsch; World Parliament of Religions

Thompson's Temple of Faith (Philadelphia), 1

Thompson, William Hale, 279

Tifereth Israel (Cleveland): membership in 1925, 275; M. Gries as rabbi, 172, 173, 221; Sepher Torah removal, 172, 173; A. H. Silver, 3, 271, 272, 275, 278, 279, 284; Sunday services, 142. *See also* M. Gries

Toynbee Hall settlement (London), 155

Treitschke, Heinrich, 246

Trieste, 38

Tuskegee Institute, 230

UAHC (Union of American Hebrew Congregations): founding, 98, 99; 1881 Chicago convention, 126, 127; Columbus Platform, 275; Detroit convention, 280; expansion during the 1950s, 286; member congregations, 275, 276, 286; Pittsburgh Platform, 143; Sinai Congregation, 99, 225, 226

UHRA (United Hebrew Relief Association): A. G. Becker, 228; Chicago Fire, 83; on Chicago

Ghetto, 160; founding, 50; M. M. Gerstley, 57; I. Greensfelder, 150; H. Hart, 256; E. G. Hirsch as driver for modernization, 154; merger with FOJC in 1923, 271; model for other institutions, 156; perception of Jews from eastern Europe, 158, 160; reorganization and name change to Associated Jewish Charities in 1899, 154; scientific approach and name change to United Hebrew Charities in 1888, 153; struggles to support Jews in need during 1870s, 106; ties to Sinai Congregation, 149–54. *See also* J. Addams; I. Greensfelder; E. G. Hirsch; J. Mack; J. Rosenwald

Ullmann, Joseph, 22, 89

Union of American Hebrew Congregations. *See* UAHC (Union of American Hebrew Congregations)

Unitarian congregations: All Souls Church as a social congregation, 209, 210, 221, 225; collaboration with Chicago Reform Jews, 62, 133, 208–11; J. L. Jones, 208–11; potential competitors with Jewish Reform congregations, 133, 210

United Garment Workers (UGW), 256, 257

United Hebrew Charities. *See* UHRA

United Hebrew Relief Association. *See* UHRA (United Hebrew Relief Association)

Unity Church (Chicago), 62

University of Chicago: donation of Sinai's Sepher Torah, 172, 236; E. Felsenthal as trustee, 156; founding, 155, 156; E. G. Hirsch as professor, 208; influence of the German research university, 117; Regenstein library, 290; support by L. Mandel, 156; support by J. Rosenwald, 156, 228, 229; support by Sinai members and leaders, 155, 156, 193, 228, 229, 290; urban renewal in Hyde Park, 288–90. *See also* W. R. Harper; E. G. Hirsch; KAM; E. Levi; J. Levi; L. Mandel; J. Regenstein; J. Rosenwald

University of Illinois at Chicago, 1

University of Pennsylvania, 115–17

urban historiography and religion, 6, 7

urban renewal in Hyde Park, 288–90

Verbürgerlichung (embourgoisement), 26–28

Vienna, 22, 157, 180